A TRAGIC BEGINNING

A Tragic Beginning

*The Taiwan Uprising
of February 28, 1947*

LAI TSE-HAN
RAMON H. MYERS
WEI WOU

Stanford University Press   Stanford, California
1991

Stanford University Press
Stanford, California
© 1991 by the Board of Trustees of the
Leland Stanford Junior University
Printed in the United States of America

CIP data are at the end of the book

We dedicate this book to all those who suffered on account of the tragedy we have tried to understand

Acknowledgments

THIS WORK could not have been completed without the assistance of certain institutions and individuals, and to them, as well as to other, unmentioned individuals, we express our deep gratitude and thanks.

We are grateful for the assistance rendered by the following libraries and their staffs: the Central Library and the Taipei Branch Library of the Republic of China; the Fung Ping Shan Library of the University of Hong Kong; the Library of the School of Oriental and African Studies (London); the Foreign Records Office of the United Kingdom; the British Museum; Trinity College; the libraries of the University of Illinois, the University of Chicago, and Yale University; and the Harvard-Yenching Library of Harvard University.

The following individuals read parts or all of the manuscript and provided helpful critical comments: Dr. Wu Wen-hsing (National Taiwan Normal University); Dr. Hsü Hsüeh-chi, Professor Su Yün-feng, Professor Chang Yü-fa, and Dr. P'eng Wen-hsien (Academia Sinica); Ms. Lu Hwei-hsin (University of Illinois); Dr. Chang Wei-an (National Ch'ing-hua University); Mr. Ch'üan Lin, who supplied the photograph of Ch'en I; and our assistants, Mr. Yeh Ch'uan-hung, Ms. Cheng Yen-hsia and Ms. Yü Hui-hui.

Special thanks are due to the Hoover Institution, which provided financial support for preparing the maps and photographs presented in this study and financed the travels of Drs. Lai Tse-han and Wei Wou when they visited the Hoover Institution.

We also are grateful to Professors Lloyd Eastman, Tien Hung-mao, Frank S. T. Hsiao, John K. Fairbank, Lucien Bianco, and C. Henriot. They gave generously of their time to comment on earlier drafts, and many of their criticisms were invaluable. Dr. Hsieh Kuoyeng-wo corrected errors pertaining to her participation in the Uprising, and we are grateful to her, too. Professor Takahashi Hisashi of the National Institute for Defense Studies in Japan provided statistics of Japanese troops stationed in Taiwan at the end of the war.

Acknowledgments

Special thanks go to Mrs. Lin Ying of the Hoover Institution for the valuable assistance she rendered Dr. Myers in preparing the final manuscript for editing and printing.

We interviewed around sixty individuals who were living at the time of the Uprising and were observers or participants. We cite only those individuals who allowed us to use their names: Yang Liang-kung (October 5, 1986); Hsü Chin-te (October 26, 1986); Ch'en Chien-chih, who was P'eng Meng-chi's secretary for many years (November 15, 1986, at P'eng's home); Yang Yüan-ping (October 20, 1986); Yeh Ming-hsün (June 20, 1986); Wang Ming-ning (November 11, 1986); Shen Yün-lung (October 16, 1986); Hsieh Kuoyeng-wo (April 20, 1987); Chung I-jen (April 10, 1987, in Boston); Chung Chao-cheng (February 27, 1987). To these individuals and other informants, we owe special thanks for their kind assistance and willingness to share their memories with us.

Our greatest debt is to Dr. Thomas A. Metzger, whose encouragement and support inspired us to finish this study. Metzger made three major contributions, but disagreed with our conclusion that he had a right to be listed as an author. First, he provided us with the framework for this study, as outlined in Chapter 1, where we set forth seven questions around which to organize our data. Second, Metzger used P'eng Ming-min's memoirs to provide us with an analysis of his life, making clear the complexity of his thought and the great influence Japanese education had on his world view. Third, he carefully edited various drafts, making suggestions about how to organize the material.

Yet although he helped complete this work, he cannot be blamed for any errors, omissions, or failings, for which the three authors are responsible.

L. T. H.
R. H. M.
W. W.

Contents

CHAPTER 1 Posing the Problem   1

Progress Under a Cloud, 1; Current Interpretations of the Uprising, 3; Our Approach and Sources: Seven Basic Questions, 6.

CHAPTER 2 Taiwan Under Japanese Rule   13

Historical Background, 13; The Evolution of the Taiwanese Elite, 15; The Taiwanese Struggle for Political Rights, 23; Japan's Initial Wartime Policies, 26; Total Patriotic Mobilization, 29; The Educational Campaign, 33; Mobilization Efforts During the Last Years of the War, 35; The Thrust Toward Industrialization and Its Social Implications, 38; Expanding the Role of Taiwanese in Local Government, 41; Taiwan on the Eve of Retrocession, 44.

CHAPTER 3 The Establishment of Nationalist Rule   50

The Nationalist Government on the Mainland, 51; Conditions on the Mainland in 1945, 55; Preparations for Retrocession, 56; The Arrival of the Nationalists, 62; Understaffing and the Loss of Governmental Positions for Taiwanese, 63; The Beginnings of Electoral Politics in 1946, 67; Arguments About Property, 71; Corruption and Troop Misbehavior, 73; Other Political Problems: The Role of the Media and Ch'en I's Leadership, 76; The Economic Crisis, 80; Social Ills, 89; Linguistic and Cultural Barriers, 93; No Calm Before the Storm, 96.

CHAPTER 4 The Uprising   99

The Uprising Begins: Taipei, 102; Keelung, 121; Pan-ch'iao and Neighboring Towns, 122; T'ao-yüan and Neighboring Areas, 123; Taichung, 124; Chia-i, 128; Tainan, 129; Kaohsiung and Neighboring Areas, 130; Hua-lien, 131; The Pescadores, 134; The Pattern of the Uprising and the Role of the Communists, 135.

x   *Contents*

CHAPTER 5   The Nationalists' Response   141

The Nationalists' Shift from Conciliation to the Use of Force, 142; The Time of Terror, 151; The Extent of the Terror, 155; Moving Toward Reform, 164.

CHAPTER 6   The Nature and Aftermath of the Tragedy   168

The Nature of the Tragedy, 168; Ch'en I's Fate, 180; Early Chinese Reactions, 182; The Reactions of Taiwanese, 183; The Taiwan Independence Movement, 188; KMT Policy in the Wake of the Uprising, 192.

Appendixes   197
Notes   217
Bibliography   251
Index   267

Eight pages of photographs follow p. 116.

A TRAGIC BEGINNING

CHAPTER I

Posing the Problem

Progress Under a Cloud

The progress of Taiwan over the past forty years from a state of extreme poverty and political and social backwardness to one of prosperity, widespread literacy, and increasingly democratic institutions is one of the great success stories of the developing world. The achievement of the Republic of China (ROC) is all the more remarkable because it required the absorption of over 2 million refugees from the Chinese Mainland beginning in 1949, and the overcoming not only of poverty and backwardness but of enormous tensions between native Taiwanese and governing Mainlanders. Today, Taiwan's president, Lee Teng-hui, is a Taiwanese who took office in 1988 with the strong support of Mainlanders.

For many Taiwanese, however, these successes have a hollow ring. A dark cloud hangs over Taiwan's political life. On February 28, 1988, large demonstrations took place in the main cities of Taiwan. Their purpose was to commemorate the events of February 28, 1947, when Taiwanese rose up to protest the policies of the Mainlander-run ROC government. The recently formed Democratic Progressive Party (DPP), which participated in these commemorative rallies, called for "noisy yet harmonious demonstrations."[1] When a dozen people assembled in the plaza in front of the railway station in the city of Chia-i to hold a memorial service, a fight broke out between demonstrators and police. "When the service had ended, Ch'en Chen-wei, a member of the DPP's Action Committee in Chia-i, and several others began to burn funeral paper. At that moment, several policemen moved in to stop them, and a violent altercation erupted." Police immediately arrested Ch'en and stamped out the blaze.[2]

That same day, President Lee gave reporters his view of the February 28 Uprising: "Not long after Nationalist China recovered Taiwan, a tragedy took place. Society must have tranquility, and that incident should be treated with sincere understanding."[3]

On the next anniversary of the Uprising, in 1989, there was another upsurge of activity. On February 28, some DPP members of the Legislative Yüan proposed that the legislature demand government compensation for the victims of the February 28 Uprising. Although the proposal did not carry because the majority refused to support this proposal, a majority of DPP and Kuomintang (KMT) members finally demanded a report from the ministers of the Interior, Defense, and Justice on the February 28 Uprising, who would then come to the Legislative Yüan for interpellation.[4]

Commemorative rallies were held around the island that same day. In the city of Chia-i, some 2,000 people, including many DPP members, paraded with cars and banners and then assembled at the plaza in front of the railway station. Their ire was aroused by a Rotary Club emblem that had been placed at the site where a large bronze statue of Wu Feng, a famous hero of nineteenth-century Taiwan, had once stood. They pressed forward to remove the emblem. A large contingent of police stood ready to control the crowd. The atmosphere was tense. "At that moment, Chang Po-ya, Chia-i's mayor, appeared and ordered the Rotary emblem removed. The wave of potential violence immediately receded."[5] The next day, the Chia-i city council approved a DPP request to build a memorial to commemorate the February 28 Uprising.[6] On August 19, 1989, a ceremony was held for the completion of the memorial, which was also intended to honor peace.[7]

As the anniversary of the February 28 Uprising neared in February 1990, another burst of activity took place. On the morning of February 23, the DPP membership in the Legislative Yüan expressed condolences for the February 28 Incident by standing silently for a full minute while KMT members remained seated. Later that day, the KMT membership stood silently to express condolences for the death of the National Assemblyman and parliamentarian Chiang Kung-liang, who had passed away suddenly at a dinner party hosted by President Lee when a group of Assemblymen overturned the dining tables.[8] On February 28, 1990, members of the Legislative Yüan agreed to stand silently for a minute to express condolences for victims of the February 28 Uprising, but government cabinet officials were excused from attending.[9] On that same day, the Minister of the Interior, responding to political demands, publicly stated that the government had no plan to designate a national holiday commemorating the February 28 Uprising.[10] Meanwhile, the press reported the conflicting views of academics about the appropriate way to commemorate the Uprising.[11] Then on February 28, a resolution was advanced at a meeting of the National Assembly for members to stand silently for a minute in honor of the Uprising; only a portion of the body stood, whereas others remained seated, and some rose only to quickly resume their seats.[12]

The memory of the events of February 28, 1947, thus continues to burn in the minds of many Taiwanese. This memory, at the heart of the movement demanding that Taiwan become an independent nation, constitutes the last major obstacle to political consensus in the Republic of China.

Could a full account of 2-28, as the event is known throughout Taiwan, help dispel the cloud? We do not know, but we write this book in the hope that it will. In this work, we describe and analyze the events of 1947 and put them in their historical context. Thus we deal with the society, economy, and political orientations of Taiwan under Japanese colonial rule (1895–1945); the ideological, political, and administrative character of the ROC in 1945, when it established its rule over Taiwan; the problems and tensions that subsequently occurred and led to the Uprising; the Uprising and the ROC's response to it; and the main events and trends occurring in the wake of the disaster. Before turning to these topics, however, we first review current interpretations of the Uprising and then raise the questions they have left partly or wholly unanswered.

Current Interpretations of the Uprising

Over the years, and especially since 1986, a flood of articles and books has appeared about the Uprising. Today there are four main interpretations.

One is that of the Communists. In late February 1975, the Chinese Communist Party (CCP) held a meeting to commemorate the event. Such high-ranking leaders as Yeh Chien-ying, Hsü Hsiang-ch'ien, Ulanfu, and the famous philosopher Feng Yu-lan attended the meeting, chaired by Hsü Te-heng, a member of the CCP Central Committee. On February 28, 1975, they issued this statement:

> Twenty-eight years ago, on February 28, 1947, the patriotic and anti-imperialistic Taiwanese people heroically rose up. They were inspired by the great leader, Chairman Mao, who had just declared that the people *should welcome the high tide of the Chinese Revolution*. Moreover, the Taiwanese people were influenced by the entire nation's revolutionary victories at that time. This action of the Taiwanese people shocked the reactionary ruling clique of Chiang Kai-shek and linked up with the revolutionary struggle of the Chinese people. The February 28 Uprising was part of the New Democratic Revolution under the leadership of the Chinese Communist Party.[13]

Officially, the CCP has never wavered from this interpretation of February 28. Its leaders argue that the Taiwanese people were patriotic and anti-imperialistic, and that the Uprising of 1947 was part of the great revolutionary tide that swept across China in the late forties "under the leadership of the Chinese Communist Party."[14]

A second view is that of the Taiwan Independence Movement (TIM), which, as discussed in Chapter 6, arose after the Uprising. The TIM views the Uprising as an angry reaction to KMT-inflicted oppression, as one phase in the continuing Taiwanese struggle for self-rule and democracy. Writers like P'eng Ming-min also assert that the KMT killed "20,000 or more" of Taiwan's native elite, not simply to restore order but also to destroy any possible political opposition by eliminating two overlapping classes, the "middle class" and the "landlord class." According to P'eng, the KMT pursued this strategy in two phases, the "slaughter" of "more than 20,000" Taiwanese in early 1947, following the Uprising, and the land reform beginning a couple of years later, which he sees as an effort "to impoverish the well-educated middle class."[15]

For another example of the TIM view, one can turn to an article in the Japanese journal *Taiwan seinen* (Taiwan Youth), the leading TIM organ in Japan. The February 20, 1961, issue contains the following view of the Uprising's significance:

The flowing tide for an independent Taiwan began with the National People's Movement in 1920, and continued with the efforts to abrogate the June 3, 1896, law, the movement to establish a Taiwan Parliament, and the awakening of the masses of farmers and workers. Therefore, the Uprising of the Taiwanese people on February 28, 1947, [is] merely a continuation of that great tide. . . .

This heroic act of the Taiwanese people occurred because they demanded basic freedoms in terms of human rights, the democratization of government, self-rule for Taiwan, and a secure life. Naturally, this Uprising was a sacred struggle based upon the people's just demands for their fundamental rights. We will definitely overcome all distorted slanders and derisive sneers from our enemies, and we will make very clear the real facts of the February 28th Uprising.[16]

The TIM view of KMT policy in Taiwan is shared by many Western scholars, though the latter do not necessarily share the TIM view of Taiwan's history.

A third view is that of the Nationalist Party, or KMT. Pai Ch'ung-hsi, the Minister of Defense of the Nationalist government in Nanking at the time of the Uprising, advanced an interpretation with which many KMT members would probably agree. The Nanking government sent General Pai to Taiwan to investigate the causes of the Uprising. He arrived in Taiwan on March 17, 1947, left on April 2, and presented his report on April 7. His public position was that the Communists had played an important role in triggering the Uprising. In the May 1, 1947, issue of the journal *Cheng-ch'i yüeh-k'an*, he referred to the Uprising as an "unfortunate incident" and explained it as follows:

Background Causes: The Taiwanese people had received a sordid, evil education from the Japanese, and had been misled by depraved propagandists. Proximate Causes: The Communist Party and mad, ambitious schemers had used the case of an arrested smuggler to launch their uprising.[17]

According to Pai, fifty years of Japanese education as well as the distortions and lies of devious individuals misled many Taiwanese, causing them to riot. Moreover, Communist Party cadres and "ambitious" individuals manipulated events to incite the riots that broke out after the arrest of a woman selling contraband cigarettes. Together, these complex factors produced an "unfortunate incident." In public, therefore, he largely agreed with the Communists about their pivotal role. In a memorandum for the government's internal use only, however, he presented a more complex, realistic picture and downplayed the role of the Communists.[18]

The fourth interpretation is that of the *China White Paper*, issued by the U.S. Department of State, which argued that "the economic deterioration of the island and the administration of the mainland officials became so bad that on February 28, 1947, popular resentment erupted into a major rebellion."[19] Nationalist troops suppressed the revolt, but at high human cost. To make matters worse, the report continued, "hatred of the Mainland Chinese was increased."[20] General Wedemeyer on August 17, 1947, using information provided by U.S. consular officials in Taipei at the time of the Incident, reported to the Secretary of State on the principal causes of the "rebellion":

The administration of the former governor, Chen Yi [Ch'en I], has alienated the people from the Central Government. Many were forced to feel that conditions under autocratic rule were preferable. The Central Government lost a fine opportunity to indicate to the Chinese people and to the world at large its capability to provide honest and efficient administration. They cannot attribute their failure to the activities of the Communists or of dissident elements. The people anticipated sincerely and enthusiastically deliverance from the Japanese yoke. However, Chen Yi and his henchmen ruthlessly, corruptly, and avariciously imposed their regime upon a happy and amenable population. The Army conducted themselves as conquerors. Secret police operated freely to intimidate and to facilitate exploitation by central government officials.[21]

Wedemeyer also pointed to the great natural wealth of the island, the efficient infrastructure built by the Japanese, and the high literacy rate of the populace. Despite these advantages, conditions had become so bad that public sentiment strongly favored political independence.[22]

Which of these four interpretations, if any, is persuasive? More basically, what questions should we ask about this momentous historical event?

How can we go beyond a television reporter's view of history, depicting a violent incident as a simple contest between good and evil, without understanding the ideas and values of the people involved, the way these ideas were formed, and the nature of the problems people were trying to solve?

Our Approach and Sources: Seven Basic Questions

First, it seems to us, we must ask to what extent the Uprising was caused by patterns or circumstances deeply rooted in Taiwan's historical background, as opposed to circumstances arising after 1945, when the island returned to Chinese rule for the first time in fifty years. In 1945, there were already irreconcilable differences between the KMT's worldview and that of the politically conscious strata of Taiwanese. Each group was angrily perceived by the other as outrageous and immoral—perceptions that were bound to inflame the disagreements necessarily accompanying retrocession in 1945.

This divergence stemmed from the historical experience of the Taiwanese as well as that of the KMT. To be sure, Chinese elites on Taiwan who had lived under the Japanese viewed themselves as Chinese and were still influenced by China's cultural legacy. Yet a good number had come to respect the Japanese and their ability to use the new technology from the West. Not a few had studied in Japan and adopted many Japanese or cosmopolitan perspectives, including those of Japanese liberals. Moreover, many Taiwanese felt that because they had long suffered under Japanese control, the returning Nationalists should put the highest priority on satisfying their economic and political demands, not on mobilizing Taiwan's resources to prosecute the war against Mao Tse-tung.

Such Taiwanese attitudes necessarily led to tensions with Chinese officials from the Mainland, who had been fighting the Japanese for eight years and regarded Japanese imperialism as China's ultimate foe. Seeing themselves as the liberators of Taiwan, they expected their Taiwanese brethren to gratefully and enthusiastically support the central government, caught as it then was in a life-and-death civil war. Whereas the Mainlanders expected gratitude and respect from the Taiwanese, however, many Taiwanese expected respect and solicitude from them. Whereas Mainlanders were disgusted by Taiwanese admiration for the Japanese, many Taiwanese compared Mainlanders unfavorably with the Japanese.

The second issue to be addressed is how strains or tensions increased after the island came under Nationalist rule on October 24, 1945. One of our central theses is that KMT misrule was *a* cause of these tensions, not *the* cause. Many Taiwanese felt victimized by the KMT and adopted a "we-versus-them" attitude, but this sense of victimization was not caused solely by KMT misrule.

We have already mentioned the fundamental clash in worldviews. Distrusting the Taiwanese, the KMT refused to allow them an important role in the government. Because ROC officials did not appreciate the intensity of Taiwanese political expectations, they failed to respond to growing Taiwanese resentment and anger. Moreover, instead of giving aid to Taiwan to speed up its economic recovery, the KMT believed that Taiwan's economic resources should be mobilized in the fight against the Communists. The KMT also followed economic policies that inhibited recovery; inflation and unemployment worsened in 1946, hitting urban groups particularly hard. These economic strains greatly exacerbated tensions between Mainlanders and Taiwanese, as did other factors discussed in Chapter 3.

Even so, the Uprising would not have spread as it did but for the reduction of the ROC military-police presence in 1946 from 48,000 to 11,000 men. Once reinforcements began arriving on March 8, order was quickly restored.

Third, we ask who actually participated in the Uprising. We will show that only the cities and larger towns were involved. The vast majority of the Taiwanese—up to 80 percent—were rural folk who played little if any role. Of the remaining 20 percent, only a fraction played any role at all, and of these, only some had serious political grievances. Eyewitness accounts show that the activists were a mixture of unemployed (many recently returned from service in the Japanese military), professional people, and, possibly, members of the underworld. Our study shows that the Taiwanese Communists did not instigate the Uprising and that only a few Communists actually took part in it.

A focal point for the interpretations described earlier is a fourth question: What were the motives or goals of those carrying out the Uprising? We found no compelling evidence that the Uprising was deliberately organized by Taiwanese who planned to turn Taiwan into a separate, sovereign nation. On the other hand, many dissidents wanted to end KMT rule and set up a government that, whether ultimately sovereign or not, would be run by Taiwanese largely unconstrained by a Chinese central government. In other words, a significant part of Taiwan's urban minority wanted to take over the government of Taiwan.

Therefore, the violence they perpetrated for nearly two weeks beginning on February 27, 1947, constituted an uprising or rebellion. Both the KMT and the TIM publicly prefer the term "Incident"—the KMT to minimize the episode and dispel divisive feelings, and the TIM to minimize the violent rebellion that provoked KMT repression. Yet, as illustrated by the secret April 1947 report made by General Pai Ch'ung-hsi, the ROC leaders perceived the Uprising as an attempt to overthrow the Government and seize power.[23] Similarly, the 1947 report by General Wedemeyer referred to the Uprising as a "rebellion."

After all, for more than a week, provincial government organs and police forces lost control over Taiwan, or at least its urban sector. The nine largest cities were taken over by rebel committees and militia units. During this period, mobs destroyed buildings and other property and savagely beat hundreds of Mainland officials and civilians, killing a good number. The casualties they inflicted totaled at least 1,300. The fury they vented on property and persons they associated with the Mainlander presence is not a matter of dispute. Neither is the fact that their leaders repeatedly called on the government to disarm and demanded the power to govern Taiwan. To call the episode an "incident" is to place a veil over its actual nature.

Our fifth question concerns what actually happened during the Uprising and its suppression. How did events unfold? How many people were killed? We focus on three main phases, or aspects.

First, from February 27 to March 5, rebels took the offensive, rampaging at will, occupying the cities, and presenting a series of demands to the authorities. For a week or so, the government responded by trying to meet some of these demands, but the rebels rejected attempts to solve the crisis through negotiation, apparently believing that the government was not acting in good faith.

In the second phase, March 5–8, the leadership of the central government shifted from a policy of conciliation to a hard line, determined to crush the Uprising at all costs and to set a stern example in order to prevent a recurrence. The third phase, March 8 to May 15, involved the implementation of that stern position: KMT troop reinforcements arrived in Taiwan and, together with provincial and military police, easily and ruthlessly suppressed the Uprising. They also arrested thousands of alleged leaders and participants, killing many of them. Presenting his secret report to the Control Yüan in April 1947, Yang Liang-kung agreed that "the work of cleansing society" (*ch'ing-hsiang kung-tso*) should be rapidly concluded.[24]

Describing these three phases, we try to ascertain the extent to which Chiang Kai-shek was directly responsible for the switch from conciliation to repression. We cannot exclude the possibility that the shift stemmed from a vicious circle of hostility and misunderstanding: At least some dissidents perceived the government's reform proposals as merely an attempt to stall until reinforcements arrived. How many people died in the government counterattack? Our research indicates that perhaps as many as 8,000 Mainlanders and Taiwanese were killed in the Uprising, a slaughter largely due, we find, to brutality or lack of discipline in the field rather than to orders given from above.

Did the KMT instigate the Uprising as a pretext for eliminating the native elite? It strikes us as preposterous, at the very least, to claim that there was such an intention before the Uprising. On the contrary, the Uprising was a frightening shock to Ch'en I, who in 1946 had been seeking cooperation with all Taiwanese within the context of a rather free press, local elections, and KMT guidance, and who optimistically felt Taiwanese would support his policies. Unaware that urban Taiwanese had become dangerously disaffected, he responded to the outbreak by seeking conciliation. Had he been looking for an excuse to carry out a massive purge, he would hardly have transferred more than 90 percent of the Nationalist troops out of Taiwan in 1946. Unless one believes that the KMT was guilty of a very risky kind of entrapment, the view that the Uprising was engineered by the KMT is unsupportable. Moreover, while the number killed (some 8,000) was much less than the number of elite (which at 1 percent of the population would have been 65,000), it is inconceivable that the 8,000 included *only* members of the elite.

Sixth, from the standpoint of historical or sociological analysis, what kind of event was 2-28? Was it part of a nation-wide revolution against a declining regime (the view of the Chinese Communists)? An incipiently nationalistic movement trying to throw off the rule of a "colonial" power (the view of the TIM)? Or was it the kind of mass urban violence that has often accompanied the evolution of Chinese regimes? We prefer the last of these interpretations, keeping in mind three main patterns of urban violence.

First, Chinese cities have long been the locus of organized violence directed against government authority or misrule. C. K. Yang recorded over 6,000 cases, in only six provinces, of urban violence involving groups of more than five persons between 1769 and 1911.[25] Almost half were anti-government protests, and the next-largest share were aimed simply at replacing certain officials accused of misconduct. Although we lack statistical studies for other periods, it seems clear that Chinese society has often exhibited this pattern of urban violence.

Second, while the misrule or the unpopularity of authorities has often provoked urban violence, the establishment of a new regime which rearranges the distribution of power, wealth, and prestige has often made previously established local elites fear the loss of their hard-won position in society and has thus dangerously escalated local tensions. Although the Ch'ing established their dynasty in 1644, not until 1681 did massive resistance to the new dynasty end on the Mainland.[26]

Third, apart from misrule and the establishment of a new regime threatening entrenched local interests, we must consider the complex ramifications of a shift from native to foreign governance, and vice versa. As the Ch'ing case illustrates, a shift from native to foreign rule often aroused deep feelings of patriotism or loyalism, which reinforced the resentment entrenched elites felt toward the new regime. Yet, paradoxically, a shift back to native governance could unbottle local demands repressed by foreign rulers, whose lack of respect for Chinese expectations was taken for granted by the colonized population. Taiwanese did not expect democracy from the Japanese but demanded it from the KMT. At the same time, when colonial power was exercised by nations more modern than China, reversion to Chinese rule effected a disappointing decline in administrative efficiency. An example is provided by Weihaiwei, which reverted to Nationalist control in 1930, after 32 years of British rule. Riots plagued the Chinese administration throughout the 1930s, which reacted with bewilderment, attempts to modernize, and increasing brutality.[27]

The Taiwan Uprising of 1947 resembles in some ways each of these three types of violence, exhibiting as it does urban reactions to misrule; the nervousness of local elites resenting the new regime's redistribution of power, wealth, and prestige; and the particular disappointments caused by restoration of Chinese authority over an area previously governed by the colonial administration of a nation more modern than China. The 1947 Uprising, however, also had distinctive characteristics: a basic clash between the highly moralistic, if not Manichaean, worldview of the local Chinese elite and that of the Mainlanders arriving to re-establish Chinese authority. And it had a distinctive combination of trends and events, including a severe economic crisis, controversy over disposition of the colonial power's economic assets, social ills, cultural-linguistic barriers, and the reduction in 1946 of the military-police presence to a minuscule force.

Who, then, should be held responsible for the 1947 Uprising and the subsequent period of repression and terror? This is our seventh question, that of moral evaluation. Our main contribution in this regard, distinguishing our effort from the four interpretations discussed earlier, is to detach this moral issue from the first six questions, which are factual and analytic, and must be addressed as such. For instance, whether the dissidents' acts in February and March amounted to sedition is a factual question that lacks a moral dimension. George Washington's actions were seditious relative to British law, but many people today regard them as moral, whereas the revolutionaries who overthrew the Czarists in 1917 and opened the way to Communist totalitarianism are often judged less favorably. Sedition can be viewed as praiseworthy or reprehensible. Only by separating factual questions from moral ones can we debate the latter reasonably. Given the powerful political passions that still envelop the 1947 tragedy, a differentiation of moral and factual issues could be a major step forward in the quest for a just historical judgment.

To reach such a judgment, it seems to us, one has to consider, in addition to the factual issues, the degree to which the actions and demands of the dissidents were justified; historical perspective; and the relation of moral judgment to the needs of people in Taiwan today. With regard to historical perspective, for instance, we can condemn the bloody excesses of the government in the spring of 1947 while keeping in mind both the world political situation at that time and the range of behavior of governments fighting to maintain their sovereignty.[28]

We believe that readers who seriously reflect on the complex circumstances leading to the Uprising will regard it not as a contest between heroes and villains, but as a tragic event. This tragedy was a reflection of China's struggle in the 1940s to turn itself from a traditional society into a modern one, with an efficient, democratic government. In 1947, there was no political organization able to give China that kind of government. Forty years later, there still is not, except in one small part of China, Taiwan. Until this struggle is successfully concluded in other parts of China, tragedies like the February Uprising are likely to occur again.

In the next four chapters, we answer our seven questions in much greater detail. But what of the sources on which this study is based? How credible is the evidence on which we base our interpretation?

We have examined every important article and book written about the Uprising since it occurred, including previously secret reports made by ROC officials in 1947 and published only in 1988. We have also tried to introduce a historical dimension to our analysis of the Uprising by examining the previous decade in greater detail than any other study of 2-28. We have examined a large body of Japanese historical material that sheds new light on the complex relationships between the Chinese living in Taiwan and their Japanese colonial rulers, particularly during the Pacific War. Further, we have drawn on declassified U.S. State Department documents prepared by American officials in Taipei during the eighteen months prior to the Uprising, including the private papers of an American official serving in Taipei at that time. We have also examined numerous memoirs by Taiwanese and Mainlanders who wrote about the Uprising and its antecedents. Permission to examine some rare documents held by government organizations of the Republic of China has, we believe, enabled us to present a clearer, more complete picture of the Uprising than has previously been possible.

Of course, we would have liked to know even more. We asked the Garrison Command in Taipei for permission to examine its records. At first they promised to grant permission, but after numerous telephone calls to confirm, permission was denied. We did, however, interview around sixty men and women who had participated in the Uprising.[29] Some were Taiwanese, others were former Communists, and still others were Mainland officials who held high positions in Ch'en I's provincial government or who knew Ch'en I personally. Finally, we visited the site where the Uprising began, the street where provincial Monopoly Bureau officials arrested a woman for selling contraband cigarettes, and an innocent bystander was accidentally killed. We interviewed people living in the area today. While many still remembered the event that caused the Uprising, they recalled few details.

That we have drawn on a wider range of historical sources than any previous study has, we believe, enabled us to provide an analytic and a narrative framework for the Uprising that will remain valid as additional facts become known about the tragic events of February 28, 1947. In regard to the facts we have assembled, we have tried to be honest and fair. As the famous twentieth-century philosopher Yin Hai-kuang said, "Whatever something is, that is what you say it is" (*Shih shen-mo, chiu shuo shen-mo*).

CHAPTER 2

Taiwan Under Japanese Rule

Historical Background

Taiwan is about one hundred miles east of Mainland China, some seven hundred miles south of Japan, and only two hundred miles north of Luzon (the northernmost, largest Philippine island). On the same latitude as central Mexico, it straddles the sea lanes between Southeast Asia and Japan. About 240 miles long and 98 miles wide from west to east at its broadest point, Taiwan is about half again as big as Massachusetts. Its semi-tropical climate encourages agriculture, but much of the area is mountainous, and there are few animal or fossil resources.[1]

Aboriginal people began living in Taiwan perhaps 6,000 years ago, and Mainland Chinese may have been aware of Taiwan by the third century A.D.[2] Yet serious immigration from the Mainland began only about four centuries ago, around 1600. In contrast, the Japanese islands, which are no nearer the Mainland, supported a large population by A.D. 600. Why Taiwan remained a generally undesirable piece of land for a millennium is not clear.

There were few Chinese in Taiwan even in 1590, when Portuguese navigators found the island and called it Formosa ("beautiful"), the name by which it became known in the Western world.[3] In 1622, the Dutch established a military base on the Pescadores, just southwest of Taiwan, and in 1624 they built Fort Zeelandia on the island itself, just outside today's Tainan city. After routing Spanish settlements from the northern part of the island, the Dutch expanded their garrison and used Taiwan as a trading center.

The rule of the Dutch ended in 1661 when the forces of Cheng Ch'engkung (Koxinga), the famous Ming loyalist, defeated them. The regime established by Cheng lasted until 1683, when troops under the Ch'ing K'ang-hsi emperor crushed units under Cheng's grandson. The emperor vowed that the Ch'ing would "establish a proper administration for protecting the people, crushing all traitors, and bestowing a culture to make local customs conform to our own."[4] For the next two hundred years, the Ch'ing state administered the island like any other prefecture, but anti-Ch'ing sentiment, united around the memory of Koxinga, persisted.

By the late seventeenth century, the Mainland was experiencing an unprecedented population explosion. Emigrants from Fukien and Kwangtung provinces sailed illegally to Taiwan, founding villages and market towns in the arable western plain. After the 1720s, emigration accelerated because the Ch'ing court no longer tried to enforce the laws against it.[5] Settlements then spread to the north and east of the island.[6] Urban and rural communities were modeled on those of the Mainland, and trade flourished between the two sides of the Taiwan Strait.

The Ch'ing state stationed troops to maintain order and sent civil officials to govern from their yamens in the walled cities of Tainan and Taipei. These officials, as well as wealthy local leaders, also established the traditional academies (*shu-yüan*) to train a class of literati from which to recruit new officials. By the early 1800s, Taiwan's schools had produced more literati than had old frontier areas like Kansu. There were about 5,000 of them out of a population approaching 2 million.[7]

The legal exclusion of foreigners from Taiwan ended only in the mid-nineteenth century. The Treaty of Tientsin, in 1858, designated Anping as a treaty port, and the Treaty of Peking, in 1860, opened Tamsui. Three years later Keelung and Kaohsiung (Takao) were also opened to foreign trade.[8] British and American merchants began trading at these centers, and missionaries soon followed. Especially influential was the Presbyterian Missionary Association (*Chang-lao chiao-hui*), which arrived in 1865, established medical, printing, and school facilities, and attracted enthusiastic converts, who formed a prominent social network.

Presbyterian missionaries first arrived in Taiwan in 1865, and their work produced meager results in the next three decades. By 1900, however, there were 77 places of worship in which some 10,000 Christianized Taiwanese frequented and made annual contributions totaling around US$7,000.[9] By the 1930s, the Presbyterians had greatly expanded in number, although they still were less than 1 percent of the population.[10] The church now had four schools offering a Western-style education to young students. Each minister or elder, whether Chinese or a foreigner, had voting rights in the church instead of being governed by a missionary council of foreigners. The Presbyterians already pursued a policy of instilling in their members the principles of "self-organization, self-cultivation, and self-promotion" (*tzu-chih, tzu-yang, tzu-ch'uan*).[11] In other words, the internal structure of the church order reflected and emphasized a British-Canadian concept of democratic management of officers, which conflicted with the authoritarian political environment of Japanese colonial rule and the Chinese Confucian tradition. The Presbyterians had, however, the premier foreign religious-cultural association on the island, attracting many members of the Taiwanese elite, such as the family of P'eng Ming-min. This religious network continues to exert influence today, having played a significant political role in the post–World War II movement to make Taiwan an independent nation.[12]

Between 1870 and 1895, repeated threats by foreign powers to annex Taiwan induced local officials to initiate a land survey as well as a tax reform to raise the revenue needed for "self-strengthening" projects. High-ranking Ch'ing officials came to Taiwan to strengthen the island's military defenses, develop mining, construct roads, and build telegraph lines and a telegraph cable between Taipei and Foochow. In 1885, the court demonstrated its concern for the island's security by making Taiwan a province, detaching it from the province of Fukien. Some Taiwanese have claimed that as a result of these changes Taiwan became the most modernized part of the Ch'ing empire and anti-Ch'ing feeling finally subsided.

These efforts, however, failed to keep Taiwan within the empire. On April 7, 1895, in the Treaty of Shimonoseki ending the first Sino-Japanese War, Japan compelled the Ch'ing court to cede Taiwan as well as the nearby Pescadores.

The Evolution of the Taiwanese Elite

The Japanese landed on Taiwan on May 29, 1895, but they met fierce resistance from the Taiwanese, who had proclaimed the establishment of a Republic of Taiwan on May 25. The Republic lasted only ten days, but the Taiwanese fought the Japanese troops for four months before surrendering Tainan city in October 1895. Sporadic guerrilla resistance to the Japanese continued for another five years (and some say for as long as twenty). More than 10,000 Taiwanese died. Eventually, the Taiwanese acquiesced, and only a tiny minority accepted the Japanese offer to leave the island with their property. The local elites then resorted to practices that Chinese of all regions have long used in dealing with invaders: they tried to preserve their cultural heritage, retain ties with other provinces, and derive whatever advantage they could from their new rulers' policies. To some extent, they oscillated between co-optation and alienation.

Although some literati moved to the Mainland, after the spring of 1897 the youngest, especially, became nostalgic for the island and returned. Meanwhile, the Japanese began co-opting those who had remained by presenting public awards to prominent people, some of whom were sent to

Tokyo for an audience with the emperor. Wang Shih-lang recalls that the Chinese "accepted these awards, wore them on occasion, but they later regarded the Japanese policy as deceiving the people, and they discarded these medals." [13]

Co-optation took many forms. The Japanese recruited members of the elite to serve as leaders in the new organization to police and supervise household activity (the *hokō* system, which was based on the Chinese *pao-chia* arrangement), as officials in the new prefectural (*ken*) and department (*chō*) administrative units below the central bureaucracy of the colony, and as officials in the bureaucracy itself.[14]

But some literati resisted co-optation. They continued to identify themselves with the Ch'ing empire and dreamed of expelling the hated Japanese. Many dropped out of public life and became recluses. Some, like Lien Heng, Lo Hsiu-hui, and Hu Tien-p'eng, went to Amoy in 1905 and worked on a newspaper that supported the T'ung-meng-hui revolutionary organization dedicated to overthrowing the Manchus.[15] Yet when such literati eventually returned to Taiwan, they quickly learned that the ubiquitous Japanese police, with their household surveillance system, made promoting revolutionary activity very risky. As a result, these literati ceased their conspiratorial activity.

This pattern of alienation and co-optation was reflected also in Chinese reactions to Japanese reforms, which began in earnest in 1897. In the next decade, the Japanese restricted the use of opium to legalized dens and banned the drug elsewhere, forbade foot-binding, and urged males to cut off their queues. Some older scholars opposed these reforms and withdrew from public life. Others preferred teaching the doctrines from *ssu-shu* (The Four Books) in the old-fashioned Chinese schools.

Many literati accepted the reforms and became teachers in the new Japanese system. As already mentioned, some agreed to serve in the new colonial administration as officials. A significant number turned to conventional occupations. Many literati visited Japan and became interested in the modern ways they observed on their travels. Some, like Huang Ch'un-ch'ing of Shu-lin in Taipei prefecture, urged rural reforms, while others, like Lin Yao-t'ing, introduced new technology to farmers.[16] As more of the elite became exposed to Japanese culture and society, they began to admire Japanese bureaucratic efficiency.

Fifteen years after the Treaty of Shimonoseki, Japanese policies had borne fruit. Specialization and trade were increasing rapidly; the technical improvement of agriculture was progressing at a fast pace; a modern sugar industry had sprung up; exports had soared; and finance and railway transport had been revolutionized. Rising per capita income made it possible for Taiwanese to increase the funds they spent on schools, temples, charities, and parks.

These new opportunities encouraged many Taiwanese, including literati, to go into business and become wealthy. Many if not most of the literati remained deeply attached to Chinese culture, however. Some "who still treasured the Chinese literary tradition, came to play leading roles in their communities."[17] Some, like Ts'ai Kuo-li in Tainan and Hung I-nan in Taipei, formed a poetry association in 1900 to preserve the essence of Chinese culture. Members met at restaurants, elected leaders to manage the association, recited poetry, and discussed literature. Wu Te-kung of Changhua, who in 1899 had lamented the fate of the literati under Japanese rule, wrote essays praising Confucian thought and urged young people to cultivate Chinese literary skills and moral qualities. Cheng I-lin, who taught Chinese literature at a secondary school in Lukang, criticized anyone who did not advocate studying the Chinese language and Chinese culture in the schools. When his school canceled instruction in the Four Books, Cheng resigned in protest.[18] Such individual efforts and poetry associations helped keep Chinese culture alive. Long before the Ch'ing dynasty fell in 1912, however, most literati had lost hope that it would liberate them from Japanese rule.

The 1910s and 1920s saw a new kind of elite begin to emerge. The status of its members was less dependent on pre-Japanese social structure than that of the literati, landowners, and merchants who had already enjoyed wealth or position under the Ch'ing. In many cases, members of this new elite had been poor before 1895 and saw the opportunities created by the Japanese or, more broadly, by the non-Chinese elements in Taiwan, including the missionaries, as a way for them to rise from misery and obscurity. They did not actually fully absorb Japanese culture. They simply had less nostalgia—or perhaps even none at all—for the Chinese social order under the Ch'ing and tended instead to identify everything good in their lives with the changes brought about in Taiwan by the Japanese or Westerners.

In 1895, many members of this new elite had been the children of very poor families, but by 1920 they were acquiring under Japanese auspices a professional education—typically medicine—that would be their ticket to wealth and prestige. Their children, born in the 1920s, would from kindergarten on receive a Japanese education and identify personal success with success in the Japanese academic world, whether in Kaohsiung, Taipei, Kyoto, or Tokyo.

This kind of elite was bound to have weaker emotional ties to the Chinese political and cultural order than those of families already well off under the Ch'ing dynasty. In other words, the Taiwanese elite under the Japanese exhibited a spectrum of orientations one pole of which included far more commitment to the inherited Chinese cultural and intellectual order than the other pole, though at both poles Taiwanese continued to take for granted the everyday norms and customs of Chinese family life and, probably, to feel some patriotic commitment to China.

The pole with little or no sense of debt to Chinese culture can be illustrated by the history of P'eng Ming-min's family. P'eng's great-great-grandfather had arrived in Taiwan from Fukien around 1840, roughly the time his great-grandfather was born.[19] The family were the poorest kind of fishermen and farmers, who probably first heard of "Western barbarians" on the island around 1850. P'eng's grandfather was born around 1865, just when Presbyterian missionaries first arrived. The family fortunes began to change around 1885, when P'eng Ming-min's grandfather was hired as a cook for one of these missionaries, became a Christian, and, greatly interested in the Western ways he encountered, "gradually left behind the life of the traditional Chinese," as P'eng Ming-min describes it.[20] P'eng Ming-min's father, P'eng Ch'ing-k'ao, was born around 1890, one of eight children, most of whom did menial work to support the family. Around 1910, however, P'eng Ch'ing-k'ao was able to go to Taipei on a Japanese scholarship to study medicine. In one generation, then, he raised the P'eng family from poverty to elite status.

While at medical school, P'eng Ch'ing-k'ao, moving in Presbyterian circles, met his future wife, who came from a landowning merchant family engaged in making rice-wine.[21] After graduating, he married, opened up a clinic in Ta-chia (central Taiwan), and enjoyed a fine income. He also invested in a considerable amount of paddy land, was an influential and respected community figure, supported the movement for Taiwanese political rights, and raised a family in which more than twenty members eventually went on to earn medical degrees.[22] P'eng Ming-min was born into these happy, comfortable surroundings in about 1924: "I clearly remember that when we went north on the train, Father would always point to yellow paddy fields and proudly say, 'Those paddy fields are all ours.'"[23]

Around 1929, when P'eng Ming-min was about five, his parents took him to visit the Mainland. Years later, he remembered walking up the many steps at the tomb of Sun Yat-sen in Nanking. His parents "were deeply impressed by how big China was and felt some sadness and nostalgia when visiting their ancestral home area, but with regard to social development, industrialization, education, and public hygiene, they felt that China compared with Taiwan was backward in many ways."[24]

About this time, P'eng Ming-min, his mother, and his two older brothers and older sister moved to a Japanese-style house that they rented in Taipei near the U.S. consulate, living there in order to obtain a Japanese education. By this time, the law allowed any Taiwanese child who spoke Japanese properly to go to one of the schools that the Japanese had set up for their own children. P'eng Ming-min thus entered a Japanese kindergarten and then a primary school in Taipei, studying and playing with his young Japanese friends. P'eng then transferred to a Japanese primary school in Ta-chia, where the Japanese principal was especially fond of him and where he was chosen to be class representative.[25]

Around 1935, P'eng went to Tokyo to live for more than a year with his father and older sister. His father went there to receive training in obstetrics, his sister entered a women's medical school, and P'eng attended primary school. The day the family left Ta-chia, the Japanese principal of P'eng's school led the students—almost all of them Japanese—to the train station to see the P'engs off. When he and his father returned from Tokyo, his father opened a hospital in Kaohsiung, which the Japanese were then developing into a major harbor city to support their empire's expansion in China and to the south. P'eng was now about twelve and entered the fifth grade in a Kaohsiung Japanese school, where he made the baseball team. He was a "lousy" hitter but a good second baseman. He then entered a high school in Kaohsiung where three-quarters of the students were Japanese.[26]

By this time, Japan was at war with China, Japanese patriotism filled the school, and P'eng participated in evening lantern parades congratulating the Japanese army on its victories. Yet as a Taiwanese, he felt "pained and embarrassed" by this situation.[27] His family avidly read the newspapers and discussed international events. P'eng started studying English, seeing it as an opening into the world of the West—a world that clearly appealed to him as a progressive alternative to the worlds of Japanese imperialism and Chinese backwardness. Around 1940, because his Kaohsiung principal refused to allow him to take the college entrance examination, P'eng went to Japan and entered a Japanese high school, from which he eventually managed to go to a prestigious school in Kyoto and then to Tokyo Imperial University. He thus circumvented a decision discriminating against him as a Taiwanese.

P'eng stayed in Japan throughout the war. He acquired many Japanese friends and especially enjoyed his time in Kyoto, before wartime conditions deteriorated. Not drafted into the Japanese army, he lived in Kyoto on a generous stipend from his father and fell in with a crowd of zealously intellectual students who discussed philosophy with the idealistic enthusiasm of young people eager to read every new book and solve every old problem. Already proficient in English, he now became fascinated with the French language and everything French.[28] The student atmosphere tended toward individualistic, liberal, and anti-militarist thinking, and P'eng may have begun to move a bit toward the vision of Taiwan's independence that crystallized in his mind some two decades later (see Chapter 1). The initial impulse may have been his reading of Joseph Ernest Renan (1823–1892), who blended scientific rationalism with Hegelianism to arrive at the conclusion that modern nationhood is based not on a shared language, culture, or ethnic origin but a "shared sense of destiny," to use P'eng's words. In 1945, P'eng's left arm was blown off by a bomb in Nagasaki, and he was also near Nagasaki when it was hit by the atom bomb.[29]

In January of 1946 P'eng returned to Taiwan, although a number of Taiwanese students in similar circumstances chose to continue their studies in Japan and P'eng himself was just a year short of graduation from Tokyo Imperial University. His memoirs give a picture of his years in Japan—years filled with the kindness of his Japanese acquaintances, the personal respect he felt for many of them, warm personal relations, and the pride he felt at repeatedly passing the difficult examinations needed to enter top Japanese institutions. As P'eng grew older, he concluded that many Japanese teachers, intellectuals, and ordinary people disagreed with Japanese policies discriminating against Taiwanese and sympathized with the Taiwanese desire for equality.[30] Readers familiar with the period of British rule in India will notice that much of the Japanese presence in Taiwan does not fit the stereotype of a haughty ruling community keeping a great social distance between itself and its colonial subjects.

The twenty-two-year-old P'eng Ming-min who returned to Taiwan to complete his undergraduate degree at National Taiwan University had an outlook that must have been somewhat typical of many young Taiwanese intellectuals who had excelled in the Japanese educational system and whose families' elite status was based entirely on the opportunities and institutions created by the Japanese administration of Taiwan, not on the socioeconomic order of the Ch'ing era. This outlook, combined with the difficult conditions under the KMT in 1946 and 1947, could easily grow into the demand for Taiwan independence described in Chapter 4. Nonetheless, there was also to be found in this outlook a certain patriotic attachment to China, manifest in the embarrassment felt by P'eng when he had to join his Japanese friends in celebrating Japan's victories in China. There was, too, a concomitant strong resentment about being treated as a second-class citizen by Japanese authorities, such as P'eng's Kaohsiung high school principal. Still, the young intellectuals felt strongly that fifty years of Japanese rule had freed Taiwan from "backwardness, bad government, and chaos" and brought it economic and social progress.[31] With this came a propensity to feel superior to the Chinese who had not benefited from this experience.

P'eng's father already felt that Taiwan owed its progress to Japan when he visited China in the 1930s. He felt this even more strongly in October 1945, when, as chairman of the Taiwanese Reception Committee, he watched with embarrassment as ragged Chinese troops disembarked at Kaohsiung to be greeted by an immaculate delegation of Japanese troops lined up at the dock:

The first man to appear was a bedraggled fellow who looked and behaved more like a coolie than a soldier, walking off carrying a pole across his shoulder, from which were suspended his umbrella, sleeping mat, cooking pot, and cup. Others like him followed, some with shoes, some without. Few had guns. With no attempt to maintain order or discipline, they pushed off the ship, glad to be on firm land but hesitant to face the Japanese lined up and saluting smartly on both sides.[32]

P'eng's father was mortified by this "nightmare" and later recounted that "if there had been a hole nearby, I would have crawled in."[33] From then on, people like the P'engs saw the KMT as an institution that would drag Taiwan down to the level of general Chinese backwardness. This was hardly the reward they expected for having been subjected to the humiliation of colonialism.

The P'engs' feeling of Taiwanese superiority was intensified by the elitism of a family accustomed to being honored in society and—in the case of P'eng Ming-min—by the natural pride of a young man in his legitimate academic accomplishments. Such people could not fail to feel outrage when Chinese they perceived as slovenly and ignorant received high positions denied them. In addition, P'eng Ming-min felt he was part of a superior, cosmopolitan culture—a culture of individualism and liberalism he had won access to through his knowledge of French and English. This cosmopolitan culture, however, exhibited little if any fascination with either Japanese or Chinese literature, philosophy, or history. At least, no such fascination surfaced in P'eng's memoirs. His interests lay in the science and liberalism of the West. Nothing in his memoirs indicates any serious interest in the modern Chinese intellectual *Problematik* which, going back to K'ang Yu-wei and Liang Ch'i-ch'ao at the turn of the century, wrestled with how to reconcile Confucian values to an age of modernization. For P'eng, there was a right answer to this question (Hu Shih's iconoclasm), but the question itself did not interest him much. With a grandfather who had thankfully left Chinese culture behind, a family educational tradition centered on modern medicine, a life spent in Japanese schools since kindergarten, and a largely scientific, liberal Western philosophy, P'eng had no conceptual access to the evocation of Confucian ideals that was to become central to the ideology and culture of Taiwan under the KMT.

We cannot determine with any precision how widespread P'eng Ming-min's worldview was among the roughly 6.5 million Taiwanese in the 1940s, but the available figures suggest that it was very widespread in elite and sub-elite circles. We know that in 1945, 47,353 Taiwanese were serving in the bureaucracy under the governor-general. With their immediate families, averaging around seven persons per household, they constituted a group of about 300,000. We also know that an overlapping group, Taiwanese members of district, city, and town councils, numbered 3,455 in 1944. When their immediate families are included, they numbered about 24,000. Another overlapping group numbered some 700,000 by 1942: the families of the 100,000 Taiwanese reported to have adopted Japanese surnames after 1941. Still another overlapping group consisted of professional people, like P'eng, who owed their elite status to social conditions promoted by the Japanese.

Obviously, not everyone belonging to one of these categories thought the way the P'engs did. However, these figures do suggest that a great number of people in elite circles had institutional or other reasons to identify themselves with Japanese perspectives, at least in part. We may get some idea of the actual numbers if we estimate that 5 percent of the population, or 325,000 people, were elite. Because 300,000 of these were economically dependent on the state bureaucracy, it is theoretically conceivable that most of the elite had views similar to the P'engs. If we increase our estimate of the elite to 10 percent, our theoretical approach would still lead to the conclusion that 40 percent or so of the elite viewed the world somewhat as the P'engs did. It is very possible that the actual figure was well below 40 percent. That it was significant, however, cannot be doubted.

Nevertheless, as already mentioned, many members of the elite, perhaps because of family roots in the pre-1895 elite world, had a stronger commitment to Chinese culture than did the P'engs. Lin Hsien-t'ang is an example. In 1914, Lin, a wealthy, influential landowner in Taichung, invited the famous Japanese politician and founder of the Liberal Party Itagaki Taisuke to tour Taiwan at his expense. Itagaki's call for "the people of Taiwan and the Japanese to strive to achieve the goal of greater assimilation" caused a great stir among the Taiwanese.[34] In response, the more politically active Taiwanese quickly formed the Assimilation Society to promote harmonious relations between Japanese and Taiwanese—but on the basis of racial equality.[35] Yet in his personal life Lin Hsien-t'ang was "most thoroughly anti-assimilationist."[36] He never spoke a word of Japanese, even though he had served as a district chief since the age of twenty. Although he had constant contact with Japanese officials, he never used the Japanese language to communicate with them. His life-style was never influenced by Japanese fashions and ideas. When the Japanese ordered public schools not to teach Chinese language, history, and culture, he petitioned the officials to restore those courses to allow the people to have contact with Chinese culture. Lin's tactic of cooperating with the Japanese while preserving his Chinese heritage was one adopted by many members of the elite.

Certainly in the writings of Taiwanese intellectuals during the period between the world wars, one finds few if any arguments for abandoning Chinese culture. In the 1910s, Liang Ch'i-ch'ao and Tai Chi-t'ao had told the Taiwanese that China could not help them—that they would have to struggle along on their own. Thus, although Taiwanese intellectuals and elites developed a spectrum of attitudes toward Chinese civilization and Japanese rule, even many of those most indebted for their status to the Japanese joined in the Taiwanese demand for additional political rights. The P'eng family was only one example.

The Taiwanese Struggle for Political Rights

At first, the Japanese had hoped to apply the same laws to the Taiwanese as to their own people, but that did not occur, because the governor-general's office on Taiwan insisted on retaining Special Law No. 63, enacted by the Diet in 1896, which gave it the authority to impose any laws it believed necessary to keep the peace and ensure Japanese control. Therefore, the Japanese colonial administration had jurisdiction over the Taiwanese through a system of colonial courts. Because colonial laws applied only to the Taiwanese, not to the Japanese, the Taiwanese never had the same rights as the Japanese.[37] Moreover, the Japanese created a dual economic structure which gave them a privileged position. The highly commercialized and industrial processing sector, primarily urban, remained in Japanese hands. The primary sector of handicraft, agriculture, forestry, and fishing was left to the Taiwanese. The island's economic surplus eventually passed through the Japanese-controlled commercial sector, usually at exchange rates favorable to it. Japanese wealth and privilege were never challenged.[38]

In education, most Taiwanese fared little better, which eventually proved troublesome for the Japanese. Colonial officials initially wanted to limit the Taiwanese to "the lower track of the two-track Meiji education system." For this purpose, they increased the number of elementary and vocational schools in the early years.[39] The first civilian governor-general, Den Kinjirō, set up additional schools in the 1920s for the Taiwanese and even allowed some outstanding students (like P'eng) to enter the prestigious primary and middle schools reserved for the children of Japanese residents. This spillover of Taiwanese into the higher education track continued into the 1930s, when several thousand Taiwanese were studying in Japanese schools every year. Paradoxically, this new educational training, coexisting with inherited Chinese Confucian values of benevolence and justice that had been nurtured by families and Chinese private schools, caused many young Taiwanese to feel outraged by the whole structure of colonial inequality.

We have seen how Itagaki Taisuke's tour of Taiwan in 1914 stimulated the formation of the Assimilation Society to promote Japanese-Taiwanese relations based on equality. In March 1920, Taiwanese students in Tokyo, funded by wealthy Taiwanese, established the New People's Society, dedicated to reforming Japanese colonial rule. The society began publishing a magazine to enlighten Taiwanese back home and to solicit their support to end Japanese discrimination. Several years later, the society divided on the issue of support for Lin Ch'eng-lu's proposal to establish a separate Taiwanese legislature, which emerged after the Japanese Diet had upheld Law No. 63 without setting any time limit for terminating it. Lin viewed a Taiwanese legislature as a means of restraining the colonial executive, and he led the Taiwanese elite in submitting petitions asking the Japanese Diet to create such a legislature in Taiwan. The League for Establishing a Taiwan Parliament, created by Lin and his supporters, was active between 1921 and 1934. At first, the League obtained fewer than 1,000 signatories, but after 1926, it received many more. Great courage was required for a signatory to go public, because disclosure made one vulnerable to government pressure. Colonial officials adamantly opposed the movement, using different means to destroy it. They dismissed signatories from their government jobs and forced banks to recall loans made to Taiwanese considered politically undesirable. They even arrested leaders such as Ts'ai P'ei-huo. Eventually, the movement failed for lack of support from top government leaders in Tokyo.

In addition to this movement, Taiwanese found other ways to express their frustrations. In October 1924, Chiang Wei-shui set up the Taiwan Cultural Association. Chiang perceived the Taiwanese as "suffering from a disease" caused by "mental malnutrition." He contended that the only cure was mental nourishment through Chinese culture. The Association also wished to promote harmony among Asian peoples. Association branches quickly formed around the island.

In the mid-1920s, socialist and Marxist ideas began filtering into Taiwan. These ideas radicalized many young Taiwanese, some of whom even went to the countryside to work with farmers and tenants and organize them into a Farmers' Union (*Taiwan Nōmin Kumiai*). Once formed, this union instigated a number of strikes on sugar plantations to prevent the harvesting of sugarcane. The strikes usually led to violence and the arrest of the strikers.[40]

The Popular Party (*Min-chung-tang*) was formed and approved by the Japanese authorities in July 1927 by moderates like Chiang Wei-shui and Ts'ai P'ei-huo, who withdrew from the Taiwan Cultural Association and the Farmers' Union because of the increased radicalism of their members. The goals of the Popular Party were democracy, economic fairness, and social justice. The new party worked to legalize labor unions and win a large role for Taiwanese in local governance. In 1930, the Popular Party split, with Ts'ai and others forming the League for the Attainment of Local Autonomy. Those who remained, like Chiang Wei-shui, called for a united front representing "the interest of the people without property" and including all political parties in Japan and elsewhere.[41] This proved too much for the Japanese police, who quickly arrested Chiang and his colleagues.

By 1930, all Taiwanese political opposition to Japanese rule ended, except for the League. Finally, in 1936, the governor-general's office disbanded the League too, arguing that local councils had met the League's demands. In 1940, however, Taiwanese were given a bigger role in these councils, and elections were held to fill some of the seats on them.

To summarize, Taiwan's political history under Japanese colonialism can be roughly divided into three phases. The first, lasting for at least a few years after the Japanese assumed control in 1895, was marked by violent resistance to the imposition of colonialism. During the third phase, beginning around 1940, wartime mobilization took precedence over everything else. The in-between or second phase, which began around 1914, was marked by strong, widespread Taiwanese reactions against Japanese legal, educational, and economic discrimination. Taiwanese formed the Assimilation Society, the New People's Society, the League for Establishing a Taiwan Parliament, the Taiwan Cultural Association, the Farmers' Union, the Popular Party, and the League for the Attainment of Local Autonomy. Also founded in this period was the Taiwanese Communist Party, whose history will be sketched in more detail in a later chapter. Created in Shanghai in 1928, the Taiwanese Communist Party sent its members to the island to try to build a revolutionary movement there, but police surveillance prevented them from having much success, and in the 1930s all its important members were obliged to flee back to the Mainland.

Although varying in their degree of radicalism or Marxism and possessing no clear vision of Taiwanese self-determination, all these groups expressed political consciousness and a demand for equality and political participation. Despite Japanese colonialism, therefore, Taiwan's society was far from immune to that mix of liberal and radical political ideas so important on the Mainland during those decades. When the KMT began to establish an electoral process in Taiwan in 1946, it was responding to a Taiwanese demand for political participation that had taken shape over a number of decades, as well as building on an electoral process begun by the Japanese in 1940.

Japan's Initial Wartime Policies

By 1937, Taiwan had enjoyed four decades of peace and unprecedented economic prosperity. The island's gross domestic product, the barometer of its wealth, had risen 2.6 times by that year. Thus, per capita income may have been nearly twice that of the Mainland.[42] Moreover, the island's infrastructure of railroads, roads, harbors, telecommunications, health services, and educational institutions far exceeded that of the Mainland. A "green revolution" had swept the island, providing an expanding food supply that far outstripped population growth. Chinese visitors from the Mainland reported their amazement at Taiwan's material progress.[43] People were not afraid to leave their homes unlocked.[44] Criminals were quickly apprehended and sentenced. Yet legal and economic discrimination against the Taiwanese persisted, and the Taiwanese clung to their cultural heritage while at the same time assimilating much of Japanese culture. At this point, the Taiwanese were faced with a situation filled with ambivalence and agony: war between Japan and China.

Although tensions between the Taiwanese and the Japanese seemed to have eased, they quickly escalated after Japan invaded China in July 1937. Within a few days, the authorities prohibited all Taiwanese from listening to radio broadcasts from the Mainland.[45] Within six months, there were more than 1,000 reported cases of Taiwanese cursing Japanese officials and police.[46] Isolated incidents of espionage and sabotage also occurred, allegedly in support of the Nationalist government in Nanking.[47] Such displays of public anger seem to have declined before the outbreak of the Pacific War, and they became rare after 1940. Japanese criminal statistics certainly bear this out, as reported by the island's premier newspaper, the *Taiwan nichi-nichi shimpō* (*Taiwan Daily*), which proudly announced in January 1942 that island-wide crime had rapidly declined (see Table 1).

TABLE 1
Crime in Taiwan, 1936–42

	No. of crimes by type						
Period	Petty theft, etc.	Burglary	Gambling	Public indecency	Navy & army crimes	Other	Total
Dec. 8, 1936– Dec. 7, 1937	983	–	393	38	4	1,087	2,505
Dec. 8, 1937– Dec. 7, 1938	1,212	2	460	3	8	731	2,416
Mid-Dec. 1938– Mid-Nov. 1939	2,418	4	910	0	1	2,344	5,677
Mid-Nov. 1939– Mid-Dec. 1940	2,480	30	1,523	0	0	3,398	7,431
Dec. 1940– Jan. 7, 1942	901	0	916	3	3	537	2,360

SOURCE: "Dai Tōa senkaishi irai hanzai wa kyū ni genshō" [Crime has suddenly declined since the Great East Asian War commenced], *Taiwan nichi-nichi shimpō*, Jan. 25, 1942, p. 2.

Although some scholars claim that Taiwanese resistance to the Japanese remained widespread and significant between 1940 and 1945,[48] such claims are based upon questionable information. True, we have no firm evidence to deny that sporadic sabotage and anti-Japanese sentiment persisted among the Taiwanese in these years. Yet there are two reasons why it is reasonable to suppose that criminal acts reflecting anti-Japanese behavior declined in this period.

First, the authorities successfully controlled all information about the conflict on the Mainland. Told only about Japanese victories, the Taiwanese probably knew nothing about the Chinese military resistance and the spirit of nationalism that had filled many on the Mainland. Second, the Japanese greatly improved their policies to co-opt the Taiwanese, especially the youth, by launching new campaigns to encourage additional contact and legitimize social equality between Taiwanese and Japanese. This latter point should not be exaggerated, but it also cannot be ignored. These island-wide campaigns eventually affected every household in Taiwan. They were related to Tokyo's efforts to build the Greater East Asia Co-Prosperity Sphere made up of Japan, its colonies, and its newly occupied territories.

These campaigns began in earnest when Admiral Hasegawa Kiyoshi, Taiwan's seventeenth governor-general, arrived on December 16, 1940. On April 22–24, 1941, Hasegawa called a meeting of all leading officials and presented a new strategy to mobilize the Taiwanese in support of the Japanese war effort.[49] Hasegawa first pointed out that Taiwan had a most important role to play, and that all its people would have to assume new obligations to serve the emperor and imperial Japan. Japanese officials and military personnel were also expected to carry out their duties as loyal subjects of the emperor.

Hasegawa then stressed that the international situation still favored Japan, and that the nation had taken several steps to improve its position. The Japanese were developing Manchukuo (Manchuria) to help the imperial cause. They had also joined the Axis with Italy and Germany in September 1940 and had just signed a neutrality pact with the Soviet Union. Furthermore, Japan was now establishing the Greater East Asia Co-Prosperity Sphere, an event of great historical significance. Taiwan's role was to become a new base for Japan's march to the south, and Taiwanese officials must prepare for that thrust. The key was to expand education, "that fountainhead for unswervingly cultivating the foundations of the country."[50] Therefore, the administration must redesign the educational system to develop a sense of national purpose and duty among the Taiwanese. Such a plan required the reform of the educational system to make it suit Taiwan's special conditions but still meet the needs of Japan's historical mission. For such a reform to take root, the administration had to instruct the Taiwanese, turning them into true imperial subjects (*kōmin*).

According to Hasegawa, "the purpose of training people to become imperial subjects was to make them acquire the Japanese essence (*kokutai*) by developing in them the concept of being accountable for the nation's destiny and the spirit of glorious national martial preparedness."[51] The life-style most compatible with this new spirit consisted of frugality, hard work, and a willingness to sacrifice and cooperate. Hasegawa pointed out that there still "did not exist any system in Taiwan whereby all the Chinese could devote their services directly to the military and make national duty the first line of battle."[52]

In addition to educational reform, Hasegawa proposed a new industrial plan to develop the island's sources of energy, produce more raw materials, process them, and ensure their distribution. This plan called for the massive mobilization of labor and raw materials to build new electrical power stations, maintain port facilities, and construct new metallurgical, chemical, machine tool, and construction industries. All these resources could be mobilized under the control of the colonial administration if the administration created a "controlled economy" (*tosei keizai*) to supply and allocate labor, raw materials, and consumer goods.[53] The administration and the people, from the top to the bottom, would be mobilized as the emperor's subjects to industrialize the economy and turn Taiwan into a base for Japan's thrust to the south.[54]

Several weeks after Hasegawa's secret meeting with top officials, the administration made public this three-pronged strategy stressing education, industrialization, and total mobilization. The public learned that all Taiwanese would be educated to become the "great subjects of the emperor."[55] Taiwan's "most important industries would become metallurgy, chemical products, and synthetics, for which an unlimited [sic] supply of raw materials existed. Agriculture would undergo a 180-degree turnaround and a second takeoff to fuel the industrialization of Taiwan."[56] Finally, Taiwan would serve as Japan's main base for the southward thrust because of its proximity to South China and Southeast Asia, regions that offered unlimited resources that Japan and Taiwan could exploit. Moreover, these southern regions would be colonized.[57] Because the Taiwanese would work so closely with the Japanese, they would have to behave the Japanese way.

Total Patriotic Mobilization

The Japanese had tried to impress upon the Taiwanese the significance and superiority of Japanese religion and culture as early as their takeover of the island. To commemorate the death of the 49-year-old Prince Kitashirakawa in Tainan on October 28, 1895, they had quickly built a huge Shintō shrine in Taipei and lesser shrines throughout the island.[58] After 1931, the authorities stepped up the pace of imposing Japanese religion and customs on the Taiwanese. They constructed even more Shintō shrines and began asking prominent Chinese families to discard their ancestral tablets and Buddhist statues and pictures.[59] They urged Taiwanese to bow in the direction of the Shōwa emperor's dwelling and worship at the numerous Shintō shrines. Step by step, the Japanese tried to discourage the use of the Taiwanese language, first by terminating radio broadcasts in Taiwanese, then by urging families to adopt Japanese names, and finally by encouraging Taiwanese to take on Japanese customs, such as wearing Japanese-style clothing and instructing young girls in the tea ceremony.[60] The authorities also insisted that students in church schools like those of the Presbyterians "bow at Shintō shrines."[61] These ad hoc policies naturally produced only mixed results and were met with some resistance by the Taiwanese. Then in 1941 the administration abandoned its strategy of gradualism and moved to that of the island-wide "mobilization movement."

On April 19, 1941, Admiral Hasegawa's office launched the first campaign to turn the Taiwanese into imperial subjects through public service for the emperor (*kōmin hōkō undō*) that stressed total patriotic mobilization. All of the island's people had to take seriously and adopt Japanese ideals. The Taiwanese had to accept a single vision of unified benevolence (*isshi dōjin*) and form one great family (*Taiwan ikka*), as had the people of Japan.[62] The Taiwanese also had to believe in the Japanese imperial system and its values. For the first time since they ruled Taiwan, the Japanese committed themselves to assimilating their subjects and making them learn about and acquire the cultural values of Japan. Fully aware of the great differences in religion, ritual, customs, and even entertainment between them and the Taiwanese, the Japanese still hoped to introduce Japanese culture on a crash-course basis of massive mobilization and compulsory education.

This campaign was organized by the *Kōmin hōkōkai* (the Association for Rendering Public Service on Behalf of the Emperor). Governor-General Hasegawa served as the *Kōmin hōkōkai*'s (KHK's) first president from his Central Department headquarters, located at the corner of the Taipei New Public Park in a building called Harmony Hall (*Kyōwa kaikan*).[63] The KHK's control center managed a general affairs office and sections for information, training, and cultural affairs, with regional branches spreading out into every district, township, village, city, ward, and street.[64] There were KHK squads (*hōkōhan*) in every neighborhood association (*hokō*) of every city or village.[65] These squads recruited their members from the neighborhood associations, performed public service at the request of local officials, and met at the neighborhood association halls.

The KHK had its song, which all members sang to stir up patriotic fervor for public service:

> Our Japanese flag flies high, fluttering back and forth.
> We who are born in Taiwan deeply appreciate Japanese might.
> Our bravery is unwavering. Six million Taiwanese
> Now march forward on the road, officers and people,
> Side by side.

> We will vigorously protect Taiwan, its
> Hamlets and towns. Our fighting power
> Shall grow and victory will be ours.
> Our public service will reverberate to the heavens.

> Japan looks to the south, and we support its efforts.
> As our people go forth into Asia, we are united
> And will protect our national security.
> Singing the Japanese national anthem, our
> Blood burns like fire in our breasts, ready
> To blossom forth like flowers for the emperor.
> Our volunteer army displays the brave Yamato spirit
> Under the flag of the armed forces.

> The sun has ascended over Niitaka Mountain*
> And radiates its brilliance across Asia. Our
> Six million brethren now perform service for
> The emperor. With great determination, we
> Will build a new order in the world.[66]

These passionate words were supposed to make young Taiwanese identify with the Japanese. Japan's emperor was their emperor. The Japanese Yamato spirit was to be their spirit. KHK units sponsored dramatic performances to teach Japanese traditions and culture.[67] Other KHK units distributed movies and picture-card shows (*kami shibai kyōkai*) each week in the cities and hamlets to describe Japanese education, homemaking, and living habits.[68]

The KHK became the largest island-wide organization to mobilize the Taiwanese for the war effort. By the end of 1941, over 6,000 administrators worked in every region to coordinate KHK activities. Besides the weekly lectures, movies, dance troupes, and so on, the KHK developed other programs. Seven training centers in Kaohsiung, Taichung, and Tainan ran three-month rotating sessions for 500 young people to learn tropical agricultural technology.

In Taipei's Baba-machi, a unit trained youth being sent to help develop resources in Japan's newly conquered territories in Southeast Asia in six-month courses, graduating 150 candidates every cycle. The young people, selected from graduates of the public schools, learned carpentry, construction, and machine technology. In Maruyama-machi of Taipei, another KHK unit trained young people in navigation and sailing. Established by Hasegawa and staffed partly by naval officers, it instructed groups of fifty young Taiwanese every three months. Similarly, the KHK created a young people's association for public service (*hōkō sōnendan*) which had 219 chapters and 11,971 members by April 28, 1942.[69] Still another KHK-sponsored organization had 27 chapters that instructed unmarried women in how to become model Japanese ladies. The KHK also established work squads in agriculture, industry, mining, and fishing to perform industry-wide public services (*sangyō hōkōdan*).[70]

These efforts undoubtedly had some impact on the tens of thousands of young Taiwanese who participated in the training programs, weekly meetings, and public service activities. Most participants had some education and came from urban families of average or higher means. All spoke Japanese. They probably discussed the war and took part in the island-

---

*The highest mountain in Taiwan.

wide celebrations of Japan's early victories in the Pacific War. Courses in subjects like carpentry and sailing may well have elicited the enthusiasm of young students.

The newspaper *Taiwan nichi-nichi shimpō* reported huge, three-day celebrations throughout the island at the announcement of the Japanese occupation of Manila on January 4, 1942. On that day, 10,000 students in Taipei, Taichung, Chia-i, Tainan, Kaohsiung, and Hua-lien waved Japanese flags, sang patriotic songs, and screamed *"Banzai!"*[71] Tens of thousands of officials and citizens pledged their support to fight to the end and win a decisive victory for Japan.[72]

It is difficult to know whether this public support of the Japanese war effort was genuine or false. Perhaps the participants felt that sense of "overlooking" (*kan-ka*) their participation that P'eng Ming-min spoke of. We do not know. Yet in Taipei city alone, thousands of Taiwanese youths reportedly committed themselves to support Japan's quest for all-out victory.[73] Schools across the island began training students in the Japanese spirit of discipline to emulate the victorious imperial troops in the Philippines.[74] To sustain such mobilization, the press began featuring stories of heroic young Taiwanese who had enlisted in the Imperial Army and lost their lives in China.[75]

By the end of 1942, perhaps 10 percent of the population had adopted Japanese surnames.[76] Although many Taiwanese appeared to have willingly complied, others adopted an attitude of passive resistance. One example is Wu Hsin-jung. Wu wrote in his diary that he changed his name because of Japanese pressure but that he deliberately chose a new name linking himself to Chinese culture and demonstrating his Chinese identity:

> One of the concrete methods of the Kōminka campaign was that the government encouraged the islanders to change their Chinese names. I had heard that in Korea the Japanese practice of creating a new surname had been successful. However, in Taiwan the practice was for changing one's surname. If one were forced to create a last name, then one should consider one's tradition and give that name a new meaning. I looked in a geographical dictionary under the character *Wu* and found that the site of the country Wu during the Spring and Autumn and Warring States Periods was called Yen-ling. The character "Yen" was in the name of Yen-p'ing-chün-wang (Koxinga), whom I admired very much. "Ling" could be replaced by "Kang"; both characters meant the mountain ridge. If I combined "Yen" and "Kang" and then converted the two Chinese characters into Japanese, they became "O-ka," and "O-ka" became a perfect new name for me.[77]

We do not know how many Taiwanese behaved like Wu Hsin-jung. Yet thousands of Chinese students continued to volunteer for public service and assemble in public parks to declare their patriotic intentions and strong resolve.[78] The authorities then ordered all KHK organizations to issue new rules for marriage and funeral ceremonies.[79] The new rules compelled KHK members to simplify marriage and funeral rites and display greater frugality. A flood of press reports appeared describing how Taiwanese, by the tens of thousands, were enlisting in the imperial armed forces.[80] Physicians also formed teams to perform public service throughout the island, even offering their private clinics for the war effort.[81] School children raised money and donated it to buy equipment and weapons.[82]

These island-wide mobilization campaigns certainly influenced some Taiwanese, probably those who were not yet in their mid-twenties and lived in the cities. When teenagers volunteered for the Japanese military forces or performed public service—whether they did so under pressure or not—they worked and lived like the Japanese, even absorbing some Japanese customs and discipline. Whether the young graduates of the urban training centers who became instructors and activists in the KHK could impart to other young people their own patriotic fervor is unknown. Nevertheless, more Taiwanese than ever before experienced direct contact with Japanese leaders, professionals, military men, and officials. Some Taiwanese certainly became good friends with their Japanese counterparts. A few perhaps began to think and behave like Japanese. After all, as P'eng Ming-min's case shows, the Japanese they met often treated them in a kind and warm way as equals, and Japanese ways, organizational and personal, were often admired in Taiwan.

Older Taiwanese, however, remained deeply resentful of the Japanese efforts to turn them into loyal Japanese subjects. Tomisawa Shigeru served in the Japanese army air force in Taipei in 1944–45 and recalls making friends with and visiting the family of a female Taiwanese worker in an aircraft factory on the west side of Sung-shan Airfield (the present Taipei Municipal Airport). When Tomisawa asked her father, Chou Hsiao-ming, what he thought about the Kōminka campaign, particularly the changing of Taiwanese surnames into Japanese, the elder Taiwanese bitterly said, "I cannot accept it at all."[83] Some months later, Tomisawa learned that Japanese police had arrested Mr. Chou.

The Educational Campaign

As early as August 1939, the Hasegawa administration had expanded elementary schooling to teach the speaking and reading of Japanese. At this time, the governor-general's office had set up a Provisional Education Investigation Commission to review education in Taiwan and establish rules for developing a new public school system. In March 1941, the rules stipulated that Taiwanese and Japanese primary schools were to be standardized and unified under a single system (*kōgakkō*) as in Japan. There were, however, minor differences. Parents did not have to send their children to public school if they were self-employed and short of labor, and from the fifth year girls had to learn homemaking.[84] Although this new system incorporated the elementary public schools (*kokumin gakkō*), remedial schools, high schools, vocational and technical schools, universities, and special schools for the handicapped, curricula were still not standardized. The course content for Japanese and Taiwanese children still differed.

In 1943, elementary school became compulsory for all Taiwanese. A year earlier, only about 65 percent of school-age Taiwanese attended public schools.[85] In that year, the colony had a total of 1,029 elementary public schools, 13,182 full- and part-time teachers, and 797,503 children in both elementary and high schools.[86] By April 1944, however, more Taiwanese parents sent their children to primary school than ever before. The total number had jumped to 932,525, or about 71 percent of all Taiwanese children of school age.[87] The proportion of children in school increased more rapidly between 1937 and 1945 than during any other equivalent time period of colonial rule.

If nearly three out of every four children attended school by 1944, what were they learning? Extant school readers show that Taiwanese children had to learn about Japanese culture, especially Japan's divine origins. A typical reader began by instructing children about the founding of Japan by Jimmu Tennō.[88] To win young people's support for the war, these texts argued that a "divine spirit" was the only true source of the Japanese emperor system. Taiwanese children learned that they should help the Japanese people in the virtuous task of building a new order in East Asia under the Japanese aegis. This is how one textbook argued the case:

Already the power of our enemies throughout Asia, the United States, England, and so on, has been entirely shattered. The people of China and Southeast Asia, under the spirit of our country and with our leadership, will work together enthusiastically, with a common purpose, to establish the Greater East Asia Co-Prosperity Sphere. In this way, the great spirit that founded our country will radiate forth and glitter like the rays of the sun throughout China, Southeast Asia, and even the world, by the august virtue of His Majesty, the Emperor.[89]

These readers contained excellent maps along with their historical arguments to teach students that the Western powers had tried to help Chiang Kai-shek's regime deny Japan her rightful access to raw materials in China.[90] They also informed students about the activities of the KHK and presented histories of exemplary young Taiwanese whom the students were asked to emulate.

Schoolchildren read about the virtuous young Taiwanese who had volunteered to serve in the imperial armed forces. These volunteers described their background, education, and reasons for enlisting. A young volunteer might extol the Japanese Imperial Army and Navy for "having destroyed the American Pacific fleet at Hawaii," "having occupied Guam," and "having sunk the main Asian warships of the English, occupied Hong Kong and Malaya, and [for] now attacking Singapore."[91]

One volunteer, Ch'en Chien-ti, cited the new opportunities for young people if they enlisted by saying, "By actively participating in the imperial forces, this island's young man now has an extremely fortunate opportunity. I hope that all who are qualified will eventually become volunteers and work for the betterment of Taiwan."[92] Other volunteers described how the "Imperial Army bravely fought on the front line after the China Incident," while others glorified their wartime experiences in Central China.[93]

The final year for statistical information on education numbers, 1942, shows that 3.3 million out of 6.2 million Taiwanese, or 58 percent, had already received at least an elementary school education and had learned sufficient Japanese to be functionally literate.[94] By 1945, the number must have been higher, with even more Taiwanese functionally literate in Japanese. Among urban youth, the number able to read, write, and speak fluent Japanese must have been very high. Among elite families, many had probably achieved near-bilingual proficiency in both Taiwanese and Japanese.

Although the Japanese educational reform was undoubtedly very successful, particularly in terms of the number of Taiwanese learning the Japanese language, a relatively small number of Taiwanese assimilated Japanese cultural values. Those who did lived mainly in the cities, and many prided themselves on being part of the new elite. In 1945, then, their world outlook would be very different from that of their counterparts in Mainland China.

Mobilization Efforts During the Last Years of the War

Throughout 1944, the Japanese brought additional villages under KHK control. In early February, they published new rules to recruit additional Taiwanese into the army.[95] The KHK also instructed all its squads to promote virtue and elevate popular consciousness on behalf of the war effort. Squad leaders were to use Japanese at all times, to mobilize old and young alike for public services, and to extend KHK activities into the villages.⁹⁶ Japanese officials often met with KHK regional leaders to report on local difficulties. Squad leaders at the village and ward levels also attended these meetings.⁹⁷ Hasegawa traveled around the island and exhorted KHK officials to work harder to win over the populace to support the war effort.⁹⁸

By late 1943, the drafting of so many Taiwanese youth for the war effort had created a severe farm labor shortage. As a result, rice became scarce. Sixty-three-year-old Lin Hsien-t'ang wrote in his diary on November 16, "We had no rice to eat last night."⁹⁹ In 1944, the rural labor shortage became even worse. More and more women and schoolchildren began performing rural work, because all the young males were away in the military forces or working in factories and on construction sites. In Taichung city, schoolgirls joined teams to go into villages and help the farmers.¹⁰⁰ Over 10,000 students from Taichung reportedly farmed 100 hectares of land with only simple tools.¹⁰¹ In the Hsin-chu area, the KHK also organized work teams to help.¹⁰²

The KHK continued to organize public meetings to educate Taiwanese in Japanese culture. On February 12, 1944, massive celebrations were held on the island to commemorate the anniversary of the founding of imperial Japan.¹⁰³ Japanese officials publicly declared that the island's 6.5 million Taiwanese were the emperor's people. They exhorted the Taiwanese to cultivate Japan's "great spirit" (*dai seishin*). Japanese educators continued the steady drumbeat of moral instruction for Taiwanese parents, urging them to raise their children like good Japanese children. Accounts appeared daily in the press touching on all aspects of child-rearing and domestic life.¹⁰⁴

By early 1945, B-29 bombers from Okinawa, flying in numbers of about 500, were bombing Taiwan's cities every day.¹⁰⁵ The large cities were nearly empty, though, because the year before the administration had begun preparations to evacuate city people to the countryside.¹⁰⁶ When General Andō Rikichi replaced Admiral Hasegawa as governor-general in January, Andō tried to accelerate the pace of island-wide mobilization by ordering on February 2, 1945, that all middle-aged and elderly people be mobilized. Andō referred to the Taiwanese as "already being people of a great imperial country."¹⁰⁷ Moreover, "the Taiwanese are no different from Japanese. All of the people of this island are Japanese, and as people of this great empire who have been educated for many years, they definitely believe that."¹⁰⁸ On February 11, 1945, Andō urged the people of Taiwan to develop a warrior-like spirit and always display it.¹⁰⁹ Even though the war was going badly for Japan, Japan's leaders were determined to mobilize the people of Taiwan to fight to the bitter end.

In mid-April 1945, the administration began streamlining the KHK by eliminating various organs and combining four agencies into two bureaus, one for planning and the other for management.[110] KHK officials also held island-wide celebrations to commemorate the fourth year of the association's activities.[111] Then on April 21 the chief of the KHK's general affairs bureau urged that new KHK teams be set up in every village so that the KHK could control all rural areas.[112] The Japanese command now feared that after the capture of Okinawa and the daily bombings of Japan, the Allies might invade Taiwan. Andō's plan called for mobilizing every Taiwanese community into squads and giving the people weapons to assist the military in a final stand.

Throughout May and early June, the Japanese continued to form paramilitary teams.[113] Then, on June 17, Governor-General Andō personally appealed to the Taiwanese people, called them the servants of the emperor (*kōmin*), and urged them to show self-discipline and support a new military recruitment system (*chōhei seido*). Andō reminded the Taiwanese that they had enjoyed fifty glorious years under Japanese rule and now possessed a remarkable spirit of loyalty. This spirit made it possible to "cultivate those war capabilities needed to win a decisive victory."[114] Andō further urged that the "people and all their officials join as one to establish volunteer organizations for public service and firmly integrate all of these organizations." With this strong spirit of public service, Andō claimed, "we will persevere and remain loyal to the emperor."

On the very next day, roughly two months before Japan's unconditional surrender, the administration announced the new rules for a national people's volunteer corps.[115] Now the Japanese and Taiwanese would fight side by side, with all officials and people united. The corps would have a new central headquarters in the governor-general's office, with branches in all districts, counties, townships, cities, wards, and villages. These units would coordinate the activities of the new people's volunteer corps (*giyūtai*). The integrated police and household system (*hokō*) would remain intact, as would the old KHK.

The *giyūtai* would be responsible to local officials, and its paramilitary brigades would assist the imperial armed forces. By June 26, the people's volunteer corps even had their new song.[116] As Andō Rikichi described it, the *giyūtai* would combine with the KHK "to form a powerful defense organization."[117] Andō reminded the people that the KHK movement adhered to the spirit of self-sacrifice on behalf of the emperor and the empire and said that "the KHK would be absorbed into the powerful *giyūtai*."[118] The General Affairs Bureau's chief repeated Andō's claim by saying that the *giyūtai* was really designed to strengthen the island's defense, and their volunteer squads would work without pay, as the KHK teams had. He then added, "The Japanese, the island people, and the aborigines are people of the empire, and there is no need to refer to them as separate entities. Because our people have been thrust into war, we have organized the people's volunteer corps, *giyūtai*."[119]

Giyūtai squads began springing up all over the island.[120] These volunteer units went into the villages and helped the farmers. When one reporter asked a corps member what the *giyūtai* did, he replied, "The purpose of forming the *giyūtai* is to strengthen the country's unity by making the place of birth the centerpiece and developing that sense of national spirit [*kokutai*] which everyone now shares."[121] *Giyūtai* members spoke only Japanese, and they worked closely with Japanese military and officials.

Even at the end of the war, then, the Japanese military did not relax its efforts to mobilize the Taiwanese into the war effort. Whether a significant number of young and middle-aged Taiwanese became assimilated is not entirely clear. The written record reveals little of what people thought or believed in these years, but leading Japanese believed that many Taiwanese had become like the Japanese. Only eleven days after the Japanese surrendered, Andō Rikichi stated publicly that Taiwan's 6.7 million people still traveled the same road as the Japanese. He pointed out with pride that the Taiwanese had committed no acts of violence against the Japanese, and that there had not been any sentiment in favor of self-rule.[122] Indeed, as we have seen, public protests against the Japanese apparently ended by 1940. Volunteer corps continued to farm, preserve stocks of grain, and maintain public order.[123] Japanese officials and their organizations performed as usual until retrocession.

The Thrust Toward Industrialization and Its Social Implications

Other events that altered Japanese-Taiwanese relationships occurred during the war years, besides the Japanese efforts to make Taiwanese behave and think like Japanese. There was also a rapid growth in industrialization.

In late 1935, some 68,000 factory workers throughout the island labored in 7,000 factories, mainly of small size.[124] Although colonial officials worried about the shortage of industrial technicians and low worker productivity, they did little to solve those problems. The Sino-Japanese War dramatically changed the situation. At the beginning of the war in 1937, factory workers had increased to 87,000. By late 1941, however, their number had jumped to 137,000, a 57-percent increase.[125] By mid-1943, the number of workers in manufacturing plants had reached an all-time high of 147,000;[126] combined male and female participation in the non-agricultural work force (mining, transport, communications, and services), excluding construction and military-related employment, was around 214,000.[127] An overlap of nearly a half million workers would include those needed to maintain the island's transport, communications, airfields, naval stores, and so on.[128] As more and more able-bodied workers moved into areas like manufacturing, construction, and services, an increasing number of older people, children, and women entered the agricultural labor force to replace those who had left for the cities, ports, and mines.

This large influx of workers (40 percent of whom were females) into mines, construction sites, and new industries greatly expanded the manufacturing sector's contribution to gross domestic product, increasing its share to 33 percent in 1937 and then to a high of 37 percent in 1942.[129] Meanwhile, the manufacturing sector's output increased at nearly 4 percent per annum after 1937, reaching a peak in 1942 and then leveling off. Thereafter, it declined, as labor shortages and bombings disrupted production.[130] On the other hand, the share of gross domestic product from the primary sector (agriculture, forestry, and fishing) declined after 1937, as did services. Wartime demands diverted considerable labor and materials away from farming and services to the manufacturing sector and military activities. For example, when the Japanese navy accelerated the expansion of Kaohsiung's port after 1940, it mobilized workers at the rate of 300 people per day for construction and other related jobs.[131]

If industrialization and military needs required a total work force of some 400,000 or more in the 1940s, how was so much labor mobilized? As early as October 1939, the governor-general's office had created a new Labor Cooperative Association (*rōdō kyōkai*) responsible for supplying labor for heavy industry and naval construction. In August 1940, the administration also established in every district of the island the Taiwan Central Labor Cooperation Association (*Taiwan chūō rōdō kyōkai*) for mobilizing labor for industrial work.[132] This association later became the Association for Performing Public Work in Industry (*sangyō kōkōkai*) and was managed by the KHK.

The Japanese tried to recruit the young people graduating from elementary public schools who possessed enough Japanese reading and writing skills to become partially and fully skilled factory workers and managers. In April 1940, the governor-general's office established a youth corps (*hōkoku seinentai*) to perform free labor on behalf of the state.[133] The administration also set up training centers for the youth corps, the first of which opened in Kaohsiung in April 1940. Teams of 200 youth corps workers labored in squads for three-month cycles, building tunnels, roads, and other structures. The Kaohsiung center was followed by centers in Taichung, Hua-lien, Taipei, and other cities.[134] Japanese and Taiwanese young men served as regional chiefs to manage the corps. By 1942, probably as many as 20,000 youth corps workers labored on urban industrial project sites each year. Between the ages of twelve and thirty, they lived in barracks and submitted to a military, disciplined life-style.

The first administrative mobilization plan for industrialization, electrification, and the upgrading of mining came on September 17, 1938, when Ordinance No. 645 stipulated that the Taiwan Heavy Industry Control Commission (*Taiwan jūyō sangyō chōsei iinkai*) be created to plan the island's rapid industrialization.[135] The commission discussed how to expand transportation networks to facilitate additional railway traffic and motor carrier tonnage and to build new industrial projects in major cities.

By late 1941, officials realized that trade between Taiwan and Japan might be disrupted and that Japan could not be expected to supply the consumer goods and materials vitally needed for Taiwan's markets and industry. A move toward self-sufficiency began. Taiwan, for example, had imported around 250,000 tons of limestone each year from Japan for its sugar processing industry. Now the administration informed officials in Hualien and elsewhere on the island's east side that they must expand limestone production to meet demand.[136]

As the economy turned toward self-sufficiency, the cities mushroomed, with more workers than ever before needing to be fed. Officials restricted land use for non-food products and diverted irrigated land and fertilizers to increase the output of rice, sweet potatoes, and wheat—foods critical to the people of the island. Officials also mobilized the farmer associations to produce more food grain. The Association for Rice Delivery (*beikoku nōnyū kumiai*) and the Rice Distribution Association (*beikoku haigō kumiai*) handled rationing. Prefectural officials used these two associations to purchase food grain from farmer associations, stock the surplus, and sell at fixed prices to designated wholesalers and retailers. Officials allowed farmers to have 3.8 liters of grain per day.[137] After 1941, the total area used for crops declined because of acute labor and other input shortages. Yet food grain reached a peak in 1942, declining thereafter.

The thrust toward industrialization caused other changes. Not only did cities mushroom, but so did education. The number of young people in primary schools and other educational institutions reached an all-time high. This led to an enormous concentration of youth as well as workers in cities. Both groups, who often lived in barracks and worked under regimented conditions, had more personal contact with Japanese than ever before.

We can only conjecture how industrialization and urbanization influenced young and old Taiwanese alike. Those from villages were exposed for the first time to Japanese discipline and organization. Even city people, who had long experience of the Japanese and had benefited from previous contact, could now receive more education than before, train in crash-course industrial programs, and work as skilled workers and lower-level managers.

It is significant that these new experiences spawned no large literature of resentment or suffering. No memoirs written about the early 1940s depict these years as a fearful time of Japanese cruelty and oppression. If there were bad memories and nightmares, no one was inspired to make them public after the war. Neither were there any significant incidents of sabotage or underground activities designed to damage the Japanese war machine. In fact, during the war years, an increasing number of Taiwanese behaved like Japanese in dress and manners. Taiwanese in their teens and twenties probably came to respect, if not admire, Japanese ways.

Expanding the Role of Taiwanese in Local Government

After 1940, the role of Taiwanese in government grew. To understand why this happened, one must first take into account the bureaucracy under the governor-general. In 1945, it had 84,559 people on its staff. Presumably, this 84,559 included the police force, constituting about 11,000, which was backed by a military force of at least 195,500.[138] This was a huge civil and military presence compared with that under the ROC from 1945 through at least 1947.

The military and civil bureaucratic structure penetrated every territorial-administrative unit. The Japanese had divided colonial Taiwan into five districts, three prefectures, and eleven cities, all of which were under the office of the governor-general. Districts and prefectures had villages and towns under them. Cities and towns were in turn divided into wards. Wards and villages contained neighborhood associations, often with neighborhood association halls. As illustrated by the KHK, state-led activities were sometimes organized on a street-by-street basis. At the grass roots, moreover, there was a network of informants, household registration, and "self-policing."

To grasp the large governmental role of the Taiwanese, one must first note that of these 84,559 people in the bureaucracy, 46,955, or 56 percent, were Taiwanese. With their families, they constituted a stratum of some 300,000 Taiwanese who had a stake in the bureaucracy. (This does not take into account the many other Taiwanese serving in the military or the police.) Even in the top six administrative grades, Taiwanese held 35 percent of the jobs.

Besides this basic Taiwanese presence in the bureaucracy, Taiwanese came to have a greater say in local leadership as executives and council members. Each territorial-administrative unit had an executive leader: cities were headed by mayors; districts, by governors; prefectures, by chiefs; towns and villages, by elected leaders. Executives at each level worked with a council. On the city, district, and prefecture levels, councils were only advisory, but town and village councils had greater decision-making powers. The number of council members varied from three to five, depending on the level, and terms of tenure varied anywhere from two to four years. Before 1940, all positions were appointive, but a fair number of those appointed were Taiwanese, especially at the town and village level.

After 1940, the mayors and other leaders were still appointed, but at the city, district, and town levels, about half of the council members came to be elected. At the town level, the council members, whether appointed or elected, were eventually all Taiwanese, and these town councils actually took charge of community affairs to a large extent. The same must have been true of village councils. At the other levels, however, Japanese council members continued to outnumber Taiwanese. On April 1, 1944, 179 elected and appointed Taiwanese began serving on district and city councils. On that same date, 3,276 Taiwanese became town council members—1,748 of them appointed and 1,528 elected. (See Table 2.)

More work is needed to understand the nature of the elections, the extent of the suffrage, the frequency of elections, the number of candidates running for office, media coverage, platforms (if any), and so on. We do have information, however, on the social background of the elected and appointed Taiwanese who served on the councils. On the whole, they were well educated, with many having graduated from Japanese middle schools. On the average, they were in their fifties or sixties, but even younger Taiwanese joined these councils. Many had adopted Japanese names. Most were businessmen or officials in the colonial administration.

Take the case of Hsü Yen-shou, who had adopted the Japanese name

TABLE 2
Composition of Councils at Different Administrative Levels
(April 1, 1945)

Administrative level	No. of council members	Appointed		Elected	
		Japanese	Taiwanese	Japanese	Taiwanese
Taipei District	40	15	5	11	9
Hsin-chu District	22	7	4	6	5
Taichung District	36	16	2	7	11
Tainan District	38	15	4	11	8
Kaohsiung District	28	10	4	9	5
Taitung Prefecture	12	8	4	–	–
Hua-lien Prefecture	15	11	4	–	–
Pescadores Prefecture	10	7	3	–	–
Taipei City	37	14	6	8	9
Keelung City	21	8	3	6	4
I-lan City	22	7	5	2	8
Hsin-chu City	27	10	4	3	10
Taichung City	25	9	4	6	6
Changhua City	25	10	33	–	12
Tainan City	29	12	48	5	8
Chia-i City	25	9	4	4	8
Kaohsiung City	30	13	33	9	5
P'ing-tung City	24	10	3	3	8
Hua-lien City	20	9	1	6	4
Taipei District Towns	476	79	164	11	222
Hsin-chu Towns	501	96	189	6	237
Taichung Towns	778	137	267	11	363
Tainan Towns	880	167	295	17	401
Kaohsiung Towns	486	97	178	11	228
Taitung Towns	97	27	23	14	33
Hua-lien Towns	86	28	15	13	30
Pescadores Towns	57	9	22	2	24

SOURCE: Taiwan sōtokufu, *Taiwan tōji gaiyō* [A Summary Report of Taiwan's System of Administration] (Taipei, 1945), pp. 19–21.

Takayama Motomasa and owned several business enterprises. Born in Hsin-chu city on December 5, 1892, by 1942 the 50-year-old Takayama had already been elected to the Hsin-chu city and district councils.[139] Or consider Wang Lin. Born December 16, 1884, in Changhua city, he graduated from Changhua public high school in February 1914. He served with the police force in Taichung for a number of years and was, in November 1939, elected a councilman for Changhua city.[140] Thousands of such cases existed in the large and medium-size cities of Taiwan at this time.

The Japanese, of course, continued to restrict the political role of the Taiwanese. They not only kept tight control of all these councils, but they exercised power through the Japanese-appointed mayors, chiefs, and governors, the huge, centralized bureaucracy under the governor-general, and the massive police-military establishment. Yet, because of the war, Taiwanese increasingly found themselves officially discussing public affairs, often with Japanese colleagues.

The increased participation certainly whetted the political appetite of the Taiwanese elite, who had long been attracted to the ideal of self-government (a popular idea going back to the turn of the century in the Chinese world) and who had earlier demanded a Taiwan Parliament. Moreover, the Taiwanese started to become accustomed to the idea of basing local government on local elections. This was certainly one of several reasons why the KMT initiated local elections in Taiwan as early as it did, in April 1946.

Taiwan on the Eve of Retrocession

There is considerable evidence, then, that in the course of Taiwan's colonial experience, many if not most members of the Taiwanese elite came to share to a great extent the Japanese view of the world. To be sure, one cannot claim that Japanese culture supplanted Chinese culture in their minds. For the most part, they continued to take for granted many inherited Chinese norms, especially those endorsing the patrilineal descent line of the family and ancestor worship. Some of them even made conscious efforts to cultivate knowledge of the Chinese language and of China's history and civilization. Moreover, there was widespread Taiwanese resentment that Taiwanese were denied equal status with the Japanese and that they were not allowed a greater role in the government of the island. Their patriotic attachment to China, evidenced by their original resistance to the imposition of colonialism, was clearly muted as Japanese rule continued, but that it had not disappeared showed in the joy with which they greeted retrocession.

Despite these facts, a significant part of the Taiwanese elite was clearly co-opted into making the best of a colonial situation forced upon them. In many cases, they owed their professional opportunities and elite status to the Japanese order or, to a smaller extent, to missionary influence. By the 1940s, the second generation of this elite stratum had emerged. Their sense of identity and status derived from their success in top Japanese schools and universities and from the access to a cosmopolitan culture which their Japanese education had given them. Members of this second generation often enjoyed warm relations with gifted Japanese friends and remembered with happiness the years they lived in Japan. By 1940, their expanding role in local government complemented the large Taiwanese presence in the bureaucracy, which as noted above employed some 47,000 Taiwanese, supporting a social stratum of some 300,000, perhaps 5 percent of the population.

The Japanese influence, however, clearly reached well beyond such elites and sub-elites. One cannot dismiss as ineffective all the Japanese efforts to enlist the Taiwanese masses in their cause. After all, many Taiwanese—not only elites like the P'engs—had feelings of respect and admiration for the Japanese, and the objective grounds for such admiration were obvious. In April 1947, a secret ROC report made by an official of the censorate (Yang Liang-kung) not only, noted that the Taiwanese all praised the efficiency and integrety of Japan's civil and military personnel in Taiwan but also itself expressed great admiration for Japan's economic and administrative methods there, regarding them as a model useful for all of China.[141] In the 1940's, therefore, similar feelings clearly facilitated mass Taiwanese participation in the KHK patriotic program, with its staff of some 6,000. This huge, dynamic propaganda program aimed at young and old sought to turn Taiwanese into loyal subjects of the emperor excited by the dream of realizing the "Japanese essence." Propaganda infusing children with the same spirit reinforced an expanding educational system. Propaganda and education were in turn supplemented by many programs teaching desirable technical and homemaking skills. Some half-million workers were mobilized to support industrialization and the war effort. All these propaganda, educational, and occupational activities involved increasing contacts with Japanese. The shared suffering in 1945 under U.S. bombing must have further strengthened ties of solidarity.

It is true that we lack sufficient data about the Taiwanese response to Japanese efforts to assimilate them. We do know, however, that perhaps 100,000 Taiwanese—with their families, perhaps 10 percent of the population—adopted Japanese surnames. This was not a trifling act. We also know that many Taiwanese in Japan at the end of World War II preferred to stay there, that there was no significant underground resistance in the 1940s, and that Japanese wartime mobilization spawned no literature of resentment or resistance expressing outrage at Japanese abuses. This contrasts with other parts of the world after World War II, where free people did speak out publicly about their sufferings under defeated oppressors, as did the French about Nazi occupation.

Although the comparative study of colonial rule is still in its infancy, scholars have already begun to consider similarities and contrasts among different empires by referring to certain variables. These variables include: (1) the nature of the colonized area, which varies from empty land to the existence of a large, densely populated, complex society; (2) the goals or interests of the imperialists, which range from strategic aims to different kinds of economic goals and include the need of elites to distract the restless proletariat of the colonizing country, the career interests of various military and civil elites, and the quest for international prestige; (3) the ethos, social origins, and organizational structures of the elites carrying out colonial administration; (4) elite attitudes—ranging from contempt to respect—toward the colonized populations; (5) the modes of colonial control, which to varying degrees mix coercion, discriminatory policies, and possibly some degree of political participation with policies promoting educational and material development while calibrating the social distance between ruling and subjugated elites; (6) the image of the imperial rulers in the eyes of the subjugated population—an image ranging from that of a cruel tyrant to that of a stern master having admirable qualities worth imitating; and (7) the political responses of the subjugated population, ranging from cooperation and submission to peaceful protest, subversion, and rebellion.

We cannot use such categories here to systematically compare Japanese colonialism during the first decades of the twentieth century with colonial empires elsewhere, or even to compare Japanese colonialism in Taiwan with Japanese colonialism elsewhere. Yet available studies suggest that in Taiwan relations between the Japanese and their subjects were relatively tension-free and more harmonious than in Korea, for example. Although "the Japanese respected Chinese culture," they "held the Koreans in contempt," with only some exceptions. As one writer has noted, "Japanese rule in Taiwan was far from unpopular, especially at a time when the Chinese Mainland was in the hands of quarreling warlords."[142] On the other hand, the Japanese destroyed the Koreans' own dynasty, the Yi, in order to impose their colonial regime, and "Koreans had nothing for which to thank them and the liquidation of Korean sovereignty for which to hate them, along with their Korean collaborators."[143]

The Taiwanese elite who flourished in Taiwan under the Japanese system—such as local government council members or those working in the governor-general's bureaucracy—were seldom if ever regarded as traitors by other Taiwanese. Koreans who worked with their Japanese masters, however, were indeed stigmatized as collaborators. In fact, this subject is so painful for South Koreans today that most cannot and will not discuss it.

Similarly, violent or other kinds of illegal resistance to colonial rule were more extensive in Korea than in Taiwan. Again citing a recent study on Japanese colonialism, "More than 140,000 Koreans supposedly participated in the independence struggle between 1907 and 1911. . . . When Japan launched its conquest of Manchuria in 1931, it faced a strong anti-Japanese resistance in this new semi-colonial sphere. . . . Koreans served as many of these insurgents and bore the brunt of Japanese repression. . . . Japanese repression was felt in Korea as well, and thousands of Communists were jailed, many of them imprisoned until August 15, 1945."[144]

Clearly, the Korean image of the Japanese was more that of the cruel tyrant than was the Taiwanese image. Furthermore, Korean resistance to Japanese rule was more vigorous, and the Japanese view of Koreans tended more to contempt than did their view of the Taiwanese. This contrast makes still more plausible our thesis that many Taiwanese came to admire the Japanese and to share many of their attitudes, including a tendency to see them as more progressive than the Mainland Chinese.

Most basically, the kind of ambivalence that has often accompanied cultural diffusion developed in Taiwan. Since the late nineteenth century, many Chinese both hated Western imperialism and admired many Western ways. Similarly, a number of Taiwanese resented their status as colonial subjects while simultaneously appreciating many Japanese ways, liking many Japanese individuals, taking for granted the validity of many Japanese values and perspectives, and feeling superior to Chinese without these values.

As the war ended, however, this ambivalence quickly gave way to euphoria. The Taiwanese regarded the Mainland as their homeland, the source of their culture, and the home of their ancestors. When news of Japan's surrender became known, many Taiwanese reacted with disbelief. After the news was confirmed, each ward in Taipei and other large cities began to organize young men's associations named after the Three Principles of the People,[145] whose leaders assumed their responsibilities without pay. Every district organized groups to welcome the Nationalists. In Taipei, "on each street and on every door, people pasted ornamental banners and firecrackers to commemorate the recovery of Taiwan by Nationalist rule."[146] When people in Kaohsiung, Taipei, and Keelung learned which day the Nationalist troops and officials were scheduled to arrive, a state of delirium overwhelmed them. Here is how one observer described the scene:

From across Taiwan, the old and the young, women and men, had converged on Taipei and Keelung. Hordes of people had come, living in hotels and crowding the homes of relatives and friends. No hotel vacancies could be found, and even the inns in the cities' outskirts were filled about a week before the troops were to arrive. Every day and night, people lined up on the fifth floor of the Keelung Harbor Service Office, or climbed to the top of the hills on Sheliao Island to look out over the waves rushing in from the Pacific, wondering all the while when the troop ships from the mother country would arrive. Upon seeing a troop ship, crowds began to set off firecrackers and wave the national flag. Line after line of people clapped and cheered. This crazy swirl of welcoming cries rent the sky, and it seemed as if the earth shook.... Never had the Taiwanese people assembled in such a way to greet military troops. At that time, even the poorest villagers had come to build a great decorative archway to welcome the soldiers as they passed through. Throngs of people slaughtered pigs and fowl to feed the weary warriors. In one very poor village, it seems, 300 farms had slaughtered 500 pigs to welcome the officials and troops.[147]

The Nationalists, however, could hardly have hoped to meet Taiwanese expectations. The Taiwanese anticipated not only the end of Japanese colonialism but also an economic well being that would replace the hardships of war; an efficient, modernizing administration like the one the Japanese had given them; the successful outcome of their long struggle to take over the political management of their island; and the warm embrace of compatriots sympathetically aware of what they had endured as the subjects of a foreign empire. Some even referred to the hope for "perfect government."

At the very least, Taiwanese who had preserved or acquired wealth, professional status, and a sense of social importance under the Japanese expected that their achievements and status would be respected by the Mainlanders, who, many felt, had yet to learn as much about modern ways as the Taiwanese had under Japanese tutelage. Few if any of them dreamed that the fruits of this tutelage would be regarded as "poison" by the Nationalists, who had fought bitterly for years against the brutal Japanese invasion of their country. Nor did they stop to think that the brutal war and the long life-and-death struggle with Mao Tse-tung had left the Nationalists unable to give them at that time the peaceful, prosperous, and democratic society which they believed history owed them.

Furthermore, the Taiwanese had excelled—as their compatriots in Hong Kong later excelled—at the task of efficiently carrying out economic activities under an umbrella of sovereign political authority erected by another nation. They now imagined that they and their compatriots from the Mainland could easily erect a sovereign system if everyone acted with good will and common sense. Indeed, this kind of euphoria was common around the globe at the close of World War II, especially in the vast areas becoming free of colonial rule.

For their part, the Nationalists, unlike the Japanese, had a confusing political message for the Taiwanese. They intended to impose authority from the top down, but they were seemingly committed to doing this while nurturing democratic impulses. They expected to be embraced as liberators without being prepared to offer the concrete political and economic benefits that the Taiwanese perceived as integral to liberation. Far from looking up to the Taiwanese as Japanese-trained experts on modernization, they tended to regard them as unfortunate compatriots too long deprived of the benefits of Chinese civilization, and indeed morally infected by their exposure to Japanese culture.

The Nationalists were also confident that they could quickly take over the economy and run it as efficiently as the Japanese had. They not only misjudged the complexities of such a takeover and lacked the experienced personnel needed for the task, but they also failed to realize how severely they would be evaluated by the Taiwanese, who would compare their abilities with those of the departed personnel of a more modernized nation. As clashing expectations and KMT misrule aggravated the tensions of an inherently difficult situation, the bright hopes of October 1945 quickly faded.

CHAPTER 3

The Establishment of Nationalist Rule

KNOWING LITTLE about what had happened on the Mainland during World War II, many Taiwanese never appreciated the seriousness of the problems confronting the Nationalist government in 1945. In contrast to the euphoria aroused in Taiwan by Japan's defeat, the Nationalist government in Szechwan on August 15, 1945, greeted the victory soberly, stating that "at this time there are still great difficulties and heavy work tasks."[1] The KMT knew that the government was ill-prepared to extend its authority to other provinces and to revive the economy. It had come to depend largely on informal, patron-client ties with regional military commanders, local elites, and secret societies, rather than on the use of official and party organs, falling into this predicament as a way of dealing with the militarization of China in the 1920s and 1930s. The Sino-Japanese War had claimed many of the KMT's best troops, generally enervated civil and military personnel, and made it difficult to establish party cadres.

When they arrived in Taiwan in 1945, the Nationalists therefore lacked the administrative capabilities needed to meet Taiwanese expectations. Their political premises, moreover, were at odds with much of Taiwanese thinking. As we noted earlier, many Taiwanese saw themselves as deserving respect and sympathy from the Mainlanders: respect for their social status, academic achievements, and modern ways; and sympathy for the hardships they had endured under Japanese rule after being abandoned by China in 1895. They were also inclined to look down on Mainlanders as less modern than they and as, for example, tending to fall back on the ideology of Confucianism. Mainlanders, on the other hand, considered the Taiwanese misguided because of their exposure to the culture of a hated enemy but were prepared to be compassionate in return for support and respect. Nothing was more offensive to Mainlanders than the idea of looking up to the Taiwanese elite as Japanese-trained experts on modernization when Chinese had just fought and defeated the Japanese.

Moreover, Mainlanders believed the Taiwanese should be grateful for the Nationalist government's efforts to erect a new provincial administration for the island. Some Taiwanese felt they were owed immediate self-government and democracy, but the KMT, which was only then moving from the stage of "tutelage" to that of "constitutional rule," saw democratization as a gradual process contingent on suppression of the Communist rebellion. Many Taiwanese also assumed that liberation from Japanese colonialism would immediately lead to economic prosperity and continuing administrative efficiency, but neither of these could have been provided by the KMT in the mid-1940s.

These contradictions between the expectations of many Taiwanese and the premises of the KMT made it difficult for the two groups to maintain any consensus in late 1945 as they faced the problems arising from the change in government: the great decline in the size of the bureaucracy and the resulting shortage of official posts for Taiwanese; controversy about the social composition of the remaining bureaucratic staff; problems regarding the disposal of confiscated Japanese property; corruption; troop misbehavior; the irresponsibility of the press; and the style of KMT leadership. Other problems caused tension, too: the economic crisis and the KMT brand of socialism aggravating it; social ills such as crime, exacerbated by rising unemployment and the underworld; and linguistic and cultural barriers to mutual understanding and harmony. Although these problems weighed heavily in provoking the crisis in early 1947, the minor incident on February 27 in Taipei could not have grown into a large uprising if the KMT had not decreased the size of the police and security forces during 1946 to less than 14,000 men (a mere 6 percent of the military and police presence in 1945 under the Japanese).

The Nationalist Government on the Mainland

The Revolution of 1911 led to the establishment of the Republic of China on January 1, 1912, whose provisional president was Sun Yat-sen, a leader of the political party called T'ung-meng-hui, an organizational ancestor of the KMT. Sun died on March 12, 1925, after struggling in the south for some years with "the threefold problem of foreign imperialism, party disunity, and civil strife."[2] With Soviet advice, he had reorganized his party in 1923–1924, forming the KMT and working with members of the newly born Chinese Communist Party.

After Sun died, the KMT established the National Government in Canton and the National Revolutionary Army, led by Chiang Kai-shek and other generals, and started a campaign to subdue the warlords ruling central and northern China. That campaign, the Northern Expedition, lasted two years but was ultimately successful. On July 6, 1928, in a temple in the western hills outside Peking, the commanders of the Four Army Groups assembled at a solemn ceremony before the coffin of Sun Yat-sen, their late leader.[3] There they reported that their Northern Expedition had been victorious, having achieved the capture of Peking and to a large extent the unification of the country. But a casualty of these years was cooperation between the KMT and the Communists.

Yet although warlords like Wu P'ei-fu, Sun Ch'uan-fang, Chang Tsung-ch'ang, and Chang Tso-lin had been overthrown, they had now been replaced by generals who had participated in the Northern Expedition.[4] Most of the country was now divided into five clusters of military power: a group proclaiming itself the National Government, based in Nanking in the lower Yangtze Valley; the Kwangsi military faction holding much of Hopei, Hunan, and Kwangsi; Feng Yü-hsiang's National People's Army (*Kuo-min-chün*), with its base in Shensi and populous Honan and now stretching into Shantung and Hopei; Yen Hsi-shan in Shansi, with subordinates in the Peking-Tientsin area; and Chang Hsüeh-liang and other Manchurian generals in the Northeast. Moreover, local commanders ruled parts of Szechwan, Kweichow, and Yunnan, and Kwangtung was only loosely connected with the Nanking government.

To be sure, the KMT regime had by 1935–1936 extended its political influence from the two provinces that it initially controlled, Chekiang and Kiangsu, to six others, Anhwei, Kiangsi, Hupei, Honan, Hunan, Fukien, and, to a lesser degree, to Kansu and Shensi.[5] Yet China remained afflicted by warlordism, even in the KMT's base area of Chekiang and Kiangsu. The result was weak administrative control and an inability to promote modernization in other than a few cities. For example, when the Party and government tried to initiate a land survey and a tenant rent reduction program in Chekiang in 1929, members of the rural elite successfully lobbied to make the government desist, and the Nanking government failed to make Chekiang into a model province with a modern fiscal system.

In addition, the KMT was never able to expand its membership beyond 600,000, which constituted only about 0.003 percent of the country's total population. Because the KMT was more militarized than civilianized,[6] KMT cadres were unable to form new organizations and set up model counties in order to elicit grass-roots support for the new central government. Instead, cadres and local government officials had to negotiate with local elites to raise taxes, build roads, construct schools, or initiate other modernization programs. In fact, the impressive economic development that did occur between 1928 and 1937 took place only in and near the large cities of the lower Yangtze Valley, such as Shanghai and Nanking, where a great construction boom occurred, resulting mainly from provincial road building.[7] Similar progress never took place in the middle Yangtze, the Northwest, or the Southwest.

The Nationalists soon became caught in a vicious circle.[8] Hampered by a small membership and by the continuing power of regional military commanders and local elites on whom they had to depend to extend their authority, they were unable to reconcile divergent class interests, to expand the role of state and party organs, to carry out fiscal and agricultural reforms, and to achieve modernization in other than a few cities. As a result, they could neither raise revenue for their modernization programs nor obtain the popular support such programs could have generated. At the same time, many intellectuals, long predisposed to radicalism and utopianism, were critical of KMT performance. Seeing in the KMT's predicament not the tribulations of modernization but a basic lack of morality, many of them turned to Marxism.

Amid these difficulties, the Nationalist government's most important achievement was the buildup of a modern army trained by German advisers. The new army routed Communist forces from their base areas in Kiangsi province in the early 1930s and enabled the central government to extend its influence to other provinces. Military success, however, did not bring about a substantial increase in KMT membership or lessen the power of local leaders. Moreover, the Nationalists' problems were compounded first by the Japanese invasion and, increasingly, by the ability of the Communists to turn KMT difficulties to their advantage.

The Japanese, invading in July 1937, quickly seized the major coastal cities, the centers in which initial modernization had just taken root. The KMT decided to slow the Japanese advance at whatever cost, to gain time to move to the Southwest and establish a new capital at Chungking (Szechwan province). This decision probably allowed the Japanese to conquer the government's two base provinces and to destroy its best divisions by 1938. Nevertheless, the central government continued the war from Szechwan and the undeveloped provinces of Kweichow and Yunnan.

Military disaster was accompanied by political decline, with the KMT's registered membership in 1939 falling to "less than one-third of its prewar strength."[9] Moreover, it remained unable to control local officials and ordinary people at the district (*hsien*) level. In 1940, the chief party secretary of Chungking, Ch'en Fang-hsien, admitted that "even if the party committee made the slightest criticism, the *hsien* government would regard it as interference."[10] As in the past—or perhaps to a larger extent—

government officials and Party cadres could govern, raise taxes, and draft soldiers only by relying on local elites and their clients as well as on local secret societies, such as the *ko-lao-hui*.[11]

KMT attempts to deal with the situation were unsuccessful. Unable to recruit and train enough Party members and worried about Communist subversion, it organized a "surveillance network for party members."[12] This policy, however, backfired, because it did not enhance discipline, alienated many Party members and intellectuals, and led to further decline in party morale and efficiency. Many professionals, intellectuals, and businessmen believed that government corruption and incompetence were pervasive. By 1944–1945, even middle-level officials demanded personnel changes at the top in order to revitalize the Party and reform government policies.[13]

Popular dissatisfaction existed in rural as well as in urban areas. The government had to establish a new food grain tax system and to conscript young men—actions that heavily burdened rural society. Unable to introduce reforms that could have raised farmers' incentives and lacking the new technology and capital needed to increase farm output, the government could barely feed its army and administrative personnel. Meanwhile, food crop production stagnated, the supply of non-food crops declined, and living standards deteriorated.[14]

To make matters worse, in December 1943, Japanese Imperial Headquarters conceived of a two-stage military campaign to destroy the cream of the Nationalist government's military forces.[15] The first stage of Operation Ichigō called for an attack on Hupei province to link Japanese-controlled areas in North China with sections in Hupei province along the Peking-Hankow railway. The second stage involved the Japanese occupation of territories between Hunan and Kwangsi provinces. On April 18, 1944, some 140,000 men launched this massive operation by crossing the Yellow River in central Honan. By early September 1944, Operation Ichigō had dealt the Nationalists a devastating blow, even though the Japanese had suffered enormous losses. The Nationalists lost 23,000 tons of weapons and ammunition—enough to supply forty divisions—and some 750,000 troops *hors de combat*.[16] The central government also lost control of Hunan, depriving it of resources it needed to support about a half million troops.

To be sure, the Nationalists still had some six elite divisions that had been transferred in 1943 to General Stilwell's command and were returning now that the Allies had driven the Japanese from Burma—a victory that allowed the U.S. to accelerate its flow of lend-lease aid to China in early 1945. Yet, except for these few elite divisions and the additional supplies received from the U.S., the government had few resources with which to extend its control over the rest of the country and to deal with the Communists and other regional military commanders.

The Communists, having established numerous base areas throughout North China, had enlarged their armed forces, totaling by April 1945 some 910,000 men, divided between the Eighth Route and the New Fourth Armies. Communist Party personnel now numbered around 1.2 million.[17] Although KMT recruitment had also increased—to some 2.5 million by the end of 1944—its social composition was more rural and less educated than before. The Communists, on the other hand, profited from a large urban intelligence network made up of intellectuals and professionals alienated from the KMT and also from a bureaucratic network that penetrated even the villages, mobilizing popular support for the Communist military.

Conditions on the Mainland in 1945

By the summer of 1945, eight years of war and Japanese occupation of key provinces had left the Chinese economy in a shambles. Many sections of the railroad system had been destroyed, the number of trains and the amount of rolling stock had been greatly reduced, roads were in disrepair, and important bridges had been damaged and destroyed. Urban services, such as gas, electricity, water, sanitation, telecommunications, and transport, were almost nonexistent. Although new factories had emerged in the Southwest, overall industrial production had declined.[18] In agriculture, the area of cultivated land had declined because of a decrease in such resources as livestock, farm tools, and able-bodied workers. As farmers had switched to producing food grains, the supply and marketed surplus of industrial crops had decreased, causing severe shortages of raw materials for urban factories. These scarcities, coupled with a flood of worthless paper money, caused hyperinflation, with a fivefold increase in prices occurring between June 1944 and December 1945.[19]

Facing these conditions, the KMT and the central government followed the same style of governance that had become routinized after 1928. The Party tried to mobilize enough resources to promote economic development, support a large bureaucracy, and strengthen its military forces.[20] Instead of building up support at the grass roots, however, it depended on coercion and on the help of local elites—an unpopular, ineffective mixture of policies. When local elites, their client networks, and urban intellectuals withheld support and urban groups organized themselves to oppose the central government, this mixture was still less effective.

The Nationalists had had trouble governing before the Japanese invasion, which only compounded their problems by leading to a military decline that strengthened the Communist insurgency, increasing the moral support it received from radicalized intellectuals. Moreover, as the war with Japan was supplanted by that with the Communists, continuing economic devastation aggravated the suffering and alienation of the Chinese people. Coercive efforts to contain political opposition backfired, and inflation spun out of control. In this desperate situation, factionalism aggravated the corruption and ineptitude of the bureaucracy, and as conditions worsened, the image of the KMT was damaged almost beyond repair.[21] It was from this weakened political organization that the Taiwanese in 1945 expected a solution to the economic and political problems inflicted on them by Japanese colonialism and World War II.

Preparations for Retrocession

In the Cairo Declaration of December 1, 1943, President Roosevelt, Generalissimo Chiang Kai-shek, and Prime Minister Winston Churchill announced that "all the territories Japan has stolen from the Chinese, such as Manchuria, Formosa, and the Pescadores, shall be restored to the Republic of China."[22] A Taiwan Study Committee having already been established to collect information about the island's history and conditions, the Nationalist government immediately began to consider how Taiwan should be administered.[23]

Four views of Taiwan's future political structure emerged.[24] Kuo I-min, a former Chinese consul-general in Taiwan, proposed that the central government appoint a high-ranking official as chief administrator of Taiwan. After this administrator had restored order, Taiwan should then be administered like any other province in China. Two Taiwanese who had lived on the Mainland, Hsieh Nan-kuang and Hsieh Cheng-ch'iang, proposed that Taiwan have its own provincial constitution and that the central government use the constitution as a model for all other provinces. K'o T'ai-shan, a Taiwanese youth, presented a petition to the central government titled "Problems Concerning the Rehabilitation of Taiwan." He proposed that Taiwan become a province directly under central government rule, with the provincial capital in Tainan. Another Taiwanese, Huang Ch'ao-ch'in, suggested that Taiwan be considered an experimental province. He felt that because the island had been under Japanese colonial rule for fifty years, conditions in Taiwan were very different from those in other provinces.

These four opinions were reviewed by a special Taiwan Investigation

Committee, created in April 1944. General Ch'en I, the former governor of Fukien province, was the leader of the committee, whose members included Shen Chung-chiu, Wang P'eng-sheng, Ch'ien Tsung-ch'i, Hsia T'ao-sheng, Chou I-o, Ch'iu Nien-t'ai, Huang Ch'ao-ch'in, Hsieh Nan-kuang, and Yu Mi-chien. The committee favored a provincial government with joint administration by the KMT and the military. This meant that the island would be governed as a special province under rules different from those for other provinces.

Eventually, two approaches emerged out of all these discussions.[25] Ch'en I advocated that the KMT, the government, and the military should jointly govern the island for a transitional period. Taiwanese who had long lived on the Mainland took the other position—that Taiwan should not be governed too differently from the rest of China, but that there should be a provincial constitution or an experimental provincial status for Taiwan, allowing it some degree of local administrative autonomy.

Meanwhile, the Taiwan Investigation Committee organized three subcommittees to establish the island's subprovincial structure, plan the management of land, and consider the operation of publicly owned industries. Another group of six officials—Ch'en Kuo-fu, Wu T'ieh-ch'eng, Chang Li-sheng, Tuan Hsi-p'eng, Hsiung Shih-hui, and Ch'en I—began to plan the training of administrators who would govern Taiwan. On December 22, 1944, in Chungking, this group established the Taiwan Administration Cadres Training Class, with Ch'en I as the director.[26] The group set up seven units that would train officials to manage departments dealing with civil affairs, education, judicial matters, finance, agriculture, forestry and livestock, commerce, and transportation. Training classes for 120 people began in December 1944 and ended in April 1945. Forty more people were trained in Chungking in banking, and another 932 in Chungking, Fukien, and other areas were trained in police work.

On August 14, 1945, the central government announced that General Ch'en I was to be appointed governor-general of the Taiwan Provincial Administration (*T'ai-wan-sheng hsing-cheng chang-kuan*) as well as the head of the Garrison Command (*Ching-pei tsung-ssu-ling*). On September 1 in Chungking, the office of the governor-general was established as the Taiwan Provincial Administrative Executive Office (*T'ai-wan-sheng hsing-cheng chang-kuan kung-shu*). (See Table 3.) Thus, it controlled the Taiwan Provincial Administration. With military and civilian authority centralized in his hands, Ch'en I had much more power than the governors of Mainland provinces.

On September 2, he met with Chinese journalists and outlined his plans for the new province. Ch'en I said that he intended "to act in accor-

TABLE 3
Organization of the Taiwan Provincial Administration,
Oct. 25, 1945–May 15, 1947

TAIWAN PROVINCIAL ADMINISTRATIVE EXECUTIVE OFFICE	
Governor-General	Ch'en I
Chief Secretary-general	Ko Ching-en
Administrative Executive Office	
Nine Departments:	Head of Department
Secretariat	Chang Yen-che*
Civil Affairs	Chou I-o
Education	Fan Shou-k'ang*
Finance	Yen Chia-kan
Agriculture and Forestry	Chao Lien-fang
Industry and Mining	Pao K'o-yung
Transportation	Jen Hsien-ch'un*
Police	Hu Fu-hsiang
Accounting	Wang Chao-chia
Three Commissions	Chairman of Commission
Adjudication	Fang Hsüeh-li
Propaganda	Hsia T'ao-sheng
Planning and Evaluation	Hsü Tao-lin
Three Sections	Chief of Section
Confidential Secretariat	Lo Wen-chao
Personnel	Chang Kuo-chien
Councilors	Chao Te-hsin
Two Commands	Commander-in-chief
Taiwan Provincial Garrison Command	Ch'en I
Taiwan Provincial Security Command	Ch'en I

SOURCE: T'ai-wan-sheng hsing-cheng chang-kuan kung-shu jen-shih-shih [Personnel Office of the Taiwan provincial Administrative Executive Office], *T'ai-wan-sheng ko-chi-kuan chih-yüan-lu* [Record of Taiwan Provisional Organs and Administrators] (Taipei: Kuang-hua yin-shu kung-ssu, 1946). The Administrative Executive Office directly managed four bureaus (food grain, monopoly, trade, and meteorology), five commissions (land, school property, handling of Japanese emigrées, Japanese property, and coal), seven research and experimental institutes, the Taiwan Provincial Library and Museum, and an orchestra. We have omitted these organs and their personnel leaders.
* Other officials also held these positions, but we list only those who served the longest.

dance with the teachings of the Republic's founding father [Sun Yat-sen], carry out the Three Principles of the People, liberate our Taiwan brethren from slavery, and then persevere to build a strong, healthy, prosperous Taiwan."[27] On September 20, 1945, the government published the new administrative regulations for Taiwan province, and on September 26, General Ch'en I met with foreign correspondents and explained how the central government would administer its new province. His statement reflected the Taiwan Investigation Committee's basic conclusion that Taiwan was a special case and could not be administered like other provinces:

After the retrocession of Taiwan to Nationalist China, we will first consider the problem of education. We will rapidly expand the use of *kuo-yü* (Mandarin), restore the study of Chinese history and education, and encourage our Taiwan brethren to develop freely their capabilities. Second, Japan's imperialistic economic organizations must be dismantled, but we will still protect the existing productive enterprises. Their profits must be used to raise the living standards of the people and increase their wealth. Third, we will take over the enterprises and wealth of all Japanese on Taiwan and make plans to allocate those resources to agricultural enterprises and publicly owned enterprises. Fourth, within the scope of our capabilities, we will make every endeavor to employ our Taiwan brethren as officials in the provincial government.[28]

Ch'en I understood the Japanese and had lived for many years in Fukien, the province most closely connected with Taiwan. Born in Chekiang province's Shaohsing County in 1883, Ch'en I had studied in Japan and graduated in 1907 in the fifth class of the Rikugun Shikan Gakkō, the Japanese army's chief military academy.[29] He later married a Japanese woman (his second wife). He joined the army in Chekiang, where he served as commander of the First Division in 1924–1925, and then participated in the Northern Expedition.

When the Nationalist government was established in Nanking in 1928, Ch'en became head of the Military Works Division (*Ping-kung-shu*) of the Military-Political Department (*Chün-cheng-pu*). The government sent him to Germany to study political and economic organization and recruit talent. He selected a small group of overseas students like Yü Ta-wei, Hsü Hsüeh-yü, Chiang Shao, Chang Kuo-wei and Pao K'o-yung, some of whom later became important subordinates of his. On returning to China, he was promoted to deputy of the General Affairs Section of the Military-Political Department, whereupon he immediately appointed Yü Ta-wei to fill his old position as head of the Military Works Division.

After the Nationalist government suppressed the Fukien rebellion in 1934, the central government appointed Ch'en chairman of the Fukien provincial government, a post he held until 1944. Like many provincial leaders and warlords of the 1920s and 1930s, Ch'en I carefully cultivated his coterie of followers, moving them upward as his fortunes improved. While governor of Fukien in the 1930s, he began to acquire dependable lieutenants like Shen Chung-chiu, who later helped him recruit officials in Chungking to serve in the first Taiwan provincial government.[30]

By 1940, Ch'en I was 57 years old and had won the respect of his peers, such as Chiang Kai-shek, for his loyalty to the KMT and its leaders and for his unswerving commitment to Sun Yat-sen's doctrine. His steady career advancement in the bureaucracy of the ROC was the result of not only his ability but also of his character and leadership style—qualities that would influence his policies in Taiwan, his performance as an official, and his relationship to the Taiwanese, especially members of the elite.

Just as Ch'en I was loyal to his leaders, he expected loyalty from his subordinates. When Ch'en favorably evaluated a key subordinate, he completely supported that person. While he was in Fukien, some of his officials formed factions and fought each other. When one official asked Ch'en how he determined which official to support, Ch'en replied, "Take the case of two strong thieves who incessantly attack each other. They attack each other not because they are two strong thieves. One of them must be right, and you must believe the report submitted by that person."[31]

Ch'en I's support for his key subordinates was buttressed by his conviction that a leader should back a subordinate even if that person were criticized for incompetence. For that reason, many Taiwan provincial officials suspected of corruption were not removed from office because Ch'en refused to turn his back on a friend unless the evidence was overwhelming. This streak of stubbornness was even commented upon in some newspaper reports of his execution on June 18, 1950.

One unconfirmed story revealing his stubbornness involved an incident during a parade held in Chungking on June 14, 1945, to honor the United Nations' flag. When marchers drew close to Ch'en I's vehicle, he refused to avoid them, telling his driver not to detour. But the driver was finally forced to stop when throngs surrounded the car and demanded that its occupants get out and walk. Ch'en I had no choice but to obey.[32]

Along with the loyalty and stubborn support for his officials that marked Ch'en's bureaucratic qualities were his strong beliefs. For example, throughout his career he firmly believed that only the national language could unify the country and keep the Chinese true to their heritage. As Fukien's governor, Ch'en I never learned Minnan (Hokkienese) or any other local dialect but insisted on speaking the national language. Ch'en I adopted this same principle when serving as Taiwan's first governor, refusing to speak Japanese, even though use of the language would have improved communication with the Taiwanese elite.[33] Strong adherence to principles isolated Ch'en from the local elite and prevented him from detecting and understanding the deep grievances they held against his administration.

The same stubbornness extended to Ch'en's ideology—his fervent adherence to Sun's Three Principles of the People, especially that of promoting local self-government.[34] Ch'en's commitment to Sun's aim of first introducing democracy at the grass-roots level of society under single-party rule prevailed over the objections of his officials in late 1945 and early 1946.

The Establishment of Nationalist Rule   61

Along with these qualities, Ch'en I followed a work style of frugality and spartan discipline that confined him to his office and residence when it would have been useful to interact with officials, mix with the local elite, and meet ordinary people. A colleague remarked of Ch'en's work style:

> Ch'en I always went to his office one hour before the government offices opened. He remained there an hour after all offices had closed before he returned to his official residence. He remained in his office at noontime for a lunch that usually consisted of vegetables, a bowl of soup, and a portion of meat. After eating, he stayed in his office and took no nap. Upon returning to his official residence and eating his evening meal, he liked to read the newest books as well as continuing to handle office work. He retired late at night.[35]

Inflexible in his administrative management style and firm in his ideological principles, Ch'en I had still scaled the bureaucratic heights to become the chief architect of Taiwan's new provincial administration and its first governor.

Before Ch'en assumed his new post in Taiwan, Chiang Kai-shek asked Ch'en I for a list of the persons he intended to appoint as Taiwan's provincial department heads.[36] Chiang reviewed the list and found that most appointees were officials from Fukien and Chekiang provinces. Saying nothing, he turned the list over to Ch'en Kuo-fu, his most reliable official in charge of personnel matters and a leader of the KMT's famous right-wing faction, the "CC Clique." This faction, led by two Western-educated brothers, Ch'en Kuo-fu and Ch'en Li-fu, was loyal to Chiang and greatly influenced him in the building of a modern political party. Alarmed at not finding many KMT cadres or members of his own faction among the candidates, Ch'en Kuo-fu persuaded Chiang Kai-shek to have Ch'en I confirm Li I-chung as head of the KMT Party section in Taiwan. Li I-chung was charged with closely supervising Ch'en I and other officials to make certain they recruited and promoted administrative personnel committed to KMT principles and policies. Although Li's appointment later spawned rumors about discord between the Party and the new provincial governor, available records neither confirm nor disprove the rumors.

On August 30, 1945, the leading officials of important departments were announced: The Chief Secretary-General was Ko Ching-en; head of the provincial secretariat, Ch'ien Tsung-ch'i; head of civil affairs, Chou I-o; head of education, Chao Nai-ch'uan; head of finance, Yen Chia-kan; head of agriculture and forestry, Chao Lien-fang; head of industry and mining, Pao K'o-yung; head of transportation, Hsü Hsüeh-yü; head of police, Hu Fu-hsiang; and head of accounting, Wang Chao-chia.[37] None of these officials was Taiwanese, all coming from Fukien or Chekiang provinces.

Another group of officials consisted of Taiwanese who had lived many years on the Mainland and had returned to Taiwan in 1945.[38] The islanders called them *pan-shan*, people "half from beyond the mountains, half from here," in contrast to the Mainlanders, who were *a-shan*, "people from beyond the mountains." One example was Hsieh Tung-min, the first magistrate of Kaohsiung District under the new administration. Hsieh had grown up in Taiwan and graduated from Taichung city's top Japanese middle school, then moved to the Mainland and eventually graduated from the Faculty of Law of National Sun Yat-sen University in Canton.[39] Another example was Wang Min-ning, who had also been born in Taiwan, and graduated in 1929 from the same Japanese military school Ch'en I attended before moving to China and serving in various military posts. Upon his return to Taiwan in late 1945, Wang held a high position in the Garrison Command.[40]

In addition to filling government posts, many Taiwanese who had lived in China acquired other important positions in Taiwan after retrocession. Lin Chung, for example, became director of the Taiwan Broadcasting Company, and Li Wan-chü became the publisher of the island's premier newspaper at that time, the *T'ai-wan hsin-sheng-pao*. This new *pan-shan* elite moved in official circles and advised the new administration, playing an important role in integrating the new province into the central government's administration of China. But its members did not find it easy to establish friendly ties with members of the local Taiwanese elite, who had risen under Japanese auspices to become landlords, doctors, council members, and minor officials.

The Arrival of the Nationalists

For some weeks after Japan's formal surrender, Japanese officials in Taiwan continued their rule, waiting for someone to arrive to whom they could hand it over. On October 16, an advance party of Nationalist troops disembarked at Keelung, followed the next day by forty small U.S. ships bringing the 70th Division to Keelung.

Meanwhile, top KMT officials and provincial government bureaucrats flew into Taipei's airport and began occupying the few buildings still standing. On October 24, Ch'en I landed in Taipei. Speaking *kuo-yü* (Mandarin) through an interpreter, he said:

I come this time not as an official but to offer my services to Taiwan. On the one hand, we must plan to make the people better off; on the other hand, we must strive to build up the country. I will work and strive to see that we fulfill six lofty aims: First, we will not lie; second, we will not be idle; third, we will not seek to gain advantage; fourth, we will strive for exemplary behavior; fifth, we will be patriotic; and finally, we will behave with responsibility. From today onward, with these ideals in mind, we will strive to build a new Taiwan. And we hope our Taiwan brethren will cooperate in achieving these six aims. This is the precious gift that I bear with me today.[41]

At 10:00 A.M. the next day, a ceremony at Taipei's Public Auditorium marked Japan's transfer of Taiwan to the national central government. The Japanese side was represented by the governor-general of Taiwan and commander of the Tenth War Theater, Andō Rikichi; the chief of the Taiwan General Staff, Isayama Haruki; the head of the General Affairs Bureau, Suda Hifumi; and the police chief of Kaohsiung (Takao), Nakazawa Yū.[42] Andō signed the surrender document in front of Ch'en I, who then declared:

On this October 25, 1945, at 10:00 A.M., in the public auditorium of Taipei city, we hold this ceremony for the surrender and return of Taiwan to the Republic of China. As the procedures have been completed, from today onward Taiwan and the Pescadores are formally part of China. Therefore, all the land and people, and all administrative matters will be under the authority of the government of the Republic of China.[43]

On October 30, the administration ordered all Japanese troops to turn their weapons and equipment over to the new administration.[44] During November and December, Chinese troops and officials collected weapons from Japanese troops and assigned the internees, both military and civilian, to camps to await repatriation to Japan. The numbers involved were so large, though, and the lack of transport so acute, that as late as February 1946 there were still 322,149 Japanese, of whom 13,917 were Okinawans, in detention camps in Taiwan.[45]

Understaffing and the Loss of Governmental Positions for Taiwanese

To understand the conflicts arising out of the evolution of Taiwan's political structure, we should first note that by 1946 the territory of the Province of Taiwan, consisting of the island of Taiwan and the Pescadores, was divided into eight districts, twelve cities, and a number of townships. (See Map 1.) There were villages under the districts, and wards under the cities and towns, and within the villages and wards people were organized into neighborhood watchdog associations (*lin* and *pao*). At first, districts, cities, and townships were all directly under Ch'en I's Taiwan Provincial

64 *The Establishment of Nationalist Rule*

Map 1. Taiwan Province, Showing District Boundaries as of 1946.

Administration. By late 1946, however, the familiar "three-tier" structure of the Japanese era had reappeared: Townships were put under districts, while districts, and cities remained under the Taiwan Provincial Administration. However, the Japanese system of local councils and elections was not continued at this time. The provincial administration appointed all district chiefs, magistrates, city mayors, and township heads.

Much of the inefficiency of the provincial structure during these first months was no doubt caused by drastic understaffing. In 1945, the Japanese colonial bureaucracy had a staff of 84,559 people. An additional 12,980 people served in the police force, which was backed by a military force of 195,500. Mainly because of a shortage of funds, the ROC could send only some 28,000 officials and police to Taiwan. Together with Taiwanese officials, the Taiwan Provincial Administration's bureaucracy totaled some 44,451 in 1946, only half of the Japanese total.

A still more striking decline in the size of the police and military greatly reduced the government's ability to deal with crime and to respond to a popular uprising. In August 1946, the police force numbered 9,337 persons, about 90 percent of the full force under Japanese rule,[46] but thereafter it declined to 8,378.[47]

In October 1945, the Nationalists had sent the 72nd Army, made up of the 107th, 75th, 157th, 95th, and 151st divisions, to Taiwan to supervise the surrender and repatriation of Japanese troops, but within a year most of these troops had been transferred to the Mainland because of the worsening civil war.[48] Of the fewer than 5,000 troops remaining in the autumn of 1946, only 3,000 were battle-ready, and part of this force consisted of military police and special forces. These forces were dispersed to Keelung, Kaohsiung, Feng-shan, Kang-shan, and Taichung.[49] With fewer than 5,000 troops and a police force of little more than 8,000, the total security force of the Taiwan Provincial Administration totaled around 13,000—only 6.4 percent of the total military-police presence under the Japanese during World War II.

The new provincial governmental structure also suffered a reduction in size, which angered the many Taiwanese officials thrown out of work. Under the Japanese, the bureaucracy of 84,559 had included 46,955 Taiwanese, but under the ROC, the bureaucracy of 44,451 included only 9,951. In 1946, therefore, some 36,000 former Taiwanese officials had lost their jobs. If the average household size of these officials numbered around seven persons (the average household size for that period), then about a quarter of a million people were affected by the staff reductions.

Economic hardship fueled Taiwanese resentment. Taiwanese angered by job losses did not fully appreciate that they were caused by cutbacks in

TABLE 4
A Comparison of Japan's Governor-General Administration
and the Taiwan Provincial Government
(Oct. 1945–Oct. 1946)

A. Distribution of Japanese and Taiwanese Officials in Japan's Governor-General Administration

	Total		Taiwanese		Japanese	
Total number of staff	84,559	(100%)	46,955	(56%)	37,604	(44%)
Number of staff in upper six grades	40,314	(100%)	14,128	(35%)	26,186	(65%)
Number of staff in lower two grades	44,245	(100%)	32,827	(74%)	11,418	(26%)

B. Distribution of Mainlander, Taiwanese, and Japanese Officials under Taiwan Provincial Administration

	Total		Taiwanese		Mainlander		Japanese	
Total number of staff	44,451	(100%)	28,234	(64%)	9,951	(22%)	6,266	(14%)
Number of staff in upper six grades	21,845	(100%)	13,419	(61%)	7,526	(39%)	0	(0%)
Number of staff in lower two grades	22,606	(100%)	14,815	(66%)	2,425	(11%)	6,266	(23%)

SOURCE: T'ai-wan-sheng hsing-cheng chang-kuan kung-shu hsüan-ch'uan wei-yüan-hui [Taiwan Provincial Propaganda Commission] (comp.), T'ai-wan i-nien lai chih jen-shih hsing-cheng [Personnel Administration After One Year in Taiwan] (Taipei: Kuang-hua ying-shu kung-ssu, 1946), pp. 7, 8.

the size of the government. Other Taiwanese were bitter because they had not been appointed to top-level jobs in the administration. Furthermore, the Nationalists had insisted on repatriating Japanese but had retained about 6,000 top officials and technicians to assist in economic recovery and to operate transportation, communication, and services systems, and many Taiwanese believed that they should have these positions rather than the Japanese. Table 4 shows that Taiwanese impressions accorded with the facts. Although the percentage of Taiwanese in the bureaucracy declined drastically from 56 percent under the Japanese in 1945 to 22 percent in 1946, 14 percent of the staff was Japanese in 1946.

The new administration did employ a slightly higher percentage of Taiwanese officials in the top six administrative grades (39 percent) than had been employed in the Japanese period (35 percent). Yet almost all department heads were Mainlanders. Moreover, when the Taiwan Provincial Administration appointed the district chiefs, city mayors, and township heads in 1945 and 1946, almost all were Mainlanders. For instance, only two of the eight district chiefs were Taiwanese.

The Taiwanese share of official positions had declined dramatically, both in absolute and in relative terms. Instead of being co-opted, the Taiwanese elite in the bureaucracy had been dispossessed and grossly insulted. As Wu Cho-liu recalls in his memoirs:

After the recovery, the intellectuals thought they would have far more opportunity in politics than under Japanese rule. The result was that the majority of intellectuals were extremely disappointed. Those lucky enough to gain official positions regarded them as unimportant, not to mention that it was difficult to become a cadre or section chief. Thus, having waited for so long, intellectuals strongly felt that after retrocession, the new conditions were no different than under Japanese rule, and they were greatly disappointed.[50]

Wu compared the frustration of Taiwanese not acquiring political jobs to "water boiling in a pot with only a small spigot from which steam could escape."[51] As frustration turned to anger, their mood resembled the "pent-up steam in a tea kettle about ready to blow off the lid."[52]

Yet many Mainlander officials also became bitter because they believed they had granted more political power to the Taiwanese than had the Japanese. The Chinese had trained 2,200 Taiwanese, compared with only 305 Mainlanders, for the top six grades.[53] Between October 1945 and October 1946, they had also recruited and trained 4,296 Taiwanese policemen, compared with only 396 Mainlanders.[54] The Chinese justified other hiring practices with the argument that most former Taiwanese officials could not speak *kuo-yü* and were not trained to work in a Chinese administration.

The Beginnings of Electoral Politics in 1946

Forced to cut back the civil bureaucratic staff by half and reluctant to bring in more Taiwanese officials at the expense of Mainlanders and Japanese, the Ch'en I regime sought to enlist Taiwanese support by developing the electoral system. (The Japanese, as we have seen, had allowed some elections to local councils beginning in 1940, giving Taiwanese a little experience in electoral politics and whetting their appetite for more.) The Nationalists had long accepted Sun Yat-sen's goal of local self-government based on elections, and as early as October 1926 had planned to set up provincial and district popular assemblies.[55] In 1946 a new national constitution was being developed, and it provided for elections in each province to select a provincial council and elections in each district to select a district council.[56] (It was adopted by the National Assembly on December 25, 1946.)

Acting in this spirit, Ch'en I called for elections in April 1946 to select the members of a council for the province and councils for the districts, cities, and townships. Many of Ch'en I's advisers counseled him not to hold these elections, but he ignored their advice, deciding to approve council elections "at various levels, with no misgivings at all." He believed that there was "nothing to fear from the people," and that "lying ahead is the wide and smooth path leading to democracy."[57] Chou I-o, a top official under Ch'en I at the time, recalls that early in 1946 Ch'en ordered him to draft a plan for "establishing popular elections for district, municipal, and provincial officials by 1950."[58]

The April 15 elections were a major political event for the Taiwanese. Competition for council posts was intense. Some 36,968 people competed as candidates for all of these provincial council elections, four times the number of seats available.[59] For the Tainan district council alone, 481 people contended for 77 seats.[60] As a result of the elections, Taiwanese membership on councils greatly increased from what it had been under the Japanese, and the Taiwanese were given a greater voice in local and provincial government than were people in other provinces.[61]

As of April 1, 1944 to April 1, 1945, a total of only 179 Taiwanese served on district and city councils.[62] However, after the elections on April 15, 1946, 523 Taiwanese served on the district and city councils—roughly a threefold increase.[63] Similarly, there was a dramatic increase in Taiwanese membership in small city and town councils. As of April 1, 1944, the Japanese had appointed 1,153 Taiwanese members and allowed another 1,528 to be elected, bringing the total to 2,681 Taiwanese.[64] In the 1946 elections, however, 7,771 Taiwanese were elected to these same urban councils—more than a twofold increase.[65]

At the same time that elections were held for district, city, and township councils, a provincial assembly was established for the first time in Taiwan's history. A Taiwan Provincial Council of thirty members was elected to represent the entire island. This council advised the administration and interpellated top provincial administrators, but it did not have the power to draft laws or approve budgets.

The council convened for the first time on May 1, 1946, in Taipei.[66] At this first meeting, delegates elected Huang Ch'ao-ch'in as speaker and Li Wan-chü as deputy speaker. The Provincial Administrative Executive Office appointed Lien Chen-tung as the council's secretary-general.[67] This was the first time in the island's history that a distinguished group of elected Taiwanese had convened at the provincial level to discuss their responsibilities, and their lack of parliamentary experience was immediately evident. As the discussion of how to interpellate top officials became heated, some council members became extremely vocal, unruly, and discourteous. They allowed their fellow council members few opportunities to speak or frequently interrupted their speeches. Others complained that the meeting place did not seat enough observers. When one member urged that future meetings be shifted to the city hall, "some observers . . . began applauding the proposal, with the result that it became nearly impossible to maintain order."[68]

Speaker Huang reluctantly arranged for the move, and the Provincial Council then reassembled at the Restoration Hall of the city hall building several days later. Spectators came from as far away as the south of the island, with the result that the meeting place was so "jam-packed that not even an ant could get in." The meeting, as Speaker Huang recalled it, dissolved into anarchy.

On that day, as many as 300 spectators had crowded into city hall. This showed the enthusiasm of the people for democracy and their concern for the council. However, some people came to have a good time and out of curiosity about the heated speeches of some members. This was proved by the fact that after certain council members spoke, those people left even though the meeting was still in progress. However, when other spectators heard the impassioned speeches, they became carried away and began to applaud. So the meeting became more and more chaotic. When the meeting was adjourned at noon, some members stayed in the hall. The observers then unexpectedly crowded into the chambers. Someone sat in the speaker's seat, declaring that they were holding a people's meeting and beginning to severely criticize the council. Some council members even supported them. Was this not scandalous? Consequently, the order and dignity of the council were all but destroyed.[69]

Huang resigned in disgust but eventually returned at the urging of council members.

The Provincial Council remained in session from May 1 to May 15, meeting every day including Sundays.[70] Despite the shaky beginning, members of the Provincial Council continued to inquire relentlessly into the behavior of certain officials and into provincial administration policies. Councilman Kuo Kuo-chi explained why so many Taiwanese council members had severely questioned provincial government officials at the interpellations held during the first two weeks of May 1946:

The Taiwanese, through the fifty years of oppression and grief under the Japanese government, were seething with hope of liberation. After the restoration they also placed great hope in the government personnel [from China]; therefore they tendered them a very warm welcome. But the government personnel, upon their arrival, disappointed the people. You must know that our mother country has suffered the oppression of imperialism for the past hundred years, and for this reason the political administration of our national government [will certainly], and as a matter of course, not be able to give the people perfect satisfaction; hence the burden of representing the zeal of our people throughout the province is shifted to the shoulders of the counselors. However, most of the people do not understand the nature of the provincial political council.[71]

Another member of the Taiwanese elite recalled in his memoirs that because of Taiwanese disillusionment with the Nationalist administration of Taiwan in the months just after retrocession, "they naturally felt everything was totally hopeless."[72]

Kuo's comments to top provincial officials during the early May interpellations reflected views already shared by many of the Taiwanese elite, although the *pan-shan* elite were undoubtedly more sympathetic toward the central government. A particular grievance was the diminished share of government jobs available for Taiwanese. On learning from a top official that the provincial administration had not hired more Taiwanese because of their inability to speak Mandarin, Councilman Kuo probably spoke for most Taiwanese elite when he angrily declared, "It is absolutely intolerable that the government refuses to employ Taiwanese on the pretext that, unversed in Mandarin, they are ignorant of Chinese. Such a view is not only unreasonable, it is an unendurable insult to Taiwanese."[73]

During the interpellations, some council members also pointed out that the provincial administration hired Japanese personnel for jobs that should have gone to Taiwanese.[74] The same complaint had surfaced in the press with regard to Mainland cities formerly under Japanese rule, because Nationalist officials had insisted upon employing many Japanese rather than local people.[75] In the May interpellations, Ch'en I tried to justify his policy on the grounds that the use of Japanese officials, who were already trained in administration, would speed up economic recovery:

When Japan ruled Taiwan, only the Japanese governed in the top echelons of the governor-general's office and below in the districts, townships, cities, wards, and villages. Not many Taiwanese held any official position. There were only a few Taiwanese above the recommended-appointee rank, and none at the higher levels. In taking over from the Japanese, there were many difficulties. Because we had to have some governance, and because of the shortage of high-quality personnel, it was difficult for us to accept the resignation of Japanese officials. Thus, we were compelled to employ the Japanese.[76]

Because of this view, the administration continued to employ Japanese experts in publicly owned enterprises like the Monopoly Bureau, railroads, and the postal service, as well as in the judiciary and even the police, much to the chagrin of the Taiwanese. While the development of electoral politics gave Taiwanese a voice in the governance of Taiwan, it also gave them a forum in which to protest their limited participation in the management of the provincial administration.

Arguments About Property

Another troubling issue related to confiscated Japanese property. Japanese wealth—ownership of private and public assets—was immense. The Taiwan Provincial Administrative Executive Office expropriated all Japanese public wealth, including land, mines, buildings, publicly owned companies, and so on. Japanese private wealth—land, buildings, paper assets, and business enterprises—became the object of great rancor between Taiwanese and the new administration.

On January 14, 1946, the administration set up a special committee to estimate the value of Japanese private assets and manage their allocation and use. The committee's seventeen branches, which immediately went to work, had by late April estimated private assets at 3.8 billion old Taiwan dollars, with another 2.5 billion in bonds and 3.2 billion in postal savings, making for a sum of 9.5 billion.[77] This huge sum amounted to roughly 17 percent of net domestic product in 1946.[78]

The provincial government began selling some of the confiscated assets to private buyers, among whom were many Taiwanese. Nevertheless, Taiwanese were unhappy with this policy, claiming that the new administration had confiscated most of the Japanese wealth for its own use rather than selling it. Indeed, much Japanese property, public and private, ended up in the state economic sector built by Ch'en I. Han Shih-ch'üan recalls in his memoirs how this was viewed by many Taiwanese: "Scheming managers and Japanese linked up with Mainlanders to rent from Japanese, but in fact they really came to own that property. Those people used all kinds of actions, and I myself was often bothered by requests to behave in this way. Because Japanese properties were so highly valued, many would have liked to own them."[79]

Some Mainland officials and their relatives seized Japanese property illegally for personal gain, a practice that became so widespread that even the government-backed newspaper *T'ai-wan hsin-sheng-pao* complained, "There have been cases where an individual occupied many homes and buildings, using the illustrious name of some association as a pretext for owning that real estate. In reality, those structures are never used for the purposes for which they were originally intended."[80] The *T'ai-wan hsin-sheng-pao* urged the government to enact a law requiring any buyer to make public the purchase price and seller's name, and to use the property for the purpose given at the time of purchase.

At the interpellation of government officials in early May 1946, Councilman Kuo Kuo-chi probably spoke for many when he denounced the

Trading Bureau's illegal acquisition and use of Japanese private property, particularly the wealth of business enterprises, and demanded that such property be auctioned to the Taiwanese: "All the Japanese properties in Taiwan belong to the Taiwanese. Is it possible that the Japanese moved these [properties] in from Japan during fifty years? Taiwanese, therefore, should be given the right to use Japanese properties."[81]

The Nationalist government, however, regarded Japanese property and stocks of materials as war booty dearly acquired through sacrifices in the long struggle with Japan. After the provincial government's commission made an inventory of Japanese wealth, a process requiring many months, the commission sold off a few properties and some small companies to Taiwanese at public auctions. These acts, however, did not soften Taiwanese anger at what was perceived to be outright theft from people who should have been compensated for a half century of Japanese oppression.

Another issue associated with property involved the many Taiwanese who, decades before, had fled to China to build a new life. Many had bought property on the Mainland that had been confiscated during the war by the Japanese or the Nationalists. They now wanted compensation so they could return to Taiwan. Taiwanese associations in large Mainland cities wrote to Ch'en I's administration and pleaded for help in recovering their assets. Ch'iu Nien-t'ai, a distinguished local leader on the Mainland, also urged President Chiang Kai-shek to help the Taiwanese to return home. Although Chiang agreed,[82] his government and Ch'en's administration, lacking staff and legal authority, could do little to help.

To further complicate this same problem, on January 14, 1946, the central government's Executive Yüan passed a law providing for the disposal of property forcibly confiscated during the war.[83] The law placed Taiwanese and Koreans in the same ethnic category, requiring them to prove original ownership, make formal applications, and then receive official approval to recover the confiscated property. These procedures required a significant amount of time and effort to submit detailed information. Because property deeds had been lost by owners or officials during the Sino-Japanese War, Taiwanese were unable to verify their claims, and most were discouraged from taking advantage of the law. As a result, Taiwanese residents on the Mainland recovered little of their property, and as this situation became known on Taiwan itself, it increased the islanders' hostility toward the Mainlanders. In the eyes of many Taiwanese on both sides of the Strait, then, the Mainlanders should have at least auctioned off confiscated property in a fair manner. By not doing so, Mainlanders were accused of having cheated the Taiwanese out of their property.

By late 1946, much of the urban business stratum was unhappy with the policies of the provincial administration. Rumors, fed by newspaper reports, circulated to the effect that the administration had shipped large amounts of raw materials to the Mainland: 87,962 tons of sugar, 45,325 tons of coal, 217,138 tons of salt, and 97,269 tons of cement.[84] The Taiwanese felt that their resources should be used for their own needs, not those of the Mainland.

Corruption and Troop Misbehavior

For many Taiwanese, the problem of resolving property claims merged with that of corruption. The amount of corruption under Ch'en I is hard to assess, especially given the Chinese penchant for denunciation of administrative shortcomings. In any case, the arrival of around 100,000 Mainlanders in late 1945 quickly focused major attention on this problem. Rumors began circulating that the Mainlanders were engaging in all kinds of corrupt behavior, from bribery to nepotism.

In the summer of 1946, a U.S. consular official in Taipei said of the police that "corruption is rife at all levels in the organization."[85] Accusations were made connecting graft and venality with the disposition of Japanese wealth. In October 1946, a report stated that the "Japanese property takeover investigation mission returned to Nanking on September 14 after hearing reports on 384 cases of political and criminal bribery during its 42-day stay."[86] At the same time, the "heads of both the Taiwan Trade Bureau and the Taiwan Monopoly Bureau were dismissed on charges of corruption, and their cases referred to the courts for investigation and trial."[87] An editorial in the February 20, 1947, edition of *T'ai-wan hsin-sheng-pao* described how an official had bilked a government-owned textile firm: "Fei Mien-ch'ing used his authority to steal the company seal and falsify company letters. After being apprehended, he escaped, and the government posted a $100,000 [in old Taiwan dollars] reward for his capture. Fei was charged with using considerable public funds for illegal exchange in which he allegedly earned more than $300 million."[88]

Then there was the case of a clerk in the Monopoly Bureau: "A clerk named Shao Yin used a counterfeit letter to obtain 300,000 tons of camphor. He next stole the bureau's and the director's seals and arranged to sell the camphor to merchants, netting himself over $3 million. He then used an official guarantor document and fled."[89]

As for administrative nepotism and corruption, some examples had already come to light during the early May 1946 interpellations. The following exchange took place between a council member and the director of the Inspection Bureau of the Department of Civil Affairs.

74 *The Establishment of Nationalist Rule*

"How many persons are in the Bureau?"
"There are 114 persons, of whom 23 are Japanese."
"Are they employed on the basis of technical ability?"
"Yes."
"Is there a person named Fan Chin-tang in the office?"
"No. He has resigned."
"Is there a person named Hsieh Chin-chiu in the office?"
"No . . . yes."
"What qualification has this person?"
"This person is a graduate of Chekiang University."
"What official rank does this person hold?"
"Technical expert."
"Is she your concubine?"
"Yes."
"Fan Chin-tang, with thirty years' technical experience, was dismissed. Why is his salary allotment still requested from the senior office?"
"Salaries for March have not yet been paid."
"Yes. You requested the Finance Department to allot salaries for 186 persons, while in reality your staff consists of only 46 persons. The average salary is 1,200 old Taiwan dollars per person. Your total income from November through March has been 1,000,000 old Taiwan dollars."[90]

A former Mainland newspaperman, writing under the pen name Hsüeh Mu, commented after the Taiwan Uprising that pervasive corruption had been largely responsible for the hatred that eventually exploded into violence:

Yet when I had settled down for a year after Taiwan's retrocession, the rotten, corrupt, and incompetent official activities had already produced widespread unemployment, hunger, poverty, unrest, and all sorts of evil consequences. These evil consequences created in the hearts of our Taiwan brethren a burning hatred. That hatred was like a powerful bomb that eventually would have to explode. Moreover, such an explosion could not be averted, because the people of this island are very strong-willed. They simply could not tolerate any kind of suffering and oppression for a long time. The heart of each Taiwanese is like a time bomb ticking away.[91]

The provincial government made some efforts to stop corruption. On March 19, 1946 it charged Liang K'o-ch'iang, a high-ranking member of the committee taking over Japanese organs, with corruption, sentencing him to seven years in prison.[92] On April 5, the police arrested the director of the Taiwan Monopoly Bureau, a man named Tsai, on charges of pilfering 100,000 old Taiwan dollars.[93] On May 21, 1946, Governor Ch'en I ordered that officials desist from hiring their relatives to fill public offices, a widespread practice.[94] To improve the image of officials, the provincial government announced on June 15 and again on July 20, 1946, that officials should not dance in public places.[95] On June 17, 1946, Ch'en I spoke out again on corruption, threatening severe punishment to any found guilty of it.[96] On September 18, 1946, the administration suspended the district heads of the Monopoly and Trade bureaus, without announcing any reason.[97] These efforts to reduce corruption, including the harsh punishments often given to officials, were largely unsuccessful. Moreover, Taiwanese and Mainlanders had different views of what constituted corruption. To Mainlanders, it was legal and proper to use Japanese wealth to create an economic empire that provided generous salaries to Mainlanders, but to the Taiwanese this was simply another example of corruption.

Linked in many people's minds with government corruption was the behavior of Nationalist troops. Although billeted outside major cities, Chinese servicemen had to purchase their food and other necessities in local markets. Bitter arguments frequently led to refusal to pay shopkeepers. Many soldiers stole bicycles. Behavior like this quickly undermined the initial goodwill that existed between Taiwanese and the troops. A U.S. Consulate report reviewing the period from October 1945 to January 1946 pointed out that "military misbehavior is perhaps the greatest single liability of the new government, for the demands of the roving troops on local shopkeepers and households have an immediate effect."[98] Even as late as February 11, 1946, when troop withdrawals had reduced ROC military strength to fewer than 5,000, the Taiwanese People's Association urged Yang Liang-kung, an influential official of the central government's Control Yüan, to ask the government to discipline the Nationalist troops in Taiwan: "There should be tougher control over military discipline. Troops should be assigned to defined areas, and all personnel should be severely limited in their off-duty activities. The troops should avoid disturbing the people."[99] Taiwanese contempt for Mainland troops was reinforced, too, by the latter's "poor physical condition and shabby equipment," which contrasted sharply with the "better mechanized forces and high discipline of the Japanese under whom the natives have lived."[100]

The loss of civilian respect for military and official authority led one American observer to speculate that "civil violence is not improbable within the next six months."[101] Civil violence did not occur, however, until almost a year later, after grievances had been exacerbated by other administrative problems.

Other Political Problems: The Role of the Media and Ch'en I's Leadership

Along with the other factors contributing to Taiwanese dissatisfaction was the role played by the media. Ch'en I's belief in Sun Yat-sen's teachings, and thus in the gradual democratization of China, led him not only to organize the local and provincial elections of April 1946 but also to give largely unlimited freedom to the press.

On March 13, when Ch'en listed the causes of the Uprising, he included the behavior of the press, claiming that it had abused the freedom it had enjoyed under his administration by excessively criticizing the government and thus sowing seeds of conflict between Taiwanese and Mainlanders. Although this claim may or may not be valid, it is clear that the press criticized the government in vehement, across-the-board terms, helping to mold public opinion.

The largest newspaper was *T'ai-wan hsin-sheng-pao*, which by March 1946 had expanded in size and was distributed even in southern Taiwan. In 1946, "one could say anything with complete freedom" under the provincial government's policy, which made it "unnecessary to request permission to publish" and proclaimed that "the press will not be censored."[102] On February 20, 1946, the *Chung-hua jih-pao* began publishing in Tainan. Between March and September 1946, about ten newspapers sprang up in Taipei and another five in various districts and cities, many of them published on only a single sheet. By the time of the February 1947 Uprising, there were around twenty newspapers throughout Taiwan.[103]

Some, like the *Tzu-ch'iang-pao (Self-Strengthening Tribune)* and the *Ho-p'ing jih-pao (Peace Daily)*, reported the opinions of reporters and officials alike. The opinions were often unfavorable to the government, blaming it for Taiwan's problems. For example, an editorial in the *Ho-p'ing jih-pao* in early August 1946 criticized the provincial government's handling of Japanese assets by saying:

> The better caretakers merely know how to confiscate property without knowing how to use it, relegating all to waste. These bad caretakers either openly rob or secretly steal. Nothing holds them back. National pride has been swept away. These caretakers have obtained material goods, but the Nationalists have lost the hearts of the people. The people's feelings have turned to hate of the motherland. Most people cannot hide their disappointment with the takeover by the central government. Some have incurred enormous losses in the process. Until now, 6 million Taiwanese still have no way to petition and no way to solve their problems.[104]

Several days later, the same paper ran an editorial condemning the provincial government for not satisfying Taiwanese hopes and expectations.

After the takeover, the central government's policies were not as good as what people had been hoping for. These policies could not meet the people's hopes and desires. The worst part is that a few corrupt bureaucrats have engaged in illegal activities, using their powers to abuse the populace, thus arousing hatred and complaints in the hearts of the people.[105]

The *Ho-p'ing jih-pao* also singled out certain remarks of leading officials in order to criticize the provincial administration. For example, it quoted Yeh Ming-hsün, director of the Central News Agency, as saying, "Thinking back to when Taiwan returned to China, the enthusiastic welcome of the Taiwanese for the Nationalists was very moving. However, because the caretakers were incompetent in redistributing resources and mishandled affairs, the Taiwanese were enormously disappointed. Now their warm feelings for the central government have cooled."[106] Then it quoted this from Director Lin Chung of the Taiwan Broadcasting Station: "The Taiwanese hope the government of the motherland will develop innovative political and economic policies. However, what they see so far departs too much from the ideals of the people. Thus, the gulf between the two sides has widened. This is really very sad."[107]

Still another article emphasized how the Taiwanese sincerely wanted democracy and gave readers the impression that the administration was not sincerely trying to fulfill those hopes: "The Taiwanese are passionate and sensitive; all of them have received at least some basic education, and this has proved to be beneficial to their overall development. Furthermore, the Taiwanese are very interested in politics. This is a very good foundation on which to establish a democratic system."[108]

Reports often depicted complex events in a way that made the administration seem inept. On September 11, 1946, the *Tzu-ch'iang-pao* reported an account by a journalist who had interviewed the assistant of General Shih Hung-hsi concerning friction between Chinese troops and the local people:

The cannons turned over by the Japanese in the garrison were in complete sets, and some were even brand new. There were several types, both low- and high-trajectory cannons. However, the caretakers were incompetent, and there have been many losses due to theft and corruption. This problem occurs quite often. So the government was forced to use very harsh measures to deal with the problem.[109]

We can therefore argue that, given the freedom to criticize the government, the press often did not provide balance. After the spring of 1947, when the press became more strictly controlled, it blamed the Uprising on the "poisonous" influence of Japanese colonial rule, underworld elements, and riffraff, claiming that citizens had been misled into robbing and looting stores, public buildings, and residences.[110]

However, while newspaper criticism of the administration may not have been balanced, Ch'en I's administration continued to nurture grass-roots democracy, first through the April 1946 local elections and, second, by allowing the provincial council to interpellate administration officials in May. These interpellations, moreover, received widespread publicity in the newspapers, giving many politically conscious Taiwanese an opportunity to press for reform. Therefore, at a time when Taiwanese felt the administration might respond to their concerns, their elected councils made it possible for Taiwanese to confer with officials and resolve some of their problems.

Finally, the rich organizational life that accompanies the familism of the Chinese was clearly flourishing in 1946. There were associations formed by people in a particular kind of business (for example, tobacco sellers), a youth association, student associations in high schools and colleges, the Political Construction Association (*Cheng-chih chien-she hsieh-hui*) formed in late 1945, labor, farmer, and women's associations, and so on. This entire organizational network facilitated the kind of horizontal and vertical communication that has for many centuries been basic to the vitality of Chinese society—and perhaps served to mitigate the tensions that had arisen in late 1945 and early 1946. As members of the Chinese elite expressed their frustrations to higher government organs, they hoped that the government would take action. For this reason, perhaps, there was constant grumbling from the Taiwanese but as yet no well-organized opposition to the provincial administration, particularly opposition that would involve drastic action like labor strikes or public demonstrations. One foreign observer noted this by remarking: "Although dissatisfaction and disillusionment with the present regime are heard in all directions, there is no evidence that this feeling is likely, in the foreseeable future, to crystallize into organized resistance against the government."[111]

Ch'en I, moreover, had set an example for many officials with his hard work and self-discipline, and he was notably frugal in his living habits. He seemingly devoted himself solely to his work and public duties.[112] While rumors and actual examples of official corruption circulated more widely with each passing month, no one could criticize the Governor-General for corrupt behavior.

Chou I-o, a high official under Ch'en I who later fled to the Mainland after the Uprising, later wrote that when Nationalist officials first arrived in Taiwan, the island appeared to many of them like a "ripe piece of meat" for the taking.[113] Factions immediately tried to stake out spheres of privilege and power. Ch'en I resisted them, attempting to centralize power under himself. Infuriating many officials, he decided that different bureaus would manage Japanese public enterprises, regulate trade, control the supply and distribution of food grains, operate the monopoly bureaus, and print provincial currency different from that of the Mainland. Ch'en I's policies prevented the administration from disintegrating into conflicting fiefs, although Ch'en I's enemies surfaced after the Uprising, blaming him for precipitating a rebellion that their management had helped to bring about.[114]

Among Ch'en's shortcomings, however, was his failure to build informal ties throughout the bureaucracy and among members of local elites. Upon arriving in Taiwan, he vowed he would never utter a word of Japanese, serving notice to his officials and to the Taiwanese that the era of Japanese influence in Taiwan had ended. His close associates report that he was true to his word; he never spoke a word of Japanese in Taiwan, even though he was fluent in the language.[115] Although Ch'en's attitude is understandable, it handicapped him because he did not know Taiwanese (the Minnan dialect), and thus could not mingle easily with the Taiwanese.

Ch'en I's handling of his subordinates, moreover, caused additional problems. Ko Ching-en, his chief secretary-general, recalls that Ch'en I's habit was "to harbor no doubts about any official when employing him, but never to employ an official about whom he had doubts."[116] Therefore, when officials he trusted made mistakes, he took no action against them, even if they turned out to be corrupt or incompetent. Many of his subordinates were sycophants, afraid to give him information that might cast doubt on his policies. A large number of his department heads were cronies from his days in Fukien, including Chou I-o, head of Civil Affairs; Chao Nai-ch'uan, head of Education; Hsü Hsüeh-yü, head of Transportation; Pao K'o-yung, head of Industry and Mining; Chao Lien-fang, head of Agriculture and Forestry; Hu Fu-hsiang, head of Police; and Ch'ien Tsung-ch'i, head of the Secretariat.[117] In surrounding himself with such people, Ch'en I gradually lost touch with political reality and thus failed to appreciate how serious conditions had become for his administration by the winter of 1946–47.

Ch'en I's leadership style, then, made it difficult for him to assess the tensions provoked in urban areas by the inefficiency of the understaffed bureaucracy, the loss of government jobs for Taiwanese, his insensitive program for the disposal of Japanese property, bureaucratic corruption,

80   *The Establishment of Nationalist Rule*

and military misbehavior. Nor is there any indication that he understood that the combination of urban dissatisfaction and a greatly reduced military force signified danger for his administration. At the same time, he pursued statist economic policies that, although intellectually respectable in his day, proved to have a disastrous impact on the war-ravaged economy.

The Economic Crisis

Of the problems facing Ch'en's administration, none was more serious than the economic crisis, which became worse in 1946 with the deepening of political tensions between the Taiwanese and the new administration. Its severity played an important role in eroding urban patience with the new regime and creating the sense of moral outrage that fueled the 1947 Uprising.

Until the end of 1944, the Japanese had maintained much of the island's modern system of transport and communications, kept factories running, and produced enough grain for the rationing system. The Allied bombings of 1945, however, leveled sections of cities, devastated harbor and railway facilities, and halted some manufacturing. The Nationalists' most urgent problems were reviving transport and communications and guaranteeing enough food for the populace. There was a limited number of skilled workers, however, and the provincial government could not depend upon the Mainland for help. To make matters worse, the government placed too much money in circulation and adopted policies constricting the free market. Thus, by early 1946, commodity shortages, inflation, and unemployment had dramatically increased.

When a team of Western and Chinese journalists arrived in Taipei on August 31, 1946, to inspect the island, they received briefings from Ch'en I and other officials and visited nearby factories. The next day they also flew to Kaohsiung and Tainan. One of the journalists reported on the transport shortage existing after the Japanese surrender:

The shortage of transport equipment was a major obstacle preventing the rehabilitation of Taiwan. Before, Japanese ships had assembled in Taiwan's harbors under the protection of the Japanese navy, but during the war the bombings and their damage made it impossible for any ships to deliver their goods on time, thus causing a great shortage of transport materials and equipment. There was only the China Steamship Company, which sent a ship to Taiwan three times each week.... Because of the bombings and the shortage of equipment, Taiwan's roads and railroads had deteriorated; there were great difficulties in purchasing vehicles, and they were in scarce supply. Railroad tracks and roadbeds had also been severely damaged, and trains still had to wait for fixed periods to pass each other.[118]

The Establishment of Nationalist Rule 81

In 1945, the total number of railway cars hauled came to only 25 percent of those hauled in 1944.[119] Even at the end of 1946, only 80 percent of the railway system, tracks, and tunnels had been restored, and roughly the same amount of freight and passengers was hauled in 1946 as in 1945.[120] Because of transport problems, many factories never received enough raw and semifinished materials to stay open. The provincial administration found that of 356 Japanese factories, only 156 still operated in the fall of 1945.[121] Only about 70 percent of all factories remained in operation,[122] and around one-quarter of the large-scale factories had closed down.[123] Factory production had declined to about 25 percent of the 1942 output level.[124] By the early fall of 1946, six out of nine key industrial commodities were in shorter supply than a year earlier.

Taiwan's dependence upon Japan for chemical fertilizer, textile materials, and machinery also made recovery difficult. Even before Japan's surrender, the island had been forced to break this dependence and become self-reliant. Taiwanese agriculture had used 250,000 tons of fertilizer of all kinds annually, but by late 1945, the island could supply only 5,000–6,000 tons to farmers.[125] In late 1945, farms produced only 584,973 metric tons of rice, an amount just below the rice output for 1904, and about half the output for 1943.[126] Rice production rose to 894,021 metric tons for 1946, but demand far exceeded supply because of hoarding, population growth, and the return of tens of thousands of Taiwanese from China and elsewhere. In 1946, agricultural output was higher than in 1945 for four out of five main crops but still lower for peanuts.

Agricultural shortages contributed to inflation, which the Japanese had suppressed through price controls and rationing. Between 1938 and 1942, the price level had risen only about 1.5 times (Table 5). Prices continued to rise at a slightly faster rate in 1943 and 1944, but still much less than on the Mainland, especially in areas controlled by the Nationalist government. Moreover, Japanese rationing and effective controls over the food supply allowed the price for one peck of native rice (*tsai-lai*) to rise only 6 percent in these same years. Between 1944 and 1945, however, there was runaway inflation, with a 530-percent increase in the price level.

In 1945, the money supply exploded when note issue rose to almost four times the amount issued in 1944.[127] In 1946, the administration failed to raise enough tax revenue to meet island-wide administration expenses, despite cutbacks in government staff. It responded by printing more currency,[128] which drove note issues up another 20 percent.[129] A tremendous increase in prices took place. Between October 1945 and August 1946, the price level rose 3.5 times.[130] After October 1945, accelerating inflation caused great anxiety throughout urban society. Food prices, for instance,

TABLE 5
Taipei City Retail Price Index, 1938–46
(1945 = 100)

	Total index	Food grain	Clothing	Fuel	Misc.
1938	3.77	4.30	2.27	3.65	5.36
1939	4.37	5.03	2.78	4.62	5.43
1940	5.13	6.01	2.79	5.21	6.51
1941	5.22	6.22	3.11	5.31	6.97
1942	5.56	6.58	3.23	5.55	7.25
1943	9.62	8.10	8.33	28.16	9.30
1944	18.85	18.61	16.65	32.67	15.47
1945	100.00	100.00	100.00	100.00	100.00
1946	324.90	324.43	281.97	224.76	487.03
1946:					
Jan.	163.54	147.05	134.94	133.30	305.63
Feb.	202.83	194.40	158.92	166.06	331.40
Mar.	250.01	224.28	238.99	195.71	443.84
Apr.	285.64	248.08	321.95	196.54	519.75
May	326.97	309.49	326.87	209.02	506.71
June	322.95	328.86	338.94	206.17	509.92
July	350.82	304.49	319.70	223.31	503.07
Aug.	361.71	388.62	287.15	256.46	496.81
Sept.	346.68	364.56	276.09	265.06	481.80
Oct.	364.29	387.66	310.88	251.80	490.58
Nov.	372.59	401.80	311.90	261.04	486.99
Dec.	406.94	439.45	313.93	295.30	497.34

SOURCE: Tai-wan hsing-cheng chang-kuan kung-shu t'ung-chi-shih, [Taiwan Provincial Office Administration Executive Office, Statistical Bureau] (comp.), *Tai-wan-sheng t'ung-chi yao-lan* [A Statistical Summary of Taiwan Province] (Taipei: T'ai-wan-sheng hsing-cheng chang-kuan kung-shu t'ung-chi-shih, 1946), 3rd issue (March 1947), p. 110.

increased rapidly through the first half of 1946. Between January and February 1946, the price of one peck of rice in Taipei markets increased 230 percent. It rose another 130 percent by March—more than doubling each month.[131] Food prices stabilized during the harvest of the second rice crop but then continued their rise. Between January and February 1947, the Taipei retail price for third-class rice rose 130 percent, that of second-class rice, 93 percent, and that of top-grade rice, 103 percent—the largest monthly increase in rice prices since retrocession.[132] Similarly, inflation for other categories of goods worsened in early 1946, moderated during the remaining year, and then escalated again in early 1947. Clothing prices followed this pattern, as did fuel prices, skyrocketing in the first month of 1947, when the price of a catty of wood rose by over 100 percent.[133] This surge in prices just after the Chinese New Year in 1947 greatly alarmed the public.

While low industrial and agricultural production stimulated inflation,

TABLE 6
Production of Selected Commodities in Taiwan
(metric tons)

		Pre-1945 peak year output		Avg. monthly prod.	
	Year	Annual	Monthly	Oct. 1945	Aug. 1946
Industrial commodities					
Cement	1937–38	293,780	24,451	60,000	10,000
Electricity (kwh)	1943	321,029	26,752	40,000	145,429
Sulphate	1937	24,768	2,064	2,203	136
Nitrogen	1942	12,778	1,064	7,933	252
Paper	1940	16,535	1,377	827	246
Soap	1941	5,407	450	179	72
Coal	1941	2,853,832	237,819	13,540	88,334
Carbon black	1939	2,229.8	191	24	59
Agricultural commodities					
Sugar	1937–38	1,418,731	118,227	87,544	7,172
Tea	1942	11,586	965	119	243
Peanuts	1942	12,907	1,075	963	3,114
Pineapple fiber	1942	264	22	20	19
Rice	1942	1,116,715	93,059	48,747	74,501
Sweet potatoes	1942	1,556,390	129,699	97,105	110,875

SOURCES: sugar, Chung-kuo kung-ch'eng-shih hsüeh-hui [Chinese Engineer Association], *T'ai-wan kung-yeh fu-hsing-shih* [History of Taiwan's Industrial Recovery] (Taipei: Chinese Engineer Association, 1948), p. 239; cement, electricity, paper, soap, coal, and carbon black, see *Tung-chi t'i-yao*, pp. 87–89; sulphate and nitrogen, *WCT*, p. 44; agricultural commodities, Chinese-American Joint Commission on Rural Reconstruction, *Taiwan Agricultural Statistics, 1901–1965* (Taipei: Joint Commission on Rural Reconstruction, 1966): p. 23 for rice; p. 39 for peanuts; p. 48 for tea; p. 61 for pineapple fiber; p. 36 for sweet potatoes.

they also increased unemployment. In 1946, employment had still not regained the 1942–43 levels. Although the official estimate of unemployment for the year was only 8 percent of the work force, this figure was lower than the actual number out of work.[134] Acute labor shortages still afflicted agriculture during the sowing and harvesting seasons, but unemployment in the cities remained high.

Much of Taiwan's economic crisis could be traced to World War II, which deprived Taiwan of economic aid from the Mainland as well as its previously vital trade connections with Japan. More directly, the military destruction of production and transportation facilities had created great shortages in industrial and marketed agricultural output. These shortages contributed to the breakdown in manufacturing, processing, distribution, and storage, exacerbating raw material and commodity shortages. (See Table 6.) Moreover, the lag in production caused serious unemployment, particularly in the towns and cities, at a time when thousands of Taiwanese were returning from overseas. These returnees added to the ranks of the unemployed, increasing the demand for basic goods and thus serving as another inflationary pressure.

Clearly, the most astute governor would have been hard-pressed to deal with the economic crisis. Ch'en I, however, lived in an ideological environment in which the accepted economic ideas were—as many economists today would agree—likely to make a bad situation worse. These were the statist economic ideas used in KMT circles to interpret Sun Yat-sen's doctrine of "The Principle of the People's Livelihood," which emphasized state regulation of property values through a fixed tax and state leadership in developing and owning infrastructure. For example, when Hu Ch'iu-yüan praised capitalism in the 1930s, he considered himself a lonely voice in KMT circles, even though he argued that his view accorded with Sun's.[135] Many central government officials, especially the technocrats of the Resource Commission (*tzu-yüan wei-yüan-hui*), interpreted Sunist doctrine to mean that the state should take the lead in economic development by creating public enterprises—as large as possible—to modernize agriculture and industry.

Ch'en I's statism, probably motivated partly by his desire to build up the KMT patronage network, was also based on ideology. He took Sun Yat-sen's economic policies seriously, interpreting them to justify his administration's intervention in all economic activities. For Ch'en I, economic planning was a serious goal:

> The purpose of economic planning is the people's welfare. Sun's outline for state building stated, "The road to construction requires the Principle of the People's Livelihood." The Taiwan administration's outline plan requires that economic construction, national income, and profit should raise the living standards of the Taiwanese. After I arrived in Taiwan, I stated that we should use capital and knowledge for the benefit of the greatest number of people. Because we want to implement the Three People's Principles, we must concentrate on the people's livelihood. The purpose of economic construction is to realize that goal.[136]

Planning entailed that the state take the lead to administer prices, control supply, and establish "a system of public enterprises."[137] Ch'en I, like many central government officials of this period, believed that public industries were more cost-effective, produced higher-quality goods, and could increase supply more rapidly than the private sector.[138] In this view, even textile products, paper, and other common consumer goods should be under public-enterprise control. For agriculture, Ch'en wanted to increase the number of cooperative farms using machinery and new technology.[139]

Ch'en I's interpretation of Sunist doctrine led him to believe that the state should expand the public sector and regulate economic activity. State-

The Establishment of Nationalist Rule 85

owned public enterprises and rural cooperatives would serve as models to increase productivity and use new technology. Ch'en I already had demonstrated his commitment to state control in Fukien by backing the Fukien commissioner Hsü Hsüeh-yü when the latter had established complex regulations for "setting up various departments and bureaus in every district where all kinds of transport existed, and then allowing those organs to control every form of transport."[140] Every coolie worker, with his small cargo, either paid a fee or was branded a criminal. Ch'en I also set up a bureau to control Fukien's foreign trade. "Merchants who did not rely on the provincial government could neither export nor import any commodities."[141] Such policies "led to the rise of commodity prices, especially those for rice, caused goods to be delayed and perishable items to rot, and made transport costs higher than before."[142] Even after his statist policies had adversely influenced economic recovery in Fukien and Taiwan, Ch'en did not abandon his commitment to state economic planning. While governor of Chekiang in 1947–48, he expressed great interest in studying socialist planning in the USSR and its European satellites.

In Taiwan, Ch'en I's unpopular policy on expanding the state's economic role merged with his equally controversial policies on the disposal of Japanese property. He justified turning many private and publicly owned Japanese enterprises over to Chinese official managers on the grounds of economic efficiency and justice.[143] His statism thus also made him vulnerable to the charge of creating an economic empire generating ample salaries for a Mainlander patronage network. Many of the 28,000 Mainlanders in the bureaucracy in 1946 were part of this empire.

In addition to the publicly owned firms that soon controlled over 70 percent of all industrial and agricultural enterprises,[144] there was a new Monopoly Bureau, which controlled the supply and marketing of salt, camphor, opium, matches, liquor, tobacco, weights and measures, and so on. The Monopoly Bureau managed 22 factories, of which two produced matches, two manufactured cigarettes, eleven were distilleries, four turned out camphor, and two made boxes.[145] It distributed its products to licensed wholesalers and retailers and relied on police power to eliminate any private activities that competed with it. Indeed, the provincial administration controlled an immense economic empire (Table 7), which included not only former Japanese publicly owned firms but also Japanese private enterprises that had been confiscated.[146]

In addition to owning or managing a large number of agricultural and industrial enterprises and controlling a marketing network, the state had set up a bureau to regulate trade. No sooner had this bureau opened its doors than its actions "brought a stop to all private trade between private

TABLE 7
Taiwan Provincial-Government-Owned Enterprises
(by industry, 1946)

1. Petroleum	11 factories (including 6 petroleum factories for the Navy)
2. Aluminum	2 factories (one in Kaohsiung and one in Hualien)
3. Bronze	2 factories
4. Electrical power	Former Japanese corporation with power stations in Philippines, Hong Kong, Manila, Indonesia
5. Fertilizer	4 factories
6. Soda	4 factories
7. Shipbuilding	3 yards
8. Paper	7 factories
9. Sugar	16 plants, and canefields occupying 16 percent of Taiwan's arable land
10. Cement	11 factories
11. Coal	11 mines
12. Textiles	7 factories for cotton and synthetics
13. Tile and ceramics	2 factories
14. Glass	8 factories
15. Oil pressing	7 factories
16. Electrical engineering equipment	Manufacturing of electrical materials, communications equipment, and turbines
17. Printing	Inkmaking equipment and factory
18. Machine tools	More than 22 factories which manufactured tools and equipment
19. Steel	5 factories, including a metallurgical plant to handle scrap iron
20. Chemical products	A factory producing India rubber
21. Construction	4 companies established during the war, and one road construction company
22. Mining & its equipment	11 factories manufacturing assorted equipment, and 2 factories producing high explosives
23. Fisheries	1 factory producing boats, and 1 plant processing fish
24. Mitsubishi Corp.	7 large plants in Taipei
25. Pineapple	Pre-war factory that ranked among the world's largest processing establishments
26. Abattoirs	17 plants
27. Agricultural processing	13 factories
28. Agricultural products	11 factories
29. Pharmaceuticals	10 factories

SOURCE: *WCT*, pp. 41–43.

parties except through the office of the provincial administration's Trade Bureau."[147]

Similarly, administrative controls were extended to the private sector of food grain production and distribution. In late 1945, the provincial authorities had abolished the Japanese food rationing system and permitted free markets to operate.[148] Rather than allow producers to respond to market-driven prices, administration officials reacted to information received about rice hoarding and to rising food grain prices in December 1945 and early 1946 by quickly moving to control the supply and distribution of all food grains. In March 1946, a Food Grain Bureau with departments in every district began monitoring the purchase, storage, and distribution of rice and sweet potatoes under the supervision of a Food Regulation Committee directed by K'o Yüan-fen and three vice-directors.[149] Farmers and landlords were forced to sell their food grain to agents of bureau warehouses at fixed prices rather than to private merchants. The police arrested offenders and confiscated their grain. The bureau stored the food grain and sold it only to licensed distribution outlets throughout the island, which in turn sold to consumers.

The administration also controlled the former Japanese military and commodity stores located in each of the island's counties (see Map 2). By the end of 1946, Ch'en I's administration probably controlled even more economic activity than had the Japanese. Yet Chinese officials could not manage this vast economic empire as effectively and fairly as the Japanese, because their administration had fewer personnel, a smaller budget, and less understanding of local conditions. For these reasons, the new economic controls spawned widespread corruption. Virtually all commercial transactions required the supervision of some bureaucratic agency and its officials. There was great temptation for officials to charge fees far above the rates legally permissible. Some also granted special favors in exchange for gifts or privileges their customers might grant. More seriously, these bureaus and publicly owned enterprises were inefficient and unprofitable, and they required large administration subsidies,[150] which increased administrative expenses met to a large extent by printing money during a time of inflation.

In other words, statism generated additional problems that aggravated the economic crisis created by the war. As state regulation inhibited production and commerce, inflation increased, and living standards declined. Suppliers reacted by withholding their products and selling through illegal "black markets." This merely provoked more police surveillance, more arrests, and further food shortages. The street disturbance on the evening of February 27 that led to the Uprising illustrates the pervasiveness of government controls; rumors of even a small illegal shipment of cigarettes and matches could quickly bring out a police team of ten men. As we have seen, rice prices had moderated for only a few months after the Food Grain Bureau began operating, before rising yet again. In Taichung and Tainan, rice for the markets became so scarce that several rice riots erupted, although police quickly restored order.[151]

In spite of these economic policies, Ch'en protected his administration

88   *The Establishment of Nationalist Rule*

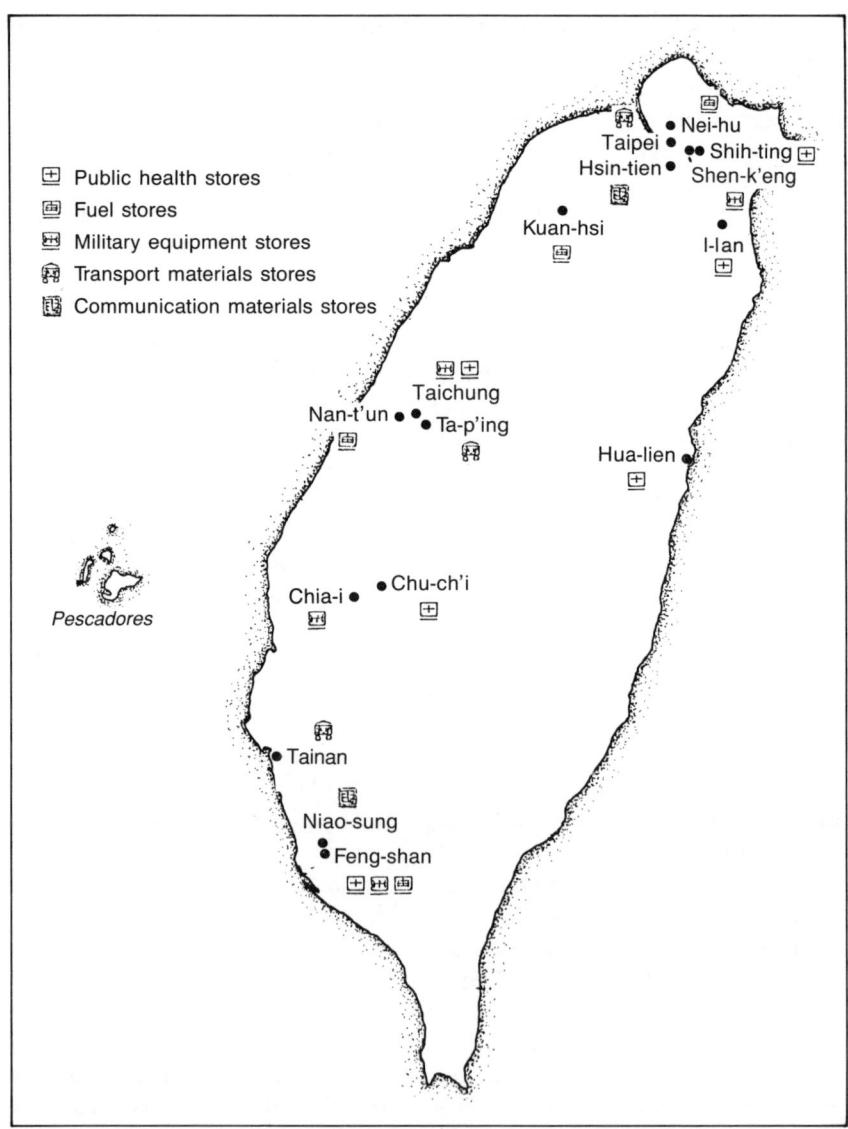

Map 2. The Location of Former Japanese Military Stores and Other Matériel in Taiwan, 1946.

and the island's economy from the interference of powerful members of the Nationalist government and the financial and business community. Perhaps trying to check inflation in Taiwan, he sealed the island off financially from the Mainland by issuing old Taiwan dollars from the Bank of Taiwan, rather than using the *fa-pi* currency circulating throughout Nationalist-controlled China.[152] When several representatives from the four major banks controlled by the powerful and influential H. H. Kung and T. V. Soong, along with representatives from two government bureaus, tried to land in Taiwan shortly after Taiwan's retrocession, Ch'en I ordered their aircraft to be prevented from landing. They had to return to the Mainland.[153] When Director Weng Wen-hao of the National Resources Commission dispatched a representative to Taiwan to take over all Japanese wealth and property, the representative was rebuffed by Ch'en I and sent back to the Mainland.[154] Ch'en I, moreover, insisted that the KMT not become dependent upon government wealth and income to cover party expenses. For example, when the KMT tried to force Ch'en I to place all movie theaters under the party's control in order to provide it with a new source of revenue, Ch'en I resisted vigorously. After much negotiation, he conceded only a movie house on Taipei's Hsi-ning South Road as a party-run enterprise.[155]

On the whole, however, his statist, interventionist economic policy exacerbated rather than alleviated Taiwan's economic crisis—a crisis that heightened tensions between Mainlanders and Taiwanese. Contributing to the crisis, too, was the inability of the provincial leadership to deal with inflation and the desire of many officials to build an economic empire with lucrative openings for well-connected Mainlanders.

Social Ills

The economic crisis naturally led to increased crime and disorder, which may have resulted, too, from the shortage of police and security personnel on the island. As already noted, after the fall of 1946, the Nationalists never had anywhere near the force of 208,480 military and police personnel with which the Japanese had so easily kept order in the early 1940s. From late 1945 through early 1947, police personnel stood at less than 10,000. Soldiers, moreover, were mainly located outside the cities, and their numbers were too few to suppress the Uprising that broke out in February of 1947. (See Map 3 for the distribution of forces on Taiwan in late 1945.)

Table 8 offers figures regarding the geographical distribution of police. In mid-December of 1946, for example, Taipei's police force totaled 486

Map 3. The Disposition of Provincial Military Police and Nationalist Army Troops in Taiwan, December 1, 1945.

The Establishment of Nationalist Rule 91

TABLE 8
Police Power in Urban Taiwan, Nov. 16, 1946

				Sept. 1946	
Location	Police officers	Policemen	Total population	Male population	Female population
1. Police Bureau	169	–	–	–	–
2. Police Training Center	164	–	–	–	–
3. Railway Police	66	356	–	–	–
4. Police Brigade	31	415	–	–	–
5. Police Telecommunications	43	–	–	–	–
6. Police Detention	3	–	–	–	–
7. Taipei District	89	644	774,230	393,604	380,626
8. Hsin-chu District	73	712	761,179	380,549	320,360
9. Taichung District	104	802	1,332,485	669,561	662,924
10. Taiwan District	97	894	1,297,863	648,163	649,700
11. Kaohsiung District	71	663	649,794	326,743	323,051
12. Taitung District	35	292	91,352	46,457	44,895
13. Hua-lien District	41	390	142,432	73,682	68,750
14. Pescadores District	28	81	73,442	35,248	38,194
15. Taipei City	56	430	277,587	137,796	139,794
16. Keelung City	46	186	68,102	34,061	34,041
17. Hsin-chu City	34	182	118,947	59,780	59,167
18. Taichung City	37	120	82,444	41,424	41,020
19. Changhua City	19	85	59,144	29,270	29,874
20. Chia-i City	33	172	115,814	58,241	57,573
21. Tainan City	45	214	165,334	82,562	82,772
22. Kaohsiung City	56	270	142,577	72,655	69,922
23. P'ing-tung City	29	98	97,677	49,482	48,195
Total	1,369	7,006	6,250,403	3,139,275	3,111,128

SOURCES: Police officers, *T'ai-wan-sheng t'ung-chi yao-lan*, December 1946, pp. 131, 137; policemen, ibid., p. 13.
NOTE: Of the 1,369 police officers, about one-third (423) were Taiwanese, 930 came from the Mainland (518, 197, and 142 from Fukien, Chekiang, and Kwangtung, respectively), with 8 Japanese and another 8 unidentified. See p. 135 for an ethnic and provincial breakdown. Of this police force, 483 (about one-third) had graduated from a college, university, or technical college. Another 111 had attended the same schools but never graduated. The remainder had an elementary and high school education. Generally speaking, the educational background of the police force was rather high. (See p. 134 for background on education.) Of the 7,006 policemen, 6,431 were Taiwanese; 407 were from Fukien; and the rest came from other Mainland provinces (p. 140). All the policemen had a primary education, and some had gone to high school (p. 139).

for a city of 277,587, or a ratio of 571 persons for every police officer. Although this ratio was not much different from that during the Japanese occupation, Japanese authority had been buttressed by a much larger military presence.

Moreover, the Japanese police had used an efficient network of informants, household registration, and self-policing (*hokō*) to keep down the crime rate. Although the new police force took over the existing household registration and self-policing system, their unfamiliarity with conditions on the island led to the deterioration of the system's effectiveness within months after the start of Nationalist rule.

Official reports include only a few incidents of crime and unrest, but other sources reveal a large increase in kidnappings, theft, and killings after the last quarter of 1945. For the first ten days of January 1946, the U.S. Consulate in Taipei reported 144 kidnappings.[156] In August 1946, another report mentioned "a sharp increase in numbers of beggars and impoverished peddlers and a great increase in petty theft."[157] In October 1946, thieves reportedly took 400,000 old Taiwan dollars from a Taipei rice shop, and a street vendor, robbed of his day's earnings, was found decapitated in the Tamsui River.[158] On the morning of October 31, 1946, "ten armed robbers entered a leading commercial bank in Taipei and, after taking 300,000 old Taiwan dollars drove away in a truck."[159] The robberies continued in November 1946, the largest involving 950,000 old Taiwan dollars' worth of mining equipment.[160] Robbers also stripped factories of their machinery.[161]

Violent incidents were not limited to the Taiwanese alone, however. The police themselves sometimes were the cause of disorder. For example, an armed clash erupted in the Taichung city police station between policemen and officials sent by the Taichung municipal court to apprehend a policeman wanted for questioning in a civil suit. The judicial officials demanded that the policeman be turned over to them, and in the ensuing struggle one policeman was killed, others were wounded, and the judicial officials were verbally abused and manhandled.[162] In another incident, a police chief at Hua-lien Harbor who had refused to pay his electric bill arranged for several workers at the city electric power company to be beaten. Their colleagues responded by walking off their jobs, leaving the city without electric power.[163]

We noted earlier that unemployment increased because of the worsening economic crisis after 1945 and the rapid growth of the urban population. Added to this was the return of nearly 100,000 Taiwanese from Asia and the Pacific by the end of 1946, many of whom had served in Japanese labor battalions.[164] Most of these returnees found no work and joined the growing pool of unemployed. Many young men, some of whom undoubtedly had dependents, were forced to turn to crime to support themselves.

Taiwan's cities and coastline had long been the haunt of underworld elements, or hoodlums, called *liu-mang*. Efforts to eliminate them failed during the period of Japanese rule, and their ranks swelled after Japan's defeat, especially when Ch'en I ordered the release of all prisoners soon after Japan's surrender of Taiwan on October 15, 1945.[165] Although information to confirm this trend is impressionistic, one report estimated the number of underworld hoodlums in Taiwan at around 100,000.[166] The unemployed and hoodlum elements thus overlapped, producing an expanding stratum of people who were alienated from the provincial administration and who resorted to crime and violence. Their anger frequently became directed at Mainlanders, whether officials or military personnel, whom they perceived as being non-Taiwanese and supportive of the "hateful" administration.

Linguistic and Cultural Barriers

Urban tensions were bound to divide society along new ethnic lines— the Mainlanders versus the Taiwanese. Signs of Taiwanese unhappiness were soon observed by foreigners living in Taipei. In December 1945, only months after the retrocession of Taiwan, a U.S. Consulate report noted that the "disillusionment after one month is apparent and, though there is an atmosphere of watchful waiting, a deep ground swell of resentment and reaction is developing." [167]

Native resentment was soon being translated into song to display Taiwanese contempt for Mainlanders. The Taiwanese had always referred to the Japanese as "dogs" (*kou*), and now they called the Mainlanders "pigs" (*chu*), a pejorative term used to describe their greed.[168] A five-line Taiwanese poem about Mainlanders quickly became popular:[169]

Ching-t'ien tung-ti	Both heaven and earth trembled.
Huan-t'ien hsi-ti	Both heaven and earth then rejoiced.
Hua-t'ien chiu-ti	Women and wine they enjoyed.
Hei-t'ien an-ti	Heaven and earth darkened; we suffered.
Hu-t'ien huan-ti	O heaven and earth, please save us.

This poem refers to different events experienced by Taiwanese and their reactions to the events. "Both heaven and earth trembled," the first line, refers to the period before Japanese surrender when Allied bombings obliterated the island. When the Taiwanese learned of the Japanese surrender and the pending Mainlander takeover of the island, "Both heaven and earth then rejoiced." After the Mainlanders recovered Taiwan, their behavior became more despicable: "Women and wine they enjoyed." Also, Mainlanders preferred hiring more Japanese than Taiwanese: "Heaven and earth darkened; we suffered." Then as factories closed down, transport came to a halt, and prices skyrocketed: "O heaven and earth, please save us."

Language not only mirrors social attitudes and judgments but can also create misunderstanding when different languages are spoken by different groups. Few Mainlanders spoke Japanese or the Minnan dialect of Fukien, and few Taiwanese spoke the Chekiang dialect or Mandarin. Language difficulties were bound to aggravate the tensions already emerging between the two groups. One such difficulty was recalled by Tu Ts'ung-ming soon after Taiwan's retrocession:

> Most Taiwanese could not understand Mandarin very well. One day, a military officer who had been wounded arrived at the National Taiwan University hospital. The doctor informed him that his wound was not serious. The doctor's pronunciation was not very clear in Mandarin. The military officer thought the doctor had insulted him by saying, "You are a traitor." As a result, the officer beat the doctor, and the soldier who had brought the officer in even joined in the beating. This matter was brought before the police for judgment, and both parties realized that language misunderstanding had been the cause of the violence. The doctor had said, "Ni-te ping hen ch'ing" [Your illness is not serious], and the officer had mistaken that to mean "Ni shih Han-chien" [You are a traitor].[170]

Language problems could also heighten tensions between Taiwanese and the government. A speech by a provincial government official in the spring of 1946 set off a firestorm of anger when his comments were mistranslated by the interpreter, misunderstood by the audience, and misreported by the press. Han Shih-ch'üan recalls what happened when Fan Shou-k'ang, the Head of the Department of Education, spoke to a group in Taipei on April 29, 1946:

> According to the newspaper *Min-pao*, his lecture had insulted the Taiwanese people. He had sarcastically commented about their independent way of thought and their desire to expel all Mainlanders. Fan had been reported as saying that the Taiwanese held the idea of governing Taiwan. But, according to Fan, the Taiwanese just stood around idly while the Mainlanders did all the work, and almost all Taiwanese had been Japanized. When the Taiwan Provincial Council met soon after, Mr. Kuo, a Councilman, addressed this issue and the provincial council approved his proposal to have Mr. Kuo and Mr. Su investigate the facts about the speech and report back to the assembly.[171]

The Taiwan Provincial Council's secretary-in-chief reported the results of the investigation as follows:

> Although there were aspects of Director Fan's lecture that one could criticize, he had not delivered an outrageous lecture as the newspaper had reported. The reason for the misunderstanding was probably Director Fan's Mandarin pronunciation, which was not very clear. Moreover, the interpreter seems to have misinterpreted the speech. This case caused 6 million Taiwanese to misunderstand China's provincial government. I proposed that Director Fan's speech be published in the newspaper in order to clear up any misunderstandings and soothe the people's bad feelings.[172]

The damage, however, had already been done.

Recognizing that language was a barrier, the provincial government had authorized the publishing and distributing of printed materials in Japanese for yet another year, to be followed by the gradual phasing out of Japanese in late 1946.[173] Foreign and Chinese journalists reported that in spite of serious language difficulties, Japanese newspapers were being phased out after the first year of Nationalist rule.

A major difficulty in administering Taiwan is the language difference. The majority of Taiwanese came from Fukien as immigrants, and they speak the language of southern Fukien. Under Japanese rule, they were forced to learn to write and speak Japanese. Therefore, the Taiwanese lost the opportunity to use the Chinese language spoken on the Mainland. Governor Ch'en I deeply believes that by the summer of 1947 every school will use Mandarin [*kuo-yü*], and that 60 to 70 percent of all students will have entered Chinese-speaking schools and will be already speaking that language. There are mainly Chinese newspapers on the island, but there is still a Japanese paper that will go out of business in October. There have been requests to extend that paper into the future. [This paper closed on October 25, 1946.][174]

Sensitive to the growing bitterness and resentment toward their presence in Taiwan, Mainland officials who had arrived on the island with the sincere intention of reuniting the two societies became frustrated and bitter. One former official recalled a sentiment shared by many of his colleagues after they assumed their new positions in the provincial administration.

When the Mainland public servants first came to Taiwan, their purpose was not to make money. The majority had the spirit of performing public service, and they wanted to strive for the reconstruction of Taiwan. They sympathized with their island brethren who had suffered the slavery and oppression of some fifty years of Japanese imperialism. They wanted to liberate the Taiwanese from their shackles and restore to them their national freedom.[175]

Many public officials shared these views and tried to perform their duties competently. However, their new working conditions were unfamiliar, and their living conditions difficult. Life in a semi-tropical environment required adjustment, and officials, most of whom could not bring their families, experienced loneliness and frustration. Another public servant remembered his first difficult year in Taiwan with bitterness:

The Mainland public servants did not enjoy a good life. Their salaries were no better than those in comparable jobs anywhere on the Mainland. Their work, compared with similar duties on the Mainland, was more tension-ridden. They unconditionally gave everything to serve the Taiwanese. Among the thousands of wounded and dead Mainlanders [after the Uprising], how many were corrupt officials? How many were villains?[176]

To be sure, such tensions were interrupted by new efforts to open up lines of communication. Many Taiwanese elite had access to high-ranking Nationalist officials. On July 18, 1946, for example, delegates from the Taiwan People's Association on the Mainland, the Shanghai branch of the Taiwan Construction Cooperation Society, and the Taiwan Provincial Construction Cooperation Society went to Nanking to consult with the Legislative Yüan, the Executive Yüan, and the Kuomintang Central Committee.[177] The delegates pointed out that too much power resided in the top leadership of the provincial administration, which they felt should be abolished so that Taiwan could be governed like any other province. One spokesman also proposed that the central government "abolish the Bank of Taiwan's note issue so that the government would not have a monopolistic control over the currency." He wanted the central government to "open up Taiwan's financial markets to the outside world."[178] Other delegates complained that the Monopoly and Trade bureaus restricted trade, which resulted in factory closings, increased unemployment, and worsening inflation.

Yet these appeals apparently fell on deaf ears, because the central government did not respond by taking major actions. By the end of 1946, frustration and grievances had become widespread in Taiwan, especially in the cities, and tensions ran high. One observer recalled that the "Taiwan provincial government and the people hate each other, and cataclysmic change could erupt at any moment."[179]

No Calm Before the Storm

By the end of 1946, a U.S. Consulate official in Taipei was again preparing "gloomy predictions of impending violence."[180] On February 2, 1947, a Chinese journalist reported, "Today, there is crisis everywhere in Taiwan; at every moment there is danger; a riot or great upheaval could erupt at any time."[181] A Taiwanese, Wu Cho-liu, recalled in his memoirs how tense Taiwan had become in the first few months of 1947:

I recall that between January and February 1947, I had just purchased a factory, and the social situation was already very complicated. Among the Mainlanders, there were some who were satisfied with their positions and others who were very disappointed, and these two groups fought with each other. Even among the returned Taiwanese there were some who were satisfied and others still bitter. These groups quarreled with each other. The most serious problem was that [Ch'en I's] government and the KMT were opposed to each other and could never agree on anything. For example, the KMT headquarters in Taiwan continuously claimed to carry out the Three People's Principles and to implement democracy under that banner. That simply was not the case. The Mainlanders monopolized political power.[182]

Wu saw factionalism and bitter struggle everywhere, even within the provincial administration. The gap between the people and the administration had widened so far that only a final ingredient—wild rumors or mass hysteria—was needed to trigger a violent explosion.

Between December 1946 and February 1947, fantastic rumors began to circulate, according to U.S. Consul Ralph J. Blake. "Taiwan is alive with rumors that America and Russia are, or shortly will be, at war, that America is about to initiate large-scale military activities here and that the government here is secretly preparing for military action on the island. It is alleged in another rumor that Taiwan has been sold to the United States government in return for a huge credit for military use."[183] Some rumors reported that the island would be returned to Japan. Blake also reported in mid-February 1947 that fear gripped the island:

Public uneasiness reflects the uncertainties of political and economic conditions both on the Mainland and on Taiwan. The seeming imminence of large-scale civil war on the Mainland is felt here. The continuing influx to Taiwan of people of all classes from the coastal areas (with a rising percentage from the poorest levels) brings conflicting interpretations of conditions across the channel. The police system does not improve. Large-scale robberies continue to take place.[184]

Visitors to Taiwan at this time observed a society slipping out of control. As one leading member of the Taiwanese People's Association on the Mainland said, "One hears of all kinds of people alarming others by suggesting that the current conditions of governance are going to provoke an uprising."[185]

Governor-General Ch'en I, however, had a very different view. Like most provincial governors, Ch'en I stayed at his desk, conferred with his staff, and did not often attend social gatherings. He rarely toured the island or associated with the Taiwanese elite. His provincial departments spent their time publishing impressive statistics, which do provide the only extant record about Taiwan between 1945 and 1949.[186] Ch'en I seemed oblivious to the rapid economic deterioration, the growing social violence, and the deep social, cultural, and ethnic tensions that increasingly beset the cities.

His radio speech to the people of Taiwan on December 31, 1946, conveyed little awareness of the new crowd hysteria that had begun to grip some cities only weeks before the Chinese lunar New Year. He boasted of his administration's accomplishments in 1946, saying that Taiwan's new councils now expressed the people's will. The schools had a new educational curriculum with more instruction in Chinese, and his officials had not only "restructured the old, but had created more new projects."[187] Transportation had recovered and production was increasing. Ch'en I was very optimistic about the future:

> After having spent considerable time and effort to successfully complete several projects, and having solved certain problems, I have come to the conclusion that there is no issue without challenge. However, all dilemmas can be overcome through meticulous planning and a systematic approach, and with undaunted courage and persistent effort. Instead of retreating under pressure, we must face reality with courage and overcome our difficulties through positive action. Based on the experience of the past year, we should have full confidence in our capabilities to undertake reconstruction.[188]

In closing, Ch'en I urged everyone not to "forget to build a new Taiwan based on the doctrine of the Three People's Principles."[189]

He exuded confidence that his administration could manage Taiwan's civil and military affairs. When Chiang Kai-shek informed Ch'en I in early January 1947 that Nanking would soon send a leading military official to Taiwan to take charge of security affairs, Ch'en I wired Chiang on January 11, 1947, requesting that he not send such an official. Taiwan province, he said, was a very special case, and the provincial governor ought to handle both civil and military matters.[190] Ch'en I confidently informed Chiang that "he could do the job." Chiang Kai-shek immediately sent a telegram to Ch'en I stating that no military official would be sent to Taiwan, but that, according to reports he (Chiang) had received, Communist elements were reported to be organizing in Taiwan. Chiang asked Ch'en to "please take strict precautions." Chiang also agreed that Taiwan was very different from the Mainland provinces (*T'ai-sheng pu-pi nei-ti*), but that Ch'en I's administration must adapt to the island conditions as best it could.[191] Some six weeks later, Taipei and eight other large cities were engulfed in riots, and the blood of Mainlanders and Taiwanese flowed in the streets.

CHAPTER 4

The Uprising

AS WE HAVE SEEN, tensions between Taiwanese and Mainlanders did not escalate in a uniform, linear way. Instead, the Uprising involved a series of violent actions taken by crowds expressing grievances and anger arising from the tensions described in the previous chapter. Erupting like a flash fire, the Uprising was triggered by a street disturbance that attracted crowds, who soon directed their anger at provincial government buildings, persons, and vehicles. The following table (Table 9) presents a brief chronology of the day-to-day events, which lasted roughly two weeks and involved a large part of the urban population.

As the Uprising progressed, a series of meetings and negotiations were held to consider the choice between violent confrontation and conciliation. The first of these meetings began no later than Friday evening, February 28, and involved Governor-General Ch'en I's own Executive Office and other administrative offices; different groups elected the previous April (especially the Taiwan Provincial Council and the Taipei City Council); local organizations, such as those formed in schools or universities or by merchants; and a sequence of newly formed committees, especially the famous "Resolution Committees" (*ch'u-li wei-yüan-hui*). The meetings were often attended by audiences of a hundred or more angry citizens expressing the rage felt by those in the streets. The process itself often evoked misunderstanding and anger and overcame efforts to conduct negotiations calmly and reach a speedy, peaceful end to the Uprising.

The chief problem was that of finding a common ground between Governor-General Ch'en I's administration and the different groups that more or less spoke for the crowds in the streets. Although Governor-General Ch'en I eventually agreed to a number of the dissidents' basic demands, he could not agree to the more revolutionary ones. Moreover, dissident actions in the streets or in other cities were often at odds with the views expressed in the Resolution Committees. That the demands escalated and took on a revolutionary character is indisputable—and that in itself explains the breakdown of the negotiations.

100   *The Uprising*

TABLE 9
The February 28, 1947, Uprising: A Chronological Outline

February 27 (Thursday):
  Evening incident takes place at T'ai-p'ing Street in Taipei.
  Angry crowd gathers at Taipei Police Bureau.
  Violence begins in Keelung.
February 28 (Friday):
  More crowd violence occurs in Taipei.
  The Incident takes place at the Taiwan Provincial Administrative Office.
  Mainlanders flee Taipei.
  In the evening, the Taipei City Council meets in the first of many meetings about the crisis.
  Governor-General Ch'en I begins to favor conciliation.
  Martial law is imposed.
  Violence begins in Pan-ch'iao, T'ao-yüan, and Taichung.
March 1 (Saturday):
  More crowd violence occurs in Taipei.
  Taipei City Council organizes the first Resolution Committee.
  At 5:00 P.M., Governor-General Ch'en I makes a broadcast promising that martial law will be lifted, and victims and their families compensated.
March 2 (Sunday):
  Martial law is lifted at 12:00 A.M.
  Meeting in Chung-shan Auditorium, Taipei, at 9:00 A.M., results in more radical demands.
  Resolution Committee meets in Taipei at 2:50 P.M.
  Governor-General Ch'en I, at 3:00 P.M., makes a conciliatory broadcast. Wang T'ien-teng then broadcasts denunciation of Governor-General Ch'en I.
  Taichung radicals elect as chairperson the Communist Hsieh Hsüeh-hung.
  Chia-i and Tainan uprisings begin.
March 3 (Monday):
  Resolution Committee meeting in Taipei moves to set up a self-defense corps.
  Executive Office agrees to requests made by Resolution Committee.
  Uprising begins in city of Kaohsiung.
March 4 (Tuesday):
  Taipei Resolution Committee becomes increasingly radical.
  Governor-General Ch'en I warns that demands must be limited to local administrative matters.
  Order is restored in T'ao-yüan.
  Revolutionary demands are made in Hua-lien.
March 5 (Wednesday):
  Alliance of Youth for the Self-Government of Taiwan meets in Taipei's Chung-shan Auditorium and calls for self-rule and elections.
  Three ROC destroyers arrive in Keelung.
  Generalissimo Chiang Kai-shek plans to send Twenty-first Division to Taiwan.
March 6 (Thursday):
  Governor-General Ch'en I's third broadcast is again conciliatory; Taiwan Provincial Council telegraphs Generalissimo Chiang Kai-shek to explain the Uprising and suggests ways to end the riots.
  General P'eng Meng-chi tries to restore order in Kaohsiung, in a massacre that goes on for days.
March 7 (Friday):
  Taipei Resolution Committee issues radical 32 Demands.
  Taiwan Self-Governing Alliance's branch is established in Hua-lien.

TABLE 9
Continued

March 8 (Saturday):
  Taipei Resolution Committee retreats to take a conciliatory position.
  Crowds engage in violence in Taipei-Keelung area.
  First reinforcements arrive—in Keelung, at night.
  Ministry of Defense in Nanking plans reforms once order restored.
March 9 (Sunday):
  Nationalist troops arrive in Keelung after 12:00 A.M.
  Fukien and Taiwan Censor Yang Liang-kung arrives.
  Martial law is reimposed at 6:00 A.M.
  An order requires that all Resolution Committees be disbanded.
  Order is restored in Pan-ch'iao.
March 10 (Monday):
  Two army divisions arrive in Kaohsiung.
  Generalissimo Chiang Kai-shek publicly denounces "32 Demands" of March 7, adopting a stern tone.
  Governor-General Ch'en I publicly condemns "seditious" behavior in Taiwan.
March 11 (Tuesday):
  Tainan uprising ends, as well as much of the Taichung uprising.
  Governor-General Ch'en I publicly denounces Taipei Resolution Committee for issuing 32 Demands of March 7.
March 17 (Monday):
  Taichung uprising ends.
  Governor-General Ch'en I offers to resign.
March 21:
  All fighting has ceased.
May 15:
  Wei Tao-ming replaces Governor-General Ch'en I as head of the Taiwan Provincial Government.

Although P'eng Ming-min and others later charged that Governor-General Ch'en I was negotiating in bad faith, we do not think that the evidence supports this thesis. The series of proposals he made, some of which were broadcast over the radio, strike us as serious ones, but the chief point is that his own interests would have been best served by a quick and peaceful resolution of the crisis.

There is little doubt that the Uprising embarrassed Ch'en I in the eyes of his superiors and that he dreaded asking them to transfer troops badly needed on the Mainland back to Taiwan. The only alternative for Ch'en I, if he was to keep the KMT in power, was conciliation with the dissidents. Regardless of the governor-general's position, however, some of the dissidents' demands would never have been acceptable to the central government. To understand the nature of the demands, we can divide them into three categories.

Demands falling into the first category were made by those who wanted the government to accept responsibility for its violent actions from February 27 on, make amends for them, and promise not to take similar actions in the future. Dissidents asked that the government apologize, guarantee that no such incidents would occur again, punish guilty officials, compensate victims' families, bring a wider circle of citizens into the investigative process, and so on. We shall call these demands ones emphasizing the government's culpability.

The second category of demands involved restriction of the government's power to act coercively against dissidents. Advocates of this viewpoint asked that the government end martial law and press censorship, release all suspects and enact an amnesty, restrict the movement of troops or use of their weapons, and so on.

The third category focused on the restructuring of the polity or even on the transfer of power from the KMT to people who viewed themselves as the true representatives of the Taiwanese. The request that the government employ more Taiwanese was, of course, a common one, but there were also demands for self-rule, including the suspension or abolition of the government's police or military units and the delegation of police powers to certain citizen groups. Taiwanese with this viewpoint increasingly demanded immediate democratization of the government in a way that would effectively end the central government's ability to impose policies on the Taiwanese. Because such demands would have in effect ended the sovereign authority of the ROC in Taiwan, they can be called "revolutionary."

The following account shows that Governor-General Ch'en I was willing to make concessions about government culpability and even about restriction of the government's power to act coercively. (For example, he ended martial law on Sunday, March 2.) The dissidents, however, did not limit their demands to the first two categories and began to insist on a revolutionary political solution, which led them to ignore Governor-General Ch'en's concessions. This unrealistic attitude is reminiscent of the euphoria with which Taiwanese greeted the ROC forces in 1945, expecting the rapid realization of a sympathetic government and a prosperous economy. Our evidence demonstrates that as the crisis developed, wiser people on both sides sought compromise but could not prevail—a familiar situation in modern Chinese history.

The Uprising Begins: Taipei

At 11:00 A.M. on Thursday, February 27, 1947, the Taipei City Monopoly Bureau received a secret report that a boat near the little port of

Tamsui was carrying some fifty boxes of illegal matches and cigarettes. Even such a small shipment could elicit a major police effort, and in fact the Bureau immediately dispatched six investigators and four uniformed policemen to the scene.[1] When the team arrived, it found only five boxes of cigarettes. Later, the Bureau received another secret report that the missing contraband was being sold at the T'ien-ma Tea Store on T'ai-p'ing Street in Taipei (now called Yen-p'ing North Road). (See Map 4.) Smugglers were known to frequent the T'ai-p'ing Street area, so the investigative team drove there, ate an early supper at the Hsiao-hsiang-yüan Restaurant on T'ai-p'ing Street, and then, probably sometime between 7:30 and 8:00 P.M., went to the store, only to discover that the dealers had fled.

The investigators then saw a forty-year-old widow, Lin Chiang-mai, selling what they thought were contraband cigarettes. Not even a solitary peddler could escape the attention of officials, and the team demanded that she hand the contraband over. The widow Lin replied, "If you confiscate everything, I will not be able to eat. At least let me have my money and the cigarettes provided by the Monopoly Bureau." When the investigators refused, Lin grabbed hold of one of them, who reacted by hitting her on the head with the butt of his pistol, producing a bleeding gash. Lin's daughter began to cry, and some of the crowd that had now gathered began to taunt the team, screaming, "You unreasonable *a-shan*, you evil pigs, return her cigarettes!"[2] One of the investigators, Fu Hsüeh-t'ung, tried to flee. He took out his pistol, brandished it, and then fired, hitting a bystander named Ch'en Wen-hsi, who was reported to be the brother of a major hoodlum. Ch'en later died. The investigators managed to escape, but the angry crowd burned their abandoned vehicle and then went to the nearby police station to demand that the investigator who had fired the pistol be summarily executed.

At 9:00 P.M. on that same evening, Li Chiung-chih, the head of the Monopoly Bureau's General Affairs Committee, and Yang Tzu-ts'ai, the head of that committee's Fourth Section, drove to the scene to investigate. When they arrived, a crowd gathered around Li's vehicle and began beating upon it. Li and Yang immediately drove to the Taipei Police Bureau.

As news of the incident began to spread, a crowd of six or seven hundred people converged on the Police Bureau. Protected by the staff of the bureau, Li and Yang tried to explain to the crowd that the guilty investigator would be severely punished, but the crowd demanded that all the investigators be handed over to them. Li and Yang refused, saying that Police Chief Ch'en Sung-chien would send the six investigators to Military Police Headquarters. When the crowd demanded that the guilty investigator be executed the very next day, Li and Yang responded by saying,

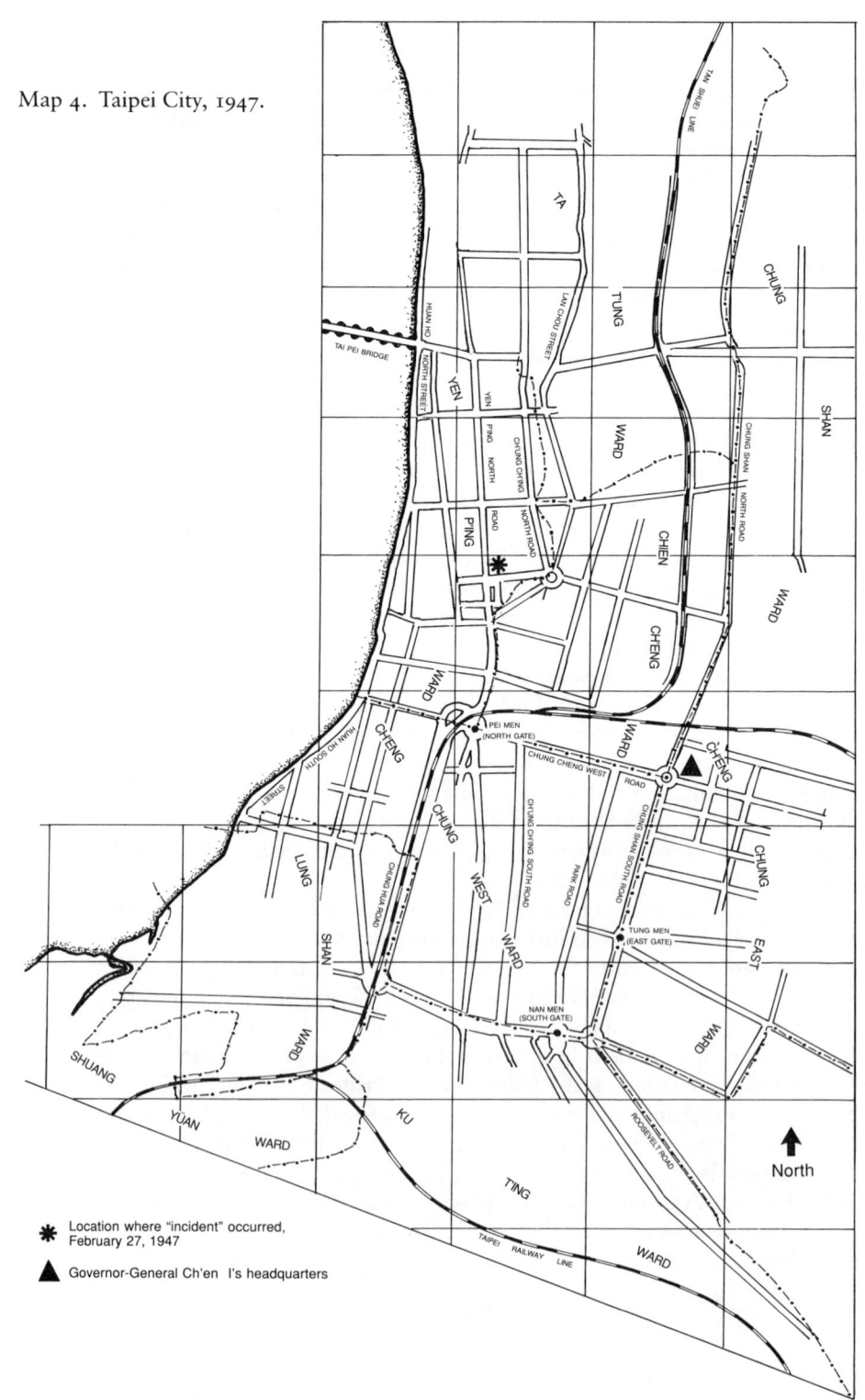

Map 4. Taipei City, 1947.

✱ Location where "incident" occurred, February 27, 1947

▲ Governor-General Ch'en I's headquarters

"Punishment will be meted out according to the crime committed. The law is very clear; we will not act without proper authority." Li and Yang repeated their position, but they failed to convince the crowd, who still refused to disperse. Some of the younger people began chanting, "The Taiwanese want revenge now!" and "Anyone who does not come out and assemble is not a real Taiwanese!"[3]

As these cries reverberated into the night, some of the crowd then moved to the office of *T'ai-wan hsin-sheng-pao* (*The Taiwan New Life Daily*), where they demanded that the paper report the incident. Someone told the crowd that the publisher, Li Wan-chü, was out of the office, but Wu Chin-lien, the chief editor, told them that the administration's Propaganda Commission had just ordered him not to report the incident. At that point, the crowd threatened to burn down the newspaper's office building, whereupon Wu suddenly produced Li Wan-chü, who assured the crowd that the incident would be printed. The account appeared in the next day's edition with only a short (one hundred characters) account.

Meanwhile, the crowd on T'ai-p'ing Street grew larger and angrier as people talked among themselves. A large group began to assemble at the Military Police Headquarters, and another group at the Taipei Police Bureau demanded that the guilty investigators be severely punished. People began beating drums and spreading news of the incident around the city.

By Friday morning, February 28, characters for "China" (*Chung-kuo*) had been removed from signs on the China Hotel and the Bank of China, and a banner in Japanese appeared, reading "Down with Military Tyranny."[4] By 9:00 A.M., people began to assemble at the Lung-shan Temple and along T'ai-p'ing Street, beating gongs and asking storekeepers to close their shops. Some shouted slogans demanding that Taiwan's 6 million people rebel.[5] Others, crying "Stop all prohibitions on cigarettes from abroad" and "Abolish the Monopoly Bureau," assembled at Erh-mu p'ai-ch'u-so, one of the police stations on T'ai-p'ing Street. When the precinct director of police, Huang, fired his weapon into the air to disperse the people outside the station, the crowd beat him, smashed glass windows, and entered the station and destroyed equipment.[6]

At about this time, Taipei's mayor, Yu Mi-chien, the Speaker of the City Council, Chou Yen-shou, and the chief of the Military Police, Chang Mu-t'ao, arrived to try to disperse the mob around the police station. These officials assured the people that the government would punish the guilty investigators, but the crowd shouted that they should be executed.

Around noon on Friday, February 28, a mob attacked a branch office of the Monopoly Bureau, beating two officials to death and seriously injuring four others. The mob burned the bureau's stocks of cigarettes, matches, and wine, as well as a vehicle and seven or eight bicycles. Office furniture and equipment were placed in the middle of the street and burned. The spectacle attracted many onlookers. When military and uniformed police arrived, they were unable to control the mob and quickly retreated.

The headquarters of the Monopoly Bureau, located at the city's south gate, became the next target. Officials there, who had already learned about the fate of their colleagues, had boarded up their doors and windows. When the mob arrived, the people could express their anger only by pounding on the doors and shattering the windows.

Around 1:00 P.M., four or five hundred people, led by individuals beating gongs and drums, threaded their way to the Taiwan Provincial Administrative Executive Office, situated in the middle of the city (see Map 4). The group gathered more and more people along the way, and soon crowds stretched from Ch'en I's headquarters to what is now Yen-p'ing North Road. Still more people were lined up from the city's north gate to the downtown bus station.

By 2:00 P.M., a mob had occupied the Taiwan radio station, broadcasting an appeal to the people to gather at the New Park and then march to the headquarters of the Taiwan Provincial Administrative Executive Office. Taiwan at the time had some 100,000 radio sets, and the broadcast must have had a wide impact. Only a few guards were on duty at the Executive Office headquarters, so they sent out an urgent call for police reinforcements from the Botanical Gardens[7] while trying to disperse the crowd and protect the office. Shots rang out, killing two people and injuring several others. This event became known as the Incident at the Square (*Kuang-ch'ang shih-chien*).[8]

As the news of the incident spread, people in the streets began to use Japanese to question passersby. Mainlanders who did not know how to reply in Japanese were beaten and cursed with cries (in the Minnan dialect) of "Beat the a-shan!" or "Kill the pigs!" (*tai di*).[9] Learning of these attacks, Mainlanders began to flee the city. The crowds refused to disperse and return home, children left school, shopkeepers bolted their doors, and government personnel closed their offices and fled.

Meanwhile, acts of violence against anything related to "China" or the "Chinese" had spread throughout the city. In the early afternoon on Friday, a Shanghai journalist, Wang K'ang, stood in his hotel room across from the Taipei Railway Station and observed mobs of Taiwanese beating up and even killing Mainlanders who happened to emerge from the railway station or be strolling along the streets.

Some Mainlanders were beaten on the head, and blood flowed; some had fallen to the ground and were gasping for breath. Just at that same moment, a passenger train had disgorged its passengers. Some of them, Mainlanders, had just emerged from the railway station only to be beaten severely; many were wounded and others killed. They never knew why they were attacked. There were two military men dressed in their uniforms strolling hand in hand down the street. They were quickly surrounded by Taiwanese, who used their fists and rocks to beat them. They were bleeding severely and groaning in pain, and the crowd still continued to beat them.[10]

Mobs attacked the Cheng-hua Hotel on Pen Street, broke the doors and windows, and took the furniture outside and burned it. Other mobs went to Piao Street, burned the shops and wares of a number of Chinese merchants, and set fire to more than ten vehicles. Whenever the crowds could identify Mainlanders, officials, or military and civil police, they beat them. The district chief of Hsin-chu, Chu Wen-po, who had arrived in Taipei that day, was badly beaten. Around 5:00 P.M., mobs took the merchandise of the Hsin-t'ai Trading Company out into Jung Street and burned it.[11]

People began shouting slogans like "Down with Ch'en I's Commercial Trading Company!" "Let Taiwan Rule Itself!" "Let's Have a New Democracy!" and "Abolish the Monopoly Bureau!"[12] The people who had occupied the city's radio station that day made broadcasts asking the public to attack corrupt officials: "The provincial government's corrupt officials and underlings are all in it together with the military police and local officials. They allow our rice to be sent abroad, so that the people do not have enough grain and are dying of starvation. Since we are dying of starvation, why not rise up and survive?"[13] Among the prominent officials singled out for attack in these broadcasts were Pao K'o-yung, head of the Department of Industry and Mining; Yen Chia-kan, head of the Department of Finance; Chou I-o, head of the Department of Civil Affairs; and Ko Ching-en, Chief Secretary-General of the Executive Office.[14]

People in the nearby cities of Keelung and Pan-ch'iao heard the appeals broadcast from Taipei and were drawn into the violence. In these cities, people poured into the streets to beat Mainlanders, destroy their shops, and burn the dormitories of Mainland officials and police.[15] Those who could not speak Japanese or the Taiwanese dialect were beaten, some so severely that they later died.[16] People shouted, "Rice is expensive because the Mainlanders are eating all of it. The Mainlanders have only come to cheat us, and we are now worse off!"[17]

Earlier that Friday, the government had responded to the escalating violence by announcing that martial law would begin on Saturday. Friday evening, however, the Executive Office broadcast that martial law would not be declared in order to reduce tensions in Taipei. (Martial law was in fact declared and then lifted on Sunday.)

Meanwhile, that same Friday, five representatives of the city's tobacco sellers' association demanded that the Taipei City Council mediate with the government to end the violence. At this emergency meeting of the City Council, the group agreed that Huang Ch'ao-ch'in, the Speaker of the Taiwan Provincial Council, should meet with Ch'en I to resolve the situation. Many also urged that Huang present Ch'en I with five demands, all of which fell into the category of what we have called "culpability": the guilty investigators must be publicly executed; the Monopoly Bureau must compensate the victims' families; the authorities must guarantee that a similar incident would never occur again; the Monopoly Bureau must meet with delegates of the people and apologize; and the provincial government must dismiss the director of the Monopoly Bureau.

The city council also appointed the council's speaker, Chou Yen-shou, to present similar demands to K'o Yüan-fen, the Chief of the General Staff of the Taiwan Provincial Garrison Command. K'o Yüan-fen in turn took their demands to Governor-General Ch'en I, who rejected all but the second one.[18] As Ch'en I realized how serious the crisis was, however, he began to reverse himself. He organized a new committee that evening, headed by Huang Ch'ao-ch'in, to explore the possibility of compensating all victims of the violence.[19]

Following these initiatives to restore order, the Speaker of the City Council, Chou Yen-shou, the Speaker of the Provincial Council, Huang Ch'ao-ch'in, the Chief of the General Staff of the Taiwan Provincial Garrison Command, K'o Yüan-fen, and an independent (non-KMT) member of the provincial delegation to the National Assembly, the physician Hsieh O, met at the Taipei radio station around 7:30 P.M. to appeal over the air for public calm. K'o deplored the beatings of Mainlanders, and he offered suggestions about how the Taiwan Provincial Administrative Executive Office might restore law and order.

First, those who broke the law in investigating this smuggling of contraband will be severely punished, so that this kind of incident will not happen again. Second, because certain violent agitators have aggravated the incident and endangered public security, the commander-in-chief has imposed martial law to restore peace and harmony. When order has been restored, martial law immediately will be lifted.[20]

In their comments, Huang and Chou expressed the hope that the people could negotiate a solution with the government. Hsieh O urged the people to remain calm. All three reported that representatives of the Taipei City Council and the Executive Office had been negotiating. However, they misled the people by claiming that the government had accepted the council's demands to abolish the Monopoly Bureau and by announcing that the government would compensate victims, when Governor-General Ch'en had agreed only to explore the possibility. Because of an erroneous report that Hsieh and the city council believed, another mistake was made: Hsieh said that no one had been killed or injured by the shots fired by the soldiers in front of the Executive Office.[21] Immediately after the broadcast, Hsieh received a telephone call informing her that shots fired by the soldiers that afternoon had caused several deaths and injuries. Although she returned immediately to the microphone and conveyed that new information to the public, the damage had been done. Some people considered her a liar who was trying to cover up the incident for the government. Indeed, the next morning a crowd went to Hsieh's hospital building and took medical instruments and her personal furniture into the street and burned them. Fortunately, Hsieh was not there at the time.

Thus, these first, stumbling efforts to achieve conciliation failed. Despite the quiet streets in the early hours of Saturday morning, March 1, the fury of the people had not abated. In this tense situation, the Taipei City Council convened at 10:00 A.M. and invited delegates from the Taiwan Provincial Council and other organizations to meet at Chung-shan Auditorium to set up a committee to investigate the recent violence. The Taipei Resolution Committee had been born. Huang Ch'ao-ch'in, Wang T'ien-teng, Lin Chung, and Chou Yen-shou were asked to submit to the Executive Office a resolution containing five demands. These five demands fell somewhere between our categories of culpability and restriction of government power: The government must suspend martial law, immediately release all people being detained, order the military not to fire, establish a committee of government and popular representatives to investigate the Incident, and ask Governor-General Ch'en I to make a public broadcast.[22] Ch'en I went on the air and said that all those who had been arrested, regardless of the violence they had perpetrated, would be released, if their families and the neighborhood watchdog associations (the *lin* and *li*) guaranteed in writing that they would not make any more trouble. For the first time, he also definitely agreed to compensation for victims of the *Kuang-ch'ang shih-chien*. The government would compensate families with a 200,000 old Taiwan dollar payment for each person killed and with 50,000 old Taiwan dollars for each person who had been wounded.[23]

However, leaders could not move fast enough to keep up with events in the streets. That same Saturday morning, some people began to organize demonstrations to oppose the government. They wrote placards and signs in large characters: "Down with Ch'en I's Empire!" "Abolish the Governor-General's Executive Office!" "Down with Tyranny!" "The Taiwanese People Should Immediately Rise Up, Struggle for Their Bread, and Fight for Freedom and Democracy!" "Don't Compromise—Use Only Armed Struggle!" and "We Will Use Guns Against Guns!"[24] At 2:00 P.M., mobs attacked the Taipei Railway Police station, and many on both sides were wounded.[25]

At 5:00 P.M. Saturday, Ch'en I made a public broadcast, declaring that the tobacco smuggling case had already been turned over to the judiciary for investigation. He added that the provincial government would compensate families whose members had been wounded or killed. Martial law would be lifted Sunday, March 2, at 12:00 midnight, but all strikes, demonstrations, and meetings were prohibited.[26] The arrested would be released if families and watchdog associations vouched for them. He also promised that delegates of the Taiwan Provincial Council would be given an opportunity to meet with representatives of the Governor-General's Executive Office to resolve the current troubles, and asked that new recommendations be discussed by those delegates. He insisted, however, that there be no further disturbances. Governor-General Ch'en then announced the names of the five representatives from the government side to sit on the Resolution Committee: Jen Hsien-ch'ün, head of the Department of Transportation; Chou I-o, head of the Department of Civil Affairs; Chao Lien-fang, head of the Department of Agriculture and Forestry; Pao K'o-yung, head of the Department of Industry and Mining; and Hu Fu-hsiang, head of the Police Department. As we have seen, at least two of these officials, Chou and Pao, were the objects of considerable popular resentment. Ch'en I obviously was aware of this fact, but given his temperament—unswerving support of his subordinates and adherence to principle—it is not surprising that Ch'en I would ignore public sentiment, particularly when he believed he had countered dissident demands with conciliatory measures of his own.

As promised, the Executive Office did lift martial law at 12:00 A.M. on Sunday, March 2. Yet peace did not return to the city. Armed patrols exacerbated existing tensions, and some people even claimed to have attacked the police headquarters on this day.[27]

On Sunday, too, there were more meetings. At 9:00 A.M., delegates from the Taiwan Provincial Council, the Taipei City Council, and the Political Alliance Association, together with members of the National Assembly, met at Chung-shan Auditorium. Out of this meeting came five recommendations: leaders of neighborhood watchdog associations (*lin* and *li*) would provide written guarantees for the good conduct of all individuals arrested in return for the latter's release; the government would pay compensation for all deaths and injuries; it would grant amnesty to all persons connected with the riots; it would promptly restore full public transportation service (Chien Wen-fa, a member of the National Assembly, was elected to see that this task was completed); and it would allow representatives from labor, farmer and student associations to join the new Resolution Committee. Another recommendation was added requesting that two more delegates representing the government be added to the Resolution Committee: General K'o Yüan-fen, and Chang Mu-t'ao, the head of the Military Police.[28]

These demands, which can be classified in our category of government culpability, were not far from the views expressed by Governor-General Ch'en I in his public broadcast on Saturday at 5:00 P.M. Shortly thereafter, however, the delegates added two more demands—that the governor abolish the police brigade and end press censorship. These fell into the category of restricting the government's coercive powers.

When the Resolution Committee met later on Sunday, it agreed to establish five subcommittees to facilitate negotiations: first, a liaison committee made up of Huang Ch'ao-ch'in, Lin Chung, Li Wan-chü, Chou Yen-shou, and Wu Kuo-hsin; second, an information committee of Wang T'ien-teng, Lin Tsung-hsien, Chang Ch'ing-chuan, and Lin Jih-kao; third, a relief and protection committee of Tu Ts'ung-ming, Chou Pai-lien, Huang Ch'ao-sheng, and Hsieh O; fourth, an investigation committee of Wu Ch'un-lin, Lo Shui-yüan, Hsü Chen-ch'ing, Li Jen-kuei, Ch'en Wu, Huang Huo-ting, Ch'en Hai-ho, Lin Shui-t'ien, Chien Sheng-yü, and Lin Ch'ao-ming; and finally, a general affairs committee of P'an Ch'ü-yüan, Ch'en Ken-huo, Wu Yu-k'o, Ch'en Pi-nan, Wang Kuei, Lin Chang-en, and Hsü Ch'ing-feng.[29]

The dissidents, however, did not unify around the Resolution Committee. Different groups repeatedly held new meetings and made demands that had not been considered by the committee. On Sunday, while the Resolution Committee was setting up its elaborate structure of subcommittees, various student leaders joined with the Political Construction Association (*Cheng-chih chien-she hsieh-hui*), headed by Chiang Wei-ch'uan, to resolve the crisis. The Political Construction Association had been formed in late 1945 to assist the central government, undertake the development of Taiwan province, and initiate reforms. The young people represented a variety of student associations from Taipei's institutions of higher learning (National Taiwan University, the Law and Commercial College, the Normal College, and Yen-p'ing College) and from many of its high schools. The meeting in Chung-shan Auditorium on Sunday at 10:00 A.M. was attended by thousands of students. Most supported the anti-Ch'en I sentiments of the people of Taipei and criticized the governor-general as well as denouncing the provincial government's management of education. Some shouted slogans like "Political democracy!" "Self-rule for Taiwan!" and "Educational freedom!"[30] Others even urged that students obtain arms and immediately attack Ch'en I's headquarters. Student demands were thus escalating in the direction of revolution. After the meeting ended, the Political Construction Association's chairman, Chiang Wei-ch'uan, and several others talked to Ch'en I, urging him to end the disturbances quickly and to meet with additional representatives from the newly organized Resolution Committee.

At 2:50 P.M. that same Sunday, March 2, the Resolution Committee met on the third floor of the Chung-shan Auditorium building. Chou Yen-shou and other committee members presided over this meeting, which was attended by hundreds of citizens. Again, those favoring conciliation were outnumbered. Chang Ch'ing-ch'uan reported on his one-hour meeting with Ch'en I at 9:00 A.M. that morning. He said that the governor-general had promised to consider the recommendations the Resolution Committee had made on Saturday and would strengthen the Resolution Committee's role: "Ch'en I promised to broaden the committee by including representatives of commercial associations, workers, students, the masses and the Political Construction Association, so that their opinions could be heard."[31]

Chou Yen-shou then reported on the Executive Office's response to the five recommendations presented to Ch'en I earlier that day and to the two additional ones that the governor-general abolish the police brigade and end press censorship.[32] Chou stated that the Executive Office had agreed to consider these recommendations, but that it did not have the authority to act immediately on all of them. Someone in the crowd then demanded that the criminals in the Monopoly Bureau and the police brigade be brought forward and photographed by the press. Another stood up and demanded that a greater number of Taiwanese be employed for important positions in the government.[33]

Around this time, at 3:00 P.M. on Sunday, March 2, Governor-General Ch'en I made a second radio broadcast, in which he promised to "do more to implement steps to make the people feel secure and to speedily restore harmony." Then he set forth his recommendations for resolving the crisis. They went far toward meeting the demands we have categorized under culpability:

As for those who participated in this incident whom the government considers as having simply lost their senses, the government will exercise leniency and release them. Second, as for those who participated in this incident and were arrested by officials or the military police, the government will be lenient and send them to the military police headquarters, where they will be released to their families or relatives; the neighborhood watchdog associations will not have to vouch for them, so we can avoid that inconvenience. Third, as for all those killed or wounded, no matter whether they were officials, educators, or ordinary people, and regardless of whether they were Taiwanese or Mainlanders, the wounded will be assisted and the dead will be compensated. Fourth, as to a final resolution of this incident, additional representatives from various groups of the people will be added to the Resolution Committee, so that more opinions can be heard.[34]

Governor-General Ch'en then said he loved Taiwan and the Taiwanese people and wanted to restore the harmony that had prevailed before February 27. He hoped that the people and the government would cooperate and work together even harder to realize a spiritual accord.[35]

After Ch'en I's radio broadcast, Wang T'ien-teng of the Resolution Committee went on the air and rejected Ch'en's attempt at conciliation. After denouncing Ch'en I and the provincial government, he praised as revolutionary martyrs citizens who had died while attacking Mainlander stores or beating or killing Mainlanders. Promising that the blood of these martyrs had not been shed in vain, Wang threatened that another crisis would erupt, and more blood would flow if the government did not speedily resolve the present crisis.[36]

Yet peace gradually returned to Taipei by early Monday morning, March 3. Shopkeepers began opening their doors and city buses operated once again. However, the price of rice in stores and markets had skyrocketed.[37] At 10:00 A.M. Monday, the Resolution Committee again met at Chung-shan Auditorium to discuss how to achieve a number of goals: freedom for those still under arrest, an end to the armed patrols still roaming the city, the prevention of the few troops that were in Hsinchu district from leaving and entering the city, the organization of groups of self-defense forces, and the transmission of news of the Incident to the central government and the outside world.

Representatives from the students and self-defense brigades asked that three student association delegates, another delegate each from the labor, farmer, and women's associations, and two more from the Youth Association, as well as Liu Ming-ch'ao of the National Assembly, Lin Chung of the National Council, and Wang T'ien-teng of the Taiwan Provincial Council, meet with Ch'en I and present their opinions to the governor-general. The Resolution Committee also elected Lin Tsung-hsien, Lin Shih-tang, Lü Po-hsiung, Lo Shui-yüan, and Li Wan-chü to go to the United States Consulate and ask it to inform the outside world of the Uprising, but this group never carried out that mission. The Committee then gave Hsü Te-hui the responsibility of organizing a self-defense corps of hundreds of thousands of people from around the island to help maintain order.[38]

On Monday, then, the Resolution Committee was beginning to undertake functions on its own, moving from the issue of culpability to that of restricting ROC powers. The delegates quickly organized two new groups separate from the Resolution Committee: the Provisional Committee for Maintaining Order in Taipei City (*T'ai-pei-shih lin-shih chih-an wei-yüan-hui*) and the Righteous Service Corps (*Chung-i fu-wu-tui*). The former would organize activities to restore law and order to Taipei city, and the latter would implement the activities. The Righteous Service Corps was assigned a leader, Hsü Te-hui, a secretary, and committees for general services, investigation, transportation, and communications and management.[39]

At 11:00 A.M. on March 3, a delegation from the Resolution Committee, including five delegates representing the people, three students, four youth representatives, one from the women's association, and one each from the National Assembly, the National Council, and the Taiwan Provincial Council, along with Chiang Wei-ch'uan and Lin Wu-ts'un, went to the Executive Office to request that "the government stop all armed patrols in the city, prohibit the police from discharging their weapons, and abolish the military police brigade."[40] Surprisingly, the government agreed to the first two requests and rejected only the last,[41] and the delegates and government officials went on to reach agreement on seven other issues:[42]

1. Military troops should be recalled to their units by 6:00 P.M. that same day (March 3).

2. Responsibility for local order should be maintained by the civil and military police; students and youth organizations should be set up to preserve law and order.

3. All transportation should be restored by 6:00 P.M., and the people should protect transportation (traffic) workers.

4. To solve the rice problem, all reserves of military food grain should be distributed to the general public.

5. If violence still continued after military troops had been recalled, the Chief of the General Staff, General K'o Yüan-fen, should deal with matters and take full responsibility.

6. If people were still being beaten and property destroyed after military units had been withdrawn, twenty representatives should take full responsibility for those disturbances.

7. The people of Taipei should not believe rumors—for example, that troops from the south would be dispatched to the north.

The Uprising 115

In the evening of the same day, March 3, General K'o Yüan-fen made a radio broadcast to the people and the military throughout Taiwan. It reflected a desire to avoid confrontation with the now increasingly assertive Resolution Committee:

I hope that harmony will prevail in central and southern Taiwan, that order can immediately be restored to Taiwan, and that all rioting and demonstrations against Mainlanders will cease. All troops will return to their units and are ordered not to come out. All disturbances should immediately cease. Peace will be maintained by the civil and military police. This incident will be investigated by the Resolution Committee. At the same time, I hope that everyone in Taiwan can cooperate and work together to restore the harmony that we once had.[43]

At 10:00 A.M. on Tuesday, March 4, the Resolution Committee met again. Discussions continued into the early afternoon as student representatives animatedly discussed the previous days' events, and delegates hammered out eight new resolutions. The focus was now on restricting the ROC's coercive powers and on setting up an island-wide Resolution Committee that would serve as a kind of government structure outside the ROC:[44]

1. Taipei city bus service should be immediately restored.
2. The Garrison Command should prohibit armed patrols throughout the island.
3. Huang Ch'ao-ch'in, Chang Ch'ing-chuan, and Yen Ch'in-hsien should ask the Chief of the General Staff, K'o Yüan-feng, to put an end to the way armed troops have been driving through the city.
4. When troops drive out from their camps to shop for rice and groceries, their vehicles should carry flags, and the soldiers should be unarmed.
5. Regarding the seizure of the Min-hsiung Broadcast Station by the people, the Resolution Committee should make an announcement to present a single story in order to avoid confusion.
6. Based on the district or city councils (in all seventeen districts or cities throughout the island), the Resolution Committees should organize branch committees as soon as possible. Representatives from these branch committees should go to Taipei for consultation.
7. Do not permanently appoint the Resolution Committee chairperson; instead, have the Taipei City Council Speaker temporarily serve in that position.
8. All information should carry the same message, so all fliers and posters should be banned.

On Tuesday afternoon at 2:00 P.M., the Resolution Committee reconvened at Chung-shan Auditorium. It urged people not to beat up or insult soldiers who left their units to buy rice and vegetables, and debated a number of issues. At the end of the meeting, the committee agreed that "the province, districts and cities should hold popular elections, and the government should immediately carry out reforms."[45]

Many people, however, did not want to leave matters in the hands of the Resolution Committee. Tuesday morning, March 4, at 9:00 A.M., crowds of students had already gathered at Chung-shan Auditorium to discuss how to deal with the issue of public safety. After much debate, they resolved that "the students should be organized into a large brigade for preserving public order."[46]

By 10:00 A.M. Tuesday, Ch'en Ch'i, Chiang Wei-ch'uan, Lin Wu-ts'un, and some forty student and popular representatives presented their views to Governor-General Ch'en I and tried to explain why the disturbances had occurred:

First, for over a year the political and economic policies that have been carried out have failed to embody the governor-general's [Ch'en I's] ideals. This failure created various contradictions and confusions and caused considerable unemployment; the Taiwanese people have not had a secure livelihood. These conditions produced the incident in Taipei. . . . Second, as for political reforms, we can have the Resolution Committee study the matter and propose some concrete measures to reform Taiwan's political system. Third, the governor-general (you) still was surrounded by subordinates, and because of the seriousness of the current crisis, we hope you can break through this ring of advisors and have a better understanding of the people's conditions and conduct discussions with openness and sincerity so that our problems can be solved.[47]

Governor-General Ch'en I replied:

My economic and political policies are correct, but I realize that my subordinates do not always clearly understand them. Unemployment is severe, and the government will try to remedy this. Any good suggestions about political reform, no matter whether from the Resolution Committee or from the general public, I will accept as well. Political matters divide into two jurisdictions: those of national administration and those of local administration. I hope your opinions, as submitted, will be related to local administrative matters.[48]

On Tuesday, conditions in Taipei remained relatively calm. Shops remained open and trains operated, although Mainlanders were still being beaten in the streets. The few Mainlanders who ventured outdoors usually did so only to flee the city.

At 10:00 A.M. on Wednesday, March 5, the Alliance of Youth for the Self-Government of Taiwan was founded at Chung-shan Auditorium. It

Taiwan's Governor-General: Admiral Hasegawa Kiyoshi. Source: *Nanpō no kyoten. Taiwan: shashin hōdō* (Tokyo, 1944).

Taiwanese Military Cadets Marching in Taipei's Main Street. Source: *Nanpō no kyoten. Taiwan: shashin hōdō* (Tokyo, 1944).

"A Mass Meeting of Young Taiwanese on September 23, 1944, Expressing Their Gratitude for Military Conscription to Commence January 1, 1945." Source: *Nanpō no kyoten. Taiwan: shashin hōdō* (Tokyo, 1944).

"The 10th Training Class of Girl Students in Close Order Marching on the Training Course." Source: *Nanpō no kyoten. Taiwan: shashin hōdō* (Tokyo, 1944).

"A Brave and Loyal Young Taiwanese Who Represents the Passion and Spirit of the Imperial Army." Source: *Nanpō no kyoten. Taiwan: shashin hōdō* (Tokyo, 1944).

Ch'en I, Governor-General of the Taiwan Provincial Administrative Executive Office during the Uprising.

Left: Ch'iu Nien-t'ai, Member, Control Yüan; *Center*: Pao K'o-yung, Head, Dept. of Industry & Mining (ca. March 1947); *Right*: Jen Hsien-ch'ün, Head, Dept. of Transportation. Source: *T'ai-wan shih-jih-chih*, vol. 1 (Taipei, 1947).

Li I-chung, Chairman, Executive Committee of the Kuomintang Taiwan Party Headquarters. Source: *T'ai-wan shih-jih-chih*, vol. 1.

Chou I-o, Head, Dept. of Civil Affairs. Source: *T'ai-wan shih-jih-chih*, vol. 1.

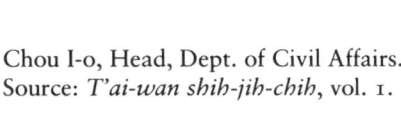

Lin Mao-sheng, Dean, College of Liberal Arts, National Taiwan University; Publisher, *Min-pao*. Source: *T'ai-wan chan-hou ch'u-ch'i ti min-i tai-piao* (Taipei, 1986).

Chiang Wei-ch'uan, Chairman, Political Construction Association.

Hsieh Tung-min, District Chief, Kaohsiung District (1945–46).

Lin Jih-kao, Councilman, Taiwan Provincial Council. Source: *T'ai-wan chan-hou ch'u-ch'i ti min-i tai-piao.*

Huang Ch'ao-ch'in, Speaker, Taiwan Provincial Council.

Lin Hsien-t'ang, Councilman, National Council.

Wang Min-ning, Head, Dept. of Police.

Yang Chao-chia, Member, Taiwan Provincial Government Committee (ca. 1950).

Yeh Ming-hsün, Director, China Central News Agency in Taipei. Source: *T'ai-wan shih-jih-chih*, vol. 1.

Hsieh O, Physician; Member, National Assembly. Source: *T'ai-wan shih-jih-chih*, vol. 1.

Hsieh Tung-min, Deputy Head, Dept. of Civil Affairs (ca. March 1947). Source: *T'ai-wan shih-jih-chih*, vol. 1.

proposed six resolutions which demonstrate the desire for drastic reform and immediate democratization:[49]

1. Establish a new high-level system of self-rule that can make Taiwan a model province for a new China.
2. Speedily carry out elections for choosing heads of the province, districts, and cities to build new political foundations.
3. Invigorate the spirit of our Taiwanese brethren to uphold the law in order to become the *avant garde* for a democratic political order.
4. Create new cultural achievements in our country for the people and for humanity throughout the world.
5. Expand production, create new industry, stabilize the economy, and enrich the people's livelihood.
6. Purify the people's spirit, promote righteousness, and improve society.

At 2:00 P.M. Wednesday, the Resolution Committee met at Chung-shan Auditorium and split into discussion groups. At 4:40 P.M., members reconvened to hear final reports, among which was that of the Righteous Service Corps:

We recommend that expenses for the Resolution Committee be covered by funds raised from large companies, banks, and public associations that represent the well-to-do and business, and that Ch'en I-sung, Wang T'ien-teng, Wu Ch'un-sheng, and Huang Ch'ao-sheng explain to the central government the truth of this Incident and discuss how to control prices and solve the grain problem.[50]

Li Tsung-hsien, a member of the Resolution Committee, stood up and declared that the Electric Power Company should be managed by the Taiwanese. Wang T'ien-teng rose and said that all organs in Taichung city were under Taiwanese control. Moderates like Li Wan-chü also spoke, saying that the purpose of the Uprising was to demand political reforms—not ask for authority to control all matters. Yet he also urged that the Resolution Committee immediately establish branches in all counties.

Despite its heated discussion, Governor-General Ch'en I conveyed to the Resolution Committee his willingness to mix with the members and even shake hands with them, and "he hoped that the people would present to him their opinions regarding political reforms."[51] However, even as the Resolution Committee was convening that day, signs printed in Japanese began to appear on many streets requesting that all former servicemen in the Japanese military meet at designated places. When Mainlanders tried to approach to read these signs, people kept them at a distance.[52] Nevertheless, normality was being restored to Taipei, and the beatings of Mainlanders steadily declined.

The Uprising

On Thursday, March 6, the Resolution Committee published its resolutions (*Kao ch'üan-kuo t'ung-pao-shu*) and stated that it wanted to "get rid of corrupt officials, try to reform the provincial government, and would not exclude the Mainlanders who were our brethren." The implication was that Mainlanders, who in fact ran the ROC, would have no role in Taiwan except at the pleasure of the Taiwanese. Some committee members argued that Mainlanders deserved fair treatment, saying, "On February 28, some Mainlanders were beaten, but these incidents were caused by misunderstanding, and we are very sad they happened. . . . Henceforth, such an occurrence will not happen again, and from now on our slogans will be directed to improving Taiwan's political conditions."[53]

Sometime that same day, Thursday, March 6, members of the Taiwan Provincial Council telegraphed President Chiang Kai-shek and other high-ranking officials to give their views of the reasons for the disturbances and suggest steps the central government should take. This long telegram described the origins of the crisis as follows:

Because the Monopoly Bureau investigated an alleged case of smuggling by a retailer, a person was killed, and this incident enraged the people. Riots of serious magnitude have broken out, and many people have been killed and wounded. These disturbances have occurred because of a widening gap between the provincial government and the people. Officials were corrupt, the administrative system has been in chaos, and some officials and police have not obeyed the law, even refusing to use Taiwanese of great talent in the administration. There also was a different wage scale for Taiwanese and Mainlanders. Of the Japanese property that had been built up through the sweat and tears of the Taiwanese people, more than half was confiscated by the officials and police. These are the main reasons why the disturbances became so violent. The incident has worsened, and to remedy the situation, we urgently recommend that you consider these proposals: First, please use more able Taiwanese for the position of the general-secretary of the provincial administration and for department heads in the provincial government. Second, place Taiwanese in charge of all schools in the educational system, and allow them to serve as judges for the local and high courts. Third, abolish the Monopoly Bureau by changing it into a publicly owned enterprise. Fourth, change the Trade Bureau into a business-managed organ and run it on a nonprofit basis. Fifth, take the people's interest into account when handling the disposal of all seized Japanese property. Sixth, as Sun Yat-sen recommended in his *Outline for National Reconstruction*, hold popular elections for local government. Seventh, guarantee free speech, a free press, and freedom of assembly. Eighth, guarantee people's security and the protection of their property. Ninth, please dispatch immediately your highest-ranking official to come to Taiwan to help resolve this incident. Avoid using military power to suppress this incident or else it will become even more serious.[54]

Another organ, the Taiwan Provincial Construction Committee (*Taiwan-sheng chien-she-hui*) also stepped forward, advancing its recommendations to the Resolution Committee. One of these was that the Taiwan Provincial Council create a large assembly with different representatives.[55] Another was that a group called the Provincial Reform Commission (*Sheng-cheng kai-ko wei-yüan-hui*) determine whether the Monopoly Bureau, the Trade Bureau, and other publicly owned enterprises should be abolished or allowed to exist, and consider whether the provincial government's Propaganda Commission, the Labor Training Camp, and other organs should be abolished or integrated.[56]

That same Thursday afternoon, March 6, the Taiwan Provincial Councilman Wang T'ien-teng made a broadcast to the people declaring that "the February 28 Incident that led to the beatings of so many Mainlanders was a gross misunderstanding. Henceforth, I hope that Taiwanese and Mainlanders can cooperate to reform the Taiwan political system."[57]

At 8:30 P.M. Thursday, Governor-General Ch'en I made his third radio broadcast, expressing his desire to reform the political system and requesting that everyone try to restore harmony and solve the food grain problem.[58] He then made these promises, which met at least some of the demands for democratization:

First, as for the organs of administration, I am considering changing the Executive Office to a normal provincial government administration; I will ask the central government to approve that request. If the central government approves, we can immediately make this reorganization. As for the officials of the Taiwan provincial government and the various department heads and their staff, I will try to employ more Taiwanese. I hope that the Taiwan Provincial Council and other legally empowered groups that represent the people can recommend people with integrity, pure thought, and talent as candidates. I will recommend these people to be approved by the central government. As for the officials of district and city administrative organs, I have already drawn up the procedures. I will order that elections be held on July 1 of this year. Before June 30, we should have an election law. I will ask the central government to approve the July 1 election for district and city officials. Before these popular elections are held, if the people believe that the present district and city officials are unqualified, I will have them dismissed. In order to fill those vacancies, if the city councils or legal groups want to participate, they can consult with the people to select qualified people to fill them. In short, I hope that through such popular representation three candidates can be nominated. I will select one of those three to be the district or city head, and they will then become responsible for setting up the popular elections. However, if the people believe that those officials currently in office can fulfill their responsibility, they can continue to carry on their duties. As for reforming all levels of the administration, after these have been reorganized, the provincial government will decide the outcome. After appointments at the district and city levels have been made, those officials will then manage their offices.[59]

By this time, however, the prospects for conciliation had reached a low point because of escalating violence and the shrill demands from the Taipei Resolution Committee. On Thursday (March 6), the Control Yüan sent a cable to Yang Liang-kung, the censor of Fukien and Taiwan, asking him to go to the island and deal with the crisis.[60] Considerable fighting had occurred in Keelung, the port of his arrival. At the same time, General P'eng Meng-chi, Commander of the Kaohsiung Fortress Headquarters, suppressed violent disturbances there.[61]

The next day, Friday, March 7, the Taipei Resolution Committee drew up a number of new demands to be presented to the Governor-General's Executive Office and the central government.[62] These became known as the "32 Demands," although in fact more were subsequently added. The first group of demands focused on handling the current crisis, and one requested that Nationalist military forces disarm and turn their weapons over to the Resolution Committees. A second group of demands related to fundamental reforms involving the military and the political system. In brief, these demands called for expanded elections based on a new law allowing for self-government—a law that would allow Taiwanese to virtually run the provincial government. Around 3:30 P.M., the Resolution Committee formulated ten more demands for reform, which merely refined other requests (for the text of all these demands, see Appendix A).

On Saturday, March 8, the Resolution Committee tried to retreat from the aggressive 32 Demands drawn up on Friday after listening to a report by Chang Mu-t'ao, the commander of the Fourth Regiment of military police. Chang told them:

You demand self-rule, and that is entirely correct. Do not let the mean and ambitious bad elements take advantage of the situation and gain political power. I urge you not to interfere in military affairs. The military police now stationed in Taiwan and the troops guarding the garrisons and airfields are only a handful, but they are still part of the national military forces of the central government. According to reports, the requests made by your committee request that, except for the military police, the military troops should disarm. I profoundly hope that you will not make those kinds of demands and that you will not involve the military in the whirlpool of politics. If you disarm the military, that can only be regarded as offending the central government. In the present circumstances, all armed military units have already accepted the people's demands, and they are not authorized to leave their military camps. Wherever any conflict takes place, it is because of attempts to disarm the military. If the masses do not try to disarm the troops, how can there be any cause for conflict? Any demands by the people in Taiwan for reforming the polity are perfectly appropriate. The central government definitely will not send troops to Taiwan.... Everyone wants each of you to have trust in the central government. Your demands for reforming the polity must be able to elicit a broad sympathy. Therefore, we hope that our Taiwan brethren will not offend the central government. We also hope that everyone will cooperate with all their power to preserve harmony. I will swear with my life that the central government definitely will not send troops to Taiwan.[63]

After listening to Chang, many committee members realized they had gone too far in their demands. Later that afternoon, the Resolution Committee published the following statement:

On March 7, this committee decided to ask Governor-General Ch'en I to accept and carry out 32 demands, because at that time the groups participating in drawing up this request were exceptionally numerous. There was no way to give the 32 demands any further review. Therefore, some of those demands—for example, dismantling the police department, disarming the military troops, etc.—were almost traitorous. These definitely did not reflect the public's opinion.[64]

The committee then expressed its new objectives: "Because corrupt officials have now been removed by the struggle for reforming Taiwan's political system, our motto is the reform of Taiwan's democratic political system."[65] Despite the committee's abrupt switch to greater conciliation, it came too late to resolve the crisis. At 6:00 A.M. on Sunday, March 9, the Garrison Command again imposed martial law, and provincial authorities reverted to the position of demanding that the violence cease, that the rebels lay down their arms, and that all public buildings, and so on, be returned to the provincial administration.

In the early hours of March 9, soon after midnight, advance units of Nationalist troops began landing in Keelung, because the Uprising had rapidly spread from Taipei to other cities. The revolt had already gained momentum because of the 100,000 radio sets on the island. As noted in the Yang Liang-kung report of April 1947, radicals seizing radio stations could effectively call for violent or revolutionary action. We must also remember that from the standpoint of the government, events in Taipei were not compartmentalized. Even if Taipei citizens became increasingly conciliatory, the government formed policy in response to events throughout the island.

Keelung

In Keelung city on the evening of February 28, harbor stevedores attacked a branch police station and began beating Mainlanders. Crowds assembled at the Kao-sa and Chung-yang theaters, and began beating Mainlanders after the films were over.[66] On March 1, Keelung Harbor's security force commander, Shih Hung-hsi, proclaimed a city curfew. In the afternoon, the vice-speaker of the Keelung City Council, Yang Yüan-ting, called an emergency meeting attended by many citizens who rose to denounce Governor-General Ch'en I.[67]

On March 3, stevedores attacked the No. 14 Pier, but they failed to occupy it and suffered many casualties.[68] On the same day, three central government navy destroyers, originally ordered to Japan for Nanking's symbolic occupation of Japan, were diverted and arrived in Keelung. This was the first sign of military reinforcements, and the ships aroused fear throughout the city. On March 6, when a rumor spread that Nationalist troops would soon arrive, fear again swept the city. On March 7 at 3:00 P.M., students held a meeting in which they and local council members called for reforms to eliminate corruption among city officials. They also appealed to all citizens to remain calm.[69] That evening, crowds clashed with Keelung military units, but there were no serious casualties.

On March 8 at 2:00 P.M., the Keelung Resolution Committee met with the Keelung Harbor security force commander, Shih Hung-hsi, to discuss how to end the disturbances. They agreed to appeal to the people to protect all soldiers and "good" Mainlanders.[70] On March 9 in the evening, Yang Liang-kung, the censor for Fukien and Taiwan, arrived by ship from Fukien, accompanied by some Nationalist troops, the first reinforcements to arrive. That evening and the next day, March 9, ships unloaded troops in Keelung who brutally restored order and reinstated Nationalist control.

Pan-ch'iao and Neighboring Towns

In Pan-ch'iao of Taiwan county, people gathered at the railway station on the morning of February 28 and began beating Mainlanders or rounding them up and assembling them in one place. A riot also broke out at the Ying-ko railway station just outside Taipei city when a truck with soldiers arrived, shooting broke out, a lieutenant was killed, and two soldiers were wounded. In Shih-lin and Hsin-tien towns, crowds attacked a supply bureau and a food warehouse. In Jui-fang, Chin-kua-shih, and Tamsui, people burned the dormitories where Mainlanders lived. In San-ch'ung, however, not until March 6 did crowds burn the police station.[71]

After violence broke out in Pan-ch'iao, town officials immediately fled, and crowds attacked the supply bureau, removed all materials, and set fire to the building. The Taiwan provincial councilmen Lin Jih-kao and Lin Tsung-hsien led the crowds in attacking the government. Lin Tsung-hsien ordered his local newspaper, *Chung-wai jih-pao*, to denounce Ch'en I's policies. On March 7, the people of Pan-ch'iao established a branch committee of the Taipei District's Resolution Committee, modeled after the Taipei committee. But on March 9, central government troops arrived, the committee dissolved, and many people fled.[72]

On March 2, in the city of I-lan in northeast Taiwan, people began beating Mainlanders.[73] Crowds poured into the streets on March 3 to show support for the Taipei demonstrators. Young people and students formed squads, and after finding weapons, attacked an air force warehouse, as well as some military camps and weapons depots in Lo-tung and Su-ao. They rounded up Mainlanders, assembled them in one area, and then formed a large military unit to attack an encampment of provincial government troops.[74] On March 13, however, government troops entered I-lan, and the streets of the city were soon filled with Nationalist flags.[75] The leaders of the revolt escaped to Su-ao and fled by sea.[76]

T'ao-yüan and Neighboring Areas

The district head, Chu Wen-po, had left T'ao-yüan (Hsin-chu district) on February 28, to go to Taipei. After going to the Land Bank about loans for irrigating farmland and the repair of schools in Hsin-chu, he drove to T'ai-p'ing Street. Crowds blocked his vehicle, demanding to know whether he was a Mainlander, and then pulled him out and began to beat him. Somehow Chu escaped, and was harmed no further after a Taiwanese concealed him.[77]

That very same evening, in T'ao-yüan, crowds began beating Mainlanders. By 8:00 P.M., many young people began forming groups to criticize officials and to denounce the government as corrupt. Around seven or eight hundred young people also held a meeting to criticize the government and to call on the people to beat Mainlanders.[78]

On March 1, around thirty young people from Taipei came to T'ao-yüan, assembled at the T'ao-yüan railway station, and organized a squad "to seize the railway police weapons and control all the trains that tried to pass through."[79] They also began beating Mainlanders, while crying slogans such as "Elevate the Power of the Taiwanese for Self-Rule!," "Stamp Out Corruption!," and "Down With an Inefficient Government!" Some of these activists cut off the head of a pig, placed it on the table of the city's largest temple, and held a ceremony, declaring that "by putting a military cap on top of a pig's head, the pig's head represents the soldiers and corrupt officials of the government."[80] The activists then searched for the property of officials like Chu Wen-po and the head of the Civil Affairs Division. Public officials fled to the police station for safety,[81] and those who did not reach it were caught by crowds and put in the city's largest temple. The crowds then proceeded to attack the district government office.

Meanwhile, the district government officials had invited some members of the Taiwan Provincial Council, high school principals, the city mayor, and other local officials to discuss policy. Knowing of this meeting, the activists went to the district government office and attacked Mainlanders. All government officials fled, leaving the district government office defenseless, and ready to be taken over, "without shedding blood."[82] Crowds at the police bureau demanded that the police hand over their weapons, and a struggle broke out. Other elements of the crowd then attacked the district government and air force warehouses. Throughout the city, firing could be heard late into the night.

Early on March 2, heavy rain pounded the city. At the police bureau, those inside prepared to resist attack. Because the rain was so heavy, some policemen were able to use it for cover and leave by the back door and flee to Taipei for help.[83] A group of activists who had captured some local officials took them to the temple, forced them to kneel before it, and then allowed local people to come and observe them. These activists then established their paramilitary branches with a headquarters for the purpose of countering the Provincial Defense Commander's Headquarters.[84]

By March 3, the riots in T'ao-yüan city had spread to neighboring towns and villages, and even to the sea coast. Some activists went aboard ships that entered the harbor, searched for Mainlanders, and beat them.[85] Crowds in Hsin-chu city began burning the city hall, the courthouse, the information office, the Monopoly Bureau's branch office, and dormitories where Mainlanders lived.[86] Local activists and those who had entered the city from other areas began to organize the people into teams that beat Mainlanders who had opened their shops, seized the weapons of officials, and attacked the local sugar factory. That afternoon, military police tried to restore order, and the rioting gradually ceased. In the evening, some people organized a Resolution Committee like that in Taipei. On March 4, the Garrison Command sent troops under General Su Shao-wen to the Hsin-chu district, and the troops quickly restored order.

Taichung

The Uprising spread to Taichung city in the afternoon of February 28 about the same time that riots were erupting in Taipei and Keelung. At 9:00 A.M. on March 1, the Taichung City Council contacted the Taichung

District Council and the Chang-hua City Council to meet and discuss the disturbances in Taipei.[87] At the meeting, some people who wanted to reform the Executive Office and change procedures for appointing district and city heads threatened to order business establishments, offices, and schools to close if their demands were not met. The group also dispatched National Assemblyman Lin Lien-tsung to Taipei to express the desires of the Taichung people.

Rioting spread from Taichung to nearby areas. Around 3:00 P.M., people in Chang-hua city began to beat Mainlanders at the train station and burned furniture and equipment they had removed from the dormitories of city officials and police.

In Taichung that evening, word spread that there would be a large meeting the next day.[88] At 7:00 A.M. on March 2, a large number of people in Taichung city gathered at the city's central theater to listen to a journalist from the *Ho-p'ing jih-pao* (*Peace Daily*) describe the Taipei disturbances and denounce Ch'en I's administration. Many agreed to follow the example of the Taipei Uprising.[89] The people then selected as their chairwoman Hsieh Hsüeh-hung, a Communist. Hsieh strongly urged that a party be organized to take political power and establish democratic self-rule.[90]

Around 11:00 A.M. on March 2, crowds began beating Mainlanders and overturning vehicles. People surrounded the police bureau and demanded that the police chief, Hung Tzu-min, hand over the weapons of the military police so that they could be unloaded and kept out of the hands of the military. Other crowds gathered at the city hall, at the city's KMT Party headquarters, at the Third Aircraft Factory, at the Sixth Services Factory, and at the Military Supply Station. In response to the large meeting the evening before, groups of young men organized squads under the leadership of Wu Chen-wu, a former lieutenant in the Japanese navy. These squads were called the Self-Administration Forces, and they quickly occupied the city radio station. Later in the afternoon, the squads encircled the Taichung branch office of the Monopoly Bureau and presented the bureau with three demands: "First, abolish the monopoly organization; second, give up all weapons in the Bureau; third, hand over all materials to the people for their management."[91]

After rounding up government officials, the activists went in search of Chao Ch'eng, the head of the Monopoly Bureau, who had escaped to the house of the Taichung District Chief, Liu Ts'un-hou. Ordinary people liked and respected Liu and would not attack his house. When Liu came out of the house to talk, however, some persons in the crowd started to beat him. A policeman from the Taichung police station, Liu Ch'ing-shan, discharged his revolver into the air, and those beating Liu withdrew. Then one of the activists in the crowd hurled a grenade into Liu's home, an explosion occurred, and a fire started. A fire engine called to the scene sprayed gasoline rather than water on the dwelling, causing the blaze to increase.[92]

Officials hiding in Liu's home came running out, only to encounter Hsieh Hsüeh-hung, who had just arrived. Hsieh promised that no weapons would be used, that all officials would be protected, and that they would be taken to the police bureau. When the officials arrived at the bureau, however, they found that the police chief, Hung Tzu-min, had already surrendered to Hsieh. The activists made Hung and the other officials stand in the order of their rank, beginning with District Chief Liu, followed by Chao, the Monopoly Bureau head, policeman Liu Ch'ing-shan, and other officials. Hsieh forced them to kneel before the crowd and apologize to the people and then ordered them beaten. Liu Ch'ing-shan was so severely injured that he fainted and had to be taken to the Taichung Hospital, where a crowd entered the building and beat him to death.[93] The activists then ordered that all Mainlanders in the city be confined in the city's main hotels, the city office, the jail, and the No. 8 warehouse.[94]

On the evening of March 2, activists from Chang-hua and a group of aborigines from P'u-li attacked a nearby military camp and then organized a Resolution Committee with sub-committees for security, administrative affairs, general affairs, information, and an executive branch.[95] They then broke open the government food grain warehouse and distributed rice to the people.

The Resolution Committee then proposed that all associations under its umbrella be organized to attack the Nationalist provincial administration. On March 3, Hsieh set up and took charge of the Taichung Area Security Committee Headquarters, from which she used forces to attack the military units located in Taichung city's downtown district and in front of the city's parks. Later, she publicly announced that she had arrested thirty lower-rank officers, 300 soldiers, and an unknown number of public service officials.[96] On that evening, crowds attacked a firearms warehouse, and gunfire reverberated through the night.[97] The activists were now in total control of Taichung city and the suburbs.[98] Hsieh Hsüeh-hung issued this statement:

We are 6.5 million Taiwanese, and we must strive for real self-rule, eliminate corruption, and reform the political system. Now, all of the people of our province can become armed to fight and destroy this tyrannical government. We want to eternally struggle to achieve this righteous goal. We hope the people will join our struggle.[99]

Then she proposed three principles: Do not kill or wound Mainlanders; do not burn and destroy public property; work to have all weapons placed in the hands of the people.

Hsieh then took 28 rifles and some 100 knives from the police bureau, armed young people, and sent them to guard the transport routes. Meanwhile, she ordered the takeover of the Taichung Radio Station to control news and information.

On the morning of March 4, the Third Aircraft Factory surrendered to Hsieh's forces. At 4:00 P.M., some 500 delegates from various popular organizations met at the city auditorium and decided to set up a Taichung District Resolution Committee. The crowd agreed that Chuang Ch'ui-sheng would be chairman and passed a statement that "with military power, we must strive for self-rule by the people."[100] They then set up organs for handling general affairs, security, information, and coordination.

At this point, some delegates began to oppose Hsieh's leadership because of her Communist connections. They argued that the people would not support their committee if they knew she was the leader. One of the most powerful and well-respected local leaders, Lin Hsien-t'ang, also opposed Hsieh and disagreed with the use of weapons. Thus the Resolution Committee decided not to arm the people. Although the Resolution Committee's leaders had become divided on tactics, they remained unified in their opposition to the Kuomintang by shouting such slogans as "Down With the KMT!," "Down With One-Party Rule of a Tyrannical Government!," "Set Up Self-Government by the People!," and "Organize a Democratic Army!"[101]

On March 7, some of the young Taichung activists set up a unit called the Twenty-seventh Militia Corps (*Erh-ch'i pu-tui*) and put it under the control of a para-military unit called the No. 8 Brigade.[102] The Corps became an armed unit that repaired weapons and vehicles in preparation for an eventual battle with government troops. However, when the Corps wanted to attack a nearby military encampment, local leaders, fearing bloodshed and an irrevocable split between Taiwan and the Mainland, demanded a peaceful solution. Then on March 8, people learned that Nationalist troops were approaching Taichung. As fear spread through the city, many committees began disbanding and burning all documents.

On March 11 at 8:00 P.M., all sub-committee members and major committee members, such as Chuang Ch'ui-sheng, Huang Ch'ao-ch'in, Chang Huan-k'uei, Yeh Jung-chung, Huang Tung, Wu Yung-ch'ang, and others, held an emergency meeting to discuss whether the Resolution Committee should be continued.[103] They agreed to ask the city mayor, Huang

K'o-li, to return to his job. Although Hsieh opposed this and the resolution failed to pass, the committee's top leadership decided to disband, and in the Taichung region all opposition toward the government ended. Meanwhile, members of the Twenty-seventh Militia Corps reviewed the situation and devised an escape plan to the mountains. On March 12, they assembled weapons and food, and went to establish a base in the P'u-li city elementary school to fight the Nationalist troops.

On March 13 at 3:00 P.M., government troops of the Twenty-first Division entered Taichung and set up their headquarters.[104] The next day they dispatched 800 soldiers from the 436th Regiment of the 146th Brigade to Ts'ao-tun. In a broadcast, they informed the Twenty-seventh Militia Corps that if it surrendered, its members would not be prosecuted.

More Nationalist troops of battalion size then moved to Erh-shui, passing through Chi-chi to Shui-li-keng, where two companies independently fanned out to secure the Sun Moon Lake (Jih-yüeh-t'an) and Men-p'ei Lake areas, the site of two hydroelectric stations. After arriving in Yü-ch'ih, Nationalist troops were able to surround P'u-li. The Twenty-seventh Militia Corps still was in high fighting spirits, but its leaders, finding themselves surrounded, outnumbered, and short of supplies, decided on March 16 not to fight. At 11:00 P.M., the Corps buried their weapons and fled. On March 17, government troops entered P'u-li, and the Taichung uprising ended.

Chia-i

The uprising in Chia-i city began on March 2, influenced mainly by the events in Taichung. On that morning, many Taiwanese beat Mainlanders on the train traveling from Taichung to Kaohsiung. In the second-class compartments, Mainlanders were reportedly forced to undress down to their underwear, and when the train arrived at Chia-i, they were taken off it and beaten. A placard was then placed on the train windows stating, "We prohibit Mainlanders from boarding this train."[105] In the streets, anybody wearing the Chinese robe (*ch'i-p'ao*) whether Taiwanese or Mainlander, was beaten. Rioting quickly spread from the train station to the heart of Chia-i city. Shops closed, schools emptied, and the police fled, leaving many of their weapons.[106]

That same evening, activists attacked a military food grain warehouse and occupied the city government and police bureau offices. The city mayor fled to a nearby military police station for protection. Activists seized the city hall and set up their Fighting Headquarters. Government officials and troops of the Twenty-first Division's First Battalion, meanwhile, had fled to the Chia-i airport, which was then surrounded by activists from the city. Fighting broke out and some 50 to 60 people were reportedly killed. Some officials and their families who had not been able to flee were captured and imprisoned in the city's Chung-shan Auditorium, at the KMT party headquarters, and in city hall. The Chia-i riots spread to other towns, and the activists soon organized fighting units made up of a variety of people, including underworld elements and aborigines.[107]

On March 9, the activists made four requests, threatening an attack on the airport if the Chia-i city mayor did not respond:[108]

1. ROC military units should surrender.
2. The airport radio system should be handed over to the Resolution Committee.
3. All police weapons should be surrendered.
4. Military police weapons should be given to the Resolution Committee. Military police also could enter the city to keep order if they were unarmed.

On the next day, Governor-General Ch'en I telegraphed the mayor of Chia-i, stating, "Fight to the end; troops will arrive soon."[109] On March 11, Governor-General Ch'en I again telegraphed that "army troops will be airlifted soon,"[110] and, in fact, at 2:00 P.M., central government troops arrived by air at Chia-i airport. On the morning of March 12, all officials who had been arrested were released by the activists, and well-known antigovernment activists fled to the mountains or to the sea. In the afternoon, troops entered the city, and the uprising ended.[111]

Tainan

By March 2, when some 60 activists from Taipei arrived in Tainan city, radicals had already set up the Southern Alliance Association to oppose the government. Taiwanese policemen in the Tainan city police force had given up their weapons and abandoned their duties, enabling activists to arm themselves. City officials and security authorities held an emergency meeting to deal with the crisis.

On March 3, beatings of Mainlanders began and spread everywhere. The activists took over all official organs and the radio station.[112] The afternoon saw the appearance of banners with such slogans as "Get Rid of KMT Rule!," "We Demand Self-Government!," and "Make Taiwan Independent!"[113] At a large meeting, the following eight resolutions were endorsed:[114]

1. All students will form the No. 1 Fighting Team.
2. The Southern Alliance Association will become the No. 3 Fighting Team.
3. The city, section and neighborhood associations, and other small groups will be reorganized.
4. A unified armed forces command center for the navy, army, and air force will be set up.
5. Totally support the February 28 Uprising until the Nationalist Government's unconditional surrender.
6. All arms will be used to fight against central government troops until the end.
7. Popular elections will be held for selecting the Tainan district chief officials.
8. If there are Taiwanese hiding Mainlanders, take them to the student-military units immediately, and search each of their households.

On March 4, people stayed in their homes and all shops remained closed, and only students and other groups who opposed the central government were seen in the streets. However, on March 11, Nationalist troops arrived in Tainan, imposed martial law, and executed leaders. The uprising had ended.

Kaohsiung and Neighboring Areas

The uprising in Kaohsiung city erupted on the evening of March 3 and continued into the morning of March 4. Radicals beat Mainlanders, and government officials from the Railway Office, the Port Authority, courts, the Police Bureau, the municipal government, and the Civil Air office, as well as the military police, fled to the Kaohsiung Fortress Headquarters located in the mountains near Hsi-tzu-wan.[115]

Activists occupied city hall, and at first they discussed how to set fire to the Kaohsiung Fortress Headquarters. Then the leaders decided to negotiate with the commander, General P'eng Meng-chi. Around 10:00 A.M. on March 6, a team of delegates set forth, made up of Kaohsiung city mayor Huang Chung-t'u, the city council's head, P'eng Ch'ing-k'ao, and three activists named T'u Kuang-ming, Tseng Feng-ming, and Lin Chieh. Upon entering the Fortress Headquarters, they requested that the commander disarm. General P'eng Meng-chi was infuriated by this request, and he ordered the delegates seized, had the three activists executed, incarcerated P'eng Ch'ing-k'ao, and released Huang to return to Kaohsiung.[116] Before Huang had returned to report what had occurred to the Kaohsiung Resolution Committee, P'eng Meng-chi dispatched 300 soldiers to descend the mountain, quickly enter the city, and immediately attack the city hall. As shooting commenced, a number of city representatives including Wang P'ing-shui were killed. Upon learning of this attack and the killing, armed activists quickly assembled and attacked these troops. Fighting continued deep into the night with heavy losses on both sides. By March 7, the uprising had ended in Kaohsiung, and P'eng's forces were in control of the city.

In the southern district of P'ing-tung, the uprising broke out on March 4. The pattern was similar to that already described in other cities. First, crowds seized the city council and other organs and immediately created a Resolution Committee. That afternoon, students and crowds collected all weapons from the police bureau. On March 9, Nationalist troops arrived, and on March 10, the uprising ended.[117] No casualties were reported in P'ing-tung city.

Hua-lien

On March 2, in Hua-lien city on the east coast, the district chief, Chang Wen-ch'eng, notified all organ heads and local leaders to meet at 2:00 P.M. to discuss how to prevent an uprising. They decided to "try to stabilize food grain prices and protect living standards."[118]

On March 4, a member of the Young People's Association named Ma Yu-yüeh rallied the youth of Hua-lien by telling them why the Taipei uprising had occurred. At 3:00 P.M., he called a big meeting and requested that police not intervene. Over 3,000 persons attended and agreed to set up a local Resolution Committee. Ma then proposed six demands, as well as twelve resolutions.[119] His demands were the following: Only the Taiwanese should rule the island; the central government should send grain to Taiwan to feed the hungry; corrupt officials should be returned to China; the military and police should disarm; the Maritime Customs should be abolished; and passenger bus charges for the Suao-Hualien Highway should be reduced.

The twelve resolutions were as follows:[120]

1. All grain from the Food Grain Bureau should be allocated to the heads of neighborhood associations for direct distribution to the people; if the grain proved to be insufficient, then sweet potatoes and other substitutes should be distributed in the same way.

2. Goods imported from other districts should not be taxed.

3. Reduce the charges on passengers as levied by the Highway Bureau.

4. Disarm the military and civil police.

5. If security cannot be maintained by military police and ordinary police, members of the Young People's Association will assume that responsibility.

6. Military and civil police should not use their weapons to frighten the ordinary people.

7. Enforce the Constitution and immediately elect a provincial governor and district officials.

8. All neighborhood association heads will meet that evening at the home of Ma Yu-yüeh to discuss the uprising, evaluate it, and report to Taipei.

9. The Young People's Association should obey the orders of the Resolution Committee.

10. Even though this uprising depended upon the weapons of our Taiwanese policemen, we must recruit Taiwanese police to become the backbone of our uprising against the central government.

11. All corrupt officials and Mainlanders should be assembled at a central place.

12. The authorities should respond to these resolutions by tomorrow morning.

The evening before, the Hua-lien district chief had ordered that all weapons be sent to a nearby military encampment, but this order was blocked by some Taiwanese members of the local police force, who may have been responsible for the later disappearance of some weapons from the Police Bureau.

On March 5, a large crowd gathered in Chung-shan Auditorium at the city's center and agreed to establish a branch office of the Resolution Committee. They endorsed twelve recommendations:[121]

1. Security will be maintained by organizations of the Young People's Association, the students, the army, navy, air force, fire fighters, and police.

2. All military and local police will be forbidden to leave their stations; they will not be allowed to carry weapons; and their daily food will be provided by the Resolution Committee.

3. All surplus rice of the Food Grain Bureau and the Monopoly Bureau will be requisitioned by the Resolution Committee.

4. All organs of transport, post offices, and power plants will continue to function as usual.

5. The Chinese people on both sides of the straits should be reconciled.

6. All corrupt officials will be identified.

7. No bloodshed should take place to resolve the current crisis.
8. Three delegates will be sent to supervise the district officer.
9. The *Tung T'ai Daily News* will change its reporting and respond to the people's will.
10. All publicly owned enterprises will be transferred to the people.
11. Maritime customs will be abolished.
12. All drugs and medicines under the control of the Committee Responsible for Japanese Property will be dispensed to the poor and sick, and the present head of the Food Grain Bureau will be replaced.

Meanwhile, the Resolution Committee picked Ma Yu-yüeh as its chairman; Liu Fu-shun and 23 others would form the Food Grain Committee; Hsü Hsi-ch'ien and four others would set up the Security Committee; Cheng Tung-hsin and two others would make up the Administrative Council; Cheng Tung-mao and eleven others would serve as the Fund Raising Committee; and Ch'en Wen-chih and four others would serve on the Information Committee. If more committee members were required, aborigines could be invited to participate.

Tensions rose in Hua-lien city as more crowds massed at this seemingly endless round of meetings. Because there were only about thirty military police in the city, the district chief, Chang Wen-cheng, urged all Mainlanders be moved to the military camps located in the hills.[122] At 4:00 P.M. on March 5, Ma Yu-yüeh and a crowd went to the military camp outside the city and presented the Hua-lien district chief, Chang, with the resolutions. Chang agreed to the demands and then broadcast his acceptance on radio.

At 10:00 P.M. on March 6, some committee representatives requested that district officer Chang and the military camp commander, army Captain Wang, order all military and civil police to give up their weapons, but they refused. That same day, the committee, led by Hsü Hsi-ch'ien, reorganized various subcommittees and made the following proposals. First, Hsü Hsi-ch'ien should take charge of security. Second, Hsü Hsi-ch'ien and Lin Ming-yung should give a briefing about their negotiations with the government through radio broadcasts. Third, The Resolution Committee should be advised that judges, school principals, and district attorneys should be Taiwanese. Also, at least half of the government employees should be Taiwanese.[123]

Although no violence occurred in Hua-lien on March 6 and 7, tension continued. Then at 10:00 A.M. on March 7, Hsü Hsi-ch'ien called a meeting to establish the Taiwan Self-Governing Alliance's Hua-lien Branch Office. Hsü became the supreme commander of the branch office's air force, navy, and army. He went on the air to appeal to all young people to unite against the government, saying that the time had now arrived for Taiwan to have self-rule.[124]

On March 8, Hsü Hsi-ch'ien summoned the young people of Hua-lien to meet in front of Chung-shan Park for training exercises. The Resolution Committee assembled at 10:00 A.M. and passed additional resolutions involving the administrative organization of the committee.[125]

On March 9 at another meeting of the Resolution Committee, members agreed that they should neither act on their own nor join the Communists. At 2:00 P.M., the Resolution Committee selected candidates who might serve as the new Hua-lien district chief. They were Chang Ch'i-lang, Ma Yu-yüeh, and Lai Ch'iu-sung. About this same time, a group of youth and some returnees from abroad tried to form an assassin group to threaten local elites and persons from the military and government.[126]

On March 10, government troops arrived in Taipei, and the Taiwan Provincial Administrative Executive Office immediately went on the air, ordering that all district Resolution Committees be abolished. The Hua-lien Committee held an emergency meeting, and after some discussion, all attending agreed to support the government's order. They immediately dissolved the Resolution Committee and passed three resolutions:[127]

1. Organize a Food Grain Adjustment Committee with Ma Yu-yüeh as the chairman.
2. Pay respect to the local Security Bureau and send some money to that bureau.
3. Send funds to the Hua-lien City Fire Department, and request that the military police and local police resume responsibility for law and order.

On March 11, normalcy returned to the city, and on March 17, central government troops entered the city.

The Pescadores

Further south lay the Pescadore Islands, where radio broadcasts from Chia-i city provided the main source of news. On hearing of the Taipei uprising, some activists and ex-military people in Ma-kung who had served with the Japanese on Hainan Island planned to attack the city's police bureau and capture all weapons. However, the district chief heard about the plan and ordered the police bureau to place all weapons in a storehouse. On March 5, a number of people assembled to discuss how to organize a Resolution Committee and how to organize youth.[128] There was considerable opposition to such activities because the district chief of the Pescadore Islands had won the respect and admiration of most of the people in the islands. Thus there was no uprising and no formation of local citizens' groups in the Pescadore Islands as there was in other cities throughout Taiwan.

The Pattern of the Uprising and the Role of the Communists

Like a firestorm sweeping through a forest, between February 28 and March 3, crowds took to the streets in all the major cities of Taiwan except in the Pescadores. They formed spontaneously to assault and beat Mainlanders, killing many, occupied city office buildings and radio stations, set upon the offices of the provincial Monopoly Bureau, seized grain stored in government warehouses, and attacked police stations as well as stealing arms and ammunition. Young people, many of them unemployed and formerly of the Japanese armed forces, and members of underground groups were conspicuous participants.

Quickly, however, many responsible Taiwanese officials and members of the elite came forward to offer the cities their leadership to fill the vacuum created by Mainlander officials who had fled to the countryside and nearby towns and airfields, seeking protection under the military police, Nationalist troops, and remnants of the police. These new leaders rapidly formed Resolution Committees, held daily mass meetings to listen to popular complaints and demands, and tried to restore city services as well as end the violence. Young leaders also appeared to press their radical demands and establish paramilitary organizations to help maintain urban order as well as to attack roving bands of provincial military police, Nationalist troops, and police trying to protect government property and regain city control.

In the first week of the Uprising, Resolution Committees seemed to follow the example of one in Taipei and formulate demands to provincial and Nationalist officials to resolve local grievances and restore order and calm. At these daily committee meetings heated discussion and debate produced a mixture of practical and unrealistic demands to the provincial authorities. No single leader could dominate these sessions and establish any control.

By March 8 and 9, reports quickly spread throughout the island that central government troops were landing in Keelung and being deployed to the central and southern parts of the island to occupy the major cities and restore provincial administration rule. The Resolution Committees in each city rapidly dissolved. The numerous paramilitary units also melted away, though some took to the hills to offer guerrilla resistance to Nationalist forces.

In this turbulent period, those who formed and led the Resolution Committees and organized the paramilitary units were a mix of members of local elites and unknown young people. There seems to have been no particular group, either political or religious, which provided leadership to instigate this urban rebellion and organize the Resolution Committees to control mass violence and anger. The historical record strongly indicates that groups like the Taiwan Communists played no role in fomenting the rebellion or taking advantage of the initial violence to direct mass dissent. Given the later charges that Taiwan Communists did play an important role in the rebellion, some remarks on this issue are in order, but we must go back to the period of Japanese colonialism and then sum up the relevant events in the spring of 1947.

In April 1928, the Japanese Communist Party sent Nabeyama Sadachika to meet with a group of Taiwanese in Shanghai in order to set up the Taiwanese Communist Party.[129] After the conference, some Taiwanese Communists returned to Taiwan and attempted to build a revolutionary movement. Within seven years, they had either been arrested or had fled to the Mainland, where they went to Yenan to link up with the Chinese Communist Party (CCP).[130] Those who reached Yenan were helped by the CCP to establish the Taiwan Provincial Work Committee (*T'ai-wan-sheng kung-tso wei-yüan-hui*). In late 1945, leading members of the Work Committee, like Ts'ai Hsiao-chien, Li Yu-san, and others, secretly returned to Taiwan to establish organizations that might eventually serve as a network to support Communist operations on the island.[131]

Already a leading Communist in Taiwan, Hsieh Hsüeh-hung later was a leader in the Uprising in the Taichung area. Her life tells us something about the Communist experience in Taiwan. Hsieh Hsüeh-hung (née A-nü) was born on October 17, 1901, in Chang-hua, in southern Taiwan, into a poor family.[132] When she was twelve, both her parents died. She went to the home of her mother's sister, who raised her. When fifteen, she became the concubine of Hung Ch'un-jung, who worked in Taichung. At the age of seventeen, she escaped to Tainan and worked in the sugar fields, where she learned to read and write Chinese and Japanese. When twenty-one, in about 1922, she returned to Taichung, became a seamstress, and saved enough money to open a small store. Shortly thereafter, she went to the Mainland and began an odyssey that eventually catapulted her into the top echelon of the Taiwan Communist Party (TCP).

She studied in Shanghai, and there she began associating with Communists, who eventually sent her to Moscow to study. She attended the important April 1928 meeting in Shanghai and became a member of the TCP's Central Committee. With other comrades, she returned to Taiwan and became active in the Taiwan Cultural Association. She also joined the farmer associations to demand better working conditions for tenants and farm laborers. She continued her Party work and helped manage a bookstore in the T'ai-p'ing section of Taipei with a man named Yang K'o-p'ei.

Sometime in the 1930s, a violent factional struggle broke out in the TCP over who should become the next Party leader, and someone informed the Japanese police about Hsieh's activities. The police arrested her, and she was sentenced to thirteen years in prison. In 1939 the authorities released her because of severe illness, and she went to Taichung to live with Yang K'o-p'ei's younger brother Yang K'o-huang.[133] She opened a bar called The Glorious Nightclub (*Ta-hua chiu-chia*) and continued her secret Party work. After Taiwan's retrocession, Hsieh set up new Party operations in Taichung by creating the Taiwan Liberation Alliance (*T'ai-wan chieh-fang t'ung-meng*), which sent a delegate to Shanghai to contact the Chinese Communist liaison unit there.

The CCP had established a liaison unit in Shanghai (the *Hua-tung-chü*) and a branch office in Hong Kong called the Taiwan Work Team Hong Kong Liaison Branch Office (*T'ai-wan kung-tso hsiao-tsu Hsiang-kang lien-lo-chan*). Both units maintained communication with Ts'ai Hsiao-chien, who was trying to organize party cells on the island.[134] Because Ts'ai had not been in Taiwan since late August 1928, and was thus unfamiliar with conditions on the island, his activities bore little fruit.

Throughout late 1945 and early 1946, other Taiwanese Communist cadres began making contact with underworld elements (*liu-mang*) and various activists to drive a wedge between the Taiwanese and Mainlanders. Sometime in 1946, the CCP sent Chang Chih-chung to Taiwan to create a formal party structure called the Chinese Communist Taiwan Provincial Work Committee (*Chung-kung T'ai-wan-sheng kung-tso wei-yüan-hui*) and to follow a new strategy. Party cadres would enlist the support of middle- and upper-echelon intellectuals and popular local leaders to criticize Mainland rule. This same group also organized various underground units called the Taiwan Heroic Army (*T'ai-wan i-yung-chün*), the Taiwanese Communist Youth League (*T'ai-wan kung-ch'an-chu-i ch'ing-nien-t'uan*), and the Taiwan Work Team (*T'ai-wan kung-tso-t'uan*) to exploit the growing tensions between the people and the Kuomintang.[135]

The provincial administration's Security Bureau eventually learned about TCP activities and worried that the rumors spread by the TCP would succeed in aggravating tensions. The Security Bureau immediately ordered all police units to watch for any Communist activities and arrest TCP members.[136] However, the police and intelligence units still lacked reliable informants among the local people, and few Communists were arrested before the Uprising. Only a few weeks before the Uprising, the administration had obtained information that "there are people circulating revolutionary tracts and also saying that Communism is much better than the Three Principles of the People. . . . Therefore, the feelings of the people have been brought to a boiling point."[137]

After the Uprising, the Chinese Communist Party still tried to remain in contact with the TCP by publicly communicating with it. For example, on March 8, *Chieh-fang jih-pao* (*Liberation Daily*) reported the Taiwan Uprising, explained why it had occurred, and gave explicit instructions for the TCP to act.[138] Communists did, in fact, act. The best example is Hsieh Hsüeh-hung, a leader in Taichung. She helped organize a Resolution Committee and demanded that the Taiwanese govern the island. But very few of the Taiwanese who demanded reforms and self-rule were Communists. Our evidence clearly shows that Taiwanese supporters of the Nationalists, not Communists, dominated the Resolution Committees.

Moreover, the government's charge that Hsieh led the famous Twenty-seventh Militia Corps is incorrect, according to Chung I-jen, who was jailed in Taiwan until 1987. In his memoirs, published in 1988, Chung says that he and several others founded the Twenty-seventh Militia Corps at 4:00 P.M. on March 4, 1947. They wanted to set up self-government so that local groups could negotiate effectively with the central government.[139] The unit was able to mobilize some 4,000 men, some of whom had served in the Japanese army or had been trained by Japanese officers in Taiwan.[140] Chung, not Hsieh, commanded the unit when it used guerrilla tactics to resist Nationalist military forces. Hsieh merely sought its temporary protection when she escaped to Hong Kong in April 1947.[141]

When Nationalist forces captured Chung and other leaders, Chung lied to his Nationalist interrogators, claiming that Hsieh, not he, was the commander of the Twenty-seventh Militia Corps.[142] His testimony may have misled the authorities into believing that Communists like Hsieh played a much more important role in the Uprising than they actually had. In his memoirs, Chung I-jen also says that the Taiwanese, at least those he knew in his home town of Taichung, had no sympathy for Communists and their ideology. In his view, many decades of Japanese anti-Communist education and surveillance had strongly influenced the Taiwanese, leading them to mistrust Communism.[143]

A former Taiwanese Communist reported that the four leading cadres sent to Taiwan by the CCP to conduct Party work failed to coordinate with each other and never established any solid link with mass organizations.[144] At the time of the Uprising, he claimed, the CCP had no influence on the island and could not have orchestrated the urban riots.

Central government leaders, therefore, exaggerated the strength of TCP members and their role in the Uprising. Chiang Kai-shek might have been misled by the information from Taipei. When he informed the Kuomintang Central Committee on March 10 that Communist activity was one cause of the February 28 Uprising,[145] it is unclear whether he meant that it was the chief cause. If he did, his view did not accord with the facts.

Our analysis in this chapter demonstrates that the main tensions and circumstances leading to the Uprising had little to do with sporadic Communist activities. This viewpoint was also expressed in the April 1946 government report, publicly released in March 1988, by the censor of Fukien and Taiwan, Yang Liang-kung.[146] The multicausal analysis in this secret report bears some similarity to our own.

Other government statements leave the same impression. On March 31, 1947, Ch'en I addressed his staff, saying, "What caused the Incident is the poisonous propaganda and ideas produced by 51 years of Japanese rule. The Taiwanese behaved as though they should oppose only our country's people; and there was also a group of people who blindly followed the agitators."[147] Ch'en I then added, "Those who thought like the Japanese and opposed us were young people under 35 years of age, most of whom did not know anything about China and only looked down on the Chinese, soiled the cultural system of China, and considered that nothing was as good as the Japanese. Such people have forgotten that their ancestors were Chinese."[148] While speaking these angry words, Ch'en made no mention of Communists instigating the Uprising. Blaming Japanese cultural influence for alienating Taiwanese from China, Ch'en I believed that only intensive education of the Taiwanese could prevent another uprising. In a report to his staff in April 1947, Ch'en I urged that the provincial government's printing office publish a series of books on the eight years of heroic struggle during which the Chinese people resisted Japan, print works on Chinese morality, and extol China's great culture. Ch'en I also wanted "all schools in the province to have a flag-raising ceremony each day, with the school principal or a teacher teaching the students how to become pure Chinese."[149] Clearly, he was worrying not about Communist influence but about lack of Chinese patriotism.

Other leading Nationalist officials also minimized the role played by the Communists. In April 1947, KMT Party and military officials held a meeting in Kaohsiung to discuss measures to prevent another uprising. Addressing P'eng Meng-ch'i, then head of the Provincial Garrison Command, a Taiwanese talked about his experience during the Uprising: "When T'u Kuang-ming led some underworld elements to riot, steal, and beat Mainlanders, I saved many of their lives. However, there were two wounded Mainlanders who were carrying communication wire in their hands. One refused my efforts to help him. I thought at that time he must definitely be a Communist."[150] P'eng then replied, "Very good. I hope each of you will give me that kind of information. This shows how well the military and civilians can cooperate."[151]

P'eng, however, did not say that Communists had caused the Uprising. Again, on May 31, 1947, a reporter asked P'eng, "In Chairman Chiang's statements, he clearly says that the Chinese Communists exploited the incident. I would like to ask His Excellency how they did that."[152] P'eng replied:

Traitors broke our country's laws, endangered social harmony, and aroused the people's hatred. Taiwan's situation is a security matter in international and Chinese terms. Our people suffered for 51 years, experienced many historical lessons, and developed a great tolerance for hardship. They simply will not let themselves be harmed by scheming people. If only a few traitors and their followers unfortunately stir up an "incident," the responsible officers of the Garrison Command absolutely will not forgive them.[153]

Clearly, P'eng did not answer the journalist's question, nor did he say that the "traitors" who caused the Uprising were Taiwanese Communists. He merely blamed traitors and their followers for the Uprising. If P'eng had thought the traitors were Communist, why did he not mention "Communists" (*kung-fei*) instead of "traitors" (*chien-t'u*)? Various Chinese journalists also reported that the Taiwan Communists were never a major factor in causing the so-called Incident.[154]

CHAPTER 5

The Nationalists' Response

ON MARCH 26, 1947, a reporter asked General P'eng Meng-chi how many people had been killed or wounded in the Incident. P'eng replied that 16 officers had been killed, 135 had been wounded, and 3 were missing; 74 soldiers had died, 262 had been wounded, and 37 were missing; 64 government civil servants were dead, 1,244 were wounded, and 24 missing. He estimated 1,431 Mainlander and 632 Taiwanese casualties altogether.[1] Around that same time, the provincial administration reported 33 civil servants killed, 866 wounded and 7 missing—all of whom were Mainlanders. Mainlander casualties thus probably came to more than 1,000.[2]

Moreover, overall damage was great, if not adjusted for inflation. Official estimates of damage to public property ran as high as 175,097,331 old Taiwan dollars and damage to private property as high as 441,373,280 old Taiwan dollars—a total of 616,470,611. Another estimate placed "the loss of production output caused by the stoppage of private and publicly owned enterprises" at around 550 million, making the grand total of damage slightly over 1 billion old Taiwan dollars,[3] though this figure may include losses suffered as a result of the actions of Nationalist forces. However, the sum of 1 billion old Taiwan dollars, if adjusted for inflation, represented less than 1 percent of Taiwan's real net domestic product in 1947.[4]

The nominally high figure for damage as well as the number of Mainlander casualties created the impression of a major rebellion, as did repeated rebel demands that the Nationalists disarm and for all practical purposes let the rebels rule Taiwan. This perception of a major rebellion was undoubtedly shared by the Mainlander elite, who had always attached great importance to having Taiwan securely under ROC rule. If Taiwan's security were jeopardized, the Nationalist leadership would be determined to make the province secure. It is not surprising, then, that Nanking's leaders used force to suppress the Uprising.

The Nationalists' Shift
from Conciliation to the Use of Force

Chiang Kai-shek had learned about the Taipei Uprising on February 28. He noted in his diary that a Monopoly Bureau official "unfortunately had fired his gun in self-defense, mistakenly killing a person."[5] Chiang then continued, "Communist elements and other evil groups stirred up crowds of people, and on the afternoon of February 28, attacked the Taipei Monopoly Bureau Section Office, beating to death two officials, severely wounding the deputy director, Ou-yang Cheng-chai, and four other people. They looted public stores, openly attacked government organs, and killed and wounded Mainlanders." Chiang lamented that "in a single moment, social harmony had turned into a great disturbance (*ta-luan*)." Moreover, just as an uprising was breaking out in Taiwan, new crises were erupting on the Mainland.

Since General Marshall's recall to the United States from China some weeks earlier, on January 6, 1947, talks had broken down between Communist and Nationalist teams negotiating a truce. In late February, a massive Communist offensive in Kirin province threatened Ch'ang-ch'un city. On March 1, 1947, Communist troops had driven within seven miles of the city, forcing the Nationalists to abandon the airfield, evacuate personnel, and send 10,000 reinforcements to the area.[6] At the same time, Communist delegates in Chungking were packing their bags and hastily departing for Yenan. The civil war was breaking out all over China. Soon Chiang was reshuffling military units in north China to thwart the Communists. Then on March 1, Chiang faced yet another crisis, this time within his government in Nanking. Premier T. V. Soong (Sung Tzu-wen) of the Executive Yüan resigned.[7]

The news from Taipei was so bleak that Chiang wrote in his diary on Wednesday, March 5, "The Taiwan incident already has become a rebellion and an attempt to seize government organs. Moreover, this Uprising already has spread throughout the north of the island and to Taichung, Chia-i, and other district cities."[8] That same day, Chiang decided to send the Twenty-first Division under General Liu Yü-ch'ing to Taiwan.[9] By Thursday, Ch'en I had begun to realize that he would probably need reinforcements, and had wired Chiang, discussing why the Uprising had occurred and suggesting means of restoring order. He blamed four groups for starting the Uprising: Communists among those Taiwanese who had recently returned from overseas, especially from Hainan Island; some of the Japanese who had not yet been repatriated to Japan; members of the

Taiwanese elite and radicals who had opposed his provincial government from the outset of Taiwan's retrocession; and ordinary Taiwanese who, he said, lacked national spirit and had gone astray because of their traditional way of thinking.[10] Ch'en I then suggested the following measures to deal with the Uprising: The people's thinking and attitudes should be changed and the political system improved to increase popular confidence in the government so that the people would not be misled by "evil forces." Evil elements and rebels should not be tolerated, however, and must be destroyed by military force.[11]

In the meantime, more views about the origin of the Uprising had reached Chiang. A special Security Bureau report sent to Chiang on March 6 cited causes different from the ones adduced by Ch'en I.[12] This report noted the impact of inflation and unemployment in 1946 and early 1947; the way economic recovery had been set back by the Monopoly Bureau and provincial public enterprises, which had absorbed so much of what had been private activity; official corruption within the provincial administration; and finally, the language barrier between Taiwanese and Mainlanders. The report then stated that the proximate factors causing the Uprising were the acute shortage of food grain in January and February 1947, and government control over domestic and foreign trade, which had alienated Taiwanese business people.[13]

Another report received by Chiang Kai-shek on March 6 came from Huang Ch'ao-ch'in, speaker and head of the Taiwan Provincial Council. Huang stated that the violence in Taiwan was worsening because the people had lost confidence in the provincial administration. He begged Chiang, "Decide quickly how to govern Taiwan and speedily send officials here to prevent the Uprising from becoming so bad that even the foreigners will have only contempt for us." [14]

Reacting to this information, Chiang wired Ch'en I on March 7:

The American Embassy has received a telegram from its consul in Taiwan requesting aircraft to evacuate U.S. personnel and their families. They believe the situation in Taiwan might worsen.

At the same time, I received a wire from the Taiwan Political Enforcement Committee via a foreign consulate, asking me to send troops to Taiwan or else the situation will become more serious.

I did not pay very much attention to the report because I knew that some rebels might be spreading rumors abroad about Taiwan.

What is the recent situation? Please report to me immediately.[15]

Meanwhile, leading officials in the Ministry of Defense urged that major action be taken to restore order in Taiwan. On March 8, Wang Ch'unghui, the general secretary to the Supreme Commission of the Ministry of

Defense, wired Chiang Kai-shek that conditions were becoming critical. He suggested that the central government send top officials to Taiwan to confer with leading Taiwanese and calm their fears; that the Taiwan provincial government be restructured to give it the same form as any other provincial administration; and that additional Taiwanese be employed immediately in the administration.[16] Thus, from the outset the KMT was aware of both the need for troop reinforcements and the need for reform.

That same day, Saturday, Chiang again wired to Ch'en I, asking for a detailed report on the available weapons and ammunition. "If rebels try to seize these items, why not destroy them first? At present, however, you should control them tightly."[17] Ch'en I immediately replied to Chiang that there were 456 warehouses with military stores, containing more than 10,000 rifles and 300 artillery pieces, and that half of the stored food grain, uniforms, and daily supplies had been stolen.[18] That same day, Ch'en I again wired Chiang Kai-shek, with a request:

In order to prevent chaos when the national army's units arrive, beginning around March 10, we should have the air force distribute propaganda leaflets over Taiwan. Their contents should read: Trust in Governor-General Ch'en and his reasonable political reforms; all students should return to their schools; return to work, do not believe rumors, and do not be manipulated by ambitious opportunists; the national army comes to protect the people, so do not panic; let bygones be bygones and assist the government to maintain order; respect the Constitution and obey the law.

I already asked the air force commander, General Chou, to assist me. Please grant my request.[19]

At about the same time that Chiang received Ch'en I's wire, he received a report from the director of the Central Investigation and Statistics Bureau (*Chung-t'ung-chü*), Chang Chen, warning that the Taiwanese would resist if the central government used military force to restore order and that on March 5 a group of 600-odd aborigines had encircled and attacked a Nationalist battalion.[20]

So far, Chiang Kai-shek had been receiving more and more information about the complex causes of the Uprising and its seriousness. As additional information was assembled in the next few days, it became clear to Chiang and the Ministry of Defense that they had been correct when they decided on March 5 to send the Twenty-first Division to Taiwan to restore order.[21] However, the division had still not left Shanghai. On March 7, Taiwan's KMT party director, Li I-chung, reported to Chiang on conditions in Taiwan and means of resolving the crisis.[22] Then on March 8, Chiang telegraphed this message to Ch'en I:

How to deal with the current conditions? We have continually deliberated. I conferred with Li I-chung, and we have considered a plan to resolve the crisis. I have already sent two warships to Keelung, and these ships will probably arrive on March 9 or 10. [Actually, three destroyers had reached Keelung on March 5.] Two contingents of the Twenty-first Division will depart from Shanghai tomorrow. Division Commander Liu Yü-ch'ing will fly to Taipei tomorrow to confer directly with you about all matters.[23]

That same day, March 8, a high-level meeting at the Ministry of Defense produced a new course of action for the central government: A mission of top officials would be sent to Taiwan to help restore order. The current administration on the island would be quickly restructured and called the Taiwan Provincial Government. At the same time, every effort would be made to staff new positions with able Taiwanese.

On Saturday, as the central government was completing its policy review, concluding that additional troops must be transferred back to Taiwan despite the Mainland crisis, the Taipei Resolution Committee adopted a more moderate tone. Having re-evaluated its 32 Demands to the central government, it publicly announced that it would retract many of them:

After examining the 32 Demands submitted to Governor Ch'en I on March 7 by this committee, we now realize that too many people participated in that action, and that the demands to abolish the Garrison Command and to disarm the Nationalist forces really were demands to oppose the central government and did not correctly represent the will of the people. Moreover, our request to abolish the Monopoly Bureau was supported by business people but opposed by the working people. These demands simply did not represent the people's real desires. We now want to reconsider some of these proposals. We recognize that Governor-General Ch'en I has decided to reform the Executive Office [of the Taiwan Provincial Government] and that he will try to select more of the able Taiwanese for official posts and as district officials. While reforming the administrative system, the provincial government alone will determine the course of reform. Your Excellency has already ordered district and city councils to begin this work so that local and provincial elections can be held and preparations for holding them made. In this way, the people of this province can participate in the management of their affairs. Therefore, from now on, this province's administration will actually represent the people's will. As for other reforms, we have no other recommendations to offer, and we have already commented on them. This committee already recognizes that the provincial reforms it has proposed have nearly been realized. From now on, this committee's duties are to encourage a return to normalcy, secure the people's livelihood, and hope that our compatriots on Taiwan will quickly return to their normal lives. We urge that everyone work hard, and that all students return to their classrooms by next Monday. We also hope that all workers from today on will return to their factories, and that the military police and regular police will cooperate to maintain law and order. Further, we request that all private and people refuse to obey the law and do not follow the natural way of the people, preferring to try to take advantage of the current situation, we ask the people to reject them.[24]

Then the Resolution Committee exhorted the people to "purify the government and strive for reform of the provincial political system," concluding its announcement with a new slogan: "Our motto is reform of the Taiwan political system."

Once again, however, dissidents in the streets remained beyond the control of negotiators. At 10:00 P.M. that same day, Saturday, extremists in Taipei attacked the Executive Office, the Garrison Command Headquarters, the police and Military Police offices, other governmental offices, and banks. Within an hour, military reinforcements had pushed back the attackers and restored order.[25] Yet disturbances continued throughout the Taipei-Keelung region.

At the same time, the rumored arrival of Nationalist troops made Taiwanese increasingly apprehensive. Shops closed, and few people ventured forth. Tensions ran high in Keelung, where all central government troops would have to debark. Militants had tried to persuade Keelung port workers to bomb the port to prevent troop landings, but the Keelung Garrison Command Headquarters learned of this plan when its men discovered some twenty vehicles packed with explosives intended for use in blowing up piers.[26] That night, Saturday, March 8, hundreds of activists attacked the Keelung Garrison Command Headquarters, but the military police repulsed them and restored order. Later that same night, a battalion of military police arrived in Keelung from Fukien with a platoon of thirty soldiers to escort the censor, Yang Liang-kung. These were the first troop reinforcements to debark. Yang and his escorts made their way to Pa-tu through a highway tunnel, where they were attacked by extremists. One of Yang's companions was wounded, but Yang and his chauffeur escaped unharmed. At 2:00 A.M. on Sunday, March 9, Yang and his escorts arrived at the Taipei Garrison Command.[27] That same day, troop ships arrived in Keelung.

The Garrison Command imposed martial law at 6:00 A.M. on March 9 because of fighting on March 8 just north of Taipei city in the Yüan-shan area.[28] Chief of the General-Staff General K'o Yüan-fen ordered troops to take over the radio broadcasting stations, transport facilities, water and electrical utilities, and so on. K'o then announced by radio that all public assembly would cease and that unofficial organizations like the Resolution Committee must be dissolved. That afternoon at 2:00 P.M., the railroad between Keelung and Taipei began operations. By the evening of March 9, Sunday, one battalion from the 21st Regiment and another battalion from the 4th Regiment of Military Police had landed in Keelung, having left Shanghai the day before.[29] General K'o then sent more troops to Chia-i by air, and the Pioneer Regiment went by truck to Taichung to restore order. After fighting in Keelung, in which troops carried out random killings, the main force of the Twenty-first Division moved into Taipei to suppress the sporadic fighting at the city's railway station, the office of the governor, the Garrison Command, and the Military Police headquarters.

On Monday, March 10, two divisions of central government troops arrived in Kaohsiung. Some troops went to Taipei and southward; others headed toward I-lan and Hua-lien on the east coast. Thus, the process of troop reinforcement, first decided on by Chiang on Wednesday, March 5, culminated in the landing of troops in Taiwan from Saturday through Monday, March 8–10.

On March 10, Chiang Kai-shek made his first public statement about the Taiwan Uprising, speaking out against the background of the troop landings:

The reasons for the unfortunate incident in Taiwan have been reported in the newspapers, and I need not repeat them in detail. Since our recovery of Taiwan last year, the central government regarded the state of the harmony and order in Taiwan as very satisfactory, and we did not send troops to be stationed there. Moreover, the military and civil police were sufficient to maintain local order and law. Last year, people in commerce, industry, and agriculture were law-abiding and sincere in their loyalty to the government. This spirit of patriotism and self-respect is no different from that of the Chinese people in other provinces. Recently, however, some people formerly mobilized by the Japanese and sent to the Southeast Asian theater to fight—and some Communists among them—took advantage of the Monopoly Bureau's smuggling case to promote their own ends and create a disturbance. They also demanded political reforms. The central government considers that the Constitution will be upheld and, moreover, it will be applied to Taiwan so that normalcy can quickly return. Because our Constitution limits the central government's powers, the central government has only limited power over local administrations. Governor-General Ch'en has followed the instructions of the central government and has decided to change the structure of government in Taiwan, replacing the Executive Office of the Taiwan provincial government. Within a defined period of time, he will implement local elections for district officials, and the people of Taiwan can express their hopes and desires. Therefore, this unfortunate incident could have ended. However, last Friday, March 7, the so-called February 28th Incident Resolution Committee unexpectedly made some irrational demands. That committee demanded that the government abolish the Taiwan Garrison Command Headquarters, that the Nationalist forces surrender their weapons, and that all security organs and the army and navy be staffed only with Taiwanese. These demands go beyond the jurisdiction of the local administration, and the central government cannot accept them. Moreover, yesterday many people illegally attacked government administrative organs. Because these incidents have repeatedly happened, the central government has decided to dispatch a military force to Taiwan to maintain security. It has been reported that a military force already has safely landed in Keelung and that harmony has been restored. We believe that normalcy everywhere will soon be established. We are also going to send a top-ranking official to Taiwan to help resolve the troubles. I have already telegraphed to military and political leaders and other staff personnel, ordering them to maintain discipline. Do not be taken in by evil persons, and do not be deceived by Japanese-style deceit. If that happens, great harm will come to our country.[30]

Chiang's statement on Monday thus pinpointed the aspects of the Taiwan situation significant in his eyes. He had counted on maintaining order there with a minimal troop presence: "We did not send troops to be stationed there." Indeed, as we have seen, troop transfers back to the Mainland in 1946 reduced the total police-troop presence to 6 percent of the Japanese level. The remaining small contingent available for security could not contain the Uprising and, just as obviously, no uprising had been possible when a couple of divisions were stationed in Taiwan. Thus, when he spoke out on Monday against the backdrop of the landings that began on Saturday, Chiang knew that the ROC's sovereignty was no longer challenged. He also made clear that his government would not accept the 32 Demands of the Taipei Resolution Committee, which the Committee had tried to retract on Saturday.

To be sure, Chiang had already decided the previous Wednesday, March 5, to send reinforcements. Moreover, on Thursday, March 6, Ch'en I had wired asking for troop reinforcements. A week had passed since Ch'en Wen-hsi had been killed in the T'ai-p'ing Street area on Thursday, February 27. What if by Monday, March 3, or Tuesday, March 4, mob violence had ceased, dissidents throughout Taiwan had decided to follow the lead of the Taipei Resolution Committee, and the committee had limited its demands to what we have called the question of culpability and to the reform of local government, instead of making its revolutionary demands on Friday, March 7? Would Ch'en I and Chiang Kai-shek have then sighed with relief, saved their troops for the deepening Mainland crisis, and pursued in Taiwan the measures that Ch'en I had set forth in his radio broadcast on Sunday, March 2, at 3:00 P.M.? (In that broadcast, he had offered leniency to all suspected of participating in the Uprising, compensation to the families of people killed or hurt by the government, and an extension of political participation.) Would Ch'en then have carried out the democratization process he set forth as late as Thursday, March 6, the same day he asked Chiang for troop reinforcements?

Or was Ch'en simply playing for time on Thursday, trying to placate the extremists with offers of democratization, but having already decided to crush them militarily? If that was his state of mind on Thursday, was that also his view the previous Sunday? Or was he on Sunday hoping to avoid the need for troop transfers then or later? Without troop reinforcements, his administration could be stabilized only by conciliating the dissidents and basing stability on popular acceptance of the administration instead of on a large military presence.

We have argued that because Ch'en and Chiang wanted to avoid transferring back to Taiwan troops urgently needed on the Mainland, Ch'en was sincerely seeking conciliation on Sunday, March 2. His decision on Wednesday and Thursday to seek a military solution was reluctantly made in response to the escalation of the rebellion and to the inability of the Taipei Resolution Committee to implement an understanding that would not challenge ROC sovereignty.

At any rate, having concluded that troop transfers were needed to uphold the ROC's sovereignty in Taiwan, Chiang also wired Ch'en I on March 13 not to take revenge on the Taiwanese: "I ask that you strongly restrain your forces, preventing them from taking revenge; I will consider any other conduct as disobeying my orders."[31] Ch'en I immediately wired back that he would vigorously carry out Chiang's order.[32] Ch'en I then ordered all troops under his command to "take prompt and effective action to wipe out these mutinous and lawless individuals in order to maintain the stability of the province."[33] He emphasized that there were no differences between Taiwanese and Mainlanders and warned his officers and men not to "plunder or shoot law-abiding people on any pretext." If proof could be provided that anyone had violated this order, he would receive a sentence of summary execution.[34]

Earlier on March 10, Ch'en I informed the people by radio that military forces were coming to Taiwan to protect them and to suppress only those elements who had rebelled against the central government. The troops "would not be used for any other purposes."[35] Ch'en then chided the Taiwanese for their broken promises and condemned their seditious behavior.

To those who had used the Resolution Committee to demand that laws be changed, I responded that I would meet those demands. I then expected that after my agreeing to your demands, law and order would be restored. However, on March 1, after I had lifted martial law, firearms were still used and property destroyed in the Taipei area, and people attacked government warehouses. The violence still continued, and then you published those articles against the country. Moreover, in every district and city armed violence took place. Officials were attacked, and government organs were besieged. . . . After the February 28 riots broke out, you wanted to resolve the problem of compensating the wounded and punishing those responsible for smuggling contraband. But then your demands extended to reforming the political system. Some among you even took advantage of this situation and spread rumors to make this situation even more serious.[36]

Finally, Ch'en I announced that martial law would be continued, and six measures enforced:

1. The staff of all transportation organs, whether railroad or highway, must return to their work; everyone will obey, and anyone refusing will be severely punished.
2. All workers will return to their factories; shops will open their doors; everyone will return to work.
3. All demonstrations are strictly prohibited.
4. No one will use titles or names to raise money from the people.
5. No commodity prices will be increased.
6. All illegal behavior will be severely punished.[37]

On Tuesday, March 11 at 8:00 P.M., Ch'en I again ordered that all Resolution Committees be abolished. He accused their members of failing to help the wounded during the disturbances. He denounced the Taipei Resolution Committee for having gone too far when it submitted the 32 Demands on March 7.[38] On March 12, General K'o Yüan-fen spoke on the radio to the Taiwanese people. He attacked extremists who had wanted to abolish the Garrison Command Headquarters, and he hoped that all the people and the nation could cooperate and restore harmony.[39]

Also on Wednesday, March 12, General Pai Ch'ung-hsi forwarded to Chiang Kai-shek two letters received from K'o Yüan-fen and Ch'en I.[40] Both K'o and Ch'en reported to Chiang that troops had arrived and restored order. Ch'en stated that he had delegated Garrison Command duties to K'o. On the next day, Ch'en I sent a long report to Chiang Kai-shek, again explaining why the Taiwan Uprising had occurred.[41] Ch'en cited seven reasons for the Uprising and also tried to justify his policy of establishing publicly owned enterprises. Ch'en began by arguing that the Taiwanese had lost their understanding of Chinese culture and their spirit of nationalism because of 51 years of Japanese rule. He then blamed the press for criticizing his administration and for sowing seeds of dissension between Taiwanese and Mainlanders. He blamed the Japanese wartime mobilization programs for the anti-Chinese attitude of many urban young people, especially those who had returned from places overseas, like Hainan Island. He also blamed Taiwanese business people for not recognizing how publicly owned enterprises had contributed to the island's recovery. Finally, he complained that because martial law had never been imposed in Taiwan and because civil law had been difficult to enforce, increasing numbers of people had unfairly blamed the provincial administration for not imposing law and order. In addition, he claimed that poor communications around the island made it impossible for Taiwanese officials on duty to leave their posts quickly when the Uprising broke out.

To restore stability, Ch'en I suggested the extension of martial law for a period of time, the holding of local elections, strict control of communications by Mainlanders, the speedy repatriation of all remaining Japanese, and the launching of a program in education and Chinese-language instruction. He concluded by advocating the continuation of his economic policies and the employment of more Taiwanese in the provincial administration.

On Thursday, March 13, two weeks after the Taipei Uprising began, Nationalist troops occupied every district on the island. Some extremists continued to resist, but superior Nationalist forces compelled them to scatter and flee. Urban transport and communication resumed. On March 14, Keelung came under martial law, and the Garrison Command imposed martial law in Taipei as well. On March 17, the defense minister of the Nanking central government, Pai Ch'ung-hsi, left for Taiwan. He issued Announcement No. 1, informing the people that he came only to investigate, report to the central government, and offer recommendations to resolve the recent crisis.

The Time of Terror

Between March 12 and May 15, when Wei Tao-ming replaced Ch'en I as provincial governor, two processes took place. Within the central government, Chiang Kai-shek and other officials introduced important personnel changes and reformed the Taiwan provincial government in order to win Taiwanese support for the Nationalists. Within Taiwan, Liu Yü-ch'ing's forces ferreted out bands of armed extremists, while provincial police and other groups carried out arrests. This was a time of terror for many Taiwanese. Killings occurred, trials were conducted, people involved in the recent Uprising were imprisoned, and in some cases innocent people were persecuted.

On March 17, Pai Ch'ung-hsi telegraphed Chiang from Taipei stating that he had conferred with Ch'en I, that peace had been restored throughout the island, and that although some Communists and rebels were still armed and active, military forces were closely monitoring their movements.[42] On the same day, Pai again cabled Chiang, having just learned that around 2,000 Communists and rebels had scattered to different areas, and that Liu Yü-ch'ing's troops, the military police, and personnel from the Fortress Headquarters were taking appropriate action to deal with them.[43] Pai also told Chiang that the 205th Regiment would be kept in reserve in case further disturbances broke out.

The same day, March 17, Ch'en I wired Chiang Kai-shek, offering to resign. Ch'en admitted that the Uprising had been caused by his misunderstanding of events and his lack of ability.[44] Ch'en I then said, "Please permit me to resign from both positions as the civil administration's governor-general and as the head of the Garrison Command."[45] Chiang wired back that Ch'en I had helped to put down the Uprising and that plans were under way to set up a new provincial government.[46] Chiang also said that Ch'en I's responsibility now was to maintain peace and order until the new administration was fully established.

On the next day, Chiang Kai-shek wired Pai Ch'ung-hsi, saying that Pai must be consulted about new administrative appointments in Taiwan: "As for appointment of provincial government personnel, you [Pai] should consult with the Executive Office [Governor-General Ch'en I] and work out a feasible plan to give me for my examination."[47] On March 19, Pai cabled to Chiang that most of the new administrators, as well as General Li Liang-jung, were from Minnan (southern Fukien). As Governor-General Ch'en I had spoken highly of Li, "it would be proper to place him in charge of military affairs."[48]

On March 19, too, Pai Ch'ung-hsi received an urgent telegram from Chiang Kai-shek informing him of news just received from Liu Yü-ch'ing. One of Liu's units had been surrounded by armed rebels, and Liu's other troops had then chased the rebels to a locale named T'a-li, where heavy fighting was in progress.[49] Chiang urged Pai to pay special attention to the situation and to wipe out the rebels. However, he also said,

> Never be careless in handling this problem, because any mistakes will only embolden the rebels. In particular, maintain military discipline and do not allow any troops to disturb the civilians. Therefore, you must supply the troops with enough materiel. Moreover, do not let the officers and soldiers make any excuses for violating military rules and discipline. If our main force pursues the rebels into the mountains, you must take great precautions. Please tell Commander Liu of these important orders.[50]

It is not clear why Liu Yü-ch'ing informed Chiang Kai-shek of the new violence and did not report directly to General Pai Ch'ung-hsi. Nor is it clear why Chiang did not cable a reply directly to Liu Yü-ch'ing instead of informing General Pai. Nevertheless, fighting in the hills of central Taiwan continued roughly a week after Nationalist troops had restored order in the major cities. However, by March 21 the fighting appears to have ceased entirely.

That same day, Pai Ch'ung-hsi cabled Chiang Kai-shek that "according to Governor-General Ch'en's plan for organizing the Taiwan Provincial Administration, there would be the following: fifteen commissioners, half to be Taiwanese, half to be Mainlanders, plus various administration bureau directors who would be Taiwanese as well."[51] On March 24, General Pai submitted a long report to Chiang Kai-shek outlining his reasons for the Uprising.[52] Pai blamed it on three factors: many Taiwanese, strongly influenced by the Japanese, had joined the Uprising to seek personal advantage; the Monopoly Bureau incident had caused crowds to form; and, finally, many of the young Taiwanese who had returned to the island in 1946, especially from Hainan Island, were Communists and hostile to the Nationalist administration. Chiang then informed Pai that he should return immediately to Nanking and discuss the selection of new personnel for the provincial administration.[53]

On March 23, Pai again cabled Chiang, suggesting that all Taiwan provincial administration officials who had remained on the job and helped to restore peace and order be congratulated for their services. Pai then said,

The truth of this Incident is not simple. . . . I am visiting many places and making some careful investigations. As for how to manage matters in Taiwan, it is best to wait until I have completed my investigation, and then you can decide. I have read in the recent newspapers that many Taiwanese organizations on the Mainland have taken advantage of this Incident and already have made many demands. Please do not make any promises right now; otherwise, that might make for more difficulty later.[54]

Chiang immediately replied, "Permission granted. We will await your complete tour and then make our decisions. I have not promised anything. I have decided not to go any further into the matter Governor-General Ch'en is investigating. Do not worry about that."[55]

Meanwhile, other officials were sending Chiang Kai-shek their proposals for reforming the Taiwan provincial government. On March 25, Chiang Meng-lin sent a long memorandum offering his views. Finally, after many meetings,[56] Nanking decided that civil matters would be handled by the provincial governor and security matters by the Garrison Command. More Taiwanese personnel would be employed even if their training and background did not match regulation standards. "As for elections [local officials and mayors], the Taiwan provincial government should discuss these with the Taiwan Provincial Council, and then work out a plan and submit it for approval to the central government."[57] Moreover, publicly owned enterprises should be reduced in number.

After March 17, Ch'en immediately shut down all newspapers critical of the provincial government. Police arrested journalists and suspended the *Chung-wai jih-pao, Jen-min tao-pao, Ta-ming-pao, Ch'ung-chien jih-pao*, and *Min-pao*.[58] One Mainlander newsman recalled that "the reason they were closed is that they represented different elements outside the Kuomintang Party. Further, they had stirred up bad feeling between the government and the people, and were deeply influenced by Japanese poisonous thought."[59] After Ting Wen-chih, a reporter for Taichung's *Ho-p'ing jih-pao*, wrote that Liu Wen-tao, a member of the Legislative Yüan from Hupei province, had criticized Ch'en I and demanded that the central government investigate his administration, Ch'en I ordered Ting's arrest and closed down *Ho-p'ing jih-pao*.[60] He also recommended that the government discuss matters with the Taiwan Provincial Council, and then work out a plan. Ch'en I's administration also initiated a new census, a counting of households and population that began on April 5, 1947.[61] Tremendous anxiety resulted from procedure 7 of the new census rules:

During the period of household enumeration, the household head must guarantee a survey and exposure of any traitors in the neighborhood association and in the unit to which the household belongs. Every village, town, and district neighborhood association head should have this guarantor system and be responsible for reporting to the census enumerator sent from the district and city administration. Henceforth, when a traitor is found in that household or within that neighborhood association, it will be the responsibility of the household head and the neighborhood association head to report to the officials of the township or the district police, who will investigate this matter. At such time, the chief official organs or the household and neighborhood association head will share equally the responsibility for that crime [harboring traitors] and will be dealt with according to the law.[62]

This new tracking method required that all citizens police each other and subject themselves to principles of collective responsibility (*lien-tso-fa*).

According to the provincial government, the police and the Garrison Command were to enforce the census regulation.[63] Many of the individuals taken away for questioning by the police were never seen again. For instance, the head of the Faculty of Letters at National Taiwan University, Lin Mao-sheng, was executed because his name allegedly appeared on a document stating that he would be the Minister of Education in the independent Taiwan government.[64] Wang T'ien-teng was executed because he "had incited people to occupy the Taiwan Broadcasting Station and had appealed to the people to take over Taiwan and expel the Mainlanders" in order to establish an independent Taiwanese government.⁶⁵ Chang Chen, director of the Central Investigation Bureau, reported to Chiang Kai-shek that Wang T'ien-teng had been involved in the Taipei Youth Corps but provided no conclusive proof that Wang was a Communist. Among the many arrested during this period, few were found to be Communists.

Some of those arrested were incarcerated for long periods. Provincial Council member Kuo Kuo-chi was imprisoned for 120 days and finally released because there was insufficient evidence to charge him with any crime.⁶⁶ A well-known leader, Liao Wen-i, who had not participated in the Uprising, had lost the Taiwan mayoral race in the spring 1946 elections and had also failed to be elected to the Provincial Council by a single vote.⁶⁷ When he expressed his unhappiness about the elections and criticized the provincial administration, Ch'en I suspected him of urging others to participate in the Uprising and ordered his arrest.⁶⁸ Like many other intellectuals, Liao fled Taiwan for Japan and became a key leader in the Taiwan Independence Movement.

Among those arrested were Li Yu-pang, a former director of the Three Principles of the People Youth Corps (*San-min chu-i ch'ing-nien-t'uan*), and Communists named P'an Hua, Hua Yün-yu, Chang I-chih, Wang P'ing, and Lo Ching-mo.⁶⁹ In a cable to Chiang Kai-shek on March 29, 1947, Chang Chen reported that Li and his associates had been arrested in Taipei on March 15, hiding in a house on Yung-lo Street. The Youth Corps, which had sub-units operating in Kaohsiung and Taipei, had organized activities against the provincial government during the Uprising.

The Extent of the Terror

Estimates of the number of people killed by Nationalist forces range from 1,000 to 100,000. Although definitive data are not available, a tentative estimate can be made from scattered information and impressionistic evidence. For instance, P'eng Ming-min recalled a relative saying that when troop ships arrived in Keelung on March 10, "Soldiers on deck had begun strafing the shoreline and docking area even before the ships had reached the pier." ⁷⁰ P'eng then gave his view of how the Uprising was put down in Keelung:

This began a reign of terror in the port town and in Taipei. As the Nationalist troops came ashore, they moved out quickly through Keelung streets, shooting and bayoneting men and boys, raping women and looting homes and shops. Some Formosans were seized and stuffed alive into burlap bags found piled up at the sugar warehouse and were then simply tossed into the harbor. Others were merely tied up or chained before being thrown from the piers.[71]

Another account of the suppression was supplied by Huang Wu-tung, a Presbyterian minister and the vice-speaker of the Chia-i district council. In his memoirs, Huang described how Nationalist troops entered Chia-i city:

> After Ch'en I's troops arrested Chia-i representatives (five of the eight-person delegation sent to meet the troops and ask them to disarm), the troops immediately left the airfield. They entered the city and began arresting many people and killing untold numbers. At the same time, everyone stopped speaking to one another and only nodded their heads in passing. Because everyone sensed the great danger, no one knew when he or she might be arrested. Among the young students, a large number had been killed in the suburbs and at Hung-mao-pei. Their bodies were then stacked in trucks, taken to a fountain, and pushed into the fountain as an example for the public. The Taiwanese had never seen such a display of cruelty. In one quick moment, our courage left us and we had no idea what to do. We could only stand idle and await death. The clever people who had realized what might happen had fled and saved their lives. As for those who had not fled, many never knew why they were arrested. When the Nationalist troops from the airfield entered the city, they immediately shot any persons they saw on the street. People bolted their doors and locked their windows, believing that what they could not see, they could not fear. Chia-i city became a dead city where neither a dog barked nor a chicken cackled. I can still visualize that episode, and it turns my heart cold; when I remember the events, my heart palpitates.[72]

Most of the people who lost their lives were probably from around Keelung, Taipei, Chia-i, and Kaohsiung, where the Uprising and suppression were both severe. The tactic of shooting indiscriminately at people and houses had long been used by KMT troops and warlord armies on the Mainland when putting down opposition. Reports like that of the American journalist John W. Powell confirm that incoming troops, who had been given names of individuals to arrest and eliminate as suspected leaders of the Uprising, rounded up these and any other suspects and executed them immediately as an example to the public.[73]

In Keelung, troops sprayed the wharfs and streets with gunfire, shooting anybody on sight, and the same probably occurred in Chia-i and other cities. News reporters described the many soldiers who behaved in a trigger-happy manner, killing innocent bystanders. When a journalist questioned an army colonel about these indiscriminate shootings, the officer replied:

> When the army arrived in Taipei, there were some rioters who still fired their weapons and offered resistance. Therefore, the army was forced to take military action. Once any soldier found people in front of him, and he asked them for the

curfew password, the soldier fired his weapon if those people did not reply or gave the wrong password . . . or if they did not stop or replied incorrectly . . . they were shot and killed. Some young and middle-aged Taiwanese did not understand these wartime regulations or did not understand Mandarin. Our soldiers also did not understand the Minnan dialect, for when our troops questioned the Taiwanese, they simply did not understand, and continued walking. Our troops had no recourse but to shoot. Later, the higher echelon became aware of these mistakes and issued orders to correct them.[74]

Presbyterian leaders in Kaohsiung and P'ing-tung districts reported the murder of innocent ministers and their children by Nationalist troops.[75] Chuang Chia-nung describes the grisly massacre in Kaohsiung that occurred after General P'eng Meng-chi ordered his troops to attack Kaohsiung city:

P'eng Meng-chi then ordered the Feng-shan troops to come and attack, and they continued killing people until March 8th. Night and day, the gunfire continued. On the streets and in the lanes and alleys there were dead bodies. Many bodies already were rotting, and blood still flowed from some. Nobody dared to go out to identify and claim them. In this way, corpses were strewn as far as Kaohsiung Mountain, and blood flowed into nearby Lake Hsi-tzu. Several thousands of people had been sacrificed, and in the end, the heroic struggle of Kaohsiung city's people had been cruelly suppressed by government troops.[76]

In Hua-lien city, there was no such massacre, but not a few persons were killed under one circumstance or another.[77]

In June 1947, a newspaper reported the following casualty estimates for the rebellion in Taichung: among public servants, 55 wounded and 4 killed; among ordinary citizens, 18 wounded and 2 killed.[78] Chiang Mu-yün, a reporter from the *Shanghai Shen-pao*, traveled in the region at this time and reported the same number of killed and wounded.[79] Chiang also claimed that in Chia-i district, Mainlander public servants suffered 11 dead and 51 wounded; the Taiwanese, 406 dead and 131 wounded, with another 5 missing.[80]

As for casualties in the Kaohsiung area, Chiang Mu-yün reported that 31 officers and soldiers had been killed and wounded guarding warehouses, 14 had been declared missing, and 2 had been shot for insubordination.[81] However, other reports of Kaohsiung's casualties say that four city councilmen (Wang Shih-ting, Huang Tz'u, Hsü Ch'iu-chung, and Ch'en Chin-neng) were shot to death, along with scores of others, either in the city hall auditorium or in their offices.[82] For the P'ing-tung area, there is evidence that four people were killed and 59 wounded in fighting around the local airport.[83]

Given such scattered impressionistic and numerical data, estimates of the total number of people killed by Nationalist forces from February 28 through May 1947 vary wildly. According to a recent Communist source, which draws upon a report submitted on April 1, 1947, by seven Taiwanese associations in Shanghai and Nanking to the Control Yüan of the Nationalist government, "The Kuomintang used military force to clean out all key elements [responsible for the February 28 Incident]; they killed untold numbers of innocent people, threw their corpses into the sea, and left their bodies in deserted fields; their number exceeded 50,000 dead."[84]

Taiwanese revolutionary organizations in Japan and the United States, especially the United Formosans for Independence, later made greatly varying claims, ranging from 10,000 to 100,000.[85] Wang Yü-te even estimated that the true number was more than 100,000: "According to an official estimate of Taiwan's population in 1953, the official household registration records are unclear, with over 100,000 names missing. Obviously, that missing number must represent the number of those killed at the time of the Incident."[86]

At the other extreme, a reporter who interviewed General Pai Ch'ung-hsi wrote in the *China Weekly Review* that the loss of life came to some 4,000 killed and wounded (2,104 dead and 1,556 wounded). This figure covered Mainlanders and Taiwanese, including officials and military personnel.[87] Pai, however, publicly denied that the total exceeded 2,000 and requested that the newspaper not quote him any more.[88] On March 31, 1947, the Minneapolis *Morning Tribune* carried a report by John W. Powell, who claimed that "a conservative estimate placed the number of Formosans killed at 5,000, with thousands more imprisoned."[89]

Another low estimate—2,000–3,000 casualties—was made by Wang K'ang, a correspondent for the *Shang-hai hsin-wen-pao (Shanghai Daily News).*[90] Ch'iu Nien-t'ai, a member of the Control Yüan, stated, "In this Incident, quite a few Taiwanese were killed by some Mainlanders, but not so many as reported by the newspapers, and certainly not to the terrible extent that seems to have been reported."[91] Ch'iu then said,

> Still another unreliable report stated that the local authorities had released news of several thousand Mainlanders killed by the rioters. People also would say that during the rioting period the Taiwanese killed and wounded came to around 10,000. However, according to my investigations, in which I asked people on both sides, the actual figure was not even one-tenth of what the rumors stated, just a percentage of those rumored figures. Why, then, have the numbers been so exaggerated? Did people think that with more people dead they could claim justice for their side? This kind of exaggeration probably reflected the abnormal mentality of that time![92]

The Nationalists' Response   159

It is evident that whereas figures in the range of 2,000–3,000 are too low, those reaching 20,000, not to mention 100,000, are too high. One hundred thousand Taiwanese killed would have equaled one-sixtieth of Taiwan's population at that time, a rate of around 1,400 killed per day over a two-and-a-half month period. If such a horrendous bloodbath had occurred, there would be more personal testimony, especially about the destruction or burial of so many bodies.

Between these two kinds of unrealistic estimates are some in the vicinity of 10,000 Taiwanese killed. Powell and Kerr, an American consular general officer, suggest such a figure,[93] but their estimate may include persons who were only arrested and jailed.[94] In fact, there is evidence that the figure was below 10,000. When the two Monopoly Bureau officials, Fu Hsüeh-t'ung and Yeh Te-ken, were on trial for instigating the riot (they had manhandled a middle-aged woman, Lin Chiang-mai, and accidentally killed a bystander), the judge admonished them with these words: "You two stand charged with the crime of instigating a great riot in which the estimated number of dead and wounded came to over several thousand, with property damage amounting to over $100 million old Taiwan dollars."[95] The judge never mentioned a figure close to 10,000 wounded and dead.

A central government report compiled shortly after the Uprising estimates total casualties at around 6,300.[96] Another, similar report blurs data on killed and wounded, and the categories do not specifically include Mainlanders (Table 10). Finally, we refer to the 1987 account of the Uprising written by Ho Han-wen, who accompanied the censorate official Yang Liang-kung to Taiwan to investigate the origins of the Uprising and to estimate the number of wounded and dead. Unlike Yang, who later fled to Taiwan, Ho remained in China to live under Communist rule. Thus, we can presume that he had no incentive to favor the KMT with a low figure.

Ho recalled that the Commander of the Kaohsiung Fortress Headquarters, General P'eng Meng-ch'i, had informed him that "From March 2 until March 13, during the violent fighting in Kaohsiung city the number of rebels (*pao-min*) killed was estimated on first account to have exceeded 2,500."[97] In the Taichung and Chia-i uprisings, "the ordinary people and soldiers fought for three days. The Taichung mayor, Huang K'o-li, and the Chia-i mayor, Ch'en Tung-sheng, reported that in the city and suburban areas of Taichung there were more than 800 corpses and in those of Chia-i over 700 corpses." After Nationalist troops arrived, "Ch'en I arrested and killed college and schoolteachers and students." On March 8 and 9, "around forty to fifty people were shot" in Taipei. Ho relates that, according to censor Yang Liang-kung's investigative report, "over

TABLE 10
Estimated Dead and Wounded, by Category,
at the Time of the February 28th Incident

Category	Dead and Wounded
1. Various organs resisting the central government	142
2. Provincial, district, city, and Party headquarters participants	8
3. Branches of youth groups	27
4. Taiwan province, district, and city activists	174
5. National Assembly, censorate, and national representatives	17
6. Police officials and policemen	33
7. Communists and other radicals	283
8. Taipei high school and college teachers and students	75
9. Red Bomb group	46
10. Other extremists	10
11. Love Taiwan Association	11
12. Min-sheng Association	9
13. District and city protesters	3,230
14. Arrested, convicted, or executed	2,252
Total	6,317

SOURCE: *Pao-an ssu-ling-pu* [Security Headquarters] (1956), pp. 32–33.

500 Taipei city people died." P'ing-tung's mayor, Kung Lü-tuan, reported that around 400 to 500 people died. Ho gives an overall estimate of between 7,000 and 8,000 dead, and with wounded included, a total casualty list of around 10,000 persons.[98]

Some, but not all, of these people were members of Taiwan's elite. The list of those who were arrested (24) or lost their lives (45), often only for making critical remarks about the administration, is incomplete, but it indicates the range of human talent that was snuffed out or incarcerated. (See Table 11.) Yet, as we have already noted, there is no basis for the common claim that the Nationalists killed all or most of the Taiwanese elite. We can assume that around 325,000 people, or 5 percent of Taiwan's population of 6.5 million or more in 1947, were members of the elite. Even an overly cautious estimate of 1 percent of the population yields 65,000. If we conclude that 8,000 persons at most were killed and that half that number were members of the elite (as illustrated by the individuals cited in Table 11), we can surmise that 0.012 percent of the elite were killed.

Who was responsible for the slaughter of so many innocent people? We know that Chiang Kai-shek and Ch'en I had instructed their subordinates to avoid reprisals and to minimize bloodshed. Ch'en I did not feel any responsibility, as one of his colleagues learned while serving with Ch'en in Chekiang after the Uprising. Ch'en said:

The Uprising occurred because I was extremely frank and I believed too much in myself. Yet I lacked a certain political caution. Because I wanted good relations between the people and the military, I sent back to the Mainland the undisciplined troops that had been stationed in Taiwan. I never dreamed that the troops that later returned to Taiwan would behave so vindictively in suppressing the people—they should not have acted in that way. I am extremely saddened by their actions, and I believe that most people, including the Taiwanese, will be able to understand me.[99]

Ch'en I felt sorrow but considered himself blameless in the brutal suppression of the Uprising. In fact, Chiang Kai-shek and Ch'en I could not have been expected to control those division and regimental commanders and officers who rounded up and shot citizens, secretly disposed of their bodies, and strafed residences and shops.

We have little information from participants or observers except for the occasional memoir like that of Ho P'ing-ju (which must be treated with caution because it is the only account by a military participant that we have found). Ho was a high-ranking officer on the staff of the Twenty-first Army, which had been sent from Shanghai to Keelung on the evening of March 8. Ho points out that the troops were extremely undisciplined. When the 438th Regiment of the 146th Division had been mustered at Woosung Harbor before leaving the Mainland, officers and soldiers had carelessly discarded their cigarettes, setting off a fire that nearly detonated the ammunition being loaded onto the ship.[100] When the 438th Regiment drew into Keelung harbor, these same soldiers began strafing the shore, where people had gathered to watch the ships, and "many people were shot and bled profusely, human organs spilled onto the ground, and not even women and children were spared."[101] Ho does not say whether officers aboard the ship had been informed of fighting in the city and for this reason landed with guns blazing.

Ho's examples underscore the undisciplined troop behavior revealed by another incident. The following day, after the same troops had moved into Taipei, they occupied Taipei Normal School, where Ho claims that members of their families, who had accompanied them to Taiwan, were bivouacked with them. The family members tore out window frames, using them and furniture to build fires, and dismantled electrical wiring and stole light bulbs.[102]

Ho also recalls that General P'eng Meng-chi, the commander of the Kaohsiung Fortress Headquarters, was so angered by the Uprising that he decided to teach the local insurgents a lesson as soon as he learned that Nationalist troops were on their way to Taiwan.[103] P'eng thus ordered the massacres in Kaohsiung and Tainan. Ho quotes him as saying, "Do not worry about killing a few people by mistake. I will bear the respon-

TABLE 11
*Members of the Taiwanese Elite Arrested or Killed
in the Taiwan Uprising and Its Suppression*

Name	Arrested or killed	Profession and/or status
Chan Jung-an	arrested	Councilman, Kaohsiung District Council
Chang Ch'i-lang	killed	Physician and National Assemblyman
Chang Chung-jen	killed	Principal of Hua-lien High School [Chang Ch'i-lang's eldest son]
Chang Kuo-jen	killed	Teacher, Hua-lien High School [Chang Ch'i-lang's third son]
Ch'en Chang-keng	arrested	Secretary, Taichung Appellate Court
Ch'en Hsin	killed	President, Board of Trustees, Taiwan Trust and Ta-kung Enterprise Co.
Ch'en Ch'eng-po	killed	Artist; Councilman, Chia-i City Council
Ch'en Hua-chung	arrested	Speaker, Tainan District Council
Ch'en Kun-lun	arrested	Councilman, Kaohsiung District Council
Ch'en Shih-jung	arrested	Public prosecutor, Taichung Appellate Court
Ch'en Fu-chih	killed	General director, Chia-i Branch, San-min Chu-i Youth Corps
Ch'en Neng-t'ung	killed	Principal, Tamsui High School
Ch'en Wan-fu	arrested	Councilman, Taichung District Council
Ch'en Wu	killed	Councilman, Taipei City Council
Cheng Ssu-ch'uan	arrested	Lecturer, Taiwan Technology College
Cheng Sung-yün	arrested	Public prosecutor, Hua-lien Court
Chien Ch'en-yü	arrested	Councilman, Taipei City Council
Chiu Chin-shan	killed	Director, Kaohsiung branch, *T'ai-wan hsin-sheng-pao*
Chuang Ch'ui-sheng	arrested	Director, Taichung Provincial Library
Chuang Meng-hou	arrested	General director, Tainan Branch, San-min Chu-i Youth Corps
Huang A-ch'un	killed	Teacher, Tamsui High School
Huang Ch'ao-sheng	killed	Councilman, Taipei City Council; physician
Huang Ma-tien	killed	Standing member, Taiwan Provincial Merchant United Association
Huang Shih	killed	Councilman, Kaohsiung City Council
Huang Shih-ch'iao	arrested	Director, Hsin-chu District Library
Huang Ting-ho	arrested	Councilman, Taipei City Council
Hsü Ch'iu	killed	Councilman, Kaohsiung City Council
Hsü Ch'un-ch'ing	killed	Councilman, Taipei City Council
Hsü Hsi-ch'ien	killed	General director, Hua-lien Branch, San-min Chu-i Youth Corps
Hung Yüeh-pai	arrested	Councilman, Taiwan Provincial Council
Jao I-jen	arrested	Director, Chia-i branch, *Ho-p'ing jih-pao*
Jao Wei-yüeh	arrested	Director, Taichung Appellate Court
Juan Chao-jih	killed	General manager, *T'ai-wan hsin-sheng pao*
K'o Lin	killed	Councilman, Chia-i City Council
Ku-shang T'ai-lang	killed	Physician
Kuo Chang-k'uang	killed	Director, Taiwan Provincial I-lan Hospital
Kuo Kuo-chi	arrested	Councilman, Taiwan Provincial Council
Kuo Wan-chih	arrested	Councilman, Kaohsiung City Council
Lai Keng-sung	killed	Judge, Hua-lien Court
Lai Yüan-hui	arrested	Director, Taichung Prison
Li Chin-tsung	arrested	Councilman, Kaohsiung City Council
Li Jen-kuei	killed	Councilman, Taipei City Council
Li Jui-feng	killed	Lawyer

TABLE 11
Continued

Name	Arrested or killed	Profession and/or status
Li Jui-han	killed	Lawyer
Liao Chin-p'ing	killed	Standing Committee member, Political Construction Association
Lin Chieh	killed	Kaohsiung resident
Lin Chieh	killed	Director, *T'ai-wan Hsin-sheng-pao* Printing Shop
Lin Hu	arrested	Councilman, Taichung District Council
Lin Jih-kao	arrested	Councilman, Taiwan Provincial Council
Lin Ko-sheng	arrested	Vice-director, Taichung Fire Department
Lin Kuei-tuan	killed	Lawyer
Lin Lien-ch'eng	arrested	Councilman, Taichung City Council
Lin Lien-chung	killed	National Assemblyman; Councilman, Taiwan Provincial Council; lawyer
Lin Mao-sheng	killed	Dean, College of Liberal Arts, National Taiwan University; publisher of *Min pao*; National Councilman
Lin Chung-hsien	arrested	National Councilman; president of the Board of Trustees, *Chung-wai jih-pao*
Lin Yu-fu	arrested	Secretary, Taichung Appellate Court
Lo Shui-yüan	arrested	Councilman, Taipei City Council
Lu Ping-ch'in	killed	Councilman, Chia-i City Council
Ma Yu-yüeh	arrested	Councilman, Taiwan Provincial Council
Pan Ch'ü-yüan	arrested	Vice-speaker, Taipei City Council
Pan Mu-chih	killed	Councilman, Chia-i City Council
Shih Chiang-nan	killed	Physician; founder of Ssu-fang Hospital
Su Hsien-chang	killed	Director, Chia-i branch, *T'ai-wan hsin-sheng pao*
Su Yao-pang	killed	Principal, I-lan Agricultural School
Sung Fei-ju	killed	Publisher, *Jen-min tao-pao*; former vice-director, Education Dept., Taiwan Provincial Administrative Executive Office
Tang Te-chang	killed	Lawyer; director, Tainan Human Rights Protection Commission
Ts'ai Tieh-ch'eng	arrested	Journalist, *Ho-p'ing jih-pao*
Ts'ai Ting-tsan	arrested	Councilman, Tainan District Council
Ts'ai Yü-pei	arrested	Secretary, Taichung Appellate Court
Tseng Feng-ming	killed	Kaohsiung resident
T'u Kuang-ming	killed	Head, Japanese Property Investigation Office, Kaohsiung city
Wang Shih-ting	killed	Councilman, Kaohsiung City Council
Wang T'ien-teng	killed	Councilman, Taiwan Provincial Council; chairman, Taiwan Provincial Tea Association
Wang Yü-lin	killed	Former public prosecutor, Hsin-chu Court; teacher, Chien-kuo High School
Wu Chin-lien	killed	Editor-in-chief, Japanese section, *T'ai-wan hsin-sheng pao*
Wu Hsin-jung	arrested	Councilman, Tainan District Council
Wu Hung-ch'i	killed	Judge, Taipei High Court
Yang Yüan-ting	killed	Vice-speaker, Keelung City Council
Yeh Ch'iu-mu	killed	Vice-speaker, P'ing-tung City Council
Yeh Tso-le	arrested	Judge, Taichung Court

SOURCE: Chuang Chia-nung, *Fen-nü i T'ai-wan*, pp. 132–34.

sibility."[104] Again, Ho's memoir can be corroborated by accounts of foreigners in Taipei. Our sources are silent, however, about who provided the lists of people for Nationalist troops to arrest, imprison, and even shoot.

As the terror continued, many influential Taiwanese petitioned the central government to order provincial officials, police officers, and troops to stop the arrests and killings. The censor Ch'en Chiang-shan appealed to the Control Yüan of the central government, asking it to send a high-ranking official to investigate conditions in Taiwan. In Kaohsiung, officials of the administration, police officers, and members of the Garrison Command held weekly meetings to discuss how to avoid another uprising. At one meeting, a local leader, Lin Chia, even asked General P'eng Meng-chi whether "many Mainlanders had taken this opportunity to seek revenge." General P'eng failed to respond. The leading censor for Fukien and Taiwan, Yang Liang-kung, personally requested that the Nanking government order the Taiwan provincial government to stop these repressive activities:

> Taiwan martial law has been suspended and mopping-up operations have ceased. These orders have been publicly announced by the Taiwan provincial government. As for the February 28 Incident, the Taiwan Provincial Garrison Command Headquarters ordered all people arrested to be placed on trial. Normalcy is supposed to have returned. However, I have recently received many reports that the military authority has used the February 28 Incident as a pretext to continue arresting people in all districts and cities. Those who were arrested after martial law was suspended have not yet been put on trial by the judiciary. These actions obviously contradict the Taiwan provincial government's orders and are against the central government's principles for handling the Taiwan incident. I ask you to order the Garrison Command Headquarters to issue orders to all local military authorities to obey the law and to immediately send those arrested to trial. Hereafter, no one should use the Incident as a pretext to arrest people or execute them willfully. Such evil trends should cease....[105]

Although the central government had forbidden reprisals after suppressing the Uprising,[106] those orders had not been obeyed. The voices appealing to the central government for leniency attest to that. Along with the other evidence we have cited, including that concerning P'eng Meng-chi's role, the data show that much of the killing was against the orders of the Generalissimo and Ch'en I. Data that have eluded us, however, may show precisely just who ordered and did what.

Moving Toward Reform

After completing his investigations, General Pai Ch'ung-hsi flew to Nanking on April 2 and reported to Chiang Kai-shek, giving his reasons for the occurrence of the Uprising and his ideas for repairing the damage. General Pai presented four recommendations on how the central government should deal with the Uprising.[107]

Pai recommended that Taiwan's political structure be reformed in two significant ways. First, the central government should abolish the title of Taiwan Provincial Administrative Executive Office and establish the Taiwan Provincial Government with an administrative structure similar to that of other provinces. That change required creating more departments and sections within the administration. Second, the central government's Ministry of the Interior should have standard procedures for electing heads of all districts and cities and members of the provincial council, as well as rules for how long they should serve. Pai also urged that these legal procedures for establishing the elections be implemented quickly in order to hold elections in Taiwan as soon as possible.

Pai also recommended some new administrative rules for the provincial government. Taiwan's provincial governor should not head the Taiwan Garrison Command Headquarters. More Taiwanese should fill top provincial administrative positions and head departments, bureaus, and sections. Salaries for Taiwanese and Mainlanders should be equal for the same administrative post.

Pai also suggested economic reforms, saying that private and publicly owned enterprises should be separated, and the power of the latter greatly reduced. The Ministry of Economics and the Resource Commission should be responsible for making certain this separation occurred. The Executive Yüan and the central government should send delegates to all branches of the Taiwan provincial government to check on the progress of these economic reforms and to determine whether further changes were required.

The urban Resolution Committees and the other organizations that had mushroomed during the Uprising already had been abolished. Pai proposed that any people connected with these groups and the Uprising should be dealt with in a most lenient way according to the law. Any Communist Party members who had been apprehended as instigating the riots should be severely punished. Nearly all of Pai's recommendations were carried out over the next two years.

On April 21, Chiang Kai-shek wired Ch'en I that Wei Tao-ming had been selected as the new governor of Taiwan and would officially take charge on May 15.[108] He instructed Ch'en I not to appoint any personnel on his own and to order all military units to remain where they were at that time. As for any lower-level appointments, Chiang wanted to be informed of them before April 23. On the same day, Wei Tao-ming offered his suggestions to Chiang Kai-shek on how the new provincial administration should be staffed and on the appointments to be publicly announced.[109]

On May 15, 1947, Taiwan's special administrative status was ended with the abolition of the Taiwan Provincial Administrative Executive Office, the single organ in which great power had been concentrated. Ch'en I had already begun hiring more Taiwanese for the new administration, and more entered the administration after he was replaced on April 29 by Wei Tao-ming.[110]

Born in 1899, Wei Tao-ming had served with distinction as mayor of Nanking, Secretary-General of the Executive Yüan, and Ambassador to the United States (1942–46).[111] Upon his arrival, Wei traveled around the island to talk with officials and local leaders, learn about local conditions, and improve Taiwanese–Mainlander relations.

On May 16, Wei wired Chiang Kai-shek that everything was moving according to plan.[112] In addition to discussing the large issue of provincial reform, Wei commented that some weapons had apparently disappeared during the Uprising and that some prisoners had escaped from jail. For these reasons, Governor Wei had ordered security to be tightened and had asked P'eng Meng-chi to look into the matter. P'eng Meng-chi immediately informed Chiang, "Regarding the weapons lost during the Incident, the Garrison Command has announced a reward for those who return them. Until now, we have recovered 216 rifles (more than the original number lost). Except for a few handguns, almost all of the weapons have been recovered by the military."[113] P'eng also said that all efforts were being made to recapture those prisoners who had escaped.

Wei remained governor until replaced by Ch'en Ch'eng on January 5, 1949. During his administration, the economic structure underwent radical change. The name of the Monopoly Bureau was changed to the Public Sales Bureau (*Kung-mai-chü*), and the bureau was revamped by restricting the number of commodities it could sell to retailers. The Trade Bureau was renamed the Commodity Supply Bureau (*Wu-tzu kung-ying-chü*) and streamlined its handling of "all commodities sold abroad and produced by publicly owned enterprises, their acquisition of machines and raw materials, and their sales to meet the demands of private enterprises."[114] The reform of these two bureaus greatly increased the number of private enterprises producing and distributing consumer goods and allowed Taiwanese business people to conduct their affairs with more freedom and certainty than before.

State-owned enterprises became responsible for producing mainly intermediate products, while the private sector specialized in the production of consumer goods. This step, along with the sale of public land to farmers, helped to prevent rising unemployment and gradually increased the production of goods and services, even though inflation worsened.

In addition to giving new encouragement to the private sector, reforms increased the role of Taiwanese in the provincial political structure. Of the eleven new provincial commissioners established, seven were Taiwanese. More Taiwanese became heads and deputies of administration departments: Ch'iu Nien-t'ai, Department Director of Civil Affairs; Ch'iu Pin-ts'un, Deputy Director of the Department of Finance; Hsieh Tung-ming, Deputy Director of the Department of Education; Ch'en Shang-wen, Deputy Director of the Reconstruction Department; Hsü Ch'ing-ch'un, Director of Agriculture and Forestry; and Yen Ch'un-hui, Director of Sanitation. For the first time, a few Taiwanese entered the highest levels of the administration.[115]

However, under Governor Wei Tao-ming's administration, the investigations and trials of those charged with participation in the Uprising continued to drag on. In January 1948, Chiang Kai-shek's secretary, Wu Ting-ch'ang, reported to Chiang that high-ranking Taiwanese were concerned about expediting these trials.[116] Wu urged Chiang to use his authority to speed up these trials, and he appealed for leniency on behalf of Taiwan Provincial Council members Chiang Wei-ch'uan and Lin Jih-kao, asking that they be released from prison because the Taiwan Provincial Government had offered to guarantee their innocence. Wu argued that Chiang and Lin were prominent Taiwanese, not guilty of any crimes during the Uprising, and people who could help to win popular support for the provincial government.

In March 1948, Chiang and Lin were still in prison, and many high-ranking officials again appealed to Chiang Kai-shek for their speedy release.[117] On June 4, 1948, Hsieh Kuan-sheng, head of the Department of Justice, reported to Chiang Kai-shek that both Chiang and Lin had finally been released because of no conclusive evidence of their guilt.[118] No doubt, there were many more instances in which people were wrongfully arrested but eventually released, or, once arrested, were not quickly put on trial and so remained in prison for a long period.

CHAPTER 6

The Nature and Aftermath of the Tragedy

> A glooming peace this morning with it brings;
> The sun for sorrow will not show its head:
> Go hence, to have more talk of these sad things;
> Some shall be pardon'd and some punished:
> Shakespeare, *Romeo and Juliet*, V, 3

The Nature of the Tragedy

1. *The Clash of World views.* We have explored the February Uprising in detail to clarify its historical background, the tensions and circumstances leading up to it, the motives and goals of its participants, its evolution and that of the government's response, its sociological character, and the moral questions it entails. The historical background of the Uprising includes the period of Japanese colonialism. Our research does not justify vague claims that Taiwanese in this period absorbed Japanese culture or in fact became "poisoned" by it. We can say, however, that Taiwanese experience under Japanese rule led many to adopt a worldview that coincided with prevalent Japanese thinking and clashed with the worldview of Mainlanders returning to Taiwan from 1945 on. In this clash, each group exhibited a way of thinking that outraged the other, causing extreme tension, especially in the context of the overarching Chinese cultural inclination to define political disagreement in hyperbolic, moralistic, and Manichaean terms.

Part of the reason for the clash lay in the contrast between the KMT's limited administrative capabilities and the euphorically optimistic expectations with which the Taiwanese awaited resumption of Chinese rule. The Taiwanese in 1945 lacked realistic understanding of the problems they would face in working with Mainlanders, even those with the best intentions, to set up a Chinese administration for Taiwan. State building in a war-ravaged land is obviously difficult, but the Taiwanese expected

The Nature and Aftermath of the Tragedy 169

immediate success, if not perfection. Having experienced the political stability and administrative efficiency of a remarkably skilled Japanese government, they assumed that the Chinese would erect a similarly efficient system, cum democracy. Yet up to that point in Chinese history, no Chinese group had ever succeeded in erecting a sovereign political system that both accorded with prevalent Chinese political ideals and efficiently focused on the practical problems of modernization.

Taiwanese also expected sympathy for having suffered under Japanese colonialism, but Mainlanders expected to be greeted with gratitude as liberators. Elite Taiwanese, moreover, expecting respect for their modern ways, academic prowess, and high social status, looked down on Mainlanders as less modern than they and as backward in still adhering to an obsolete Confucian ideology. Yet the KMT proudly regarded itself as the party responsible for ending the unequal treaties, for giving China Great Power status as one of the Big Four, and for defeating the Japanese. It now had the sacred mission of unifying China and carrying out the revolution defined by Sun Yat-sen. Expecting rather than giving respect, Mainlanders often looked down on Taiwanese for having come under the influence of the inferior culture of a hated enemy.

At the same time, Taiwanese felt that the KMT should place high priority on their economic needs, but the KMT viewed Taiwan primarily as a source of resources with which to fight important battles on the Mainland. In fact, Mainlanders felt that because Taiwan enjoyed greater wealth and higher living standards than the Mainland, Taiwanese should carry a heavier burden than other Chinese in the struggle to defeat the Communists and to modernize. Moreover, while some Taiwanese embraced the Western ideal of democracy, feeling it could be applied immediately in China, the KMT offered a confusing political message. Although it rejected Communist and Japanese totalitarianism and endorsed democracy, it insisted that democratization had to occur gradually and in combination with Confucian ethics and opposition to Communism.

In addition, the KMT was guilty of misrule, stemming from its experience on the Mainland, which had stunted the development of its administrative capabilities. We do not want to invoke the French saying that "to understand is to forgive." Yet turning China from a monarchy with a Confucian ideology into a modern, democratic state has proved to be a long and painful process. Today, in one small part of China, Taiwan, this process is now nearing completion. Even in 1990, however, more than forty years after unification of the Mainland, China is still mired in economic backwardness and political repression. Indeed, extravagant hopes to the contrary were dashed by the debacle of June 4, 1989.

In 1945, no Chinese political organization had yet acquired the political understanding and skills needed to overcome these economic and political problems. Still undergoing a learning process in the 1930s and 1940s, the KMT had been enervated by the ravages of the Japanese invasion, by dissidence based in some part on intellectual radicalism and utopianism, and by the Communist rebellion. It is not surprising, therefore, that in the 1930s and 1940s it was unable to check entrenched local elites and military forces resisting modernizing reforms.

On the Mainland, the KMT had learned to acquiesce to entrenched local elites when necessary, and in Taiwan in its land-to-the-tiller program, it displayed an ability to push them aside. What it had not yet learned was how to bargain with and co-opt these groups to form a broader political consensus, and at the same time preserve the power of government and Party organs. In 1945, the central government and the KMT lacked not only the political talent and experience to build such a consensus but also the funds to field a sufficiently large bureaucracy. At the same time, its Sunist ideology and acceptance of the widespread Chinese intellectual belief in socialism inclined it toward a statist policy that undermined postwar economic recovery. With its ability to grasp and implement effective policies already so limited, the KMT would have met with great difficulties in Taiwan even if it had avoided gross misrule, which it did not.

2. *Failed Policies.* For this failure, the KMT must be severely criticized. Responsible directly to the Generalissimo, Ch'en I's administration followed an unwise policy, which was aggravated by unfairness, corruption, and plain ineptitude. As the KMT itself admitted both explicitly in its internal reports on the Uprising and implicitly as it embarked on a course of reform in March, grievous, avoidable misrule had been a fact.

To be sure, a shortage of public funds necessitated reducing the Japanese bureaucracy of 84,000 officials. Yet only poor policy, stemming from both contempt for the Taiwanese and ignorance of the extent of Japanese bureaucratic commitment to colonial rule, could have resulted in cuts of 50 percent. Some 36,000 Taiwanese officials were thrown out of work, and the ratio of Taiwanese was reduced from 56 percent to 22 percent, not even half as many Taiwanese as the Japanese staff still serving in early 1945.

Similarly, it was unreasonable to confiscate and dispose of 9.5 billion old Taiwan dollars of Japanese property (around 17 percent of Taiwan's GDP in 1946) without taking into account Taiwanese feelings. Although the central government, preoccupied with mobilizing resources to defeat the Communist rebellion, had a legitimate interest in this property, so did the Taiwanese. There must have been room for compromise—a way of

The Nature and Aftermath of the Tragedy   171

disposing of Japanese property that met, least in part, local needs and aspirations.

Nor can the KMT escape major responsibility for the economic crisis that created urban misery from late 1945 on. War had destroyed production and commercial facilities, creating shortages and inflation, had severed vital trade links with Japan, and had precluded economic aid from the Mainland. Yet economic problems were compounded when Ch'en I confiscated Japanese assets to create an inefficient economic empire that provided fat salaries for well-connected Mainland bureaucrats and hampered the private sector by imposing regulations that further inhibited economic recovery and thus aggravated inflation and unemployment. Bureaucratic corruption and troop misbehavior were other problems for which the KMT was to some extent responsible.

3. *Poor Leadership.* More important, it was responsible for the basic problem—the obtuse, incompetent leadership of Ch'en I. Although Ch'en I supported to some degree freedom of the press and gradual democratization, he isolated himself with sycophants instead of moving through society to learn of grievances, look for ways to reduce them, and build up informal networks linking the government with the Taiwanese community. There is some truth to General Wedemeyer's report made in August 1947 to the U.S. Secretary of State: "Ch'en Yi [Ch'en I] and his henchmen ruthlessly, corruptly, and avariciously imposed their regime upon a happy and amenable population."

4. *Other Sources of Tensions and Grievances.* In addition to KMT misrule, the tensions leading to the Uprising were exacerbated by a variety of important factors: the economic misery unavoidable in an economically backward country emerging from a world war only to be plunged into a civil war; the crime spawned by unemployment; an existing underworld hostile to the KMT and given to violence; a large group of unemployed young men recently repatriated from the imperial Japanese armed services; a largely free press that sensationalized anti-government grievances; and serious cultural-linguistic barriers reinforcing the existing clash in worldviews.

5. *The Role of the Contingent: Withdrawal of Troops.* Yet were it not for still another circumstance, Taiwan's history would probably be different. Without this circumstance, only minor riots could have taken place; there almost certainly would have been no period of KMT repression; and in all likelihood, no Taiwan Independence Movement would have emerged. This circumstance was the reduction of the ROC military forces in 1946 by 90 percent, from 48,000 men to 5,000. Together with police, this left a security force of some 11,000 men, about 6 percent of the

Japanese police-military presence in the early 1940s. Without this reduction, rioting could not have seriously escalated. This becomes clear if we remember that the arrival of troop reinforcements from the Mainland, beginning on Saturday, March 8, nine days after the first riot, ended the Uprising almost as rapidly as flicking a switch turns off a light bulb.

While these troop reductions were an important part of the circumstances leading to the Uprising, the clash in worldviews of Taiwanese and Chinese was also significant. We have provided evidence of the Taiwanese worldview by quoting from the memoirs of P'eng Ming-min. There is considerable evidence that much if not most of the elite and sub-elite Taiwanese population consisted of people who, like P'eng, had made the best of the socioeconomic opportunities provided by the Japanese presence, had found life under the Japanese to be on the whole satisfactory, and so probably shared many of P'eng's views.

P'eng's life was not anomalous for one with his prosperous family background. He was not a "loner" but a gifted person with a strong and appealing personality, as is evident from his subsequently successful academic career, and he moved easily in Taiwanese society. Thus, it is unlikely that his thought or life was idiosyncratic.

The warm relations he enjoyed with his Japanese friends and teachers reflected the general social situation under Japanese colonialism, which had created much less social and political friction in Taiwan than in Korea. Most telling, in contrast with the Korean situation, was the attitude toward Taiwanese who worked with the Japanese in government or otherwise had important positions in colonial society: They were not stigmatized as traitors by other Taiwanese.

Perhaps 4 percent of the population, some 250,000 persons, consisted of families in which one or more members were employed in the Japanese bureaucracy. In 1944, some 20,000 persons belonged to families in which a member had been elected or appointed to a district, city, or town council. (The many more who served in village councils belonged to a category that overlaps that of members of the bureaucracy.) By 1942, almost 100,000 Taiwanese families—some 700,000 persons representing perhaps 10 percent of the population—had apparently adopted Japanese surnames.

To be sure, none of these statistics indicates that Taiwanese elite constituted an ideologically homogeneous group. Ambivalent, complex, varying worldviews were the rule. Moreover, some members of the elite had family roots in the Ch'ing order and stronger ties to China's traditional civilization than did the P'engs. Yet if we conjecture that roughly 5 percent of the population in 1945 belonged to the elite, this group numbers some 300,000, a figure close to the number of Taiwanese who seem to have had vested interests in or feelings of identification with the Japanese-dominated social order, and whose views could thus have been close to those of P'eng. Therefore, it is likely that P'eng's worldview was typical of views broadly shared in elite Taiwanese circles in the late 1940s.

The importance of this clash between worldviews is shown by comparing Taiwan to other parts of China.

6. *A Comparison of Mainland China's Conditions.* When the ROC liberated its coastal provinces from Japanese rule after World War II, no urban uprisings occurred in these Mainland areas. Yet there was deep dissatisfaction with KMT rule there, too. The Nationalists' failure to arrest and bring to trial leading Chinese collaborators who had served in the puppet government of Wang Ching-wei disillusioned many in Shanghai, Nanking, and elsewhere, and angered still others.[1]

The alleged mismanagement of Japanese assets seized by Nationalist officials quickly led to charges that leading Chungking officials were preoccupied with "gold bars, automobiles, houses, Japanese women, and face."[2] There also was a similar pattern of economic mismanagement in which the Nanking government's banks printed money to finance government activities. A combination of rampant unemployment and inflation nurtured the kinds of grievances and panic so widespread in Taiwan's cities. Labor strikes, large-scale student demonstrations, and attacks by intellectuals in journals and the press intensified throughout 1946.[3] Yet these vehement reactions against KMT rule in the large coastal cities never crystallized into any widespread uprising involving the seizure of government facilities, demands that ROC forces disarm, and calls for the immediate democratization of the government.

Although political conditions in Taiwan differed in some ways from conditions in these coastal cities, it is clear that in confronting the ROC, Taiwan dissidents were animated by an outlook different in kind from the views of Mainland dissidents. Their historical experience under the Japanese had given them an especially strong sense of being a clearly bounded "we-group" facing outsiders, as well as reasons for feeling superior to these outsiders. KMT misrule in Taiwan, therefore, in contrast with KMT misrule in the coastal provinces recovered from the Japanese, aroused the anger of an especially coherent, ethnically bounded "we-group" animated by a deeply shared sense of being victimized and insulted by outsiders inferior to it. It is reasonable to believe that without this distinctive sense of being a victimized "we-group," Taiwanese would have reacted to the misrule of the postwar KMT as the coastal populations did, without mounting a major uprising.

This distinctive outlook, then, was probably a significant cause of the Uprising, along with the troop reductions of 1946. KMT misrule, although a cause of the Uprising, was not *the* cause. Misrule must be considered along with these other two factors, as well as a variety of economic, social, linguistic, and cultural circumstances. Our study thus makes clear that the Uprising stemmed from a variety of circumstances, a viewpoint that contradicts currently prevalent interpretations that blame only the KMT.

7. *Social Groups Responsible for the Uprising.* Our study also clarifies the identity of those participating in the Uprising—their goals, their actions, and the evolution of the response by the provincial and national government. There is little basis for the frequent claim that the Uprising was carried out by or represented all Taiwanese. Eighty percent—the rural population—did not participate, and many of the remaining 20 percent in cities and towns played no part. There was not the link between urban and rural discontent that many scholars claim was then occurring on the Mainland. The common denominator was outrage—angry Taiwanese elite, urban people with economic grievances, a large floating group of unemployed youth, and members of the underworld. More data are needed about the social character of the Uprising, but there is little doubt about the social strata involved.

The question of social composition overlaps that of the dissidents' goals or motivations. Certainly, the most widespread motivation was a diffuse anger that KMT misrule was responsible for nearly all of Taiwan's current problems. There is no evidence that Communist ideas inspired a significant number of dissidents. Even though, in Taichung, the Communist Hsieh Hsüeh-hung played a major role, the anger and aspirations she articulated had nothing to do with Communism.

Therefore, the thesis advanced by both the CCP and the KMT that Communist influence was basic to the Uprising is nonsense. Only a rare gift for self-delusion and insincerity can explain the CCP's claim that the Uprising was "inspired by the great leader, Chairman Mao, who had just declared that the people should welcome the high tide of the Chinese Revolution." Certainly, knowledgeable Communists did not believe this.

The KMT's public claim was only slightly less extravagant: "The Communist Party and mad, ambitious schemers had used the case of an arrested smuggler to launch their uprising." Communists were indeed involved, and the KMT had reason to worry about Mao's machinations in Taiwan. KMT fears were not imaginary, but, as ROC officials acknowledged to one another, Communists were not an important factor in crystallizing tensions or causing the Uprising.

Nor can one accept the KMT official position that, apart from Communist influence, Taiwanese hostility toward the KMT was based either on misunderstanding or the influence of "depraved . . . mad, ambitious" people, along with the "sordid, evil education" Taiwanese had received under the Japanese. Leaving aside the question of Japanese influence, we must recognize that urban discontent was prevalent and was not based on delusion, misunderstanding, or wickedness. The dissidents did not objectively and fairly analyze all the causes of Taiwan's problems, but they were reasonable and justified in being outraged by KMT misrule.

8. *Demands of the Dissidents and Official Responses.* Nor is it accurate to suggest that the dissidents wanted to turn Taiwan into an independent, sovereign nation. They proposed no such concept—only the idea of "self-rule" within the framework of an ROC nation-state. Moreover, this goal was not uniformly agreed upon. Anger at KMT misrule and a demand for fundamental reforms constituted the common denominator of their movement.

Although many previous discussions of the Uprising actually ignore the Uprising itself and discuss only the reign of terror that followed, our study gives as detailed an account as possible of both phases. It shows that the Uprising quickly acquired the character of a major rebellion threatening to end the central government's sovereign authority in Taiwan at a time when civil war was raging on the Mainland. The government responded to secure its sovereign authority in Taiwan, not simply to deal with scattered riots. General Wedemeyer's report to the U.S. Secretary of State on August 17, 1947, correctly referred to the episode as a "rebellion." Its character as a rebellion is clear from the great amount of property destroyed by rioters (valued at over 1 billion old Taiwan dollars, or US$200 million at the 1949 exchange rate), from the large number of Mainlanders injured and killed (more than 1,000), and from demands that government forces disarm and allow rebellious groups a free hand in reorganizing the political administration of Taiwan.

Such demands were made by different groups in different cities. For instance, on March 2, after radicals in Taichung selected the Communist Hsieh Hsüeh-hung as chairwoman of their group, she urged that a new party be organized to take power and establish self-rule. That same day, Hsieh detained a number of officials and had them beaten. By March 3 or so, Hsieh's force controlled all of Taichung, and she announced: "Now, all the people of our province can become armed to fight and destroy this tyrannical government." The radicalization of dissident demands continued in the next days.

Most telling were the 32 Demands drawn up by the Taipei Resolution Committee on March 7. The first demand stated that "all military forces stationed in the island should temporarily disarm and turn over their weapons to the local Resolution Committees and military police, who would manage these weapons so as to prevent further bloody conflict." The third demand was to give the Resolution Committee, working with military and civil police, the power to arrest "any corrupt official" accused by "people." The first demand under "political aspects" was that "the supreme norm for political affairs within this province" be a "provincial self-government law," and other demands gave Taiwanese control over the provincial government (see Appendix A).

To be sure, on the very next day, March 8, the Taipei Resolution Committee publicly regretted these demands: "We now realize that the demands to abolish the Garrison Command and to have the Nationalist forces disarm were really demands to oppose the central government and did not correctly represent the will of the people." Nevertheless, the government cannot be blamed for believing that many participants in the Uprising wanted to end its rule in Taiwan.

There is also strong evidence that during the first days of the Uprising, Ch'en I tried to end it by offering to make reforms; that this effort at conciliation was turned down; that demands became increasingly radical during the first week of March; and that the government from March 5 on adopted a policy of military repression because its conciliatory efforts had failed.

On March 1, two days after the first incident, four members of the newly formed Taipei Resolution Committee met with Ch'en I, asking that martial law be suspended, that all people arrested be released, that a committee be set up to investigate the affair, and that Ch'en I make a public broadcast. Ch'en I responded in a conciliatory way, and martial law was lifted the next day, Sunday, March 2. The same day, Ch'en I made a broadcast promising lenient treatment for those arrested, help for all wounded, compensation for anyone killed (Mainlander or Taiwanese), and an expanded role for the public in various organs like the Taiwan Provincial Council and the Taipei City Council. A member of the Taipei Resolution Committee, however, responded to Ch'en's broadcast by denouncing him and threatening more bloodshed. Then on Friday, March 7, the Taipei Resolution Committee made the clearly rebellious 32 Demands.

Although some argue that Ch'en I's effort at conciliation was insincere, there is strong evidence to the contrary. The disturbances had humiliated Ch'en in the eyes of his superiors, and he had every incentive to restore calm before his superiors received the impression that he had lost control of the situation. Aware that military needs in 1946 had required sending back to the Mainland 90 percent of the troops then in Taiwan, he must have dreaded the prospect of having to ask his superiors to return these troops to Taiwan to put down an uprising for which he would be held responsible. He would have preferred to resolve the crisis with the 11,000 police and military then under his command, but this was impossible if conciliation failed. It seems clear that the failure of conciliation and the need to ship back troops badly needed on the Mainland led to Ch'en I's transfer out of Taiwan. Obtuse as he may have been, he surely was not stupid enough to damage his career, and thus must have sincerely sought conciliation.

Moreover, if one pictures Ch'en I happily awaiting troop reinforcements and then eagerly sending them on a mission of revenge, one not only forgets that the arrival of these reinforcements symbolized his incompetence but also brushes aside his professed goals in a gratuitously cynical way. We believe that he sincerely wanted to produce social harmony in Taiwan and that he wanted to quickly end the conflict.

Our study, therefore, shows that the policy of harsh repression was not the central government's preferred response to the crisis. We have analyzed the dissidents' demands by putting them into three categories: those emphasizing the provincial and central governments' culpability; those seeking restriction of the governments' power to act coercively against the dissidents; and those that were revolutionary, acceptance of which would have effectively eliminated the power of the KMT in Taiwan. Our data show that Ch'en I was, for some four days after the outbreak of violence, ready to compromise on dissident demands within the first two categories. Beginning on Sunday, March 2, however, some dissidents began to respond to Ch'en's conciliatory stance by moving toward demands of a more revolutionary character—a radicalization that continued through Friday, March 7.

In other words, the Uprising's flow of events can be seen in terms of two trajectories: the increasing radicalization of dissident demands and the provincial and central governments' shift from conciliation to repression. Moreover, it seems clear that the first trajectory caused the second one.

Yet the detailed documentation needed to fully corroborate this point is still missing. It does seem clear that the trajectory of dissident radicalization was steadily rising from Sunday, March 2, through Friday, March 7, and that the ROC's shift away from conciliation began at least by Wednesday, March 5, when Generalissimo Chiang Kai-shek and the central government decided to send reinforcements. Furthermore, there is, as already mentioned, solid evidence that since the previous Friday, February 28,

Ch'en I had favored conciliation. To be absolutely sure, however, that conciliation was the true ROC goal from Friday through Tuesday, we need greater access to the internal communications of the central government.

On the other hand, it must be recognized that the radicalization of dissident demands by itself precluded conciliation, whether or not Ch'en I's stance was sincere. Because the ROC could offer to make concessions only with regard to dissident demands in our first two categories (culpability and limiting the scope of the government's coercive actions), negotiations necessarily broke down once dissident demands became revolutionary—that is, calling for the end of KMT power in Taiwan. In the government's decision to use force that first week of March, the Generalissimo played a basic role. In his view, harsh steps were necessary to put down a rebellion taking place on his rear while he was fighting a civil war with the Communists.

9. *The Human Cost of the Uprising.* There is also convincing evidence that once this harsh policy was decided upon, the ensuing terror was caused partly by irresponsible decisions and lack of discipline in the field and was not the intention of the Generalissimo and the government. The Kaohsiung massacre, which continued for many days, was ordered by General P'eng Meng-chi, who apparently wanted to punish the population for rebelling. Ch'en I later said that he had not anticipated the vindictive behavior of the troops, and the leading censor for Fukien and Taiwan, Yang Liang-kung, denounced some military authorities for using the Uprising as a pretext to arrest people long after the restoration of law and order. Our study also furnishes strong evidence that in the persecution the number of Taiwanese and Mainlanders killed was around 8,000 at most, much less than half the estimate made by P'eng Ming-min and far smaller than some other estimates.

10. *Moral Aspects of the Uprising.* With regard to the moral questions raised by the Uprising and the response of the provincial and central governments, we have consistently tried to make two points. First, moral questions should be differentiated from the six other questions posed in Chapter 1, which are largely factual. Only by separating out the controversial moral issues can scholars dispassionately and thoroughly discuss the factual ones. Second, this episode was more a tragedy than a contest between good and evil.

We cannot but endorse the anger with which the dissidents reacted to KMT and provincial misrule. Yet were they wise to react so violently, to brush aside Ch'en I's conciliatory offers, and to radicalize their demands? Was the hope for "self-rule" that some of them entertained a practical possibility in that day and age?

The Nature and Aftermath of the Tragedy 179

Basic to the Uprising was a contradiction between two outlooks, both of which had equally understandable historical antecedents. Neither was demonstrably more "rational" or "moral" than the other. In this important sense, especially, the conflict between the two sides was not a contest between good and evil.

The KMT worldview was not unreasonable. The KMT was trying to save China from Communism, seeking values in the Confucian tradition of indigenous civilization, and pursuing the unification and modernization of China according to Sun Yat-sen's vision. The KMT hated the nation that had ruthlessly invaded China, was outraged by Chinese who admired the enemy, and believed in gradual democratization. The government and the Nationalists were also reasonable in considering Taiwan simply another province under their centralized control. Such nationalistic views have been common in our century.

Years ago, many Chinese and foreigners ridiculed and denounced the KMT's emphasis on Confucian ethics as unreasonable, "atavistic," and less enlightened than the Communists' iconoclastic uprooting of the Confucian tradition. Today, the scholarly view of Confucian values has been transformed, and many of the world's most established experts on Confucianism praise it for promoting moral attitudes that fit well with the needs of modernization. Yet few give credit to the ROC's leaders for having recognized its value early. Today some scholars criticize the KMT for propagating a "politicized," "vulgarized" version of Confucian values, instead of a version based on "the intellectuals' corporate, self-aware spirit of moral criticism." This is the criticism leveled at the ROC by Professor Tu Wei-ming of Harvard University when he taught and lectured on the Mainland in the 1980s.[4] But has history ever witnessed a case of state building and modernization without some "politicization" and "vulgarization"? It seems unfair that critics should use such utopian standards to evaluate the ROC's propagation of Confucian values.

While it is hard for us to regard the KMT's worldview as unreasonable, the Taiwanese response was also not unreasonable. The Taiwanese had, as Mainlanders claimed, been deeply influenced by their experience under the Japanese, coming to share a good deal of the Japanese worldview. Their relations with Japanese colonialism had been relatively benign and certainly less tense than those of the Koreans. Some members of the elite had been co-opted by the Japanese, even though they criticized the Japanese refusal to give them legal equality and the right to administer their own island. Taiwanese appreciated their progress toward modernization and identified it with Japanese guidance. When the Japanese carried out a huge, varied program of total patriotic mobilization during World War II, they were at least partly successful. The Taiwanese, even if resentful or embarrassed, did not form any effective underground to challenge their Japanese masters and did not despise those who flourished under Japanese auspices.

In 1895, however, the Taiwanese had become colonial subjects against their will and could not be blamed for adapting to a situation forced on them or for noticing the obvious contrast between the honesty and efficiency of the relatively modern Japanese administration and the misrule by the KMT from late 1945 on. Nor could Taiwanese elite be blamed for expecting to play an important role in their own province after reunification and to have a voice in the disposal of the confiscated wealth they had helped to create. With this worldview, therefore, Taiwanese were outraged by KMT-central government attitudes, just as their attitudes outraged the KMT and the central government.

A remark made in 1988 by the academician Chang Yen-hsien in a preface introducing Chung I-jen's memoir about the February 28 Uprising underscores the enormous historical significance of the Uprising: "This incident was *the* single event after World War II that influenced Taiwan in the most concrete, profound and enduring way. Until the present, numerous political and social problems in Taiwan still go back to that incident."[5] Not all these problems can be discussed here, but we can briefly outline the aftermath of this tragedy.

Ch'en I's Fate

Ch'en I could not continue in Taiwan after the Uprising and was transferred out of his post on May 15, 1947. General T'ang En-po, whom Ch'en I had once sent to Japan to study in a school for non-commissioned officers,[6] recommended that Ch'en I be given the governorship of Chekiang.[7] Chiang Kai-shek, who still trusted Ch'en, agreed, appointing him governor of his home province.

After going to Chekiang, Ch'en was suspected of having shifted his loyalty to the Communists. In later years, General Mao Sen remembered a conversation with General Mao Jen-feng, who in 1947–48 served as director of the Military Control Bureau. He said that unknown to Ch'en I, his chief subordinates (Hu Yün-kung, Shen Chung-chiu, and, later in Chekiang, Ting Ming-nan) had been Communists, and that may have influenced him to consider switching sides.[8] It seems that Ch'en I may indeed have begun to contemplate such a decision. Upon his arrival in Chekiang, he conferred with General T'ang En-po, at that time the Commander-in-Chief of the Shanghai-Nanking-Hangchow Garrison Command,[9] suggesting to him the advantages of maintaining a more independent position within the Nationalist military hierarchy.[10]

Ch'en I's main contribution in Chekiang seems to have been to strengthen the provincial Planning and Review Commission, ordering it to draft a ten-year plan for the reconstruction of Chekiang province.[11] The agency asked all departments and bureaus to provide information and ideas for this plan, and the provincial government approved it just before Ch'en I was dismissed as governor. Ch'en I still inclined toward the statism that had produced economic disaster in Taiwan. According to the memoirs of Yen Chia-li, Ch'en I became interested in economic planning in the Soviet Union[12] and the socialist countries of Eastern Europe, asking his staff to request from the Foreign Ministry books and reports from Poland and other such countries about their reconstruction plans.

As the civil war worsened for the Nationalist government in 1948, Ch'en I probably realized that Chekiang would soon be taken over by Communist forces. He probably wanted to prevent the destruction of his beloved province as well as ensure for himself some position of prominence in the new political order. Apparently filled with such thoughts, he rapidly fell from grace. On January 27, 1949, he instructed one of his sister's sons and his close subordinate, Ting Ming-nan, to take a letter to General T'ang En-po.[13] In effect, Ch'en's letter requested that T'ang stop drafting soldiers, stop building additional fortifications, and allow defensive preparations aimed at the Communists to stagnate.[14] According to the memoirs of Chang Wen-ch'i, Ch'en also mentioned that he was recommending to the Communists that General T'ang's name be removed from the list of Chekiang war criminals whom the Communists were anxious to capture and bring to public trial.[15]

General T'ang was shocked by Ch'en I's letter, which implied that Ch'en I would eventually surrender his command to the Communists. T'ang agonized over his response because he was torn between loyalty to Ch'en I and loyalty to Chiang Kai-shek, whose orders were to resist the Communist military advance at all costs. T'ang finally decided to inform Chiang Kai-shek of Ch'en I's intention. He instructed General Mao Jen-feng to take Ch'en I's letter to Chiang Kai-shek, and he asked General Mao to ask Chiang not to execute Ch'en I.[16] General Mao passed the letter to Chiang Kai-shek, but he did not convey T'ang En-po's request to spare Ch'en I's life. General Mao took his revenge on Ch'en I who, as Fukien's governor, had ordered the execution of Chang Ch'ao,[17] one of General Mao Jen-feng's closest friends.

Security officials placed Ch'en I under house arrest on February 23, 1949,[18] and on April 29, 1949, transferred him to Taiwan and put him in prison.¹⁹ A military tribunal found him guilty of consorting with the Communists and ordered that he be executed. Dressed in suit and tie, he was shot by a military firing squad in Taipei on June 18, 1950.²⁰

Early Chinese Reactions

As Ch'en I's life was coming to an ignominious end, Chinese began to digest the news from Taiwan. Little was reported in the Mainland press about the Uprising, except for reports in Amoy and other Fukien coastal cities.²¹ Fukien journalists and newspapers had close ties with Taiwan and thus great interest in developments there. In previous months, the Fukien press had reported on mounting corruption and Ch'en I's autocratic policies, regarded as the cause of the rapidly deteriorating socioeconomic conditions. In Nanking and elsewhere, many officials in the government still had little reliable information about what had taken place on Taiwan and why the Uprising had erupted.²²

By late 1947, however, a number of reports describing the suppression of the Uprising had circulated. Taiwanese communities on the Mainland, which had received many of the 3,000 or so who had fled the island, were also outraged by Nationalist behavior.²³ In Shanghai, foreign news articles reported that Taiwan might be turned into a mandated territory under United Nations rule so that elections could be held to decide the island's political future.²⁴ Mainlanders and Taiwanese on the Mainland began debating this possibility, with some arguing that even if the central government had been at fault, it was wrong to turn over the governance of Taiwan to an international agency.²⁵ The furor over the Uprising, however, does not seem to have affected the elections of 1947–48, and it eventually died down in 1949, when the Mainland passed into the hands of the CCP and its victorious armies.

The Communist leadership, however, recognized that the Uprising was a popular movement based on widespread grievances and seized upon it to create propaganda discrediting the Nationalist government. In 1947, for example, a Communist radio station in northern Shansi province transmitted this message to Taiwan: "The Taiwanese were forced to protect themselves by taking up arms against the Nationalist regime. This was a necessary, righteous, and correct course of action."²⁶ No such radio report, however, was received in Taiwan, due to the turbulent conditions on the island. Several years later, the CCP jettisoned this argument and adopted the view, maintained up to the present, that the Uprising represented a classic form of class struggle against the Chiang Kai-shek regime—a struggle that was part of the nationwide one guided by Mao Tse-tung during the 1940s.

The Reactions of Taiwanese

The Nationalist government announced on May 23, 1950, that investigations and trials of persons responsible for the Uprising had been completed and that the case was officially closed.[27] For many Taiwanese, however, the case could not be closed. Li Shih-chieh, a journalist stationed in Amoy in the late 1940s, moved to Taiwan in August 1949, and found that everyone, Taiwanese and Mainlanders alike, still talked about the Uprising. According to Li, "Everyone knew about the warlord behavior of Ch'en I, the harshly oppressive nature of his economic policies, the corrupt behavior of the officials who first arrived, and the immoral, improper ways in which the officials and soldiers behaved then—they never purchased bus tickets and would not queue up to board public transportation."[28] The Taiwanese and Mainlanders also knew that countless people, both women and men, had been killed in the streets, the marketplaces, and their homes after Nationalist troops landed in Keelung.

Taiwanese who blamed the KMT for the Uprising often directed their hatred at Mainlanders in general. Li Shih-chieh recalls a conversation he had with a Taiwanese at his relative's home shortly after his arrival in Taiwan in late 1949. Li's relative said:

"The Kuomintang massacred too many Taiwanese, and they really should never have done that. Looked at in this way, this incident already has created long-run enmity."

I said, "Didn't many Mainlanders also die? This incident really is a great tragedy! It is an enormous calamity!"

He replied: "That is right; there were great numbers of people killed. But the troops used machine guns to kill, and those who were killed in that way were Taiwanese. I also know that we should not hate the Mainlanders. For instance, we are the brothers and sisters of distant kinspeople from the Mainland. Moreover, you are a Mainlander, and I am Taiwanese. In reality, our ancestors are the same people. Is there any difference between Mainlanders and Taiwanese? But you do not realize that the government has handled the February 28 Incident in such a barbarous way. This has caused the Taiwanese to turn their hatred of the Kuomintang into hatred of all Mainlanders, hating the *a-shan* people as well as the *pan-shan* people. Although this belief is wrong, the Kuomintang should bear a large part of the responsibility."

After hearing these words, I was silent. For a long time, I lamented this state of affairs.[29]

For at least the next quarter of a century, some of the Taiwanese who had lived at the time of the Uprising despised the government and Mainlanders.[30] Their bitterness nourished an emerging movement aiming to overthrow the ROC and turn Taiwan into an independent nation. Although it is often referred to as the Taiwan Independence Movement (TIM), the groups belonging to it never coalesced to form a single, all-inclusive organization. Before the Uprising, no such movement had crystallized, although immigration and settlement under the Ch'ing dynasty and life under Japanese rule had given Taiwanese a distinct sense of destiny. Beginning in 1949, land reform also stimulated anti-KMT feeling. As Ralph Clough points out, land reform brought about "the alienation of many of the influential local gentry who were forced to give up their land." P'eng Ming-min, whose father was both a doctor and a landlord, roundly denounced it.

International circumstances also facilitated development of the TIM, especially the expulsion of the Republic of China from the United Nations in 1971 and other events compromising the ROC's legitimacy as an internationally recognized sovereign nation. Later still, growing awareness of disastrous conditions on the Mainland led to different reasoning. For many, the spectacle of Communist disaster vindicated the KMT; for others, it strengthened the feeling that reunification made no sense. Moreover, Western liberalism, increasingly powerful in Taiwan's intellectual circles, easily meshed with the demand that "Taiwan be ruled by Taiwanese" (*T'ai-jen chih T'ai*).

Chao Shao-k'ang, a KMT member of the Legislative Yüan, said in the late 1980s that the call of many Taiwanese for "democracy" has been only "an excuse with which to rationalize the demand for Taiwan independence," but Huang Yüeh-ch'in, a prominent academic and public figure, feels the substance of these popular demands is indeed a desire for democracy. Huang Yüeh-ch'in, however, also argues that as political pluralism developed with the founding of the Democratic Progressive Party (DPP) in 1986, politicians trying to woo voters away from the KMT evoked the idea of an independent Taiwan because they lacked any other significant issue.[31]

After 1947, the idea of independence came to be articulated in historical, legal, and political terms. The thought of P'eng Ming-min, a TIM leader, is a good example. In Chapter 2, we described the rise of his family to elite status after the Japanese took over Taiwan, his excellent education in Japanese schools and in Tokyo Imperial University, and the formation of his worldview as a young intellectual proud of his family status, devoted to liberalism and modernization, and filled with contempt for the KMT and its Confucian values.

In 1947, P'eng was a student at National Taiwan University who sympathized with the rioters without joining them. He had returned to Taiwan from Japan in January 1946 and promptly begun a career at the university, the Harvard of Taiwan. Cultivated as a gifted native son by famous Mainland scholars like Sa Meng-wu and Hu Shih and even by President Chiang Kai-shek, he was less than forty when he became chairman of the Department of Politics in 1961.[32] In 1964, however, he was arrested for trying to circulate 10,000 copies of a "Manifesto" calling for the overthrow of "the Chiang regime." His thought is summed up in this Manifesto and in his memoirs, written in the U.S. in 1971.[33] It can be analyzed in terms of six themes.

First, P'eng seeks to minimize the historical relations between Taiwan and Mainland China.[34] The Chinese ancestors of the Taiwanese, he implies, were already deserted by Ch'ing China, because it was the "unbearable" conditions in China that forced immigrants to hazard the settlement of that disease-ridden, uncivilized island. Moreover, far from encouraging these brave people, "China always regarded Taiwan as an island of barbarians, looking on the people there as rebels, bandits, pirates, misfits, and opium addicts."[35] In 1895, China then heartlessly abandoned them, handing them over to the Japanese without even consulting them. After that came half a century during which "Taiwan completely broke off all political and cultural relations with China."[36] Moreover, a similar break occurred in 1949 after Communist rule began on the Mainland. In other words, "the ties between Taiwan and the Chinese were loose before 1895," and from 1895 to the present, Taiwan "has been politically unified with China for only four years [1945–49]."[37]

Second, Taiwanese, loosely connected to China, "compared with Mainland Chinese, have lacked the burden of tradition" and so have been more open to modern ways, a trait already clear in the late nineteenth century, when Taiwan "became the most modernized part of the Ch'ing empire."[38]

Third, in Taiwan's experience, P'eng holds, the influence of Japan and the West has been largely beneficial, and that of China, largely harmful. Accompanied, paradoxically, by a continuing acceptance of everyday Confucian morality and customs, this low evaluation of Chinese culture has had few connections to Mainland iconoclasm and instead has stemmed from a lack of intellectual involvement in China's literary and intellectual heritage, from the practical economic mentality always basic to China's grass-roots culture, and from missionary influence. In P'eng's eyes, Western merchants, consular officials, and missionaries who came to Taiwan after the Opium War had only a beneficial influence.[39]

P'eng's ancestors, for instance, were poor farmers and fishermen until around 1885, when his grandfather became a cook for the Presbyterian medical missionary Thomas Barkley.[40] His grandfather was converted and "had a very happy relationship with the foreign missionaries and doctors, being extremely interested in Western culture and the rapid changes then occurring all around him."[41] This positive Presbyterian influence then merged with Japanese influence, when, in around 1910, P'eng's father won a Japanese scholarship to study medicine in Taipei and began the P'eng's ascent into elite circles.[42]

According to P'eng's memoirs, the modernizing Japanese influence on Taiwan was beneficial, except for the discriminatory practices imposed by the Japanese. P'eng's self-esteem was greatly enhanced by his successes in Japanese academic life. P'eng is also filled with enthusiasm for the civilization he observed in the West when he obtained his doctorate from the University of Paris in 1954 and participated in Henry Kissinger's Harvard seminars on international relations in 1956 and 1960.[43]

Conversely, P'eng feels that Chinese influence on Taiwan was almost entirely disastrous. Despite some last-minute reforms, the nineteenth-century Ch'ing administration in Taiwan was so bad that "even in China it was widely known for corruption and lack of ability."[44] Taking over in late 1945, the KMT was at least as bad, providing a shameful contrast with the Japanese colonial administration. Its officials and soldiers were corrupt, inefficient, and arrogant. It was undemocratic, not to mention its "slaughter of 20,000 of Taiwan's elite" after the February Uprising in order to destroy any potential political opposition from the landlord or middle classes.[45] It "opposed . . . any untraditional behavior, creative or critical thought, or independence of spirit . . . wanting the people of Taiwan to go back to the narrow-mindedness and conservatism of old China, a policy bound to have a frightening outcome."[46] Its goal to "Retake the Mainland" was preposterous and inflicted a huge burden of military expenses on the Taiwan taxpayer.[47]

Indeed, the KMT's entire economic policy undermined the hope of any economic growth or equity, because its heavy taxes "oppressed the impoverished, suffering masses"; unemployment was becoming ever more serious; population growth was aggravating poverty; the gap between rich and poor was creating instability; the government was guiding investment "blindly, without regard for economic principles"; and land reform was no more than a policy that complemented the terror of 1947 in order to wipe out the native landlord and middle classes.[48]

Besides bringing about economic disasters, P'eng maintains, the ROC was a weak government, dependent on the U.S. for survival and capable of selling Taiwan out to the Communists.[49] It was also an "illegal" government that "represented no one," neither the people in Taiwan nor those on the Mainland, the latter "having already chosen another government."[50]

Fourth, Taiwanese, having encountered the harmful influence of China and the hope of progress offered by the West, have always wanted the freedom to act in their own interest: "The history of Taiwan has mainly been the record of Taiwanese seeking self-determination and self-rule."⁵¹ That desire was reflected in a Ch'ing saying about Taiwan: "Every three years, a small uprising; every five years, a big one."⁵² When the Japanese took over in 1895, the Taiwanese fought back and established the Democratic State of Taiwan, which, P'eng claims, lasted 148 days.⁵³ Under the Japanese, armed resistance lasted until about 1915 and was replaced by the "movement for Taiwanese self-government" (*T'ai-wan tzu-chih yün-tung*), which forced the Japanese to allow some local, election-based consultative councils.⁵⁴ (The claim that armed resistance lasted until 1915 is not actually found in P'eng's memoirs but can be found in other TIM writings.⁵⁵) Then came the 1947 Uprising, an angry reaction to the political and economic oppression inflicted by the KMT.⁵⁶

P'eng grants that not all Taiwanese joined what he identifies as this struggle for freedom.⁵⁷ A good number have "ignorantly" or out of self-interest supported the KMT. For instance, he notes with dismay that "many people think that the Chiang regime's land reform policy was wise and benevolent."⁵⁸ When he was arrested in 1964 and assessed Taiwanese reaction to his plight, P'eng realized that he "had not yet really understood how many Taiwanese have already been corrupted to the point of voluntarily working for the KMT."⁵⁹ Nevertheless, "fellow citizens who love democracy and freedom" are to be found on every level of Taiwan's society, and so "our power to save ourselves is quickly growing."⁶⁰

Fifth, in this struggle for freedom, the need today is for a complete change of government. Though the word does not appear in P'eng's memoirs, he calls for revolution, a word appearing frequently in other TIM writings. The Taiwanese can accept neither KMT nor Communist rule, and they are deluded if they put their hope in "peacefully changing the government" or in "gradual reform."⁶¹ The only solution is to "overthrow the Chiang regime."⁶² Then "we" can set up a government that is "democratic";⁶³ that promotes economic growth free of "privilege" and "corruption";⁶⁴ that establishes a "society based on friendship, love, mutual trust, and mutual help"; and that is sovereign.⁶⁵

Taiwan's right to emerge as a sovereign nation, moreover, is supported by the controversial claim that the international documents ending Japanese sovereignty over Taiwan did not specify a formal, final transfer of sovereignty to any other political entity, and by the theory that sovereign statehood is based on a shared consciousness or will, rather than on a shared language or culture.⁶⁶

Thus, Taiwanese today need to "band together and struggle forward."⁶⁷ In 1964, P'eng said, "Our organization has already established close ties with comrades in the U.S., Japan, Canada, France, and Germany, and has obtained their enthusiastic support. When the time comes, our comrades will emerge from every corner of Taiwan and, hand-in-hand with their overseas supporters, will struggle forward."[68] This "movement of the Taiwanese people," however, welcomes sympathetic Mainlanders.[69]

Sixth, this movement is in accord with "the prevalent tendency in the world today."[70] This is illustrated by the support of prominent figures in the West, such as the Harvard professor Edwin O. Reischauer, a former U.S. ambassador to Japan, who wrote to P'eng in 1972, and Senator Edward Kennedy, who gave moral support. Moreover, the People's Republic will realize that its own interests will be served best by accepting a sovereign, friendly Taiwan.[71]

P'eng thus minimizes the historical ties between Taiwan and the Mainland, sees Taiwanese as exceptionally open to new values, and believes that China's influence on Taiwan has been harmful compared with that of Japan and the West. P'eng is proud of what he perceives as the historical struggle of the Taiwanese for self-rule, calling for a revolution to overthrow the KMT and establish Taiwan as a sovereign, democratic nation. This revolution, in P'eng's view, accords with the main tide of current world history.

P'eng Ming-min himself was trained in international aviation law, and much of the most sophisticated TIM thinking came to revolve around international law and geopolitics, thus minimizing the fuzzier questions of shared history and culture. This standpoint is reflected in a major essay written by Yao Chia-wen, the Chairman of the DPP, in early 1988. It defines Taiwan not as part of China but as the intersection between "the world's greatest continent and the world's greatest ocean," an island in the middle of the contest between "continental power" and "maritime power."[72] More radical TIM versions, however, simply deny that Taiwanese are ethnically Chinese, insist that Taiwanese culture is not a part of Chinese culture, and argue that the ROC's role in Taiwan is a form of colonialism.[73]

The Taiwan Independence Movement

Representing a spectrum of ideas, TIM leaders formed a variety of organizations and occasionally turned to violence, though sparingly, compared with other irredentist groups in the world. As a heterogeneous, amorphous movement filled with personality clashes, disagreements about whether to pursue violent revolution or peaceful reform, and tension between Taiwan and overseas elements, the TIM has survived until the present. We cannot do justice here to the complexities of the phenomenon but can give some highlights.

As the KMT cracked down on dissidence in 1947, "up to 3,000 [Taiwanese dissidents] managed to flee the island,"[74] including the Communist leader in the Taichung Uprising, Hsieh Hsüeh-hung; Thomas Lee (Liao Wen-i), a medical doctor; and Joshua Lee, his brother. Together with Hsieh, Thomas Lee founded the *T'ai-wan tsai-chieh-fang t'ung-meng* (Alliance for the Re-liberation of Taiwan) in 1948, often regarded as the beginning of the TIM.[75] In 1950, Thomas Lee started the Formosa Independence Party in Tokyo. In September 1955, a group of Taiwanese living in Tokyo established a provisional government to organize their anti-Nationalist government activities. During the 1950s and 1960s, Taiwanese activists in Japan sought in various ways to embarrass the Nationalists. They held public demonstrations at the Nationalist embassy; defaced public property belonging to the Nationalist government; published anti-Nationalist political tracts and a newspaper; smuggled their publications into Taiwan; and annually commemorated the 1947 Uprising. This movement in Japan suffered from factionalism, however, breaking up into the Democratic Independence Party, the Freedom Independence Party, the Young Formosan Association, and several small groups.[76] Personality clashes involving Thomas Lee were a major cause of fragmentation,[77] and on May 14, 1965, he left the movement and returned to Taiwan. The Nationalists pardoned him and returned his confiscated property.

In January 1970, Taiwanese dissidents in Japan, Europe, and the United States formed the Taiwan Independence Alliance (*T'ai-tu lien-meng*). A new leadership had begun to form, made up chiefly of graduates of Japanese and American universities who had studied at the best schools and universities in Taiwan, including National Taiwan University, and then gone overseas to continue their studies. The chairman of this new movement, Chang Ts'an-hung, was born in Tainan in 1936, graduated in chemistry from National Taiwan University, and obtained a doctorate from Rice University in Houston, Texas. Ts'ai T'ung-jung, another leading member, was born in Chia-i in 1935, graduated in political science from National Taiwan University and obtained his doctorate from the University of Tennessee. Wang Yü-te, one of the oldest leaders, was born in Tainan in 1924, attended Tokyo Imperial University in 1943, and after the February Uprising went to Japan to obtain a doctorate from the Faculty of Arts of Tokyo University. Huang Yu-jen was born in Tainan in 1932, graduated in economics from National Taiwan University, and obtained his doctorate in social science at Kyoto University.⁷⁸ Growing impatient, these and other young professionals in the Taiwan Independence Alliance began to advocate terrorism.

For instance, on April 24, 1970, Huang Wen-hsiung, an Alliance member, tried to assassinate Chiang Ching-kuo with a handgun in New York City. On August 9, 1979, Alliance members set off bombs at the offices of the Coordinating Council for North American Affairs (CCNAA) in Washington, D.C., and New York City. On December 4, 1979, an Alliance member assaulted an official of the Nationalist government at the Los Angeles CCNAA office. On April 6, 1980, near Los Angeles, an Alliance member detonated a bomb at the home of Wang Chih-hsiung, the son of the former Kaohsiung city mayor, Wang Yü-yün, killing the brother of Wang Chih-hsiung's wife.⁷⁹

Such terrorism reached a climax in 1979–83, reflecting a series of violent incidents occurring at that time in Taiwan, especially the December 10, 1979, riot in Kaohsiung. This riot, the major domestic political shock in Taiwan since the February Uprising, occurred when the leaders of the radical magazine *Mei-li-tao* (*Formosa*) tried to hold an illegal rally, seeking to generate a mass movement that would force the KMT to give up its hegemony. There was linkage between the *Mei-li-tao* group and the overseas Alliance—a linkage of overseas TIM and groups in Taiwan that was first established in 1977, when the famous Taiwanese politician Kuo Yü-hsin moved to the U.S. after losing an election for a seat in the Legislative Yüan. Then, in 1979 Hsü Hsin-liang, another famous Taiwanese politician, moved to the U.S. and began advocating violence.

By the late 1980s, however, radical TIM groups had declined in the face of majority sentiment in Taiwan, which put primacy on stability and peaceful change. More moderate TIM organizations include the Christian Association for Taiwanese Self-Determination (*T'ai-wan chi-tu-t'u tzu-chüeh hsieh-hui*), established in 1972 by a part of the Presbyterian Association (*Chang-lao chiao-hui*), a religious organization prominent in Taiwan since the late nineteenth century; and two organizations seeking reform by pressuring the KMT, the Formosan Association for Public Affairs (*T'ai-wan-jen kung-kung shih-wu hsieh-hui*, established in 1982, and the World Federation of Taiwanese Associations *Shih-chieh T'ai-wan t'ung-hsiang lien-ho-hui*). The United Front for Establishing Taiwan as a Nation (*T'ai-wan chien-kuo lien-ho chen-hsien*) is yet another organ. It goes back at least to 1979 and has members who also belong to one or more of the other groups.

P'eng Ming-min's role was more independent. Arrested in Taiwan in

The Nature and Aftermath of the Tragedy 191

1964 and later released from jail, he fled from Taiwan to Sweden in the winter of 1969–70. Shortly thereafter, he went to the U.S. and temporarily assumed a teaching position at the University of Michigan.

With the founding of the DPP in 1986, the TIM entered a new stage. The ideal of an independent Taiwan is shared by many if not most members of the DPP, some of whom inveigh against the "sinister culture" (*yin-hsieh wen-hua*) allegedly imposed on Taiwan by Chinese. The DPP position is illustrated by a report in the March 21, 1988, issue of the *Taiwan Tribune*, published in California. It describes a conference held March 15 in T'ao-yüan (near Taipei) by a branch of the DPP to discuss whether the DPP should break the law by inserting into its platform the statement, "People have the freedom to call for the independence of Taiwan."

More than one hundred local DPP members attended the conference, as well as DPP leaders like Yao Chia-wen, then the DPP chairman. Huang Hua, the person who insisted on inserting the statement into the platform, said, "If we want Taiwan to have a truly democratic culture, we must destroy the sinister culture formed by the dictatorship that the Chinese have so long imposed. . . . Our purpose in founding the DPP certainly does not stop with elections. It is to allow the Taiwanese to determine their own future." Arguing for a more cautious approach, another DPP member said, "I have always called for the independence of Taiwan, and I never imagined that today I would be asked to give the counterargument on such a question. . . . [Yet] the most important thing to know today is the advantage and disadvantage of placing [this statement] into our platform."[80]

As this passage illustrates, the TIM spirit is alive in the DPP, but the DPP has had to adjust to the new political environment created by the KMT, which began carrying out political reforms in 1986. Since the KMT came under the leadership of a Taiwanese in 1988 and has taken convincing steps to turn the ROC into a democracy in the Western, liberal sense, it is no longer easy to associate the ideal of an independent Taiwan with the struggle for liberation from an alien, repressive regime. The DPP has so far been unable to broaden its popular base. Even radical DPP leaders like Chu Kao-cheng were insisting in 1989 that because a new, hopeful, and more democratic era had begun in Taiwan, a revolutionary or radical line was no longer appropriate. In the increasingly pluralistic political life to come, the passions ignited by the Uprising will still play a role. Yet the economic, political, social, and cultural merging of Taiwanese and Mainlanders and a growing political spirit of moderation will also be important.

KMT Policy in the Wake of the Uprising

Can we, then, say that the KMT policy for dealing with the repercussions of the Uprising was a failure? This policy alternated between silence and attempts to blame the Uprising on Communists and "ambitious" Taiwanese. By refusing to discuss the Uprising candidly and to accept responsibility for misrule and violent excesses during the spring of 1947, the government made itself vulnerable to criticism. Yet the government may not have survived an uninhibited public discussion of the tragedy before it had built up the overall record of progress which by now has won so much Taiwanese support.

The origins of the policies that led to progress are only now being carefully studied. Yet clearly the Uprising itself served as a shock that stimulated new KMT thinking about Taiwan. This shock was quickly followed by another, still more horrendous one—the humiliating, catastrophic collapse on the Mainland. Several prescient passages in government documents written immediately after the Uprising (such as the April 1947 report by Yang Liang-kung and Ho Han-wen) called for the conversion of Taiwan into a "model" of modernization for all of China. Moreover, in 1947, officials already were becoming much more aware of the problems caused by government controls restricting trade, as illustrated by General Pai Ch'ung-hsi's recommendations in April 1947. This was an initial source for the strengthened appreciation of free enterprise that increasingly displaced the KMT's socialist bent in the late 1950s and that contributed so much to the "Taiwan miracle" of the 1960s. Moreover, in 1947, steps were already being taken to bring more Taiwanese into the provincial administration, and the need for local elections was repeatedly stressed in documents reflecting on the lessons of the Uprising.

The dictatorial aspects of the ROC have not been fully eliminated even today, but the political and economic progress made since 1947 is a familiar story that needs to be mentioned only briefly here.

There had been some local elections under the Japanese, and more were held by the ROC in 1946. In 1950, a systematic election schedule was set up for many positions below the central government level. In 1951, the first elections to the Taiwan Provincial Assembly were held. In 1969, the precedent was established, albeit on a very small scale, of elections to choose representatives at the central government level. The 1977 elections were the first marked by serious contests between KMT and non-KMT (*Tang-wai*) candidates. During the 1980 elections, it became clear that educational institutions, previously channels for the creation of propaganda for KMT candidates, began to express support for politicians opposing the KMT. During the period 1986–89, martial law was ended; opposition to the KMT crystallized into a second, major, legal political party (the DPP); and the way was cleared for full democratization of the three electoral organs on the level of the central government. This political breakthrough has been praised by observers as different as the DPP radical Chu Kao-cheng, the Mainland dissident Wang Jo-wang, and the American political scientist Myron Weiner.

We do not know precisely why this breakthrough occurred, but we can pinpoint contributing factors. Export growth led to economic growth, which in turn urbanized 80 percent of the population and created a large middle class. An excellent educational system produced the highly skilled work force needed for export growth as well as a citizenry increasingly interested in political participation. The institutionalization of a high degree of ideological or intellectual pluralism facilitated broad access to the global pool of political and economic ideas. Civic discourse was greatly affected by the government's propagation of standard Confucian values, which, emphasizing the moral autonomy and dignity of the individual as well as ascetic group norms, meshed, to some extent, with the Western, liberal ideal of democracy. The ideological commitment of the KMT as well as that of its critics to this liberal ideal greatly shaped political discourse. Pressure from media and Congressional circles in the U.S. increased that commitment. Also important were the increasingly harmonious relations between Taiwanese and Mainlanders, evidenced by frequent intermarriage. As Taiwanese entered the elite strata, playing an expanding and sometimes dominant role in the business world, the professions, the academic world, the state bureaucracy, and the KMT, not to mention electoral politics, the sharing of political power between Mainlanders and Taiwanese became both easier and inevitable. Finally, the leadership of Chiang Ching-kuo, president from 1978 to 1988, actualized his Party's ideological commitment to democracy.

The "glooming peace" that followed the 1947 tragedy covered Taiwan like a blanket of ashes laid down by a forest fire, but in these ashes the seedlings of change and hope soon appeared.

APPENDIXES

APPENDIX A

Demands presented by the Taiwan Resolution Committee to Governor-General Ch'en I on March 7, 1947

We have used the translation from Kerr, *Formosa Betrayed*, Appendix I, pp. 475–79, for rendering the thirty-two demands beginning with II.B (Political Aspects). For some reason Kerr omitted the seven demands under I (Policies to Resolve the Current Situation) and the three demands under II.A (Military Aspects), making his presentation very misleading. We have occasionally modified Kerr's translation.

I. Policies to Resolve the Current Situation

1. All military forces stationed on the island should temporarily disarm and turn over their weapons to the local Resolution Committees and Military Police, who will manage these weapons so as to prevent further bloody conflict.
2. After disarming the military forces, the Military Police, unarmed police, and the mass organizations will be in charge of public security.
3. As soon as there is no administrative military threat in any of the localities, military conflict should cease. People will notify the Resolution Committee of any corrupt officials, whether Mainlanders or Taiwanese. The committee, along with military and civil police, will then arrest them. Those officials should then be sent to the courts to await trial. They should not be killed, and further trouble should be avoided.
4. As for political reform, anyone can propose a list of demands to the Resolution Committee and await a solution.
5. Do not try to solve problems by force. The government should not mobilize any military force or request the central government to send more forces to Taiwan, because that action will cause more bloody disasters and the interference of international forces.
6. Before this political problem can be resolved, the administration should consult with the Resolution Committee before taking action, whether military or political, in order to prevent the people from doubting the administration's intentions to avoid any misunderstandings.
7. The administration will not charge any persons with responsibility for being

involved in this Incident. Neither should the administration use the Incident as a pretext to arrest people in the future. The administration will pay a proper compensation for those wounded and killed.

II. Basic Solutions to the Current Problem

A. Military Aspects

1. Military forces without strict discipline and without education should not be sent to Taiwan.

2. The central government can draft Taiwanese military soldiers to defend Taiwan.

3. Before the Civil War ends, the people will oppose any central government conscription of Taiwanese except for the purpose of defending Taiwan, in order to prevent Taiwan from becoming involved in the Civil War.

B. Political Aspects

1. A provincial self-government law shall be enacted and shall become the supreme norm for political affairs within this province, so that Dr. Sun Yat-sen's ideal of National Reconstruction may be realized.

2. Popular election of prefectural magistrates and city mayors shall be held before June of this year, and at the same time there shall be new elections of members to all prefectural and municipal councils.

3. The appointment of commissioners shall have the approval of the People's Political Council after new elections have been held. The People's Political Council shall be newly elected before June 1947. In the meantime, such appointments shall be submitted by the Governor-General to the Resolution Committee for discussion, approval, or rejection.

4. More than two-thirds of the commissioners shall be appointed from those who have lived in this province for more than [number missing from typescript] years. (It is most desirable that such persons only shall be appointed to the Secretariat and to the Department of Civil Affairs.)

5. The posts of the Commissioner for the Department of Police Affairs, and of directors for all prefectural or municipal police bureaus ought to be filled by Taiwanese. The special armed police contingents and the armed police maintained by the Railway Department and the Department of Industry and Mining shall be immediately abolished.

6. All chiefs of local courts of justice and all chief prosecutors in all local courts of justice shall be Taiwanese.

7. No government organs other than the civil police can arrest criminals.

8. The military police shall arrest no one other than military personnel.

9. Arrest or confinement of a political nature shall be prohibited.

10. Unarmed gatherings and organizations shall enjoy complete freedom.

11. Complete freedom of speech, of the press, and of the right to strike shall be realized. The system requiring registration of newspapers to be published shall be abolished.

12. The regulations in force covering the formation of popular organizations shall be abolished.

13. The regulations governing the [Nationalist Party] scrutiny of the capacity of candidates for membership in representative organs of public opinion shall be abolished.

14. Regulations governing the election of members of various grades in representative organs of public opinion shall be revised.

15. A uniform progressive income tax shall be levied. No other sundry taxes shall be levied, except the luxury tax and the inheritance tax.

16. Managers in charge of all public enterprises shall be Taiwanese.

17. A Committee for Inspecting Public Enterprises, elected by the people, shall be established. The disposal of Japanese properties shall be entirely entrusted to the provincial government. A committee for management of industries taken over from the Japanese shall be established. Taiwanese shall be appointed to more than half of these committee posts.

18. The Monopoly Bureau shall be abolished. A system for rationing daily necessities shall be instituted.

19. The Foreign Trade Bureau shall be abolished.

20. All propaganda committees shall be abolished.

21. The majority of judges, prosecutors, and other court staff members shall be Taiwanese.

22. More than half the Committee of Legal Affairs shall be Taiwanese, and the chairman of the Committee shall be elected from among its members.

On March 7 at 3:30 P.M., the Resolution Committee decided to add the following demands to those above.

1. As many Taiwanese as possible shall be appointed to the army, navy, and air force posts on Taiwan.

2. The Garrison Command Headquarters must be abolished to avoid the misuse of military privilege.

3. The Office of the Governor-General shall be converted into a provincial government. Before this reform is approved by the central government, the Office of the Governor-General shall be reorganized by the Resolution Committee through popular elections so that righteous and able officers can be appointed.

4. A Political Affairs Bureau of the Resolution Committee must be established by March 15. Rules for its organization call for a candidate to be elected by representatives of each village, town, and district, and then be elected by the prefectural or city People's Political Council. The numbers of candidates to be elected in each city and prefecture are as follows: for districts (*hsien*), Taipei, 3; Hsin-chu, 3; Taichung, 4; Tainan, 4; Kaohsiung, 3; Hua-lien, 1; Taitung, 1; Peng-hu (the Pescadores), 1; for cities, Taipei, 2; Hsin-chu, 1; Taichung, 1; Tainan, 1; Kaohsiung, 1; Keelung, 1; Changhua, 1; Chia-i, 1; P'ing-tung, 1.

5. The abolition of Vocational Guidance Camps [an internment camp for persons the government decides to mold into "useful citizens"] and other unnecessary institutions must be determined by the Political Affairs Bureau of the Resolution Committee after that body has deliberated.

6. The central government will be asked to authorize the provincial government to dispose of Japanese properties.

7. The political and economic rights and social position of the aborigines must be guaranteed.

8. Workmen's protection measures must be put into effect from June 1, 1947.

9. Detained war criminals and those suspected of treason must be released unconditionally.

10. The central government must be asked to pay for the 150,000 tons of food exported to the Mainland according to the price quotation at the time of export. [This proposal was designed to recover, if possible, some of the costs of the Resolution Committee's administrative work.]

APPENDIX B

Governor-General Ch'en I's Radio Speech on December 31, 1946

(*T'ai-wan hsin-sheng-pao*, Jan. 1, 1947, p. 4)

Today is the last day of the 35th year of the Republic of China [1946]. In my radio message last year, I had outlined the administrative program for the current year. The time is suitable to review our performance: what tasks we have done well, what tasks have not been completed, and what tasks we have not yet begun. In addition, we should also set forth our goals for the coming year.

As projected in my last New Year's Eve speech, our goals were classified according to three major categories: political reconstruction, economic reconstruction, and psychological reconstruction. Among these were such items as reorganizing the various levels of local administrative organs [from state/county/township/street/village into country/city/town/district]; establishing people's representative organs; improving the attitude of our police; promoting local self-government among the aborigines; reforming the personnel system; revising the legal codes; reviving important industrial production; reorganizing the transport system; strengthening our financial administration; developing trade; giving increased emphasis to language and history in school education; initiating refresher courses for training teachers on a rotational basis; establishing a normal college; and enlarging the enrollment in our educational institutions. Some of these goals have been accomplished and others are still being pursued. I will not delve into any details of the progress; anyone wanting to know more should check various relevant reports. However, there are some issues that I would like to briefly discuss.

The Diabolical Policy Used by Japanese Imperialists Toward Taiwan

One of the most vicious policies used by the Japanese imperialists to rule Taiwan was to keep our Taiwan brethren ignorant and restrict their opportunity to gain a higher education and achieve elevated positions in society. Our Taiwan brethren had little or no chance to develop and exercise their abilities, and they were compelled to a fate of working in middle-range or lower positions in all occupations.

According to the principles of our nation's founder, Dr. Sun Yat-sen, I firmly advocate equal opportunity for education and employment. For the field of education, we made efforts to enlarge the enrollment, to create another Normal College to train more qualified teachers, to establish more educational institutes for law as well as technical and vocational colleges, and to send qualified students to prestigious universities in other provinces. We organized preparatory classes for the benefit of students who had high potential but who had failed to pass the matriculation exams to enter National Taiwan University. If we compare [our record] with the 1944 record during the Japanese occupation, high school students show an increase of 15,000 and junior college and university students another 2,500, which reflects a significant expansion in higher education opportunities for our Taiwanese brethren.

Turning to employment in government, for 1945 we find that only one Taiwanese served at the designated-appointment rank, 27 at the recommended-appointment rank, and 3,681 at the commissioned-appointment rank. Today our records show 27 officials serving at the designated-appointment rank, 817 at the recommended-appointment rank, and 12,575 at the commissioned-appointment rank, representing an increase ranging from 400 to 3,000 percent. The number of teachers in primary and secondary schools increased by 9,000. Judiciary and civil examinations and Naval Academy enrollment exams are now entirely open to all Taiwanese.

Another nefarious policy used by the Japanese imperialists was to rule through slavery. They treated our Taiwan countrymen as slaves having no freedom, denying them freedom of speech and the freedom of assembly. Although state, county, and city councils existed at that time, the Japanese administration appointed half of them and even then on a very limited basis. The Japanese government did not allow newspapers to print any unfavorable reports. Public opinion and public representative organs simply did not exist during the Japanese occupation.

In contrast, today, representative organs of the people have been organized at different levels, with delegates elected by the public and given full freedom of speech. No matter what comments and criticisms they express, this government will always respect their freedom and will reply on the basis of law and reason. We have not imposed any restrictions or illegally interfered with newspapers, their editorial commentary, or their factual reporting. Our Taiwan compatriots have elected their representatives to attend the national administrative conference and the National Assembly meetings, as well as to participate in national affairs and to draft our national constitution. We simply cannot compare today's freedoms in Taiwan with those of yesterday.

The above two points will serve to provide a sharp contrast between the conditions under Japanese imperialism and those of the Three Principles of the People. Glancing back at last year, I cannot but be deeply impressed by the power of the human spirit. At first, we confronted many difficulties, such as establishing local administrative offices and representative organs, changing the curriculum for the schools and teachers, teaching the official Chinese language, repatriating Japanese civilians and prisoners of war, recruiting technical personnel, reviving the transport system and production in our industries, and solving the food shortage problem. After having spent considerable time and effort to complete successfully various projects and having solved certain problems, I have come to the conclusion that there is no issue without challenge. But all dilemmas can be overcome through meticulous planning, a systematic approach, and with undaunted courage and a persistent effort. Instead of retreating under pressure, we must face reality with courage and overcome our difficulties through positive action. Based on the experience of the past year, we should have full confidence in our capabilities to undertake reconstruction.

After reviewing the past year, I am now of the opinion that, although we have been persevering in our efforts, they are still not "rapid" enough, not "pragmatic" enough, and not "solid" enough. You will recall that I had exhorted each person to do the work of two or three and to accomplish in one day the tasks usually requiring two or three days. We have failed to accomplish that. Inasmuch as the current year is coming to an end, I hope that you will redouble your efforts in the new year and surpass the achievements of the past year. Here is the gist of the goals for the coming year.

The current year can be described as the year for drafting the Constitution, but the coming year will be the year for implementing the Constitution. It goes without saying that the most outstanding item is the preparatory work for implementing the Constitution, which involves two aspects: namely, administrative authority and political rights. All public functionaries carrying out their administrative duties must have a complete command of the official Chinese language, and an oral and written exam will represent the necessary prerequisite for a full understanding of the law, and hence, the proper execution of their duties. On the other hand, citizens must possess a full command of the official Chinese language in order to fully understand the meaning of the Constitution so that they can exercise their political rights. For public functionaries, who now number more than 20,000, we will conduct a daily two-hour class for one year to provide them with language training to enhance their administrative knowledge and skills. For the more than two million citizens, we will issue publications to give them knowledge about the Constitution and their constitutional rights. For national reconstruction, perfecting local self-government represents a primary condition for the Constitution's rules, which are scheduled to be implemented in the coming year. Therefore, the local self-government system first must be perfected by accelerating the role of county government in their economic functions, training people about the four powers endowed to them under the Constitution, and, finally, improving the caliber of administrative cadres in all levels of local government organs.

The cornerstone for economic reconstruction requires stepping up production in 1947, which I hereby proclaim the "Production Year." Our plan differs from the Japanese economic plan, which was designed only to rob profits from the people in order to support Japanese military aggression. Our plan is based on a close coordination of national economic development which specifically emphasizes the improvement of the people's livelihood. Our best guideline is to develop those areas that the Japanese administration entirely neglected, like mechanizing agriculture and building the fertilizer manufacturing industry, as well as the textile and glass-manufacturing industries. Our second guideline is to unify and modernize the management of government-operated enterprises with a view to improving work efficiency, so as to surpass even that of private enterprise by minimizing the number of staff and amount of waste through reducing production costs and improving product quality. We will establish standard procedures for devising efficient systems for personnel, accounting, procurement, secretarial support, production, marketing, and auditing. Our third guideline is to establish an overall agency responsible for coordinating all efforts and targets of the state-operated enterprises which are interrelated yet not independent of each other from any overall point of view. And finally, we must have long-range planning to ensure success. Hence, our plan will be called the "Five-Year Economic Reconstruction Plan."

When talking about increased production, we should not forget the aim of improving the people's living standards. What first comes to my mind is a plan to redistribute farmlands originally held by Japanese private individuals and government agencies to Taiwanese farmers who can cultivate them. Steps also should be taken to help them organize cooperative farms that utilize modern agricultural equipment and techniques which can augment farm yield and income. We hope that between 200,000 and 400,000 tenant farmers (including family members) can be elevated from tenant-farmer status to owner-farmers. Second, we hope that one-half or one-third of the farmers will join the farmers' cooperative associations, which will arrange, through their transactions, better purchasing and more efficient transportation, along with new joint public-interest programs for improving agricultural technology. That action also could enhance farmer income. Third, the past year did witness the appearance of some new, comfortable homes in villages, and the farming people wore more fashionable clothing, even though farmers' income only registered a very slight increase and living standards did not rise by any significant degree. Farmers are enjoying more opportunities for education and recreation, and suffering far less from illness and disease. Fourth, in the factories, we have set up employee welfare cooperatives to improve worker livelihood. We will place continuing emphasis on implementing these four programs. I have particularly discussed the farmers and workers because they make up the majority and have suffered the most. As the Executive Yüan has approved the "Plan for Lease of Government-Owned Land to Farmers" and the Supreme National Defense Council has approved, we will take concrete steps next year to establish cooperative farms.

Psychological Reconstruction—Emphasizing Language and History in Education

As for psychological reconstruction, we have made positive efforts to emphasize language and history in our education with the view of strengthening national awareness. We have also taken steps to train more qualified teachers, to increase the enrollment of students as a way of broadening educational opportunities, to revitalize vocational colleges and higher educational institutions as well as research institutes, libraries, and museums, and to increase translation services and publishing agencies to elevate cultural standards. These tasks have been carried out this year and they will be continued throughout next year. No effort has been initiated this year to organize any academic screening agency to increase cooperation among research institutes, among government units, or among industrial enterprises. We shall proceed with this project in the coming year on a scale to be determined by available human and financial resources.

In short, major attention this current year has been centered on the takeover of Taiwan from Japanese occupation, on reorganization, and on the maintenance of normalcy along existing patterns. For next year, we must go one step further by emphasizing creative plans to make greater improvement. Instead of stressing the "quantity" of work, which was this year's theme, equal attention will be paid to "quality" from now on. Most of the programs embarked upon this year, such as the Mandarin language and Chinese literature training, increasing opportunities for education and employment, promoting local self-government of aborigines, establishing people's representative organs, and upholding the freedom of speech, were intended to create a greater public awareness of nationalism and the rights of the people, with less being done to raise living standards. We took that course because there were too many urgent matters that required immediate attention. For next year, we will place special emphasis on raising living standards of the people by equalizing land ownership and developing national resources.

It is my sincere hope that all our Taiwan compatriots and all our public servants will join hands tomorrow, the first day of the new year, to undertake the new task of reconstructing a new Taiwan under the Three Principles of the People. That goal always remains our unforgettable aim.

APPENDIX C

Governor-General Ch'en I's Speech at an Administrative Conference

(*T'ai-wan hsin-sheng-pao*, Jan. 9–10, 1947, p. 2)

Dear Comrades:

We did not convene this administrative conference until today because of the urgent tasks connected with the takeover of Taiwan from Japanese occupation: reorganization and repatriation of Japanese civilians and prisoners of war. These matters gave us no time for consultation and discussion with you. The main purpose of this meeting is to hammer out a plan which will bring our newly recovered Taiwan speedily into the path of true democracy. I would like to discuss here two points: namely, confidence in ourselves, and strict observance of the law.

Confidence in Ourselves

Many people have been very apprehensive because China traditionally has been an autocratic monarchy. All kinds of obstacles are bound to arise to prevent our creating a democratic system. Many people fear we cannot do a good job, or that the task cannot be done at all. This psychology of defeatism must be totally rejected. We must develop an unflagging confidence in our abilities to bring about democratic rule in our country, even surpassing that of other advanced democracies. Our National Father had this kind of confidence when he first started the Revolution some sixty years ago. Each and every one of us, and the cadres for bringing about national reconstruction in particular, must forge and strengthen this confidence. If we can devote ourselves to the cause, a democratic system can, and will, become a reality.

To inspire the people to have a firm belief in democracy, we must first produce some concrete acts of representative democracy as examples for all to see; without these, there can be no foundation for trust. The accomplishments of the past year can serve this purpose. In spite of different criticisms voiced from various quarters, the foundation for winning the public's confidence for democracy has, nevertheless, been created.

But what constructive examples of democratic practice have we really achieved? One example is that upon our arrival in Taiwan, we established public representative councils. Many friends suggested to me that, because Taiwan had just been liberated from enemy oppression, there was no hurry to create such representative councils, which might cause unnecessary complications. But in my opinion, we are here to serve the people, not to behave as bureaucrats and rule over them. Once our officials reject these selfish views, the people will become as patriotic as we are. What, then, is there to fear from the people? Lying ahead is the wide and smooth path leading to democracy. With this confidence, I had representative councils established at various levels with no misgivings at all.

At the outset, the provincial and county representatives enjoyed their freedom, after having been liberated from enemy tyranny, but they engaged in far too much free speech. Those people not accustomed to democratic practices must have felt it intolerable when provincial assemblymen lashed out with severe criticisms against the government. But tolerance must be exercised in order to cultivate and build up confidence in a democratic system. Constructive criticisms should be accepted, and derogatory criticisms can be heard, but should be disregarded. In due course, people will realize the true value of free speech, and they will apply reason and intellect in using that power. This can be readily observed by the progress at the second annual general meeting of the Provincial Assembly. The representatives enjoyed the same degree of freedom, and they were as enthusiastic in their comments. Yet there was an obvious difference in progress as compared to the previous conference.

As for the media, freedom of public opinion has been given full respect to elicit a true democratic atmosphere. Taiwan's newspapers are free to publish any criticisms of the government. Criticisms with merit are accepted. Groundless charges and wild accusations, which do not merit any rebuttal, will simply be disregarded. In this age of democracy, we must have the grace to tolerate opposition, especially as it is inevitable. At one time, newspapers in Nanking and Shanghai made malicious attacks, describing Taiwan as a hell in this life. Some friends remarked that more publicity work should be done outside of this province. But in my opinion the facts are more effective than propaganda, and they are more eloquent than any argument. There is no need to overreact to reports that distorted the facts, for the truth will eventually prevail. It is true that the comments by assembly members or the newspaper editorials carry considerable influence. Public opinion has often been looked upon by many with mixed feelings of respect and fear. It is my opinion, however, that if one devotes oneself fully to public service without any selfish designs, there is no need to be afraid of public opinion, which in any case can be turned into a weapon for our use.

In fact, it is much easier to be a politician in China than in Europe or America. In the past, public functionaries in China were bureaucrats who looked down upon the people. To promote public welfare was a matter that could not have been further from their minds. If we public functionaries today could abandon such bureaucratic ways of thinking, and serve the people with sincerity, it would be very easy to win over the people's support. Even if our abilities are not sufficiently adequate, the public would still trust us. It is this belief that has given me the courage to do what I have done. Instead of being afraid, I welcome and hope to cooperate with the press. The fact that our achievements in Taiwan have effectively counteracted all the malicious reporting about us illustrates another big step forward in our democracy.

Next on our agenda for promoting a democratic system is to implement local self-government at the county level. As a basic unit, the county government will be required to exercise administrative and economic control on its own. In the past administrative system, the central government had total control over provincial governments, which in turn had total control over county governments. As a result, there was little flexibility on the part of local governments to take initiatives on their own. This change is designed to utilize more manpower for our reconstruction programs.

Our National Father, Dr. Sun, had exhorted us to catch up with the most advanced democracies. In the field of scientific research and mechanical engineering, we are still so backward that it is impossible to attain that goal in the immediate future. Yet we, as well as the 6.3 million people in Taiwan, could and should exert our maximum efforts toward achieving that goal. We will now adopt a policy to "release and delegate authority" to the county and city governments. This administrative conference is convened with a view to ensuring that the county and city administrations fully understand the motivation behind this policy and implement it accordingly.

The "release and delegation of authority" policy should also be applied beyond the county and city governments to the township and district offices. The latter units should also be allocated appropriate funds along with the appropriate authority. An efficient administrative system can thus be brought into being if all officers will tackle their duties in a responsible spirit, instead of referring them to their respective superiors for decision.

A majority of our people are very observant. They know exactly when the government works for their welfare and exactly when they are being cheated. If opposition still persists when we do everything for the public good, in all sincerity without any selfish designs, a careful scrutiny must then be made to determine whether there are any mistakes or errors in our publicity or conduct or that of our subordinates. We have to be sure that people also know our determination for democracy. During the 51 years that Taiwan was under Japanese occupation, government officials sat high up, treating the populace as dirt under their feet. All the people could hope for was that some benevolent officials would eventually come and extend small favors to them. The people were never permitted to take any initiative to participate in government. Now that the situation has been changed, we must cultivate public confidence in democratic government, make them understand the true meaning of democracy and the Constitution, and develop their ability to participate in democratic activities. We, the public functionaries, must not entertain any fear that the people have too much power. This attitude must be changed. If we have done nothing against the public interest, why should we be afraid of the people? All public functionaries must have firm confidence in leading the people onto the path of democracy.

A Law-Abiding Spirit

Intellectuals today are generally lacking a spirit to "abide by the law." They frequently claim that as long as they can answer to their conscience, minor mistakes are excused. But society must be governed by the rule of law and legal conduct, not by conscience. After all, conscience itself is invisible, and if it does exist, conduct represents it. Abiding by the law and democracy are inseparable. With our Constitution, which forms the basis of all other law codes, we must study to understand and strictly observe its stipulations. The people and public functionaries are invited to pay special attention to Chapter 2 of the Constitution. Articles 7 through 24 list in full the basic freedoms of the people, which are subject to several conditions: namely, (1) freedoms of other people cannot be violated; (2) peace and order in society must be maintained; and (3) the public interest must be promoted.

Under the monarchical, dictatorial system, emperors and their officials could do whatever they wanted in total disregard of the freedom of others, social peace and order, and the public interest. Public functionaries today are forbidden such action, as set forth in Article 24 of the Constitution, which states: "For the infringement of freedoms and rights of the people, the public functionary shall be subject not only to the penalty of the law, but also to criminal and civil responsibilities. Any citizen so victimized may appeal to the government, in accordance with the law, for indemnity for all losses sustained thereof." In the past, officials would invariably and vehemently oppose this rule, for from their viewpoint, why be an official if one is subject to such restrictions? But we must now realize that today's public functionaries are not lords over the masses, but servants of the public, and their primary duty is to diligently serve the people. All cadres should study Chapter 2 of the Constitution, try to realize the freedoms and rights of the people, and refrain from committing any acts to violate the Constitution which might subject them to the penalty of the law. To interfere with the freedoms and rights of the people, even with good intentions, is just as bad as any malicious interference. We must not have any doubt about that, and we must maintain an unswerving belief in the Constitution, which was written and approved by the National Assembly at fully attended sessions to represent the founding of the nation. Unlike a newspaper editorial or a magazine comment, the Constitution, once promulgated, must be implemented to the letter. Amendments to the Constitution may be considered only after a certain number of years, when the passage of time requires certain revisions to meet changing conditions. How could we know whether the Constitution is suitable or not when it has not yet been implemented? There is no Constitution in the world which can be billed as absolutely perfect. Even near-perfection can only be attained through revisions after making experiments. Obstacles are bound to rise in the course of implementing the Constitution. And it is our responsibility to render sincere explanations to the people, repeating these daily if necessary, until the meaning of the Constitution is fully understood. Once the people have become aware of that meaning, and approve, implementing the Constitution will be much easier.

In the old days, official status was sought for reasons of personal benefit. In the era of democracy, public functionaries must not only do what is right, but they, like artists, must enjoy the satisfaction of a job well done, such as running the government well, completing a painting masterpiece, or producing a beautiful piece of sculpture. As public servants, they must feel for the people, and feel their happiness as well as their suffering. There is no glory but the glory of the people. The public functionary glories only in the trust that people place in him, and the votes that they cast in his favor. In the monarchical system, the emperor was only one person, and could be easily isolated, deceived, and pleased. It is not so when the populace becomes the master. Only through loyal and diligent service can the public functionary win the public trust.

But if the people are ignorant, there is the possibility that ambitious politicians may work in collusion with hooligans, landlord-racketeers, and mobsters to manipulate the rights of the people for personal gain, but under the guise of democracy. In order to achieve true democracy, it is of primary importance that the people be able to differentiate between right and wrong. And here, there is a need to provide them with higher education and to improve their living standards with more financial independence. Only when the farmers and workers are not dependent upon credit from racketeers at usurious interest rates can they maintain their independent judgment and not be influenced by the racketeers. Most of the people must be adequately educated and made financially independent. In a true democracy, the voters must be able to make an independent choice and cast their votes freely according to their own will. And this task confronts the staff members of the county and city governments today.

The purpose of this meeting today is to map out a plan of preliminary work to implement the Constitution. As indicated above, impressive achievements can be expected if we only will have confidence in our ability to build up a democratic system, uphold a law-abiding spirit, and reconstruct a new China in line with the Three Principles of the People. China is ranked as one of the "four major powers of the world," and I am personally still not satisfied with that. It is my contention, without any exaggeration, that China can become the one and only major power in the world if we will relentlessly exert our combined efforts to reconstruct the nation with confidence. The steps to attain that goal include: (1) to establish concrete plans; (2) to forge ahead in an orderly manner without confusion; and (3) to intensify our efforts continuously without interruption. I sincerely hope that you will jointly work out solutions to the technical problems for implementing our program.

Finally, I want to point out for your discussion that there are many issues which were regarded as of little importance in the old days, but which now merit serious attention in this era of democracy.

During the monarchical period, there was no sense of public order. Everyone behaved as he liked, in total disregard for the convenience of others. For instance, it was not unusual for hotel guests to make annoying noises deep in the night which, of course, disturbed the sleep of other hotel guests. Yet when they were requested to be quiet, they would lose their temper. To keep cleanliness and order in public places was an act unknown to them. Writing poems and drawing paintings on the walls at scenic spots and tourist resorts were considered by the authors as artistic behavior of the culture. Yet they were really soiling and damaging public property. Crashing ticket counters or bolting through exits after the curtain falls was a common phenomenon in theaters. Correcting such behavior is a must.

Whereas one's liberty is valuable, respecting the liberty of others is just as important. Freedom must be kept within limits so that one does not infringe upon the freedom of others. Let us take a minor case as an example. To be neatly dressed or to be unkempt in appearance was regarded in the past as a personal matter of no concern to one's fellow beings, or as a matter of personal freedom. But today the viewpoint is very different. Strictly speaking, the unkempt look of a person may be regarded as an infringement of the freedom of others to admire beauty. As a human being, one should not make oneself an object of loathing. No one would vote for a person who is repugnant and disliked.

Many people are not concerned about maintaining cleanliness. For some, their outer garments might look reasonably clean, but their undergarments are dirty and unwashed. Their table manners are deplorable, providing a sharp contrast to the cleanliness of Westerners and Japanese. A large number of public functionaries might have maintained their desktops in reasonable cleanliness, but inside their drawers was another story. In many homes, the more well-to-do would hire maidservants, whereas they would not lift a finger to help clean the house. Consequently, the living room might look very clean, but the conditions of the kitchen and bathrooms were so messy that one could hardly bear to look at them. How could people living in such conditions be expected to possess any progressive spirit? Our National Father expounded that the basis for self-improvement included the maintenance of cleanliness and neatness. To that end, we must revise the old and adopt a modernized mode of living. Take eating habits. For example, we should eat three meals a day and refrain from taking snacks and junk foods. Meals should be taken at a fixed time, and snacks should not be provided at public meetings. It is not necessary to provide tea for guests visiting the office, because they usually do not touch it. That is a wasteful and unnecessary courtesy. That goes for the pattern of walking and seating as well. Dinner parties and entertainment should also be minimized, and when necessary, they should be arranged as gatherings on a "pay for your own" basis. Foods ordered should be nutritious and tasteful, and not in excessive quantity to show off one's wealth. As there is no law against serving cigarettes and liquor, locally made products should be used. For daily necessities, the principle of using locally made products should be adopted, such as wine, tobacco, fruits, towels, soap, tooth-powder, toothbrushes and socks, despite the fact that they might be inferior in quality as compared to foreign-made products of the same kind. Instead of buying from abroad, we should urge manufacturers to make quality improvements. For non-necessities which are not produced locally, one does not have to use them. No patriotic citizen would prefer foreign-made to local products. Control over these little daily items is in our own hands, and it can be complied with by a little determination by each and every citizen as his or her contribution to society and, hence, to the success of our reconstruction efforts. I am not in a position to speak for the nation, but only for Taiwan Province. I dare say that within a matter of ten years we can complete the political, economic, and social reconstruction if we will only exert our utmost efforts in this spirit. Otherwise, the proclamation of the Constitution will have no impact at all. But we should let bygones be bygones. We must regard the day to promulgate the Constitution as the day for the beginning of our new life. I hope that each of us will develop a broad-minded wisdom, cultivate a farsighted vision, and become a loyal citizen who can be proud and devoted to the country.

My expectations may be too great. But we must do our very best to achieve these targets. Do not underestimate our abilities. Let us review the past, for right or for wrong, the good or the bad, with candor, so that we can adopt a correct course in the future. The resolutions reached at this meeting must be strictly carried out. Even more important, it is not my words, which now draw to an end, but your determination to make them bear fruit.

APPENDIX D

Message from Ch'en I, Commander-in-Chief of the Taiwan Garrison Command, to Officers and Men Stationed in Taiwan, Outlining Seven Points to be Observed

(*T'ai-wan hsin-sheng-pao*, Mar. 16, 1947, p. 3)

Ch'en I, Commander-in-Chief of the Taiwan Garrison Command, yesterday issued a message to the officers and men stationed in Taiwan, the full text of which is cited below.

Dear Officers, Men, and Comrades:
 The unfortunate Incident that recently occurred in this province was perpetrated by a small number of traitorous elements and political conspirators who, by subverting the efforts of the Taiwan Wine and Tobacco Monopoly Bureau to investigate a case of tobacco smuggling, instigated people to resist the government, when they were ignorant of the facts. Hooligans disrupted peace and order, attacked government offices, and incited riots elsewhere. Both the government and the people suffered heavy losses. Indeed, this is a most deplorable and tragic event which breaks our hearts.
 We must, therefore, take prompt and effective action to wipe out these mutinous and lawless individuals in order to maintain the stability of the province and to protect the law-abiding citizens. In fact, our inalienable duty as soldiers of the national revolution is to defend the nation and the public interest. We must not relax for even one second in our efforts to achieve this sacred mission.
 In this last Incident, enemy agents and rebels used the terms "local Taiwanese" and "Mainlanders" [people from other provinces] to whip up dissension and divide their feelings. We must not be hoodwinked by such deception. There are no differences between Taiwanese and Mainlanders. We all come from the same root, and we are all countrymen of the Republic of China. We should love each other and be united.
 As officers and men stationed here, you will not at any time insult our Taiwan compatriots or entertain any intention of revenge. I have already ordered your superiors to explain to you and instruct you to comply strictly with this command. At the same time, it is my hope that when you encounter any of our Taiwanese countrymen who may not understand the causes leading to this unfortunate Inci-

dent, you will render a detailed explanation to them in a friendly way and with sincerity. Refrain from reprimanding them because of their lack of understanding. Furthermore, I would like to outline the following points that we must all faithfully comply with during this period to achieve stabilization.

1. Military police shall be held fully responsible for rooting out and arresting all traitorous elements.
2. Combat units shall be responsible only for maintaining battle readiness and carrying out combat missions.
3. All officers and men are absolutely forbidden to plunder or to shoot law-abiding people on any pretexts. Anyone who violates this order, when convicted, will receive a sentence of summary execution.
4. Military patrols shall not abuse, oppress, or insult people on the pretext of making an inspection. Violators shall be subject to the severe penalties under martial law.
5. Officers and men assigned to guard motor transport vehicles need not assume a "ready-to-shoot" posture to restore public order.
6. All officers and men are strictly prohibited from willfully firing shots to frighten the people.
7. Military police shall be responsible for strengthening patrol duties to uphold military discipline.

All our officers and men are required to fully abide by the above rules, which have been promulgated to avoid unwarranted disturbance of the public, so that while we provide adequate protection for them, we successfully accomplish our mission of stamping out the treacherous conspirators, thus restoring stability to society and enabling the people to live in peace and prosperity.

NOTES

Notes

For full forms of citations shortened in the Notes, see the Bibliography, pp. 251–64.

Chapter 1

1. "Erh-erh-pa chi-nien-hui tsai T'ai-wan" [Commemorating February 28th in Taiwan], *Shih-pao chou-k'an*, no. 158 (Mar. 1988), p. 46.
2. "Chia-i-shih i-tu fa-sheng ch'ung-t'u" [A Violent Altercation Erupts in Chia-i City], *Lien-ho-pao*, Feb. 29, 1988, p. 1.
3. "Erh-erh-pa shih-chien shih li-shih pei-chü, Li tsung-t'ung jen ying i ai-hsin k'an-tai" [The February 28th Incident Was a Tragedy: President Lee Believes We Should Treat the Incident with Sincere Understanding], *Chung-kuo shih-pao*, Feb. 28, 1988, p. 3. Generally speaking, people in Taiwan and the Mainland always refer to the February 28 Uprising as the February 28th Incident (*shih-chien* or *shih-pien*) but this has the effect of trivializing what we believe to be an uprising of great historical importance.
4. "Min-chin-tang li-wei t'su kung-pu chen-hsiang ping ts'ai pu-ch'ang ts'o-shih; Yüan-hui chüeh-i yao Nei-cheng, Kuo-fang, Fa-wu san-pu-chang pao-kao" [A DPP Legislator Calls for a Report on the Real Facts of the February 28th Incident and a Settlement to Compensate Victims; the Legislative Yüan Agrees to Call for a Report by the Ministers of the Three Ministries of Interior, Defense, and Justice], *Chung-kuo shih-pao*, Mar. 1, 1989, p. 3.
5. "Erh-erh-pa chi-nien huo-tung tsai Chia-i ho-ch'i shou-ch'ang" [At the February 28th Memorial Rally in Chia-i City, the Play Peacefully Ends], *Chung-kuo shih-pao*, Mar. 1, 1989, p. 3.
6. "Chia-i-shih t'ung-i min-chin-tang she erh-erh-pa chi-nien-pei" [Chia-i City Allows the DPP to Erect a February 28th Memorial], *Chung-kuo shih-pao*, Mar. 1, 1989, p. 3.
7. "Erh-erh-pa ho-p'ing chi-nien-pei chi-chiang lo-ch'eng" [A Memorial for the 2-28 Incident and Peace Will Soon Be Completed], *Chung-kuo shih-pao*, Aug. 4, 1989, p. 1.
8. "Liang-tang mo-ai, fen-pieh ch'i-li" [The Two Political Parties Stand but for Different Reasons], *Lien-ho-pao*, Feb. 24, 1990, p. 3.
9. "Mo-ai i-fen-chung cheng-yüan kuan-yüan pu-pi lieh-hsi" [One Minute to

Express Condolences; Cabinet Officers Need Not Attend], *Lien-ho-pao*, Feb. 23, 1990, p. 3.

10. *Ibid.*

11. Hsiao-ch'u ch'ao-yeh pu-hsin-jen hsin-chieh wei erh-erh-pa liao-shang chih-t'ung" [Dispel the Opposition's Skepticism for Healing the Painful Wound of the 2-28 Incident], *Tzu-li tsao-pao*, Feb. 26, 1990, p. 2.

12. "Kuo-tai wei 'erh-erh-pa' ch'i-li mo-ai" [In the National Assembly Some Stand Silently to Express Condolences for the 2-28 Incident], *Shih-chieh jih-pao*, Feb. 28, 1990, p. 2.

13. *Wen-hui-pao*, Mar. 1, 1975. *Ta-kung-pao* (Hong Kong), Mar. 1, 1975. In the 1980s, new scholarship from Mainland China presented a more complex interpretation, arguing that the Uprising was spontaneous and many participants only demanded more participation in government for the Taiwanese. For this new point of view, see Teng K'ung-chao, "Shih-lun T'ai-wan erh-erh-pa shih-chien chung ti min-chu yu ti-fang tzu-chih yao-ch'iu" [A Provisional Study on the Demands for Democracy and Self-Rule in Taiwan During the February 28th Incident], *T'ai-wan yen-chiu chi-k'an*, no. 2 (1987), pp. 1–11. Other studies from Amoy University in 1988 (two volumes) have been published, but because they only circulated on the Mainland, the authors have not examined their contents.

14. *Jen-min jih-pao*, Mar. 1, 1975, p. 4.

15. P'eng Ming-min, *Tzu-yu ti tzu-wei*, p. 120.

16. *Taiwan seinen* [Taiwan Youth], no. 6 (Feb. 20, 1961), p. 6. The June 3, 1896, law gave the Japanese governor-general unlimited power to enforce Japanese rule over the Chinese on Taiwan. There has still been no sophisticated study of the Taiwan Independence Movement in Japan and the United States. The best short study that we know of focuses specifically upon the ideology and tactics of key factions in the movement, and supports our assertion that the movement has, to date, been overwhelmingly influenced by left-wing theorists of the Marxist-Leninist line of thought. See Chang and Gregor, "The Taiwan Independence Movement: The Failure of Political Persuasion."

17. Pai Ch'ung-hsi, "T'ai-wan shih-pien ti chen-hsiang." A similar interpretation can be found in Hsieh A-shui, '*Erh-erh-pa shih-pien*' *chen-hsiang*.

18. Hsieh A-shui, p. 112.

19. *China White Paper: August 1949*, vol. 1, p. 308.

20. *Ibid.*

21. *Ibid.*, p. 309. The Wedemeyer report appears to be based mainly on U.S. consular reports from Taipei during 1946–47, many of them written by Lt. George H. Kerr (USNR) and others by Ralph J. Blake. See *Formosa: Internal Affairs, 1945–1949*, Reel 1 (Political Affairs Reports for 1946 and January 1947). Readers should also refer to the classic study by Kerr, *Formosa Betrayed*, which provides a detailed eyewitness account of the Uprising in Taipei. Kerr has no empathy with the KMT or with conditions in Mainland China, and describes KMT policies and official behavior in scathing terms. Rather than refer to Kerr's work when presenting our list of different interpretations of the cause of the Uprising, we refer to the U.S. State Department's interpretation.

22. *China White Paper: August 1949*, vol. 1, p. 310.

23. See report by General Pai Ch'ung-hsi and Mr. Yang Liang-kung, republished in *Shih-chieh jih-pao*, Mar. 11, 1988, pp. 6–7; and in Chiang Yung-ching, Li Yün-han, and Hsü Shih-shun, comps., *Yang Liang-kung hsien-sheng nien-p'u*. Yang's report is a dispassionate analysis which finds no evidence that the Communists played any major role in the uprising. Yang argues that the Uprising was caused by many factors: Japanese rule had influenced Taiwanese understanding of the problems and goals for rebuilding Taiwan in ways very different from the ideas of ROC leaders; economic difficulties had worsened after 1945 because of erroneous ROC policies restricting the free market; newspapers, allowed to flourish under Ch'en I, had turned public opinion against the ROC; many members of the Taiwanese elite had aspired to political power and were bitter because they failed to acquire it under the ROC; troop transfers in 1946 had produced a dearth of security personnel; and rebel control of the radio stations had incited many people who heard their broadcasts. Yang notes that some Communist agitation did occur, but mainly after the Uprising.

24. See report in *Shih-chieh jih-pao*, Mar. 11, 1988, p. 6.

25. C. K. Yang, "Some Preliminary Statistical Patterns of Mass Actions in Nineteenth-Century China," in Wakeman and Grant, pp. 174–210.

26. Wakeman, *The Great Enterprise*, vol. 2, pp. 1099–1120.

27. Atwell, *British Mandarins and Chinese Reformers*, p. 179.

28. Even before the 1940s, modern states imposed their sovereignty over distant territories. Note that the United States put down the Philippine Insurrection, directly killing 16,000 or more Filipinos and possibly causing the death of 250,000, who died because of economic disruption and health problems stemming from that military struggle. See Graff, *American Imperialism and the Philippine Insurrection*, p. xiv.

29. Since 1988, the Taiwan Historical Commission has been preparing a study of the Uprising and to that end has tried to interview eyewitnesses to the Uprising. The Commission's early findings that undisciplined Nationalist troops alienated Taiwanese from Mainlanders are in line with our own interpretation of the grievances that led to the Uprising. See "Kuo-chün san-man kung-wu-yüan ao-man" [Nationalist Troops Were Unruly, and Officials Were Arrogant and Rude], *Tzu-yu shih-pao*, Dec. 16, 1988, p. 1. The Commission has experienced great difficulty obtaining information because people are still unwilling to discuss the uprising. See "'Erh-erh-pa shih-chien k'ou-shu tzu-liao ts'ai-fang pao-kao" [A Report of Oral Interviews on the February 28th Incident], parts I–II, *Tzu-yu shih-pao*, Dec. 16, 1988, p. 15.

Chapter 2

1. For information on the geography and early history of Taiwan, see Hsieh, *Taiwan-Ilha Formosa, A Geography in Perspective*.

2. Yü, *Trade and Expansion in Han China*, p. 187.

3. Hsieh, *Taiwan-Ilha Formosa*, p. 3.

4. Quoted in Inō Kanori, *Taiwan bunkashi*, vol. 1, p. 177.

5. P'eng Ming-min, *Tzu-yu ti tzu-wei*. Before 1875, immigrants legally were "criminals"; see P'eng Ming-min, p. 3.

6. Myers, "Taiwan ... The Traditional Society," pp. 429–31.
7. Myers, "Taiwan ... The Traditional Order," p. 509.
8. Ho, *Economic Development of Taiwan*, p. 13.
9. Davidson, *The Island of Formosa: Historical View from 1430 to 1900*, p. 606.
10. Cha Shih-chieh, "Huang-min-hua yün-tung hsia-t'e T'ai-wan Chang-lao chiao-hui—i nan-pei chiao-hui hsüeh-hsiao shen-she ts'an-pei wei li," in Chang Yen-hsien, ed., *Chung-kuo hai-yang fa-chan-shih lun-wen-chi*, vol. 3, p. 138.
11. *Ibid.*, p. 139.
12. *Ibid.*
13. Wang Shih-lang, *Wang Shih-lang ch'üan-chi*, vol. 6, p. 74.
14. For evidence of the names of elite members and their number, rank, salaries, and period of service in the Japanese administration, see Wu Wen-hsing, "Jih-chü ch'u-ch'i T'ai-wan she-hui ling-tao chieh-ts'eng chih ssu-ying yü pien-tung," pp. 285–349. Wu cites 28 Chinese members of the elite who served in prefectures and departments between 1897 and 1901 and 92 officials who served at different bureaucratic levels of the colonial administration (pp. 322–38).
15. Lamley, "The Taiwan Literati and Early Japanese Rule," p. 428.
16. *Ibid.*, p. 412.
17. *Ibid.*, p. 442.
18. *Ibid.*, p. 434.
19. P'eng Ming-min, *Tzu-yu ti tzu-wei*, pp. 2–5.
20. *Ibid.*
21. *Ibid.*, p. 9.
22. *Ibid.*, p. 10.
23. *Ibid.*
24. *Ibid.*, p. 12.
25. *Ibid.*, pp. 12–14.
26. *Ibid.*, p. 16.
27. *Ibid.*, pp. 16–17.
28. *Ibid.*, p. 23.
29. *Ibid.*, pp. 33–38.
30. *Ibid.*, p. 38.
31. *Ibid.*, p. 56.
32. *Ibid.*, pp. 48–49.
33. *Ibid.*
34. In 1911, the famous Chinese intellectual Liang Ch'i-ch'ao visited Taiwan. He greatly influenced the Taiwan intellectuals to keep their Chinese heritage alive, but he warned them not to expect any help from Mainland China. See Ts'ai P'ei-huo et al., *T'ai-wan min-tsu yün-tung-shih*, p. 12. For information on Itagaki's visit, see Shih Ming, *T'ai-wan-jen ssu-pai-nien shih*, p. 455. For discussion of the events leading up to Itagaki's visit to Taiwan, see Lamley, "Assimilation Efforts in Colonial Taiwan."
35. Chen, "Formosan Political Movements Under Japanese Rule," p. 479.
36. Yeh Jung-chung, *Lin Hsien-t'ang hsien-sheng chi-nien-chi*, vol. 3, pp. 24–41.

37. Myers and Peattie, eds., *The Japanese Colonial Empire*, pp. 268–69.
38. *Ibid.*, pp. 380–83.
39. *Ibid.*, p. 308.
40. Wickberg, "The Taiwan Peasant Movement."
41. Chen, "Formosan Political Movements," p. 493.
42. Ho, *Economic Development of Taiwan*, pp. 284–86. If gross national expenditure in real terms roughly approximates the trend of gross domestic product (GDP), then GDP rose by 2.6 times between 1903 and 1937 (see Ho, p. 286). Population rose 1.7 times between 1905 and 1937, which would imply that per capita income in real terms nearly doubled between 1900 and 1937, or grew at an annual rate of nearly 2 percent over a 35-year period. Research by Thomas G. Rawski now suggests that between 1914/18 and 1931/36 the rate of growth of GDP per capita may have been as low as 0.6 percent per year, or perhaps 1.1 percent per year or even as high as 1.6 percent per year. (See Rawski, *Economic Growth in Prewar China*, p. 330.) Taking Rawski's preferred estimate of 1.1 percent per year, it still seems appropriate to assert that the Taiwanese economy was growing much more rapidly than the Mainland economy, even though Taiwan's population was also growing much more rapidly than the Mainland's.
43. See the reference to Chinese students from Fukien who visited Taiwan's research institutes and farms in 1915 and expressed their surprise at the island's agricultural development, in Myers, "Taiwan's Agrarian Economy Under Japanese Rule," pp. 461–62.
44. *Ibid.*, p. 474.
45. Minshūshugi Kenkyūkai, *Taiwan ni okeru Nihon tōchi to sengo naigai jōsei*, p. 54.
46. *Ibid.*, p. 55.
47. For an account of these incidents, see *ibid.*, pp. 55–57.
48. The best account of various incidents of Taiwanese sabotaging production and transportation (1938–39), withholding taxes and fomenting labor strikes (1939–40), and beating and murdering policemen (1939), as well as of Chinese Communist Party activities in Taiwan between 1939 and 1942 to mobilize resistance against the Japanese, is by Wu Kuo-an, "Lun T'ai-wan t'ung-pao ts'an-chia tsu-kuo k'ang-Jih chan-cheng ti huo-tung chi ch'i li-shih i-i." Wu's sources are mainly Communist newspapers like the *Hsin-hua jih-pao* and *Chieh-fang jih-pao*, and the principal years for which he cites incidents are 1938–40—precisely when a rash of anti-Japanese incidents occurred. We agree with Wu that such incidents occurred before 1940, but we disagree with Wu's assertions that Taiwanese anti-Japanese resistance remained strong and widespread after 1940.
49. Terasaki Ryūji, comp., *Hasegawa Kiyoshi den*, p. 122.
50. *Ibid.*, p. 123.
51. *Ibid.*, p. 124. It is doubtful that Admiral Hasegawa alone promoted the idea of *kōmin rensei* (retraining the Taiwanese to become loyal imperial subjects). In 1940, various officials had already expressed the view that the differences between the Taiwanese and the Japanese were not that great and that the Taiwanese could easily be transformed into Japanese. The head of the Department for General Affairs, Morikawa, expressed the following view: "For the Taiwanese

to become like the Japanese, it is necessary that the Taiwanese grasp the essence of the spirit of the Imperial Way to deal with all matters just as the Japanese do. By beginning in a formal way with the Japanese language and then moving to the external forms of our names, habits, and customs, etc., our ideal is that the Taiwanese will be no different from the Japanese. Therefore, both in spirit and in form, the Taiwanese will be the same as Japanese, and all Taiwanese can be completely Japanized." See Kō Shō-dō, *Taiwan Sōtokufu*, p. 167.

52. Terasaki Ryūji, comp., *Hasegawa Kiyoshi den*, p. 124.
53. *Ibid.*, p. 125.
54. *Ibid.*, p. 126.
55. Taiwan Sōtokufu Jōhōbu, *Jikyokuka Taiwan no genzai to sono shōrai*, p. 6.
56. *Ibid.*, p. 9.
57. *Ibid.*, p. 10.
58. Cha Shih-chieh, "Huang-min-hua . . ." (cited in n. 10), p. 143.
59. *Ibid.*, p. 132.
60. *Ibid.*, p. 148.
61. *Ibid.*, p. 149.
62. Terasaki Ryūji, comp., *Hasegawa Kiyoshi den*, p. 127.
63. *Ibid.*, p. 128.
64. *Ibid.*
65. See Myers and Peattie, eds., *The Japanese Colonial Empire*, p. 216, for a review of the origins of the *hokō* system in Taiwan.
66. *TNS*, Jan. 8, 1942, p. 3. We are grateful for the assistance of Professor Chen Tsu-yü of the Institute of Modern History, Academia Sinica, in translating this song.
67. Terazaki Ryūji, comp., *Hasegawa Kiyoshi den*, p. 129.
68. *Ibid.*, p. 128.
69. Taiwan Sōtofuku, *Taiwan jijō*, 1943, pp. 156–57.
70. *Ibid.*, p. 157.
71. *TNS*, Jan. 5, 1942, p. 4, "Manira kanraku banzai! Kinō zentō hata no nami" [Flags Flew All Over Taiwan Yesterday. Hurrah for the Fall of Manila!].
72. *TNS*, Jan. 9, 1942, p. 3, "Taiwan ikka roppyakuman kazoku senshō kansui ni kataki chikai" [Six Million People Firmly Pledge as One Great Taiwan Family to Press for a Complete Victory].
73. *TNS*, Jan. 3, 1942, p. 4, "Kōmin hokō sensen ni teishin chikau" [Pledging to Volunteer for the Front Line in the KHK].
74. *TNS*, Jan. 3, 1942, p. 4, "Nihon seishin no shūren e" [Develop and Train the Japanese Spirit].
75. *TNS*, Jan. 3, 1942, p. 4, "Kōon ni mukuyuru kakugo" [Determining to Answer for the Benevolent Reward from the Emperor].
76. *TNS*, Jan. 24, 1944, p. 2. "Hontō dōhō no kaiseimei kyoka jōken o kanwa" [Relaxing the Conditions for Permitting the Change of Surnames of Our Taiwanese Brethren]. The press reported that in 1940, 6,549 persons had changed their names to Japanese names; in 1941, 65,236; in 1942, 25,966; and by November 1943, another 28,460. Because the rules for changing names had been so strict, the Japanese decided to relax them in early 1945. We have not seen these former rules

to judge whether they were strict or not. It is conceivable that the Japanese were dismayed by the small number of Taiwanese who wanted to become assimilated in such a way, and tried to make their decision easier. However, we regard a figure of 100,000 as quite significant for a culture that greatly values the Chinese surname and reveres it through ancestor worship.

77. Wu Hsin-jung, *Wu Hsin-jung ch'üan-chi*, vol. 6, p. 102.
78. *TNS*, Jan. 14, 1942, p. 3, "Taihokushū gakuto hōkōtai asu hare no kesseishiki, gakuto ichiman rokusenmei sanka" [The Student Public Service Volunteers in Taipei District Will Publicly Assemble Tomorrow Some 16,000 Student Participants].
79. *TNS*, Jan. 15, 1942, p. 3, "Zentōmin ni reikō o shōyō" [Suggestions for Strictly Enforcing the Rules for All People of This Island].
80. *TNS*, Feb. 3, 1942, p. 2, "Kyoto shiganhei e sō shingun, shonichi no uketsuke sōsū ichimansanzenhyakukyūmei" [Over Ten Thousand Come Forth to Enlist as Military Volunteers]. Also see *TNS*, Feb. 8, 1942, p. 4, "Kakuchi shiganhei jōkyō" [The Condition of Military Volunteers All Over Taiwan].
81. *TNS*, Jan. 8, 1942, p. 2, "Zentō no ishi kessokushi, idō no shinzui kōyō, Taiwan hōkō ishidan chikaku tanyō" [Taiwanese Physicians Have United: To Promote the Essense of the 'Good Physician,' the Taiwan Physicians Corps to Perform Public Service Has Just Been Created].
82. *TNS*, Jan. 28, 1942, p. 3, "Seito kodomo no reisai na kyokin de hikōki kennō" [Students and Children Make a Present of an Airplane by Raising Small Amounts of Money].
83. Tomisawa Shigeru, *Taiwan shūsen hishi*, p. 4.
84. Terasaki Ryūji, comp., *Hasegawa Kiyoshi den*, p. 133.
85. Taiwan Sōtokufu, *Taiwan jijō*, 1943, p. 102.
86. *Ibid.*, p. 103.
87. Taiwan Sōtokufu, *Taiwan tōchi gaiyō*, p. 44. See also Tsurumi, *Japanese Colonial Education in Taiwan*, p. 148. Tsurumi contends that the compulsory elementary schooling during wartime "was not enforced with the vigor characteristic of earlier educational measures [1920s]; the colonial government's energy and funds were obviously engaged elsewhere" (p. 131). Yet she admits that during the war years, "in the last analysis, Japanization did not mean important changes in the education system, because the schools were considered to be doing a good job" (p. 132). But according to the available statistical evidence, the enormous increase in primary school attendance that took place between 1937 and 1944 attests to the remarkable upsurge in schooling among the Taiwanese because of the new opportunities opened to them during the war to attend public school and learn the Japanese language and Japanese cultural values.
88. Taiwan Sōtokufu, *Taiwan seinen tokuhon*, chap. 1.
89. *Ibid.*, p. 6.
90. *Ibid.*, pp. 62–63.
91. Umehara Ikuo, comp., *Taiwan seinen no sakebi*, p. 2.
92. *Ibid.*, p. 3.
93. Nagae Seigo, *Taiwan no gunpu*, p. 5.
94. Wu Wen-hsing, an expert on educational development under Japanese rule,

presents these statistics and argues that most Taiwanese were functionally literate in Japanese. See his "Jih-chü shih-ch'i T'ai-wan tsung-tu-fu t'ui-kuang Jih-yü yün-tung ch'u-t'an," p. 116.

95. *TNS*, Feb. 21, 1944, p. 2, "Chōhei ni sonau jissen shoshisaku, kōhō sōtoku tōsai naiyō happyō" [The Governor-General and President of the KHK Publishes the Rules for Policies to Prepare for the Military Conscription System].

96. *TNS*, Feb. 8, 1944, p. 2, "Kōtsū dōtoku no kōyō e ressha hōkōhan o soshiki" [Organize Networks of Teams for Public Services to Promote Traffic Courtesy].

97. *TNS*, Jan. 27, 1944, p. 2, "Kōhō gaishō bunkaichō kondankai owaru" [Branch Heads of Cities and Villages of the KHK End Their Roundtable Discussions].

98. *TNS*, Feb. 3, 1944, p. 2, "Zen'i no akusei arubekarazu ōkii me de kokoro de" [With a Broad Vision and an Expansive Spirit, With Good Intentions, Let's Jettison Bad Management].

99. Yeh Jung-chung, *Lin Hsien-t'ang hsien-sheng chi-nien-chi*, vol. 1, no. 31, p. 71a.

100. *TNS*, Jan. 29, 1944, p. 4, "Joshi nōgyō teishintai umaru, 'nōhon' o tsuyoku kokorogakemashō" [Women Agricultural Volunteer Corps Have Appeared; Let's Strongly Concentrate on Making 'Farming' the Key].

101. *TNS*, Feb. 15, 1944, p. 4, "Gakuto no te de suiden hyakko, ichimanmei ga shutsudō shite hiraku" [Ten Thousand Students Are Mobilized to Farm 100 Hectares of Paddy Land by Hand].

102. *TNS*, Feb. 10, 1944, "Senka ni mune odorasetsutsu" [Our Hearts Exult in the Victories Achieved in Battle].

103. *TNS*, Feb. 12, 1944, p. 3, "Kōkoku hisshō no ketsui kōyō" [Promote a Resolve for the 'Imperial Country's' Certain Victory].

104. *TNS*, Feb. 4, 1944, p. 2, "Ika ni shite shitsukeruka" [How to Raise Children]. A series of such articles appeared under the column heading "Kokumin gakkō no kyōiku" [Education of Public School Children], with various writings dealing with all kinds of family and educational problems.

105. Reports in *Taiwan shinpō* (*TS*) throughout January 1945 provide a detailed account of the number of air raids, the number of B-29 bombers, and the number of those shot down by Japanese defenses. For example, see Jan. 4, p. 1; Jan. 10, p. 1; Jan. 18, p. 1; Jan. 23, p. 1. See also Mar. 17, 1945, p. 1; and May 10, 1945, p. 1.

106. *TNS*, Jan. 27, 1944, p. 1, "Kūshū ni saizen no bōei" [The Best Form of Protection from Air Raids].

107. *TS*, Feb. 2, 1945, p. 1, "Kōhō undō ni gun mo kyōryoku, chūrōnensō no shidō ni ryūi" [Pay Attention to the Leadership of the Middle and Older Ranks and Support the KHK Movement for the Military].

108. *Ibid*.

109. *TNS*, Feb. 11, 1945, p. 1, "Seibu no iryoku o hakki" [Display the Power of That Warrior Spirit].

110. *TNS*, Apr. 12, 1945, p. 2, "Kōhō kikō o kansoka" [Simplify the Structure of the KHK Association].

111. *TNS*, Apr. 20, 1945, p. 2, "Kōhō undō koko ni yonshūnen; naitai, Ta-

kasago no senyūai" [Four Years of the KHK, Our Patriotic Comrades-in-Arms: The People of Taiwan and the Mountain People].

112. *TNS*, Apr. 21, 1945, p. 2, "Tatakau buraku o chūshin ni ganbarō Taiwan ika hisshō e hōkōhan sōshin shingeki" [A Massive Assault by the KHK Teams for a Sure Victory; Taiwan as One Great Family Must Make a Great Effort to Make the Villages the Battle Ground].

113. *TS*, June 17, 1945, p. 1, "Tōmin no sōryoku o hakki, seisen kanshō e teishin seyo" [Demonstrate the Total Power of the People of This Island; Volunteer for a Total Victory in Our Sacred War].

114. *Ibid.*

115. *TS*, June 18, 1945, p. 1, "Kokumin giyūtai hensei hōsaku" [Procedures for Forming the National People's Volunteer Corps].

116. *TS*, June 26, 1945, p. 2, "Kokumin giyūtai no uta" [The Song of the National People's Volunteer Corps].

117. *TS*, June 18, 1945, p. 2, "Kōhō wa hiyakuteki kaisan" [Rapidly Dispersing the KHK].

118. *Ibid.*

119. *TS*, June 18, 1945, p. 2, "Gun bōei ni kyōryoku" [Cooperation in Our Military Defense].

120. See the following articles in *TS*: July 13, 1945, p. 2, "Shinchikushū no giyūtai" [The Volunteers of Hsin-chu District]; July 19, 1945, p. 2, "Kakuchi giyūtai katsudō" [The Activities of Volunteer Corps All Over the Island]; July 28, 1945, p. 2, "Sakusen kōdō ni kyōryoku roppyaku nanajūman no kessoku" [Linking 6.7 Million People in Cooperative Activity for the Battle].

121. *TS*, July 28, 1945, p. 2.

122. *TS*, Aug. 24, 1945, p. 1, "Zen tōmin ichigan danketsu" [The Island's People Have Become One Great Unified Group]. But American officials in late 1945 reported that several groups of Japanese officers and Chinese had rebelled upon hearing news of the surrender and had fled to the hills, where they were followed and killed by Japanese troops. We presume these were loyal troops of the Emperor who chose to die rather than surrender.

123. *TS*, Aug. 25, 1945, p. 2, "Shokuryō zōsan, chian iji, giyūdan no mokuteki ninmu o meiji" [The Goals of the Volunteer Corps Are Clearly Expressed as Duty: Increasing Food Production and Preserving Public Security].

124. Rinji Rōmubu, "Jihenka ni okeru hontō no rōmu jijō," p. 11.

125. Terazaki Ryūji, comp., *Hasegawa Kiyoshi den*, p. 162.

126. T'ai-wan-sheng hsing-cheng chang-kuan kung-shu t'ung-chi-shih, comp., *T'ai-wan-sheng wu-shih-i-nien lai t'ung-chi t'i-yao*, p. 831. Henceforth, *T'ung-chi t'i-yao*.

127. *Ibid.*, estimated from pp. 829–36.

128. Terazaki Ryūji, comp., *Hasegawa Kiyoshi den*, p. 163. In more precise terms, around 219,429 workers. It is difficult to derive accurate figures for distribution of the workforce in 1943. Percentage figures for non-agricultural employed workers can be found in *TKN 1944*, p. 234. The precise figures for the agricultural, non-agricultural, and unemployed portions of Taiwan's population are not available from official data we have found.

129. This estimate is based on the data contained in Table A-1 in Ho, *Eco-*

nomic Development of Taiwan, p. 285. For data on male and female numbers in manufacturing and utilities, see p. 329.

130. *Ibid.*, p. 366, for data on expansion of manufacturing output between 1937 and 1942.

131. Terazaki Ryūji, comp., *Hasegawa Kiyoshi den*, p. 162.

132. *Ibid.*, p. 163. Of the total workforce actually working in 1944, only 56 percent worked in agriculture, representing a dramatic decline from the prewar numbers.

133. *Ibid.*, p. 164; *TKN 1944*, p. 145.

134. Terazaki Ryūji, comp., *Hasegawa Kiyoshi den*, p. 165; *TKN 1942*, pp. 151–53.

135. See Taiwan Sōtokufu, *Taiwan jūyō sangyō chosei iinkai kaigiroku*. This work is marked "secret" and contains the proceedings of five important meetings of the Commission's members to review plans for industrialization.

136. *TKN 1943*, pp. 40–41.

137. *TKN 1942*, p. 82. Each individual was entitled to 3,908 shaku, or roughly 3.8 liters of grain.

138. Kuwata Etsu and Maehara Tōru, comps., *Dai Tōa sensō ni okeru chiiki betsu heiin oyobi shibotsu gaisū* [Summary Data of Deaths and Various Military Personnel by Region During the Great East Asia War] (Tokyo: Hara Shobō, 1982), p. 21 (Part 2).

139. Kōnan Shinbunsha, *Taiwan jinshikan, 1943*, p. 234.

140. *Ibid.*, p. 70.

141. Yang Liang-Kung. Report on the February Uprising, reprinted in *Shih-chieh jih-pao*, Mar. 11, 1988, pp. 6–7.

142. Myers and Peattie, eds., *The Japanese Colonial Empire*, p. 516.

143. *Ibid.*, p. 486.

144. *Ibid.*, p. 509 and p. 493.

145. Wu Cho-liu, *Wu-hua-kuo*, p. 122.

146. *Ibid.*, p. 125.

147. Yang Hsing-t'ing, *T'ai-wan ch'ing-nien pai-p'i-shu*, pp. 34–35.

Chapter 3

1. *Chung-yang jih-pao*, Aug. 16, 1945, p. 2.

2. Hsü, *The Rise of Modern China*, p. 624.

3. Fairbank, ed., *The Cambridge History of China. Vol. 12: Republican China, 1912–1949, Part I*, p. 711. For the best account of this military campaign, see Chapter 11 by C. Martin Wilbur, especially pp. 581–711.

4. *Ibid.*, pp. 719–20.

5. Hung-mao Tien, *Government and Politics in Kuomintang China, 1927–1937* (Stanford, Calif.: Stanford University Press, 1972), p. 180.

6. Ch'i, *Nationalist China at War*, p. 183.

7. For evidence of such progress, see the essays in Paul K. T. Shi, ed., *The Strenuous Decade: China's Nation-Building Efforts, 1927–1937* (Jamaica, N.Y.: St. John's University Press, 1970).

8. Our concept of a "vicious circle" explains only in part why the Nationalists

failed to mobilize the Chinese rural people as so many scholars have argued. We submit that most Nationalist leaders, dedicated to building a modern society based on the Confucian principles of harmony and benevolence, were never committed to mobilizing society as the Communists were, even though Chiang Kai-shek at times revealed a penchant for transformative thinking and policy making. The Communists were dedicated to mobilizing people to carry out revolution, as some of their rural tactics demonstrated. By splitting local elite and then supporting one elite faction against another, the Communists were able to overthrow well-entrenched rural elite and replace them with loyal cadres of their choosing. For examples of this tactic see Yung-fa Chen, *Making Revolution: The Communist Movement in Eastern and Central China, 1937–1945*. The Nationalists never dreamed of splitting the elite in that way and creating civil war within society. The Nationalists, of course, were quite willing at times to use "underworld" elements to deal with terrorist, subversive elements like the Communists, as in the case of the destruction of the latter in Shanghai and other cities in 1927. They were also far more willing to allow a vast private society with its traditional customs and values to exist, only modifying that society through the gradual development of a modernization process aiming at harnessing science and technology to improve productivity and control over the forces of nature.

9. Ch'i, *Nationalist China at War*, p. 187. On the origins of modern Chinese radicalism, see Wang Fan-sen, *Ku-shih-pien yün-t'ung ti hsing-ch'i* [The Rise of the Movement to Investigate Ancient History Critically] (Taipei: Yün-ch'en wen-hua shih-yeh ku-fen yu-hsien kung-ssu, 1987), pp. 6–21, especially p. 18, n. 35.

10. Ch'i, *Nationalist China at War*, p. 193.

11. *Ibid.*, p. 194.

12. *Ibid.*, p. 196.

13. Eastman, *Seeds of Destruction*, p. 78. For an account of this reform effort, which Eastman refers to as the *Ko-hsin* movement, sponsored by middle-range party cadres to reform the party's leadership, see Chapter 5.

14. *Ibid.*

15. Ch'i, *Nationalist China at War*, p. 74.

16. *Ibid.*, p. 80. According to Ch'i, China's military records report over 310,000 military casualties (see Tables 3 and 4, pp. 80–81).

17. Fairbank and Feuerwerker, eds., *The Cambridge History of China. Vol. 13: Republican China, 1912–1949, Part II*, pp. 620–21.

18. Young, *China and the Helping Hand, 1937–1945*, pp. 354–55. Young describes the increase in manufacturing in the Nationalist-occupied areas, but overall manufacturing declined after 1943.

19. Chang Kia-ngau, *The Inflationary Spiral*, p. 57.

20. This is a major thesis in Ch'i Hsi-sheng's work; see Chapter 5. Though original and insightful, this thesis leaves aside other factors, such as the contingent, that were perhaps equally important in determining the defeat of the Nationalists between 1945 and 1949. For example, the Soviet Union's half-year occupation of Manchuria prevented the Nationalists from recovering it and establishing their rule there. Had that not occurred, the Nationalists might have prevented, or certainly delayed, the advance of Communist troops into that vast region. This in turn might have allowed them more time to link up with local elites and their client

networks, thus building enough support in the countryside to rebuff Communist base-building efforts.

21. The importance of factionalism, in particular, has been emphasized by both Lloyd Eastman (see his *Seeds of Destruction*, pp. 95 and 112) and Ch'i Hsi-sheng (*Nationalist China at War*, pp. 199–208).

22. Chiu, *China and the Question of Taiwan*, p. 207.

23. Huang Ch'ao-ch'in, *Wo ti hui-i*, p. 115.

24. These four views are described in Cheng Tzu, "Chan-hou T'ai-wan sheng-chih chih pien-ko" [The Transformation of Taiwan's Provincial System After World War II], unpublished manuscript, 1988, pp. 4–8.

25. *Ibid.*, pp. 34–35.

26. For a discussion of these training activities, see Hsü Ch'eng-tsung, "Erh-erh-pa shih-chien chen-hsiang," no. 6, p. 91; Li Chen-ming, *T'ai-wan-shih*, p. 157; and Keiji Furuya, *Chiang Kai-shek: His Life and Time*, p. 832.

27. "Cheng-ching jih-chih" [A Daily Record of Political Economy], *Cheng-ching-pao*, 1, no. 2 (Nov. 10, 1945), p. 22.

28. *Ibid.*

29. See Boorman et al., eds., *Biographical Dictionary of Republican China*, vol. 1, pp. 250–54. See also Shen Yün-lung, "Ch'en I ch'i-jen yü erh-erh-pa shih-pien," p. 57.

30. Ch'üan-kuo cheng-hsieh wen-shih tzu-liao yen-chiu wei-yüan-hui, Che-chiang sheng cheng-hsieh wen-shih tzu-liao yen-chiu wei-yüan-hui, Fu-chien sheng cheng-hsieh wen-shih tzu-liao yen-chiu wei-yüan-hui, comp., *Ch'en I sheng-p'ing chi pei-hai nei-mu* [The Life of Ch'en I and the Inside Story of the Suffering Inflicted on Him] (Beijing: Chung-kuo wen-shih ch'u-pan-she, 1987), p. 104. See account by Chou I-o about Ch'en I in Taiwan. Henceforth cited as *Ch'en I sheng-p'ing chi pei-hai nei-mu*.

31. "Ch'en I sheng-p'ing i-lin pan-chao" [Anecdotes of Ch'en I's life], *Chung-yang jih-pao*, June 18, 1950, p. 1.

32. *Ibid.*

33. Yeh Ming-hsün, "Pu-jung ch'ing-shih chin ch'eng hui: erh-erh-pa shih-chien ch'in-li ti kan-shou" [We Cannot Allow True History to Totally Become Ashes: My Personal Experience and Observation of the February 28th Incident], *Lien-ho-pao*, Feb. 2, 1988, p. 1.

34. Governor-General Ch'en I's speech, *T'ai-wan hsin-sheng-pao*, Jan. 9–10, 1947, p. 2.

35. *Ch'en I sheng-p'ing chi pei-hai nei-mu*, p. 118.

36. This information was derived from an interview with Shen Yün-lung.

37. Cheng Tzu, "Chan-hou T'ai-wan sheng-chih chih pien-ko," p. 9.

38. These photos were taken from Chang Tzu-hui, ed., *T'ai-wan shih-jen-chih*, vol. 1; and from Hsin T'ai-wan Ch'u-pan-she Compilation Committee, *T'ai-wan ming-jen-chi*, vol. 1.

39. Chang Tzu-hui, ed., *T'ai-wan shih-jen-chih*, p. 177.

40. *Ibid.*, p. 194.

41. Kao Hsien-chih, *T'ai-wan san-pai-nien shih*, p. 6. Lin Chung, *T'ai-wan kuang-fu ch'ien-hou shih-liao kai-shu*, p. 39.

42. Lin Chung, p. 40.

43. Li Chen-ming, p. 160.
44. *TNC*, Appendix, p. 1.
45. *Ibid.*, F77.
46. T'ai-wan-sheng hsing-cheng chang-kuan kung-shu t'ung-chi-shih [Taiwan Provincial Administrative Governor-General's Executive Office Statistical Bureau], comp., *T'ai-wan-sheng t'ung-chi yao-lan* [A Statistical Summary of Taiwan Province] (Taipei: T'ai-wan-sheng hsing-cheng chang-kuan kung-shu t'ung-chi-shih, 1946), 2nd issue, p. 131. Henceforth cited as *T'ung-chi yao-lan*.
47. *Ibid.*, p. 131.
48. T'ang Hsien-lung, *T'ai-wan shih-pien nei-mu-chi*, pp. 97–98; and "Formosa—Current Conditions," Mar. 15, 1946, in *Formosa: Internal Affairs, 1945–1949*, Reel 1, p. 2 (Enclosure no. 1206). U.S. forces had undertaken to move about 48,000 Chinese troops to occupy Taiwan shortly after Japan's surrender. Taipei consular official Ralph J. Blake reported on August 30, 1946, that the 62nd Army had been sent to North China, leaving only the 70th Army on the island with 20,000 troops. *Ibid.*, p. 2 (Enclosure no. 13).
49. T'ang Hsien-lung, pp. 97–98.
50. Wu Cho-liu, p. 172.
51. *Ibid.*, p. 173.
52. *Ibid.*
53. T'ai-wan-sheng hsing-cheng chang-kuan kung-shu hsüan-ch'uan wei-yüan-hui, comp., *T'ai-wan i-nien-lai chih jen-shih hsing-cheng*, p. 10, Table 2.
54. *Ibid.*, p. 13.
55. Patrick Cavendish, "The 'New China' of the Kuomintang," in Gray, ed., *Modern China's Search for a Political Form*, p. 144.
56. Copper, with Chen, *Taiwan's Elections*, p. 16.
57. *T'ai-wan hsin-sheng-pao*, Jan. 9–10, 1947, p. 2 (Ch'en I's speech at an administrative conference).
58. *Ch'en I sheng-p'ing chi pei-hai nei-mu*, p. 110. Ch'en I frequently said, "Taiwan's various foundations are superior to those on the Mainland; we want to develop Taiwan, and it is incorrect not to support and nurture the forces of this province. We must redouble our efforts when we look at this issue in this way."
59. Huang Ch'ao-ch'in, p. 137.
60. *T'ung-chi t'i-yao*, p. 385.
61. *Ibid.*
62. *Taiwan tōchi gaiyō*, pp. 19–21.
63. *T'ung-chi t'i-yao*, p. 385.
64. *Taiwan tōchi gaiyō*, p. 21.
65. *T'ung-chi t'i-yao*, p. 386.
66. Huang Ch'ao-ch'in, p. 139.
67. *Ibid.*, p. 198. Other members of the Provincial Council were Wu Ming-sen, Yin Chan-k'uei, Huang Ch'ao-ch'in, Liu K'uo-ts'ai, Hung Yüeh-pai, Ma Yu-yüeh, Li Ch'ung-li, Lin Jih-kao, Liu Ming-ch'ao, Lin Hsien-t'ang, Ch'en An-ch'a, Li Wan-chü, Liu Ch'uan-lai, Han Shih-Ch'üan, Lin Pi-hui, Li Yu-san, Kao Kung, Lin Wei-kung, Hung Huo-lien, Ting Jui-pin, Yang T'ao, Yen Ch'in-hsien, Su Wei-liang, Cheng P'in-ts'ung, Kuo Kuo-chi, Huang Ch'un-ch'ing, Ch'en Shou-shih, Lin Lien-tsung, Liu Chien-shan, and Wang T'ien-teng.

68. *Ibid.*, p. 143. The discussion of the council's behavior, based on Huang's memoirs, represents only one person's observations.

69. *Ibid.*, p. 144.

70. *Ibid.*

71. *Formosa: Internal Affairs, 1945–1949*, Reel 1, Enclosure no. 25 (Nov. 1, 1946).

72. Wu Cho-liu, p. 172.

73. *Formosa: Internal Affairs, 1945–1949*, Reel 1, Enclosure no. 25 (Dec. 4, 1946), p. 10. We have substituted the word "Taiwanese" for "Formosans," a term used by the American Consulate staff in Taipei at that time.

74. But Kerr states that Lin Hsien-t'ang and General Ho Ying-ch'in probably agreed secretly to have Japanese experts stay on in Taiwan to make Taiwan prosperous. See Kerr, *Formosa Betrayed*, pp. 65–66. Therefore, some leading Taiwanese were not at all unhappy about some Japanese remaining in Taiwan. In fact, the government had employed 6,266 persons; see *T'ai-wan i-nien-lai chih jen-shih hsing-cheng*, p. 5.

75. Chinese officials who had collaborated with the Japanese were also retained in central government positions in the recovered areas. See Pepper, *Civil War in China*, pp. 9–15.

76. Yang Chao-chia, *Yang Chao-chia hui-i-lu*, pp. 353 and 355.

77. The Japanese colonial regime issued the Taiwan bank note as legal currency convertible into Japanese currency at a one to one exchange. The colony's money supply was guaranteed by a reserve limit backed by gold and silver reserves. After Taiwan's retrocession the new provincial administration continued to print currency through the Bank of Taiwan. On May 22, 1946, the central government authorized the Bank of Taiwan to issue a new currency called the *taipi* (old Taiwan dollars) in the amount of 5,330,593,000 *yüan taipi* (issued as of December 1946) without any legal reserves. This currency exchanged with the old Bank of Taiwan notes at equal nominal value and could exchange with the currency of Mainland China at 30 *yüan fapi* for 1 *yüan taipi*. The Bank of Taiwan continued to issue *yüan taipi* until the monetary reform of June 1949. That reform called for a new currency, the new Taiwan dollar (NT$), to be convertible with the *yüan taipi* at a rate of 1 NT$ = 40,000, pegged to the U.S. dollar at the rate of NT$5 = US$1, and backed by 100 percent reserves based upon gold, silver, foreign exchange, and export commodities. See Liu Fu-ch'i, *Essays on Monetary Development in Taiwan*, pp. 7–13, for a discussion of Taiwan's monetary history during these years.

78. We estimated the 1946 net domestic product and adjusted the 1946 estimate of private Japanese wealth of 9.5 billion *yüan taipi* (assumed to be valued in 1946 prices) to 1937 prices, the same value for estimating the 1946 net domestic product. The data used for these estimates are presented below and are rough because of the inflation taking place.

	(1) price index	(2) net domestic product	(3) private Jap. assets
1937	100.00	805,700,000	—
1946	12,502.00	443,135,000	9,500,000,000

The sources for these data are as follows: for (1), Liu Fu-Ch'i, *Essays on Monetary Development in Taiwan*, p. 12 (Table 1–3); for the 1937 figure in (2), Simon Kuznetz, "Growth and Structural Shifts," p. 34; for the 1946 figure in (2), Ho, *Economic Development of Taiwan*, p. 285; for the 1946 figure in (3), the April 1946 estimate of the commission managing Japanese wealth in Taiwan province (we assume their estimate was made in current prices for 1946). When we take the figure in (3) and adjust it to 1937 prices, we can compare real net domestic product of 1946 in 1937 prices. Japanese private assets in real terms in 1946 amounted to roughly 17 percent of net domestic product—(3) ÷ (2)—for 1946.

79. Han Shih-ch'üan, *Liu-shih hui-i-lu*, p. 64.
80. *T'ai-wan hsin-sheng-pao*, Feb. 24, 1947, p. 2.
81. *Formosa: Internal Affairs, 1945–1949*, Reel 1, Enclosure no. 25 (Nov. 1, 1946, report), p. 22.
82. Ch'iu Nien-t'ai, *Wo ti fen-tou-shih*, p. 310; see also its earlier edition, Ch'iu Nien-t'ai, *Ling-hai wei-piao*, p. 246.
83. We can refer, for example, to the financial losses suffered by Yang Chao-chia on the Mainland. See Yang Chao-chia, p. 351.
84. Shih Ming, *T'ai-wan-jen ssu-pai-nien shih*, p. 720. These data differ from figures cited in official sources. See *T'ai-wan-sheng t'ung-chi yao-lan*, 2nd issue, p. 77, for quantities of exports to Shanghai through the Provincial Trade Bureau, Nov. 1945–Oct. 1946. But a special reporter for the newspaper *Kuan-ch'a* [The Observer], Mar. 29, 1947, p. 16, stated that in 1946 Taiwan had shipped 150,000 tons of sugar and 300,000 to 400,000 tons of coal to the Mainland, worth 1,300 old Taiwan dollars per ton of coal.
85. *Formosa: Internal Affairs, 1945–1949*, Reel 1, Enclosure no. 9 (Aug. 12, 1946, Taipei Consulate report), p. 8.
86. *Ibid.*, Enclosure no. 19 (Oct. 2, 1946, report), p. 3.
87. *Ibid.*
88. *T'ai-wan hsin-sheng-pao*, Feb. 12, 1947, p. 2. It is noteworthy that the author of this editorial condemning official corruption was a Mainlander, Shen Yün-lung, who was employed at the *T'ai-wan hsin-sheng-pao* at the time. See Shen Yün-lung, *Yün-lung ch'i-shih wen-ts'un*, pp. 65–67, for the same *T'ai-wan hsin-sheng-pao* editorial. Mainlanders as well as Taiwanese were outraged by these acts of corruption.
89. *T'ai-wan hsin-sheng-pao*, Feb. 20, 1947, p. 2.
90. *Formosa: Internal Affairs, 1945–1949*, Reel 1, Enclosure no. 25 (Nov. 1, 1946, report), p. 35.
91. Hsüeh Mu, "Wo ts'ung T'ai-wan huo-cho hui-lai," p. 54. The torrent of writings about official corruption in Taiwan can be found in Mainland cities in 1946–47, and these reports obviously reflect that sense of deprivation and anger shared by many city dwellers, especially among the intellectual and professional groups.
92. *TNC*, Appendix 1, p. 8.
93. *Ibid.*, p. 9.
94. *Ibid.*, p. 11.
95. *Ibid.*, pp. 12 and 14.
96. *Ibid.*, p. 12.

97. *Ibid.*, p. 18.

98. *Formosa: Internal Affairs, 1945–1949*, Reel 1, Enclosure to despatch no. 1206 (Mar. 15, 1946), p. 2. An August 12, 1946, confidential report by consular official Ralph J. Blake described the behavior of Nationalist troops: "There is a similar reaction to the misbehavior of troops from the mainland, stationed among the people, who are held responsible for thievery, illegal resort to force and alleged sharp increase in venereal diseases. These troops are required to obtain their own supplies and are often accused of forcing sales at a fraction of the value of goods acquired." See Enclosure 9 (Aug. 12, 1946), p. 8.

99. Min-T'ai t'ung-hsün-she, *T'ai-wan cheng-chih hsien-chuang pao-kao-shu* [A Report on the Current Political Conditions in Taiwan]. N.p., 1946, p. 30. Henceforth *T'ai-wan cheng-chih hsien-chuang pao-kao-shu*.

100. *Formosa: Internal Affairs, 1945–1949*, Reel 1, Enclosure to despatch no. 1206 (Mar. 15, 1946), p. 3.

101. *Ibid.*

102. Ch'en Kuo-hsiang and Chu P'ing, *T'ai-wan pao-yeh yen-chin ssu-shih-nien* [Change and Progress of Taiwan's Newspaper Industry over the Past Forty Years] (Taipei: Tzu-li wan-pao, 1987), p. 27. The remarks in this paragraph are from Chapter 1 of this excellent history of Taiwan's press.

103. *Ibid.*, pp. 28–29, for a list of these newspapers, virtually all of which were in Japanese.

104. *Ho-p'ing jih-pao*, Aug. 5, 1946, p. 1, editorial.

105. *Ibid.*, Aug. 7, 1946, p. 1, editorial.

106. *Ibid.*, p. 2.

107. *Ibid.*

108. *Tzu-ch'iang-pao*, Aug. 8, 1946, p. 3.

109. *Ibid.*, Sept. 11, 1946, p. 3.

110. See editorials in *Chung-hua jih-pao* [The China Daily], Apr. 17, 1947, p. 1, and Apr. 18, 1947, p. 3.

111. *Formosa: Internal Affairs, 1945–1949*, Reel 1, Enclosure 13 (Aug. 30, 1946), p. 2.

112. Yeh Ming-hsün, "Pu-jung ch'ing-shih chin ch'eng hui: erh-erh-pa shih-chien ch'in-li ti kan-shou" [We Cannot Allow True History to Totally Become Ashes: My Personal Experience and Observations of the February 28th Incident], *Lien-ho-pao*, Feb. 29, 1988, p. 2. See also Yeh Ming-hsün, "Pu-jung ch'ing-shih chin ch'eng hui" (cited in n. 33), p. 6; also Yeh Ming-hsün, "Hou-shih chung-hsieh tzu yu p'ing: ts'ung Ch'en Kung-hsia t'an-tao erh-erh-pa shih-chien" [Later Generations Will Judge the Righteousness and Evil: From Ch'en I to the February 28th Incident], *Chung-kuo shih-pao*, May 7, 1988, p. 18.

113. *Ch'en I sheng-p'ing chi pei-hai nei-mu*, p. 107.

114. *Ibid.*

115. *Ibid.*, p. 108.

116. *Ibid.*, p. 116.

117. Yeh Ming-hsün, "Hou-shih chung-hsieh tzu yu p'ing," *Chung-kuo shih-pao*, May 7, 1988, p. 18.

118. T'ai-wan-sheng hsing-cheng chang-kuan kung-shu hsüan-ch'uan wei-yüan-

hui, comp., *Wai-kuo chi-che-t'uan yen-chung chih T'ai-wan* [Taiwan as Seen by a Team of Foreign Reporters] (Taipei: Hsüan-ch'uan wei-yüan-hui t'u-shu fa-hsing-so, 1946), p. 26. Henceforth cited as *WCT*.

119. *T'ung-chi t'i-yao*, p. 1164.

120. *TNC*, p. J2, for report to Chiang Kai-shek that 80 percent of the transport system had been restored; and pp. J34–35 for data comparing 1945 and 1946 freight and passenger traffic carried by the railway system.

121. *WCT*, p. 74.

122. *Ibid.*, p. 18.

123. *Ibid.*

124. *Ibid.*, p. 48.

125. *Ibid.*, p. 29.

126. Chinese-American Joint Commission on Rural Reconstruction [JCRR], *Taiwan Agricultural Statistics, 1901–1965*, p. 23.

127. For such an interpretation, see *T'ung-chi t'i-yao*, p. 1096.

128. Ma Chen-tu and Ch'i Ju-kao, "T'ai-wan kuang-fu hou Nan-ching kuo-min cheng-fu tui yüan tsai-cheng chin-jung chi-kou ti chieh-shou chi ch'i kung-tso ti t'ui-chin," pp. 46–59. Between April and December 1946, the provincial government had to grant a total subsidy of 793,607,076 old Taiwan dollars to the local governments of five districts and eight cities (see p. 50) to cover a total expenditure by these same units of 988,930,129 old Taiwan dollars.

129. *WCT*, p. 71. According to research by Kenneth S. Lin and Tsong-min Wu, prices rose 73.1 percent in 1942, 96.1 percent in 1943, 430.2 percent in 1944, and 226.2 percent in 1945. Then prices rose again 300 percent in 1946, 660 percent in 1947, nearly 1600 percent in 1948, and 660 percent in the first half of 1949, only to fall dramatically after June 15, 1949, and stabilize in the latter half of 1950. See their essay "Taiwan's Big Inflation, 1946–1949," presented at the Second Conference on Modern Chinese Economic History (January 5–7, 1989), Nankang, Taiwan.

130. *Ibid.*, p. 71.

131. *T'ung-chi t'i-yao*, p. 910.

132. T'ai-wan-sheng hsing-cheng chang-kuan kung-shu t'ung-chi-shih, *T'ai-wan wu-chia t'ung-chi yüeh-pao* [Taiwan Monthly Commodity Price Statistics], Jan. 1947, p. 17.

133. *T'ai-wan hsin-sheng-pao*, Jan. 25, 1947, p. 5.

134. *WCT*, p. 70. The population in late June 1946 came to 6,336,329, with males numbering 3,194,209 and females 3,142,120, and overseas Chinese numbering 28,024. According to these data, the number of unemployed would be around 40,000 people. See also T'ai-wan-sheng hsing-cheng chang-kuan kung-shu hsüan-ch'uan wei-yüan-hui, comp. [Taiwan Provincial Administrative Executive Office, Propaganda Commission], *T'ai-wan chih-nan* [Taiwan Guide] (Taipei: Hsüan-ch'uan wei-yüan-hui t'u-shu fa-hsing-so, Sept. 1946), pp. 17–18.

135. Hu Ch'iu-yüan, *I-pai san-shih nien-lai Chung-kuo ssu-hsiang shih-kang*, pp. 214–16, 221–22.

136. *T'ai-wan hsin-sheng-pao*, Jan. 1, 1947, p. 4.

137. *Ibid.*

138. *Ibid.*
139. *Ibid.*
140. Tan Kah-kee, *Nan-ch'iao hui-i-lu*, vol. 2, p. 246.
141. *Ibid.*, p. 271.
142. *Ibid.*, p. 242; Shen Chung-jen, ed., *Ch'en Chia-keng chiu-kuo yen-lun-chi*, pp. 62–63.
143. *T'ai-wan hsin-sheng-pao*, Jan. 1, 1947, p. 4.
144. *WCT*, p. 39.
145. *WCT*, p. 37.
146. As of early May 1946, there were "46 official or semi-official companies which [had] absorbed former Japanese factories and company units. Approximately 412 small enterprises [were] being offered to the public for sale or lease." See the U.S. State Department's Nov. 1, 1946, report on the first convocation of the Taiwan Provincial Council, in *Formosa: Internal Affairs, 1945–1949*, Reel 1, Enclosure no. 25, p. 5 (May 1–15, 1946).
147. Yang Chao-chia, p. 355.
148. Huang Chen-chung, "T'ai-wan liang-shih cheng-ts'e ti shang-t'ao," p. 6.
149. T'ai-wan-sheng liang-shih t'iao-chi wei-yüan-hui mi-shu-shih [Secretariat of the Taiwan Provincial Food Grain Regulation Commission], "T'ai-wan-sheng liang-shih t'iao-chi wei-yüan-hui kung-tso pao-kao" [Work Report of the Food Grain Regulatory Committee of Taiwan Province], *Cheng-ch'i pan-yüeh-k'an*, vol. 1, no. 3 (May 1, 1946), p. 18.
150. *Formosa: Internal Affairs, 1945–1949*, Reel 1, Report 25 (Nov. 1, 1946), p. 22. Between Dec. 15, 1945, and Mar. 31, 1946, 45 percent (217,515,155 old Taiwan dollars) of the provincial government's total expenditures went to subsidize government enterprises such as railroads, the postal service, and the Monopoly Bureau. This is the figure that the Head of the Department of Finance, Yen Chia-kan, reported to the Taiwan Provincial Council in early May 1946.
151. *TNC*, Appendix, p. 8.
152. By Aug. 20, 1946, the CNC dollar, formerly exchanged on the Mainland at 30 to 1 old Taiwan dollar, rose to 40:1. See the Aug. 30, 1946, report of the U.S. Consulate in Taipei, in *Formosa: Internal Affairs, 1945–1949*, Reel 1, Enclosure no. 13, p. 4. By Dec. 1946, all Japanese banknotes were to be retired and replaced by new notes of Chinese design to be printed by the Bank of Taiwan. See Ralph J. Blake's report of Dec. 3, 1946, in *Formosa: Internal Affairs, 1945–1949*, Reel 1, Enclosure no. 30, p. 9.
153. Shen Yün-lung, "Ch'en I ch'i-jen yü erh-erh-pa shih-pien," p. 58.
154. *Ibid.*
155. *Ibid.*
156. *Formosa: Internal Affairs, 1945–1949*, Reel 1, Enclosure no. 1206 (Mar. 15, 1946), pp. 2 and 6. This report, drafted by George Kerr, was based on information provided by staff of the U.S. Consulate in Taipei.
157. *Formosa: Internal Affairs, 1945–1949*, Reel 1, Enclosure no. 9 (Aug. 12, 1946, Taipei consulate report), p. 9.
158. *Ibid.*, Enclosure no. 24 (Oct. 31, 1946, Taipei consulate report), p. 4.
159. *Ibid.*
160. *Ibid.*, Enclosure no. 30 (Dec. 3, 1946, Taipei consulate report to Ambassa-

dor Stuart in Nanking on Nov. 1946 political and economic conditions in Taiwan), p. 2.

161. *Ibid.*, Enclosure no. 24 (Oct. 31, 1946), p. 4.

162. *Ibid.*, Enclosure no. 30 (Dec. 3, 1946), pp. 2–3.

163. *Ibid.*, p. 3.

164. *Ibid.*, Enclosure no. 19 (Oct. 2, 1946), p. 4. Some Chinese viewed these returnees with contempt. "The director of the Taiwan railway administration, when approached for assistance in providing transportation from the port of debarkation, stated that he had no interest in helping the repatriates since they were 'more Japanese than Chinese.'"

165. Shen Yün-lung, "Ch'en I ch'i-jen yü erh-erh-pa shih-pien," p. 59.

166. "Erh-erh-pa shih-chien tiao-ch'a pao-kao" [An Investigation Report of the February 28th Incident], *Shih-chieh jih-pao*, Mar. 11, 1988, pp. 6–7. This source is the famous report of the Fukien censor Yang Liang-kung, who arrived in Keelung on March 9 and returned to Nanking in mid-April 1947 after conducting an island-wide tour. He reported on the reasons for the Uprising, the conditions that occurred during the Uprising, and the aftermath. This estimate can be found on p. 7 of part 3 of the report under section 1, "Liu-mang."

167. *Formosa: Internal Affairs, 1945–1949*, Reel 1, Enclosure no. 232 (Jan. 28, 1946), p. 1. The report was made on Nov. 23, 1945, by Lt. George H. Kerr.

168. Wang yü-te, p. 157. Sneider, *A Pail of Oysters*, p. 215. Kao-hsiung-shih chün-min ho-tso-chan, comp., *Kuo-chün chu-T'ai hsü-chih*, p. 10. *T'ai-wan cheng-chih hsien-chuang pao-kao-shu*, p. 9. Yang I-chou, "Hui-i erh-erh-pa min-pien ko-ming san-shih-nien" [Remembering the February 28th Incident's People's Uprising Thirty Years Later], *Wang-ch'un-feng*, no. 90 (Feb. 20, 1977), p. 15.

169. *T'ai-wan cheng-chih hsien-chuang pao-kao-shu*, p. 2; "T'ai-wan hsiao-hsi," *Hsin T'ai-wan*, no. 3 (Apr. 1, 1946), p. 8; T'ai-tu chi-k'an tzu-liao-tsu, "Erh-erh-pa ta-ko-ming ti chen-hsiang," p. 76.

170. Tu Ts'ung-ming, *Hui-i-lu*, p. 119.

171. Han Shih-ch'üan, p. 68. It should be mentioned that Han hated the Japanese.

172. *Ibid.*, p. 69.

173. Throughout the summer and fall of 1946, the *T'ai-wan hsin-sheng-pao* produced various works in Japanese on current events, for example: *Kokufu no kaigumi to Taiwan-sho seifu no seiritsu* [Establishing Governance in Taiwan Province and Reform of the National Government], June 1946; *Sanchu zenkai seiji keizai kaikaku hōan* [Proposals for Political and Economic Reform by the Third Plenary of the Central Committee of the Kuomintang], May 1946; *Nihon no baisho mondai* [The Problem of Japanese Reparations], July 1946; *Haisengo no Nihon wa do natte iru* [Where Does Japan Go After the Defeat?], Feb. 1947; *Tōnan Ajia no minzoku kaiho undō* [National Liberation Movements of East Asia], Jan. 1947; *Kokumin taikei: Chū-Bei shōyaku to kasei kaikaku mondai* [The Nationalist Party People's Congress: The China-U.S. Commercial Treaty and the Problem of Reforming the Currency System], Dec. 1946; *Rengōkoku taikei sono seiritsu to keika* [The General Assembly of the United Nations: Its Establishment and Evolution], Nov. 1946. These materials are in the East Asian Collection of the Hoover Institution.

174. *WCT*, pp. 26–27.
175. Huang Hsü-tung, "Erh-erh-pa shih-pien ssu-t'ung-lu," *Erh-erh-pa chen-hsiang*, p. 191.
176. *Ibid.*, p. 64.
177. Yang Chao-chia, pp. 354–55.
178. *Ibid.*
179. Ch'iu Nien-t'ai, *Wo-ti feng-tou-shih*, p. 352.
180. Kerr, *Formosa Betrayed*, p. 317.
181. Hsüeh Mu, p. 54.
182. Wu Cho-liu, p. 171.
183. *Formosa: Internal Affairs, 1945–1949*, Reel 1, Enclosure no. 36 (Jan. 10, 1947), p. 2.
184. *Ibid.*, p. 4.
185. *T'ai-wan cheng-chih hsien-chuang pao-kao-shu*, pp. 2–3.
186. In fact, Ch'en's administration made every effort to publish relevant statistics about Taiwan under Japanese rule.
187. Ch'en I, "Chin-nien wei hsing-hsien nien," *T'ai-wan hsing-sheng-pao* Jan. 1, 1947, p. 4.
188. *Ibid.*
189. *Ibid.*
190. *KSCW*, Doc. 1, p. 41.
191. *Ibid.*, p. 40.

Chapter 4

1. CMYWTK, "Wei 'erh-erh-ch'i' yeh ch'i-ssu fa-sheng chiu-fen shih ch'eng ching-pei tsung-pu pao-kao ch'üan-wen," p. 69.
2. *Ibid.*, p. 31.
3. Shih Ming, *T'ai-wan-jen ssu-pai-nien shih*, p. 754.
4. FWPTCC, *T'ai-wan-sheng wen-hsien wei-yüan-hui ch'ien chu-jen wei-yüan Lin Heng-tao hsien-sheng erh-erh-pa shih-pien hui-i*, p. 7.
5. Huang Ts'un-hou, *Erh-erh-pa shih-pien shih-mo-chi*, p. 51.
6. *T'ai-wan hsin-sheng-pao*, Mar. 3, 1947 (extra edition). Lin Mu-shun, *T'ai-wan erh-yüeh ko-ming*, p. 4.
7. NCPCCS, "Lo Ch'ün-yen hsien-sheng 'erh-ehr-pa shih-chien' hui-i tzu-liao," p. 1.
8. K'o Yüan-fen, "Shih-pien shih-jih-chi," p. 42.
9. Lin Mu-shun, *T'ai-wan erh-yüeh ko-ming*, p. 5; Shih Ming, *T'ai-wan-jen ssu-pai-nien shih*, pp. 755–56.
10. Wang K'ang, "Li-shih ti cheng-yen: 'Erh-erh-pa shih-pien' ch'in-li-chi," *Ch'ang-liu pan-yüeh-k'an*, no. 922 (July 1, 1988), p. 11. Wang's account was serialized in this journal in issues 922 (July 1, 1988), pp. 11–14; 923 (July 16, 1988), pp. 8–11; and 924 (Aug. 1, 1988), pp. 9–12.
11. "Erh-erh-pa shih-chien ti ching-kuo" [A Review of the February 28th Incident], *T'ai-wan hsin-sheng-pao*, Mar. 3, 1947 (extra edition).
erh-pa pei ou-chi."
12. Lin Mu-shun, *T'ai-wan erh-yüeh ko-ming*, p. 5.

13. Shih Ming, *T'ai-wan-jen ssu-pai-nien shih*, pp. 755–56. Chuang Chia-nung, *Fen-nu ti T'ai-wan*, p. 101. Lin Mu-shun, *T'ai-wan erh-yüeh ko-ming*, p. 5.

14. Lin Mu-shun, *T'ai-wan erh-yüeh ko-ming*, p. 5.

15. At that time, Mainlanders were called *a-shan*; Taiwanese who had returned from the Mainland were called *pan-shan*; and Taiwanese in general were referred to as *han-chi*.

16. Hsia I, "T'a kao-su wo-men shih-mo?," p. 56.

17. Ching Yü, *T'ai-wan shih-pien chen-hsiang yü nei-mu*, p. 3.

18. Lin Mu-shun, *T'ai-wan erh-yüeh ko-ming*, p. 5.

19. NCPCCS, "Lo Ch'ün-yen hsien-sheng 'erh-erh-pa shih-chien' hui-i tzu-liao," p. 1.

20. Lin Mu-shun, *T'ai-wan erh-yüeh ko-ming*, p. 6.

21. Dr. Hsieh provided this information in interviews and written communications. It should also be noted that Hsieh was elected to the National Assembly less than a year after the Incident, receiving the highest number of votes from Taipei and the Taipei district.

22. Huang Ts'un-hou, *Erh-erh-pa shih-pien shih-mo-chi*, p. 52. See also Lin Mu-shun, *T'ai-wan erh-yüeh ko-ming*, p. 7.

23. Huang Ts'un-hou, *Erh-erh-pa shih-pien shih-mo-chi*, p. 52. Lin Mu-shun, *T'ai-wan erh-yüeh ko-ming*, p. 7.

24. Lin Mu-shun, *T'ai-wan erh-yüeh ko-ming*, p. 7.

25. Wang K'ang, "Erh-erh-pa shih-pien ch'in-li-chi," p. 323.

26. *T'ai-wan hsin-sheng-pao*, Mar. 3, 1947, p. 1, as reported by Governor-General Ch'en I.

27. *Chung-hua jih-pao*, Mar. 3, 1947.

28. Ibid.

29. Ibid.

30. Ma Ch'i-hua ed., *Erh-erh-pa yen-chiu* (A Study of the February 28th Incident), p. 31.

31. Huang Ts'un-hou, *Erh-erh-pa shih-pien shih-mo-chi*, pp. 7–8.

32. Ibid.

33. Ibid., p. 8; *Chung-hua jih-pao*, Mar. 3, 1947.

34. *Chung-hua jih-pao*, Mar. 3, 1947. Those who had participated that day in such meetings of government and popular representatives were as follows.

Representing the government side were the five department heads and K'o Yüan-fen and Chang Mu-t'ao; other National Councilmen were Lin Chung, Tu Ts'ung-ming, Lin Chung-hsien, Wu Kuo-hsin, Lin Hsien-t'ang, Ch'en I-sung.

Representing the citizenry were all members of the Taipei City Council and members of the Taiwan Provincial Council, Huang Ch'ao-ch'in, Wang T'ien-teng, Huang Ch'un-ch'ing, Li Yu-san, Ting Jui-ping, Lin Wei-kung, Liu K'uo-ts'ai, Lin Pi-hui; and members of the National Assembly (Lien Chen-tung, Huang Kuo-shu, Li Wan-chü, Yen Ch'in-hsien, Liu Ming-ch'ao).

No representatives of Taipei's agriculture, industry, commerce, and education took part because they had yet to be elected.

35. Huang Ts'un-hou, *Erh-erh-pa shih-pien shih-mo-chi*, p. 8.

36. Ibid., p. 53.

37. *Chung-hua jih-pao*, Mar. 5, 1947; Huang Ts'un-hou, *Erh-erh-pa shih-pien shih-mo-chi*, p. 53.
38. Huang Ts'un-hou, *Erh-erh-pa shih-pien shih-mo-chi*, pp. 11–12. *T'ai-wan hsin-sheng-pao*, Mar. 3, 1947 (extra edition).
39. *Ibid.*
40. *T'ai-wan hsin-sheng-pao*, Mar. 3, 1947 (extra edition).
41. *Ibid.*
42. *Ibid.*
43. *Chung-hua jih-pao*, Mar. 5, 1947.
44. Huang Ts'un-hou, *Erh-erh-pa shih-pien shih-mo-chi*, pp. 15–16.
45. *Ibid.*, pp. 16–17.
46. *Ibid.*, p. 18.
47. *Ibid.*, p. 17. *Chung-hua jih-pao*, Mar. 5, 1947.
48. Huang Ts'un-hou, *Erh-erh-pa shih-pien shih-mo-chi*, pp. 17–18.
49. *Ibid.*, pp. 18–19.
50. *Ibid.*, pp. 20–21.
51. *Ibid.*, p. 54.
52. *Ibid.*
53. *Ibid.*, p. 22.
54. *Ibid.*, pp. 22–23.
55. *Ibid.*, pp. 23–24.
56. *Ibid.*
57. *Ibid.*, p. 55.
58. *Ibid.*, pp. 24–25 and p. 55.
59. *Ibid.*, p. 25 and p. 55.
60. *Ibid.*, p. 55.
61. Kuo T'ing-i, *Chung-hua min-kuo shih-shih jih-chih*, vol. 4, p. 614.
62. Hsia I, "T'a kao-su wo-men shih-mo?," p. 57. For a list of the 32 demands, see *T'ai-wan hsin-sheng-pao*, Mar. 8, 1947; Huang Ts'un-hou, *Erh-erh-pa shih-pien shih-mo-chi*, pp. 25–29.
63. *T'ai-wan hsin-sheng-pao*, Mar. 9, 1947, p. 1.
64. Huang Ts'un-hou, *Erh-erh-pa shih-pien shih-mo-chi*, p. 29; *Chung-hua jih-pao*, Mar. 9, 1947.
65. *Ibid.*
66. T'ai-wan-sheng hsing-cheng chang-kuan kung-shu hsin-wen-shih [Taiwan Provincial Administrative Executive Office Agency for Information], comp., *T'ai-wan pao-tung shih-chien chi-shih*, p. 3. Chan Chou, "Chi-lung wen-chien," pp. 91–96.
67. Lin Mu-shun, *T'ai-wan erh-yüeh ko-ming*, p. 18.
68. *Ibid.*
69. *T'ai-wan hsin-sheng-pao*, Mar. 9, 1947.
70. *Ibid.*
71. Ching Yü, *T'ai-wan shih-pien chen-hsiang yü nei-mu*, p. 20.
72. *Ibid.*
73. Jen Po, "I-lan ti hsü-ching," p. 103.
74. Lin Mu-shun, *T'ai-wan erh-yüeh ko-ming*, p. 20.
75. Jen Po, "I-lan ti hsü-ching," p. 107.

76. Lin Mu-shun, *T'ai-wan erh-yüeh ko-ming*, p. 20.
77. Chu Wen-po, "Erh-erh-pa pei-ou chi," p. 27.
78. Tso (pseudonym of Chu Wen-po), "Erh-erh-pa shih-chien-chung wo ho Hsin-chu hsien-cheng-fu pei-hsi ching-kuo," pp. 110–11.
79. Lin Mu-shun, *T'ai-wan erh-yüeh ko-ming*, p. 20.
80. An Hui, "Chin-shou chiao-yü ti kang-wei," p. 117.
81. Ching Yü, *T'ai-wan shih-pien chen-hsiang yü nei-mu*, pp. 22–23.
82. Chu Wen-po, "Erh-erh-pa pei-ou chi," p. 27.
83. Lin Mu-shun, *T'ai-wan erh-yüeh ko-ming*, p. 21; Ching Yü, *T'ai-wan shih-pien chen-hsiang yü nei-mu*, p. 23.
84. Tso (Chu Wen-po), "Erh-erh-pa shih-chien-chung wo ho Hsin-chu hsien-cheng-fu pei-hsi ching-kuo," pp. 112–13.
85. Ching Yü, *T'ai-wan shih-pien chen-hsiang yü nei-mu*, p. 23.
86. Ya San, "Erh-erh-pa shih-pien ti t'ou-shih," p. 4.
87. Ching Yü, *T'ai-wan shih-pien chen-hsiang yü nei-mu*, p. 25.
88. *Ibid.*; Lin Mu-shun, *T'ai-wan erh-yüeh ko-ming*, p. 22; Ch'üan, "T'ai-chung li-hsien-chi," p. 120.
89. Lin Mu-shun, *T'ai-wan erh-yüeh ko-ming*, pp. 22–23.
90. *Ibid.*, p. 23.
91. *Ibid.*
92. Ch'üan, "T'ai-chung li-hsien-chi," pp. 121–22.
93. Lin Mu-shun, *T'ai-wan erh-yüeh ko-ming*, p. 23. Ch'üan, "T'ai-chung li-hsien-chi," pp. 123–24.
94. Ya San, "Erh-erh-pa shih-pien ti t'ou-shih," p. 5. Chung Nan, "Ch'ü chih-an pen-pu," p. 130.
95. Ya San, "Erh-erh-pa shih-pien ti t'ou-shih," p. 5.
96. Lin Mu-shun, *T'ai-wan erh-yüeh ko-ming*, pp. 24–25.
97. Ch'üan, "T'ai-chung li-hsien-chi," pp. 124–25.
98. Shih Ming, *T'ai-wan-jen ssu-pai-nien shih*, p. 767.
99. Lin Mu-shun, *T'ai-wan erh-yüeh ko-ming*, p. 24.
100. *Ibid.*, pp. 25–26.
101. *Ibid.*, p. 26.
102. *Ibid.* [Chou Ming offered the following reasons for why the Twenty-seventh Militia Corps weakly resisted Nationalist forces in his memoir. First, its personnel had just taken up weapons and were still poorly trained and without any central command. Second, the unit failed to win the local support necessary to gain intelligence information, supplies, and moral encouragement. Third, the Nationalist secret police had apparently penetrated the organization's ranks and gathered relevant details about its military plans. Finally, the unit never acquired sufficient weapons and supplies, and food supplies under its control had been depleted because of theft.]
103. *Ibid.*, p. 28.
104. *Ibid.*
105. Man Hsi, "Chia-shu pao p'ing-an," pp. 137–38.
106. Shen Hsiao-shen, "Tsai-hui-pa! Chia-i," p. 146. On the afternoon of Mar. 5, some young people set up a special volunteer unit to help launch an attack on Hu-wei airport in Yün-lin county (p. 144).

107. *Ibid.*, p. 144.
108. *Ibid.*
109. *Ibid.*
110. *Ibid.*
111. *Ibid.*, p. 145.
112. Hung P'eng-wan, "T'ai-nan pao-hsing lu," p. 170.
113. *Ibid.*
114. *Ibid.*, pp. 170–71.
115. Ying, "Kao-hsiung ch'i-jih," pp. 191–92.
116. Shih Ming, *T'ai-wan-jen ssu-pai-nien shih*, pp. 775–76.
117. Fan, "La-tsa hua P'ing-tung," p. 198.
118. Mien Chih, "Hua-lien fen-jao chi-shih," p. 199.
119. *Ibid.*, p. 200.
120. *Ibid.*, pp. 200–201.
121. *Ibid.*, p. 201.
122. *Ibid.*
123. *Ibid.*, p. 202.
124. *Ibid.*, p. 203.
125. *Ibid.*, p. 204.
126. *Ibid.*, p. 205.
127. *Ibid.*
128. Cheng Che-wen, "An-ching ti P'eng-hu," p. 207.
129. P'an Chih-chün, "Hui-i T'ai-wan kuang-fu yü erh-erh-pa shih-chien ti i-tuan li-ch'eng," pp. 351–53.
130. Ts'ai Ch'ien, *Jih-pen ti-kuo chu-i chih chih-min-ti: T'ai-wan*, p. 42.
131. P'an Chih-chün, "Hui-i T'ai-wan kuang-fu yü erh-erh-pa shih-chien ti i-tuan li-ch'eng," pp. 351–53.
132. Kuo-fang-pu chung-cheng-chih-pu, *Hsieh Hsüeh-hung ti pei-chü*, pp. 6–7. Hsieh's year of birth was 1901, not 1902, as this source indicates. For correction see Ch'en Fang-ming, "Chieh-pai ti ho-hua: mien-huai min-tsu tou-shih Hsieh Hsüeh-hung."
133. *Hsieh Hsüeh-hung ti pei-chü*, p. 8.
134. In 1935, while in Yenan (northern Shensi), Ts'ai Hsiao-ch'ien changed his name to Ts'ai Ch'ien.
135. P'an Chih-chün, "Hui-i T'ai-wan kuang-fu yü erh-erh-pa shih-chien ti i-tuan li-ch'eng," pp. 351–53.
136. *Ibid.*, p. 360.
137. *Ibid.*, p. 363. Hsü Ch'eng-tsung, "Erh-erh-pa shih-chien chen-hsiang," pp. 65–66. At the time of the Incident, when government troops had not yet arrived in Taiwan, many people were deeply afraid that the Communists would somehow take over the island. See Shih Ming, *T'ai-wan-jen ssu-pai-nien shih*, pp. 788–96.
138. Chuang Chia-nung, *Fen-nu ti T'ai-wan*, pp. 106–7.
139. Chung I-jen, *Hsing-suan liu-shih-nien*, p. 480. The leader of the "Erh-ch'i pu-tui" [Twenty-seventh Militia Corps] Chung I-jen, also said that the Uprising was not directed by the Communists. Based on the authors' interview with Chung I-jen on Apr. 10, 1987. Wang Shih-hsün, "Erh-ch'i pu-tui chih hui-i," p. 12. A Communist leader who later defected to the Nationalist government also told

the authors that the CCP was never involved in the Uprising (Oct. 20, 1986, interview).

140. Chung I-jen, *Hsing-suan liu-shih-nien*, pp. 480–81.
141. Ibid., p. 555.
142. Ibid., p. 625.
143. Ibid., pp. 595–96; and *T'ai-wan cheng-chih hsien-chuang pao-kao-shu*, pp. 19–22.
144. Derived from an interview with a former Taiwan Communist named Hung.
145. Interview conducted on Oct. 20, 1986.
146. *Shih-chieh jih-pao*, Mar. 11, 1988, pp. 6–7.
147. *T'ai-wan hsin-sheng-pao*, Apr. 1, 1947, p. 1. Other eyewitnesses also corroborate this view. See Chuang Chia-nung, *Fen-nu ti T'ai-wan*, p. 97.
148. Ibid., p. 1.
149. "Cheng-wu hui-i chi-yao: Chang-kuan chih-tz'u" [Government Affairs Conference Report: The Governor-General's Instructions], *T'ai-wan-sheng hsing-cheng chang-kuan kung-shu kung-pao* [Taiwan Provincial Administrative Executive Office News Gazette], no. 11 (Apr. 12, 1947), p. 174.
150. *T'ai-wan hsin-sheng-pao*, Apr. 13, 1947, p. 4.
151. *T'ai-wan hsin-sheng-pao*, May 31, 1947, p. 4.
152. Ibid.
153. Ibid.
154. For such examples, see Wang K'ang, "Erh-erh-pa shih-pien ch'in-li-chi," p. 337; Lu Jen, "T'ai-wan erh-erh-pa chen-hsiang," p. 49. Yeh Ming-hsün also concurs with our interpretation. Interviews with Mr. Yeh, June 20, 1986, by the authors.

Chapter 5

1. *Shen-pao*, May 18, 1947.
2. Wang K'ang, "Erh-erh-pa shih-pien ch'in-li-chi," p. 336.
3. K'ou Ping-hua, "T'ai-wan hsin-chiu chih chien"; Huang Hsü-tung, "Erh-erh-pa shih-pien ssu-tung-lu," p. 17.
4. This estimate was derived by dividing the Taipei wholesale price index into the property loss figure, multiplying by the 1937 base price index figure, and using that estimate to derive the percentage of 1947 net domestic product (NDP). The 1947 NDP estimate is based on Kuznets' conjecture that Taiwan's 1947 NDP was 62 percent of the 1937 NDP, which we assume to be 805.7 million Taiwan dollars, a figure produced by Lee Teng-hui's prewar national income estimates.
5. Ch'in Hsiao-i, comp., *Tsung-t'ung Chiang-kung ta-shih chang-pien ch'u-kao*, vol. 6, pt. 2, p. 396. (Henceforth *TT*.)
6. See *South China Morning Post*, 3, no. 58 (Mar. 1, 1947), p. 12, for a report on the 250,000-man Communist attack on Ch'ang-ch'un. On March 3, Communist troops engaged in hand-to-hand combat with the Nationalists on the city's outskirts and 10,000 Nationalist reinforcements had to be rushed to the rescue. See *South China Morning Post*, 3, no. 60 (Mar. 3, 1947), p. 1.
7. *TT*, p. 396.

8. *Ibid.*, p. 397.
9. *Ibid.*, p. 398.
10. *KSCW*, Document 7, pp. 55–57.
11. *Ibid.*, pp. 57–58.
12. *Ibid.*, pp. 61–64 (a bureau report separate from Ch'en I's Mar. 6 report).
13. *Ibid.*, p. 65.
14. *Ibid.*, Document 8, p. 67.
15. *Ibid.*, Document 11, pp. 71–73.
16. *Ibid.*, Document 14, p. 77.
17. *Ibid.*, Document 16, pp. 83–84.
18. *Ibid.*, p. 85.
19. *Ibid.*, Document 18, p. 87.
20. *Ibid.*, Document 19, p. 88.
21. *TT*, p. 398.
22. *Ibid.*, p. 399.
23. *Ibid.*, p. 400.
24. *T'ai-wan hsin-sheng-pao*, Mar. 11, 1947.
25. *Ibid.*
26. *Ibid.*
27. *Ibid.*
28. See *KSCW*, Document 22, p. 100, for information on groups of extremists attacking Nationalist troops north of Taipei in the Yüan-shan area.
29. See *ibid.* for information that Nationalist troops arrived in Keelung on the evening of March 8, and some units arrived in Taipei on March 9.
30. *T'ai-wan hsin-sheng-pao*, Mar. 11, 1947.
31. *TT*, p. 403; *KSCW*, Document 38, p. 134.
32. See *KSCW*, Document 38, p. 134, for Ch'en's reply by telegram.
33. *T'ai-wan hsin-sheng-pao*, Mar. 16, 1947, p. 3.
34. *Ibid.*
35. *Chung-hua jih-pao*, Mar. 11, 1947.
36. *Ibid.*
37. *Ibid.*
38. *T'ai-wan hsin-sheng-pao*, Mar. 12, 1947.
39. *Ibid.*
40. *KSCW*, Document 35, contains a letter by K'o Yüan-fen (pp. 122–25) and another by Ch'en I (pp. 126–28) forwarded by General Pai Ch'ung-hsi to Chiang Kai-shek (p. 121).
41. *Ibid.*, Document 40, pp. 136–41.
42. *Ibid.*, Document 45, p. 156.
43. *Ibid.*, Document 47, p. 158.
44. *Ibid.*, Document 46, p. 157.
45. *Ibid.*
46. *Ibid.*, Document 49, pp. 160–61.
47. *Ibid.*, Document 50, p. 162.
48. *Ibid.*, Document 53, p. 171.
49. *Ibid.*, Document 54, p. 172.

50. *Ibid.*, pp. 173–74.
51. *Ibid.*, Document 55, pp. 175–76.
52. *Ibid.*, Document 56, pp. 177–81.
53. *Ibid.*, p. 177.
54. *Ibid.*, Document 57, p. 182.
55. *Ibid.*
56. *Ibid.*, Document 60, pp. 185–86.
57. *Ibid.*
58. Hsüeh Mu, "Wo ts'ung T'ai-wan huo-cho hui-lai," p. 56. It seems impossible to locate issues of these papers to determine how critical they were of Ch'en I and his administration.
59. *Ibid.*
60. Wang K'ang, "Erh-erh-pa shih-pien ch'in-li-chi" [A Personal Historical Record of the February 28th Incident], p. 331.
61. Bate, *Report from Formosa*, pp. 20–21.
62. *T'ai-wan-sheng hsing-cheng chang-kuan kung-shu kung-pao*, Hsia-chi-pao, Apr. 8, 1947, p. 102.
63. *Ibid.*, no. 9 (Apr. 10, 1947), p. 139.
64. P'u Jen, "I-ch'ang li-shih o-meng ti hui-hsiang: T'ai-wan erh-erh-pa shih-chien shen-li-chu," p. 343.
65. *Ibid.*
66. Chung I-jen, *Hsing-suan liu-shih-nien*, pp. 636–39.
67. Liao first went to Hong Kong and then to Japan to organize the Taiwan Independence Movement, of which he became a leader. Then in the 1960s he returned to Taiwan, made amends with the Kuomintang, and later served as the deputy director of the Shih Men Reservoir. He died in June 1986. See Li Shih-chieh, "T'ai-wan kung-ho-kuo lin-shih cheng-fu ta-t'ung-ling Liao Wen-i t'ou-hsiang shih-mo" [The Complete Story of President Liao Wen-i of the Provisional Government of the Republic of Taiwan] (Taipei: Tzu-yu shih-tai ch'u-pan-she, 1988), Preface, pp. 4–5. The Shanghai Garrison Command tried to oust Liao shortly after he arrived in Shanghai (see pp. 53–54).
68. FWPTCC, *Lin Heng-tao erh-erh-pa shih-pien hui-i*, p. 11; Li shih-chieh, pp. 55–56.
69. KSCW, Document 64, p. 191.
70. P'eng Ming-min, *A Taste of Freedom*, p. 69.
71. *Ibid.*, pp. 69–70.
72. Huang Wu-tung, *Huang Wu-tung hui-i-lu*, p. 163.
73. *Formosa: Internal Affairs, 1945–1949*, Reel 1 (Dean Acheson's report to Senator Joseph H. Bald).
74. Wang K'ang, "Erh-erh-pa shih-pien ch'in-li-chi," pp. 329–30.
75. Kuo En-hsing reported in 1988 that the Feng-lin Church members Chang Ch'i-lang and two of his sons, plus Shao Ch'ao-chin of the Kang-shan Church, were innocent victims of this slaughter. See *T'ai-wan chiao-hui kung-pao*, no. 1879 (Mar. 6, 1988), p. 7. See also Liu Feng-sung, *T'ai-wan ti hei-an*. This book describes the efforts by Chang Ch'i-lang's wife to petition the government for compensation for the death of her husband and their eldest and youngest sons.

76. Chuang Chia-nung, *Fen-nu ti T'ai-wan*, p. 135.
77. *Ibid.*, p. 151. Liu Feng-sung, *T'ai-wan ti hei-an*, pp. 1–16. See also pp. 124–34 for a description of how Wang T'ien-teng was executed in Taipei.
78. NCPCCS, "Chou Tao-yüan hsien-sheng 'Erh-erh-pa shih-chien hui-i tzu-liao,'" pp. 4–6.
79. Chiang Mu-yün, "T'ai-wan chung-nan-pu ssu-jih-hsing." Among these casualties were five Mainlanders and two Taiwanese.
80. *Ibid.*
81. *Ibid.*
82. Yang Chin-hu, *Ch'i-shih hui-i*, pp. 62–63.
83. Mei Ch'un, "Tao-shang tung-nan: sui-ching tao san-chi chih shih-san," *T'ai-wan hsin-sheng-pao*, May 23, 1947.
84. Chang Hsien-wen, *Chung-hua min-kuo shih-kang* [A Draft History of the Republic of China] (Honan: Jen-min ch'u-pan-she, 1985), p. 694.
85. Sources arguing that dead and wounded exceeded 10,000, typically ranging between 20,000 and 30,000, are the following: United Formosa for Independence, "A Declaration of Formosans," pp. 252, 254; Chai, "Taiwan for the Taiwanese," p. 2; Su Ning, *Wo-men i-ting yao chieh-fang T'ai-wan*, pp. 12–13, estimates more than 10,000. T'ai-Jen, "Ts'ung T'ai-wan jen-min ti li-ch'ang shuo ch'i," p. 95, at first estimates 32,500 victims but later reduces the figure. Wei Ming, comp., *T'ai-wan ti erh-erh-pa shih-chien*, p. 54, estimates dead and wounded at "males, females, old and young at least over 20,000."
86. Shih Ming, *T'ai-wan-jen ssu-pai-nien shih*, p. 792.
87. *Formosa: Internal Affairs, 1945–1949*, Reel 1, contains a report, later marked "Confidential," from Dean Acheson to Senator Joseph H. Bald stating that the State Department had received accounts confirming "press reports indicating harsh measures were employed to suppress the recent uprising there." Acheson's letter corroborated John W. Powell's March 31, 1947, report in the *China Weekly Review*, subsequently published in the Minneapolis *Star-Journal* and sent to Acheson by Senator Bald. Powell reported that during March 8–13 "there was a 'bloodbath' in which troops shot Formosans on sight." Powell's report was so gloomy as to conclude that "with the situation what it is in China today, there is little hope that anything constructive can be done in time to save the island economically or politically for China."
88. *Formosa: Internal Affairs, 1945–1949*, Reel 1.
89. *Ibid.*
90. Wang K'ang, "Erh-erh-pa shih-pien ch'in-li-chi," p. 336.
91. Ch'iu Nien-t'ai, *Wo ti fen-tou-shih*, p. 358.
92. *Ibid.*
93. Lee, *A Taiwanese Scholar Assails Powell's Riot Write-Up*, p. 2.
94. Kerr, *Formosa: Licensed Revolution*, p. xvi; Li, "The China Impasse: A Formosan View," pp. 445–46; Ravenholt, "Formosa Today," p. 616.
95. *T'ai-wan hsin-sheng-pao*, Apr. 6, 1947.
96. Another government report states: "An investigation of evidence collected after the Incident shows that there were another thirty leading rioters, seven members of the Political Construction Cooperation Association, and 45 Taiwan

Communists who must be included in the list of 6,317 dead and wounded. See T'ai-wan-sheng pao-an ssu-ling-pu, comp., *T'ai-wan erh-erh-pa p'an-luan chi-lüeh*, pp. 32–33. Official reports some two to three months after the Incident reported the following number of dead: officers and soldiers, 90; government employees, 64; citizens, 244. Wounded were listed as follows: officers and soldiers, 347; government employees, 1,351; citizens, 383. Missing were listed as follows: officers and soldiers, 40; public servants, 8; citizens, 24. The total casualties came to 2,601. See K'ou Ping-hua, "T'ai-wan hsin-chiu chih chien."

97. Ho Han-wen, "T'ai-wan erh-erh-pa ch'i-i chien-wen chi-lüeh" [A Brief Account of the February 28 Uprising], Chung-kuo jen-min cheng-chih hsieh-shang hui-i, Hu-nan-sheng wei-yüan-hui wen-shih tzu-liao yen-chiu wei-yüan-hui, comp., *Hu-nan wen-shih tzu-liao hsüan-chi: Ti-erh-chi* [A Collection of Historical Literary Materials of Hunan: Volume 2] (Ch'ang-sha, Hu-nan: Hu-nan jen-min ch'u-pan-she, 1981), p. 149.

98. *Ibid.*, p. 150.

99. *Ch'en I sheng-p'ing chi pei-hai nei-mu*, p. 121.

100. Ho P'ing-ju, "Chiang-chün chen-ya T'ai-wan jen-min ch'i-i chi-shih" [A True Account of the Suppression of the Uprising of the Taiwanese People by the Troops of Chiang Kai-shek], in T'ai-wan min-chu tzu-chih t'ung-meng, ed., *Li-shih ti chien-cheng*, p. 135.

101. *Ibid.*, p. 135.

102. *Ibid.*, p. 136. We doubt that any Nationalist troops were allowed to bring their families to Taiwan for this mopping-up operation. It is more likely that unruly soldiers caused such property damage.

103. *Ibid.*, p. 137.

104. *Ibid.*

105. *T'ai-wan hsin-sheng-pao*, June 3, 1947.

106. In a June 20, 1986, interview, Yeh Ming-hsün stated that, just as Taiwanese had beaten Mainlanders and then later stopped, so too had government troops gone to Taiwan and killed Taiwanese, then stopped.

107. Huang Ts'un-hou, *Erh-erh-pa shih-pien shih-mo-chi*, pp. 33–34.

108. KSCW, Document 75, p. 210.

109. *Ibid.*, Document 77, p. 212.

110. Some scholars have suggested that it was only American government pressure on the Nanking government that forced Ch'en I to be transferred and replaced by Wei Tao-ming. See Kerr, *Formosa Betrayed*, p. 325, and Riggs, *Formosa Under Chinese Nationalist Rule*, pp. 47–48. We believe that more was involved than simply U.S. pressure. Reports of the Taiwan problem had been filtering up channels to the highest levels in the Nanking government. Rather than remove Ch'en I immediately after the Uprising, discrediting both him and Nanking, the central government probably preferred to allow him to remain for several more months and then remove him, thus saving "face" for all parties concerned. Ch'en was given an advisory position in Kiangsu upon his return to the Mainland.

111. See Boorman et al., eds., *Biographical Dictionary of Republican China*, vol. 3, pp. 406–8 for a brief sketch of Wei Tao-ming's career.

112. KSCW, Document 86, p. 275.

113. *Ibid.*, Document 87, p. 276.
114. Kao-hsiung-shih chün-min ho-tso-chan, comp., *Kuo-chün chu-T'ai hsü-chih*, p. 12.
115. *Ibid.*, p. 13. This is also the conclusion reached by the American political scientist Fred Riggs in his *Formosa Under Chinese Nationalist Rule*, p. 48.
116. KSCW, Document 92, p. 283.
117. *Ibid.*, Document 96, p. 292; *ibid.*, Document 98, p. 294.
118. *Ibid.*, Document 99, pp. 299–302.

Chapter 6

1. Pepper, *Civil War in China*, pp. 9–16. Pepper states elsewhere that "by the end of 1945, virtually every sector of the population in the nation's urban centres had acquired specific grievances for which the government's policies and the behavior of its officials could be held directly responsible." See "The KMT-CCP Conflict, 1945–1949," in Fairbank and Feuerwerker, eds., *The Cambridge History of China*, vol. 13, p. 738.
2. Pepper, *Civil War in China*, p. 16.
3. *Ibid.*, Chapter 4.
4. Tu Wei-ming, *Ju-hsüeh ti-san-ch'i fa-chan ti ch'ien-chin wen-t'i* [Reflections on the Dawning of the Third Era in the Evolution of the Confucian Tradition] (Taipei: Lien-ching ch'u-pan shih-yeh kung-ssu, 1989), pp. 254–55, 112–13, 104, 52, 14. Professor Tu also grants that Taiwan's intellectual life is "flowering".
5. Chung I-jen, *Hsing-suan liu-shiu-nien*, p. 17. Dr. Chang Yen-hsien is a research staff member of the Sun Yet-san Institute for Social Science and Philosophy, Academia Sinica, Republic of China. Italics added.
6. See Fu Jun-hua, comp., *Chung-kuo tang-tai ming-jen-chuan*, p. 203, for a biographical sketch of T'ang En-po. T'ang eventually went to Taiwan after the fall of the Mainland, and he eventually died in Japan of cancer and was buried in Taiwan.
7. Mao Sen, "Ch'en I p'o T'ang t'ou-kung shih-mo" [The Entire Story of How Ch'en I Tried to Force T'ang En-po To Surrender to the Communists], *Chuan-chi wen-hsüeh*, 52, no. 4 (Apr. 1988), p. 50.
8. *Ibid.*
9. *Ch'en I sheng-p'ing chi pei-hai nei-mu*, p. 158.
10. Mao Sen, "Ch'en I p'o T'ang t'ou-kung shih-mo," p. 50. See also Mao Sen, "Pu-shih Ch'en I p'o-T'ang t'ou-kung shih-mo" [The Entire Story of How Ch'en I Tried to Force T'ang En-po to Surrender to the Communists], *Chuan-chi wen-hsüeh*, 53, no. 1 (July 1988), pp. 43–44.
11. *Ch'en I sheng-p'ing chi pei-hai nei-mu*, pp. 129–30.
12. *Ibid.*, p. 130.
13. *Ibid.*, p. 159, reproduces a copy of this letter. The same letter is also cited in *Chung-yang jih-pao*, June 18, 1950, p. 1. The only difference in the letters cited in these two sources is that for item 2 under category "B," where the letter reads "remove the names of ( )," no names are cited in the *Chung-yang jih-pao* letter, but in the Communist historiographical source the word "war criminals" has been inserted.

14. Chang Wen-ch'i, "Ch'en I yu-hsiang T'ang En-po ching-kuo," *Chuan-chi wen-hsüch*, 52, no. 1 (Jan. 1, 1988), p. 13.
15. *Ibid*. According to Chang Wen-ch'i, Ch'en I had actually stipulated that T'ang En-po's name be removed from the list of alleged war criminals. See Chang Wen-ch'i, p. 13.
16. Mao Sen, "Ch'en I p'o T'ang t'ou-kung shih-mo," p. 52.
17. *Ibid*.
18. *Ch'en I Sheng-ping Chi pei-hai nei-mu*, p. 172.
19. *Ibid.*, p. 179.
20. *Chung-yang jih-pao*, June 18, 1950, p. 1. How have historians evaluated Ch'en I as an administrator? Of all the accounts we have seen, the most fair and balanced is cited by Shen Yün-lung in his article "Ch'en I ch'i-jen yü erh-erh-pa shih-pien." Shen yün-lung. We quote the following: "When Ch'en I came to Taiwan, his intentions were to govern well. He insisted that the military strictly adhere to the law. To that end, he even had a certain General Ma, who had broken the law, publicly executed by firing squad to serve as an example of his policy. He also tried to deeply understand the problems related to the provincial administration's general affairs, finances, monetary matters, security, police affairs, food supply, industry and mining, and other concerns. His health was good. His life style was that of the military. To handle his official duties, he made his office serve as his home. In this way, even his top advisers could not stand his work style. His great failing was that when he became the top official of Taiwan's administration, he never deeply understood the character and feelings of the Taiwan people. Moreover, some of his top cadres made believe that conditions were more peaceful than they actually were, and they, as well as Ch'en I, never really understood the prevailing political conditions. Therefore, a single spark could create the February 28th Incident of 1947. For these reasons, Ch'en I lost his job. . . . Yet in other areas he could assume his duties and be responsible. He dared to adjudicate. These were his strong points. It was sad that he never had one or two really dependable, thoughtful, and competently loyal top advisers."
21. Li Shih-chieh, "Chiang-chia ch'ung-hsin Ch'en I yü 'erh-erh-pa' ti kuan-hsi," p. 11.
22. *Ibid*.
23. Chou Jih-ch'ang, "Pi 't'ou-kan' chih wang" [A Critique of the Concept of Mandate Rule], in Hsin T'ai-wan ch'u-pan-she, comp., *Sheng-li ko T'ai-wan* [To Give Taiwan Away After Victory] (Hong Kong: Hsin T'ai-wan ch'u-pan-she, 1947), p. 2.
24. *Ibid*.
25. *Ibid*.
26. Wu Yüan, *T'ai-wan ti kuo-ch'u ho hsien-tsai* [Taiwan—Past and Present] (Beijing: T'ung-shu tu-wu ch'u-pan-she, 1954), p. 25.
27. "Erh-erh-pa shih-chien i ch'üan-pu chieh-an" [The February 28 Incident Has Been Completely Resolved], *T'ai-wan hsin-sheng-pao*, May 23, 1950, p. 1.
28. Li Shih-chieh, "Chiang-chia ch'ung-hsin Ch'en I," p. 11.
29. *Ibid*.
30. Numerous examples of such Taiwanese bitterness and cases of students,

intellectuals, and others being arrested for their harsh critique of the Nationalist regime or for referring to the February 28 Incident can be found in Douglas Mendel, *The Politics of Formosan Nationalism* (Berkeley: University of California Press, 1970), Chapter 5.

31. Yin P'ing, "T'ai-wan yao tu-li" [Taiwan Wants Independence], *Shih-chieh chou-k'an*, no. 216 (May 8–14, 1988), pp. 6–12.

32. P'eng Ming-min, *Tzu-yu ti tzu-wei*, p. 99.

33. A translation of this manifesto can be found in Mendel, *The Politics of Formosan Nationalism*, pp. 249–60.

34. P'eng Ming-min, *Tzu-yu ti tzu-wei*, pp. 129–40.

35. *Ibid.*, p. 250.
36. *Ibid.*, p. 251.
37. *Ibid.*
38. *Ibid.*, p. 6.
39. *Ibid.*
40. *Ibid.*, p. 5.
41. *Ibid.*
42. *Ibid.*, p. 8.
43. *Ibid.*, pp. 89–91.
44. *Ibid.*, p. 58.
45. *Ibid.*, p. 120.
46. *Ibid.*, p. 118.
47. *Ibid.*, pp. 120 and 130.
48. *Ibid.*, p. 120.
49. *Ibid.*, p. 137.
50. *Ibid.*, p. 133.
51. *Ibid.*, p. 250.
52. *Ibid.*
53. *Ibid.*, pp. 7 and 251.
54. *Ibid.*, p. 56.

55. Ts'ai P'ei-huo et al., *T'ai-wan min-tsu yün-tung-shih*, p. 1.

56. P'eng Ming-min, *Tzu-yu-ti tzu-wei*, pp. 60–63.

57. *Ibid.*, pp. 127, 137, and 265.
58. *Ibid.*, p. 136.
59. *Ibid.*, p. 127.
60. *Ibid.*, p. 140.
61. *Ibid.*, pp. 137–38.
62. *Ibid.*, p. 140.
63. *Ibid.*, p. 138.
64. *Ibid.*, p. 139.
65. *Ibid.*
66. *Ibid.*, pp. 87–88 and 255.
67. *Ibid.*, p. 129.
68. *Ibid.*, p. 140.
69. *Ibid.*, p. 138.
70. *Ibid.*, p. 129.
71. *Ibid.*, p. 256.

72. Yao Chia-wen, "T'ai-wan hai-hsia hua-fen shih-chieh hai-lu-ch'üan" [The Taiwan Straits as the Intersection Between Continental and Maritime Power in the World], *T'ai-wan kung-lun-pao* [Taiwan Tribune], Jan. 18, 1988, p. 7.

73. *Ibid.*

74. Ying P'ing, "T'ai-wan yao tu-li" [Taiwan Wants Independence] *Shih-chieh chou-k'au*, no. 216 (May 8–14, 1988), pp. 6–12.

75. *Ibid.*

76. *Ibid.*

77. Mendel, *The Politics of Formosan Nationalism*, p. 37.

78. *Ibid.*, p. 147. Mendel's account of the first twenty years of overseas Taiwanese activities to wage armed struggle against the Nationalist government still is the best detailed account of the personalities involved in the TIM. See also Lin Ching, "Hai-wai chu-yao T'ai-tu yün-tung tsu-chih: shih-chieh T'ai-wan tu-li lien-meng" [The Major Overseas Taiwan Independence Movement Organization: The World Formosan Independence Alliance], *T'ai-wan yen-chiu chi-k'an*, vol. 1 (1986), p. 85.

79. For lists of violent acts carried out by the TIM, see Yin P'ing, "T'ai-wan

yao tu-li?," p. 10; and Gregor and Chang, "The Taiwan Independence Movement: The Failure of Political Persuasion," pp. 371–74.

80. The above quotations are at least in part not conference remarks verbatim but statements written by the *Taiwan Tribune [T'ai-wan kung-lun-pao]* reporter paraphrasing conference remarks (Mar. 21, 1988, issue).

Bibliography

Chinese-language Materials

An Hui. "Chin-shou chiao-yü ti kang-wei" [Stand Firmly Dedicated to Education], in T'ai-wan cheng-i ch'u-pan-she, ed., *T'ai-wan erh-erh-pa shih-chien ch'in-li-chi* [A Personal Memoir of the February 28th Incident]. N.p.: T'ai-wan cheng-i ch'u-pan-she, 1947. Pp. 115–18.

Chan Chou. "Chi-lung wen-chien" [Things Observed in Keeling], in T'ai-wan cheng-i ch'u-pan-she, ed., *T'ai-wan erh-erh-pa shih-chien ch'in-li-chi* [A Personal Memoir of the February 28th Incident]. N.p.: T'ai-wan cheng-i ch'u-pan-she, 1947. Pp. 91–96.

Chang Hsü-pen. *Chi-che sheng-yai ssu-shih-nien* [Forty Years in the Profession of Journalism]. Taipei: Tzu-li wan-pao-she, 1982.

Chang Tzu-hui, ed. *T'ai-wan shih-jen-chih* [A Biography of People in Taiwan Today]. Taipei: Kuo-kuang ch'u-pan-she, 1947, vol. 1.

Chang Wen-ch'i. "Ch'en I yu-hsiang T'ang En-po ching-kuo [Ch'en I Tried to Lure T'ang En-po to Surrender], *Chuan-chi wen-hsüeh* [Biographical Literature] Taipei: Chüan-chi wen-hsüeh-she, 52, no. 1, 1988.

Chang Yen-hsien, ed. *Chung-kuo hai-yang fa-chan-shih lun-wen-chi: Ti-san-chi* [Collected Essays on the History of Developing China's Maritime and Western Contacts], vol. 3. Taipei: Chung-yang yen-chiu-yüan san-min-chu-i yen-chiu-so, 1988.

Chang Yen-hsien and Li Hsiao-feng, eds. *Erh-erh-pa shih-chien hui-i-chi* [A Collection of Memoirs About the February 28th Incident]. Taipei hsien, Pan-ch'iao City: Tao-hsiang ch'u-pan-she, 1989.

Ch'en Fang-ming. "Chieh-pai ti huo-hua: mien-huai min-tsu tou-shih: Hsieh Hsüeh-hung" [The Pure Sparks: Remembering a Fighter for the Nation, Hsieh Hsüeh-hang], *Min-chin-pao chou-k'an* [Min-chin Weekly], no. 40 (Nov. 28–Dec. 4, 1987).

Ch'en I. "Chin-nien wei hsing-hsien nien" [This Year Is for Constitutional Rule], *T'ai-wan hsin-sheng-pao* [Taiwan New Life Daily], Jan. 1, 1947, p. 4.

Ch'en I sheng-p'ing chi pei-hai nei-mu [The Life of Ch'en I and the Inside Story of the Suffering Inflicted on Him]. Beijing: Chung-kuo wen-shih ch'u-pan-she, 1987.

Cheng Che-wen. "An-ching ti P'eng-hu" [Tranquil Pescadores], in T'ai-wan cheng-i ch'u-pan-she, ed., *T'ai-wan erh-erh-pa shih-chien ch'in-li-chi* [A

Personal Memoir of the February 28th Incident]. N.p.: T'ai-wan cheng-i ch'u-pan-she, 1947. Pp. 206–8.

Cheng Tzu. "Chan-hou T'ai-wan sheng-chih chih pien-ko" [Changes of Taiwan Provincial System After the War]. Unpublished manuscript. 1988.

Cheng-ching-pao pan-yiih-k'an [Political and Economical New Semi-monthly]. Taipei: Cheng-ching pao-she, 1945.

Chiang Kai-shek. "Min-sheng chu-i yü-le liang-p'ien pu-shu" [Two Supplementary Sections on Education and Recreation Added to the Principle of the People's Livelihood], in Chung-kuo kuo-min-tang chung-yang wei-yüan-hui tang-shih wei-yüan-hui, comp., *Kuo-fu ch'üan-chi* [The Complete Works of Our Nation's Founding Father]. Taipei: Chung-kuo kuo-min-tang chung-yang wei-yüan-hui tang-shih wei-yüan-hui, 1973.

Chiang Mu-yün. "T'ai-wan chung-nan-pu ssu-jih-hsing" [A Four-Day Journey to Central and Southern Taiwan], *T'ai-wan hsin-sheng-pao* [T'ia-wan New Life Daily], May 6, 1947.

Chiang Yung-ching, Li Yün-han, and Hsü Shih-shün, comps. *Yang Liang-kung hsien-sheng nien-p'u* [The Annual Chronicles of the Life of Yang Liang-kung]. Taipei: Lien-ching Publishing Co., 1988.

Ch'in Hsiao-i, comp. *Tsung-t'ung Chiang-kung ta-shih ch'ang-pien ch'u-kao* [A Preliminary Draft of Source Materials About the Major Events of President Chiang Kai-shek's Life]. Taipei: Kuomintang Central Committee Archives, 1978.

Ching Yü [pseud.]. *T'ai-wan shih-pien chen-hsiang yü nei-mu* [The Real Facts and a Behind-the-Scenes Account of the Taiwan Upheaval]. Shanghai: Chien-she shu-tien, 1947.

Ch'iu Nien-t'ai. *Ling-hai wei-piao* [The Undulating Waves]. Taipei: Chung-hua jih-pao-she, 1962.

———. "T'ai-wan-jen chüeh-pu-yüan li-k'ai tsu-kuo" [The Taiwanese Definitely Do Not Want to Leave Their Fatherland], *Chung-yang jih-pao* [The Central Daily News], Apr. 21, 1947.

———. *Wo ti fen-tou-shih* [The History of My Struggle]. Taipei: Chung-hua jih-pao-she, 1981.

Chu Wen-po. "Erh-erh-pa pei-ou chi" [Recollections of a Beating on February 28th], *T'ai-wan yüeh-k'an* [Taiwan Monthly], no. 6 (Apr. 10, 1947), pp. 27–29.

———. "Erh-erh-pa shih-chien-chung wo ho Hsin-chu hsien-cheng-fu pei-hsi ching-kuo" [The Attack Suffered by the Hsinchu District Government Office and Me During the February 28th Incident], in T'ai-wan cheng-i ch'u-pan-she, ed., *T'ai-wan erh-erh-pa shih-chien ch'in-li-chi* [A Personal Memoir of the February 28th Incident]. N.p.: T'ai-wan cheng-i ch'u-pan-she, 1947. Pp. 110–14.

Ch'üan [pseud.]. "T'ai-chung li-hsien-chi" [An Account of My Dangerous Experience in Taichung], in T'ai-wan cheng-i ch'u-pan-she, ed., *Taiwan erh-erh-pa shih-chien ch'in-li-chi* [A Personal Memoir of the February 28th Incident]. N.p.: T'ai-wan cheng-i ch'u-pan-she, 1947. Pp. 119–27.

Chuan-chi wen-hsüeh [*Biographical Literature*] Taipei: Chuan-chi wen-hsüeh-she, vol. 52, nos. 1, 4; vol. 53, no. 1. 1988.

CMYWTK. Chuan-mai yeh-wu t'e-k'an. "Wei erh-erh-ch'i yeh ch'i-ssu fa-sheng chiu-fen shih ch'eng ching-pei tsung-pu pao-kao ch'üan-wen" [A Complete Report Presented to the Garrison Command on the Incident of the Investigation of Smuggling on the Evening of February 27th by the Monopoly Bureau], in T'ai-wan-sheng chuan-mai-chü yeh-wu wei-yüan-hui, comp., *Chuan-mai yeh-wu t'e-k'an* [Monopoly Bureau Special Report], Apr. 1947, p. 69.

Chuang Chia-nung. *Fen-nu ti T'ai-wan* [Angry Taiwan]. Taipei: n.p., n.d.

Chung-hua jih-pao [The China Daily], "Hsiang T'ai-pao p'e-ch'ieh chüan-kao" [A Request to Our Taiwan Brethren], Mar. 3, 1947, editorial.

———. Issues of Mar. 3, 5, 9, 11, 12, 1947, Apr. 8, 1947, Apr. 17, 1947, Apr. 18, 1947, June 6, 1947.

Chung I-jen. *Hsing-suan liu-shih-nien* [My Sixty Years of Bitterness]. Taipei: Tzu-yu shih-tai ch'u-pan-she, 1988.

Chung-kuo shih-pao [The China Times]. Issues of Feb. 28, 1988, May 7, 1988, May 8, 1988, Mar. 1, 1989, Aug. 4, 1989.

Chung Nan [pseud.]. "Ch'ü chih-an pen-pu" [Going to Security Headquarters], in T'ai-wan cheng-i ch'u-pan-she, ed., *T'ai-wan erh-erh-pa shih-chien ch'in-li-chi* [A Personal Memoir of the February 28th Incident]. N.p.: T'ai-wan cheng-i ch'u-pan-she, 1947. Pp. 128–31.

Chung-yang jih-pao [The Central Daily News]. Issues of Aug. 16, 1945, Apr. 8, 1947, Apr. 21, 1947, June 18, 1950.

EEPC. See *T'ai-wan erh-erh-pa shih-chien ch'in-li-chi* [A Personal Memoir of the February 28th Incident].

Erh-erh-pa chen-hsiang [The Real Facts About the February 28th Incident]. N.p., n.d.

FWPTCC. Fa-wu-pu tiao-ch'a-chü [Investigation Bureau of the Ministry of Law], comp. *T'ai-wan-sheng wen-hsien wei-yüan-hui ch'ien chu-jen wei-yüan Lin Heng-tao hsien-sheng erh-erh-pa shih-pien hui-i* [Memoirs of the Former Taiwan Provincial Historical Commission's Director, Mr. Lin Heng-tao, on the February 28th Incident]. Taipei: Fa-wu-pu tiao-ch'a-chü, 1984.

Fan [pseud.]. "La-tsa hua P'ing-tung" [Random Talks About P'ing-tung], in T'ai-wan cheng-i ch'u-pan-she, ed., *T'ai-wan erh-erh-pa shih-chien ch'in-li-chi* [A Personal Memoir of the February 28th Incident]. N.p.: T'ai-wan cheng-i ch'u-pan-she, 1947. Pp. 195–98.

Fu Jun-hua, comp. *Chung-kuo tang-tai ming-jen-chuan* [Biographies of Famous People in Contemporary China]. Shanghai: Shih-chieh wen-hua fu-wu-she, 1948.

Han Shih-ch'üan. *Liu-shih hui-i-lu* [A Memoir of Sixty Years]. Taipei: Kao-ch'ang yin-shu-chü, 1956.

Ho p'ing-ju. See *T'ai-wan min-chu tzu-chih t'ung-meng*.

Ho-p'ing jih-pao [Peace Daily]. Issues of Aug. 5, 1946, Aug. 7, 1946.

Hsia I. "T'a kao-su wo-men shih-mo?" [What Is He Trying to Tell Us?], in *Erh-erh-pa chen-hsiang* [The Real Facts About the February 28th Incident]. N.p., n.d. Pp. 54–62.

Hsieh A-shui. *Erh-erh-pa shih-pien chen-hsiang* [The Real Facts About the February 28th Incident]. Taipei: Kuo-fang-pu tsung-cheng-chih tso-chan-pu, 1980.

Hsin T'ai-wan [New Taiwan], "T'ai-wan hsiao-hsi" [News from Taiwan]. no. 3 (Apr. 1, 1946), pp. 8–9.

Hsin T'ai-wan ch'u-pan-she Compilation Committee. *T'ai-wan ming-jen-chi*

[Notable People in Taiwan]. Taipei: Hsin T'ai-wan ch'u-pan-she, 1953, vol. 1.
Hsü Ch'eng-tsung. "Erh-erh-pa shih-chien chen-hsiang" [The Real Facts About the February 28th Incident]. *Chi-feng* [Violent Winds], 1, no. 6 (Jan. 1, 1980), pp. 90–96, no. 9 (Apr. 4, 1980), pp. 56–66, no. 10 (May 4, 1980), pp. 44–51.
Hsüeh Mu. "Wo ts'ung T'ai-wan huo-cho hui-lai" [Remembering My Escape from Taiwan]. *T'ai-wan yü shih-chieh* [Taiwan and the World], no. 28 (Feb. 1986), pp. 54–57.
Hu Ch'iu-yüan. *I-pai san-shih nien-lai Chung-kuo ssu-hsiang shih-kang* [A History of China's Thought in the Last 130 Years]. Taipei: Hsüeh-shu ch'u-pan-she, 1980.
Huang Ch'ao-ch'in. *Wo ti hui-i* [Huang Ch'ao-ch'in's Memoirs]. Taipei: Li-wen yin-shua yu-hsien kung-ssu, 1971.
Huang Chen-chung. "T'ai-wan liang-shih cheng-ts'e ti shang-t'ao" [Discussion of Taiwan Food Grain Policy]. *Cheng-ch'i pan-yüeh-k'an* [Righteousness Semi-Monthly], 1, no. 3 (May 1, 1946), pp. 6–8.
Huang Hsü-tung. "Erh-erh-pa shih-pien ssu-t'ung, lu" [A Painful Recollection of the February 28th Incident]. *T'ai-wan yü shih-chieh* [Taiwan and the World], no. 17 (Dec. 1984–Jan. 1985), pp. 63–66.
———. "Erh-erh-pa shih-pien ssu-tung-lu" [A Painful Recollection of the February 28th Incident], *T'ai-wan yüeh-k'an* [Taiwan Monthly], no. 6 (Apr. 1947), pp. 16–21.
———. "Erh-erh-pa shih-pien ssu-t'ung-lu" [A Painful Recollection of the February 28th Incident], *Erh-erh-pa chen-hsiang*, n.p., n.d.
Huang Ts'un-hou. *Erh-erh-pa shih-pien shih-mo-chi* [A Complete Report of the February 28th Incident]. Taichung: Sao-tang chou-pao-she, 1947.
Huang Wu-tung. *Huang Wu-tung hui-i-lu* [The Memoirs of Huang Wu-tung]. Irvine, Calif.: Taiwan Publishing Co., 1986.
Hung P'eng-wan. "T'ai-nan pao-hsing lu" [A Memoir of the Violence in Tainan], in T'ai-wan cheng-i ch'u-pan-she, ed., *T'ai-wan erh-erh-pa shih-chien ch'in-li-chi* [A Personal Memoir of the February 28th Incident]. N.p.: T'ai-wan cheng-i ch'u-pan-she, 1947. Pp. 168–74.
Hung Yen-ch'iu. "Huai i-yu Chuang Ch'ui-sheng hsiung" [My Recollections of My Good Friend Chuang Ch'ui-sheng]. *Chuan-chi wen-hsüeh* [Biographical Literature], 29, no. 4 (Oct. 1, 1976), pp. 80–87.
Jen-min jih-pao [People's Daily]. Issue of Mar. 1, 1975.
Jen Po [pseud.]. "I-lan ti hsü-ching" [The shock in I-lan], in T'ai-wan cheng-i ch'u-pan-she, ed., *T'ai-wan erh-erh-pa shih-chien ch'in-li-chi* [A Personal Memoir of the February 28th Incident]. N.p.: T'ai-wan cheng-i ch'u-pan-she, 1947. Pp. 101–9.
K'an-luan shih-ch'i chung-yao wen-chien fen-an chi-p'ien [Major Documents Classified and Compiled for the Period of the Insurrection], no. 36: "Politics—Taiwan: the February 28th Incident." Taipei, 1955; 2 vols.
Kao Hsien-chih. *T'ai-wan san-pai-nien shih* [A Three-Hundred-Year History of Taiwan]. Taipei: Chung-wen t'u-shu ku-wen yu-hsien kung-ssu, 1981.
Kao-hsiung-shih chün-min ho-tso-chan, comp. *Kuo-chün chu-T'ai hsü-chih* [Information Necessary for National Troops Stationed in Taiwan]. Kao-hsiung: Kao-hsiung-shih chün-min ho-tso-chan, 1948.

K'o Yüan-fen. "Shih-pien shih-jih chi" [A Ten-Day Record of the Disturbances]. *Cheng-ch'i yüeh-k'an* [Righteousness Monthly], 2, no. 2 (May 1, 1947), pp. 41–44.
K'ou Ping-hua. "T'ai-wan hsin-chiu chih chien" [Taiwan Between the New and the Old]. *T'ai-wan hsin-sheng pao* [Taiwan New Life Daily], June 7, 1947.
KSCW. See *K'an-luan shih-ch'i chung-yao wen-chien fen-an chi-p'ien*.
Kuo-chün chu-T'ai hsü-chih. See Kao-hsiang-shih chün-min ho-tso-chan, comp.
Kuo T'ing-i. *Chung-hua min-kuo shih-shih jih-chih* [A Daily Chronology of Historical Events in the Republican Period]. Taipei: Modern History Institute, Academia Sinica, 1985. Vol. 4.
Kuo-fang-pu chung-cheng-chih-pu [Political Affairs Dept. of the Ministry of Defense], *Hsieh Hsüeh-hung ti pei-chü* [The Tragedy of Hsieh Hsüeh-hung]. Taipei: Kuo-fang-pu cheng-chan chih pu, 1958.
Li Chen-ming. *T'ai-wan-shih* [A History of Taiwan]. Shanghai: Chung-hua shu-chü, 1948.
Li Chih-fu. *T'ai-wan jen-min ko-ming tou-cheng chien-shih* [A Concise History of Taiwan's Revolutionary Struggles]. Canton: Hua-nan jen-min ch'u-pan-she, 1955.
Li Shih-chieh. "Chiang-chia ch'ung-hsin Ch'en I yü 'erh-erh-pa' ti kuan-hsi" [The Chiang Family Condones the Ch'en I and February 28 Incident Relationship], *T'ai-wan chiao-hui kung-pao*, no. 1878 (Feb. 28, 1988).
———. *T'ai-wan kung-ho-kuo lin-shih cheng-fu ta-t'ung-ling Liao Wen-i t'ou-hsiang shih-mo* [A Complete Account of the Surrender by Liao Wen-i, Leader of the Temporary Government of the Republic of Taiwan]. Taipei: Tzu-yu shih-tai ch'u-pan-she, 1988.
Lien-ho-pao [United Daily]. Issues of Feb. 2, 1988, Feb. 29, 1988, Feb. 23–24, 1990.
Lin Chung. *T'ai-wan kuang-fu ch'ien-hou shih-liao kai-shu* [Historical Materials Related to the Retrocession of Taiwan]. Taipei: Huang-chi ch'u-pan-she, 1983.
Lin Mu-shun. *T'ai-wan erh-yüeh ko-ming* [The February Revolution in Taiwan]. N.p., 1948.
Liu Feng-sung. *T'ai-wan ti hei-an* [The Dark Age in Taiwan]. N.p., 1986.
Liu Shih-chang. "Lun T'ai-wan ti tung-luan" [On Taiwan's Turbulence], *Kuan-ch'a* [The Observer], no. 224 (Mar. 22, 1947).
Lu Jen [pseud.]. "T'ai-wan erh-erh-pa chen-hsiang" [The Real Facts About Taiwan's February 28th Incident], in *Erh-erh-pa chen-hsiang* [The Real Facts About the February 28th Incident]. N.p., n.d. Pp. 49–53.
Ma Chen-tu and Ch'i Ju-kao. "T'ai-wan kuang-fu hou Nan-ching kuo-min cheng-fu tui yüan tsai-cheng chin-jung chi-kou ti chieh-shou chi ch'i kung-tso t'ui-chin" [The Nanking Government's Promotional Work and Recovery of the Original Finance and Monetary Structure After the Retrocession of Taiwan], *Min-kuo tang-an shih-liao* [Archival and Historical Materials of the Republic of China], no. 3 (Aug. 1988), pp. 46–59.
Ma Ch'i-hua, *Erh-erh-pa yen-chiu* (A Study of the February 28th Incident) [Taipei: Chung-hua min-kuo kung-kung ch'ih-hsü yen-chiu-hui, 1987].
Man Hsi [pseud.]. "Chia-shu pao p'ing-an" [Letters Home Reporting Our Safety], in T'ai-wan cheng-i ch'u-pan-she, ed., *T'ai-wan erh-erh-pa shih-chien ch'in-li-*

chi [A Personal Memoir of the February 28th Incident]. N.p.: T'ai-wan cheng-i ch'u-pan-she, 1947. Pp. 137–45.

Mao Sen. "Chen I p'o T'ang t'ou-kung shih-mo" [The Entire Story of How Ch'en I Tried to Force T'ang En-po to Surrender to the Communists]. *Chuan-chi wen-hsüeh* [Biographical Literature]. Vol. 52, no. 4; vol. 53, no. 1. 1988.

Mei Ch'un. "Tao-shang tung-nan: sui-ching hsüan-tao san-chi chih shih-san" [Thirteen Notes on Pacification and Propaganda: Southeast of Taiwan]. *T'ai-wan hsin-sheng-pao* [Taiwan New Life Daily], May 23, 1947.

Mien Chih [pseud.]. "Hua-lien fen-jao chi shih" [A Record of the Upheaval in Hua-lien], in T'ai-wan cheng-i ch'u-pan-she, ed., *T'ai-wan erh-erh-pa shih-chien ch'in-li-chi* [A Personal Memoir of the February 28th Incident]. N.p.: T'ai-wan cheng-i ch'u-pan-she, 1947. Pp. 199–205.

Min-chin-pao chou-k'an [Min-chin Weekly], no. 40 (Nov. 28–Dec. 4, 1987).

Min-T'ai t'ung-hsün-she, ed. *T'ai-wan cheng-chih hsien-chuang pao-kao-shu* [A Report on the Current Political Conditions in Taiwan]. N.p., 1946.

NCPCCS. Nei-cheng-pu ching-cheng-shu [Police Department of the Ministry of Interior], comp. "Chou Tao-yüan hsien-sheng 'Erh-erh-pa shih-chien hui-i tzu-liao'" [Memoir Materials of Mr. Chou Tao-yüan on the February 28th Incident]. Unpublished manuscript, Mar. 1984.

———. "Lo Ch'ün-yen hsien-sheng 'Erh-erh-pa shih-chien hui-i tzu-liao'" [Memoir Materials of Mr. Lo Ch'ün-yen on the February 28th Incident]. Unpublished manuscript, Mar. 1984.

Pai Ch'ung-hsi. "T'ai-wan shih-pien ti chen-hsiang" [The True Picture of the Taiwan Disturbances], *Cheng-ch'i yüeh-kan* [Righteousness Monthly], 2, no. 2 (May 1, 1947), p. 39.

P'an Chih-chün. "Hui-i T'ai-wan kuang-fu yü erh-erh-pa shih-chien ti i-tuan li-ch'eng" [A Memoir of the Retrocession of Taiwan and a Stage in the Historical Process of the February 28th Incident], in *Erh-erh-pa chen-hsiang* [The Real Facts About the February 28th Incident]. N.p., n.d. Pp. 346–63.

———. Apr. 4, 1947, report on the February Uprising, printed in *Shih-chieh jih-pao*, Mar. 11, 1988, pp. 6–7.

P'eng Ming-min. *Tzu-yu ti tzu-wei—P'eng Ming-min hui-i-lu* [The Taste of Freedom—The Memoirs of P'eng Ming-min]. Translated into Chinese by Lin Mei-hui. Irvine, Calif.: Taiwan Publishing Co., 1984. The Chinese version contains material not included in the original 1972 English edition.

P'u Jen [pseud.]. "I-ch'ang li-shih O-meng ti hui-hsiang: T'ai-wan erh-erh-pa shih-chien shen-li-chi" [Remembering a Historical Nightmare: My Account of the Taiwan February 28th Incident], in *Erh-erh-pa chen-hsiang* [The Real Facts About the February 28th Incident]. N.p., n.d. Pp. 340–45.

Shen Chung-jen, ed. *Ch'en Chia-keng chiu-kuo yen-lun-chi* [The Collected Speeches of Chen Chia-keng for National Salvation]. Shanghai: Hua-mei t'u-shu kung-ssu, 1941.

Shen Hsiao-shen. "Tsai-hui pa! Chia-i" [Good-Bye! Chia-i.], in T'ai-wan cheng-i ch'u-pan-she, ed., *T'ai-wan erh-erh-pa shih chien ch'in-li-chi* [A Personal Memoir of the February 28th Incident]. N.p.: T'ai-wan cheng-i ch'u-pan-she, 1947. Pp. 146–50.

Shen-pao [Shen Daily]. Issues of Apr. 8, 1947, May 18, 1947.

Shen Yün-lung. "Ch'en I ch'i-jen yü erh-erh-pa shih-pien" [Ch'en I: The Man and the February 28th Incident], *Chuan-chi wen-hsüeh* [Biographical Literature], 54, no. 2 (Feb. 1989), pp. 57–59.
——. *Yün-lung ch'i-shih wen-ts'un* [The Collected Writings of Shen Yün-lung at Seventy]. Taipei: Chi-ku shu-wu, 1979.
Shih-chieh jih-pao [World Journal]. Issues of Mar. 1, 11, Feb. 28, 1990.
Shih Ming. *T'ai-wan-jen ssu-pai-nien shih* [A Four-Hundred-Year History of Taiwan's People]. San Jose, Calif.: Paradise Culture Associates, 1980.
Shih-pao chou-k'an [The Times Weekly Journal]. Issues of Mar. 1988.
Ssu Wei [pseud.]. "Shih-pien chung ti hsien-ping ti-ssu-t'uan" [The Fourth Regiment of Military Police During the Incident], *T'ai-wan hsin-sheng-pao* [Taiwan New Life Daily], May 30, 1947.
Su Ning. *Wo-men i-ting yao chieh-fang T'ai-wan* [We Definitely Ought to Liberate Taiwan]. Shen-yang: Jen-min ch'u-pan-she, 1951.
Ta-kung-pao [L'Impartial]. Hong Kong. Issue of Mar. 1, 1975.
T'ai Jen [pseud.]. "Ts'ung T'ai-wan jen-min ti li-ch'ang shuo ch'i: tao-nien erh-erh-pa sang-sheng chih shu-wan wu-ming chan-shih chi wu-ku liang-min hsi-sheng-che" [Speaking Out on Behalf of the Taiwanese People: Lamenting the Countless Nameless Warriors and the Tragic, Heroic Martyrs During the February 28th Incident]. *T'ai-tu chi-k'an* [Independent Taiwan Quarterly], no. 1 (Jan. 1982), pp. 87–95.
T'ai-tu chi-k'an tzu-liao-tsu. "Erh-erh-pa ta-ko-ming ti chen-hsiang" [The Real Facts About the Great Revolution of February 28th]. *T'ai-tu chi-k'an* [Independent Taiwan Quarterly], no. 1 (Jan. 1982), pp. 76–86.
T'ai-wan cheng-chih hsien-chuang pao-kao-shu. See Min-T'ai t'ung-hsün-she.
T'ai-wan cheng-i ch'u-pan-she, ed. *T'ai-wan erh-erh-pa shih-chien ch'in-li-chi* [A Personal Memoir of the February 28th Incident]. N.p., T'ai-wan cheng-i ch'u-pan-she, 1947.
T'ai-wan chiao-hui kung-pao [Taiwan Church News Gazette]. No. 1879 (Mar. 6, 1988).
T'ai-wan erh-erh-pa shih-chien ch'in-li-chi [A Personal Memoir of the February 28th Incident]. N.p.: T'ai-wan cheng-i ch'u-pan-she, 1947.
T'ai-wan hsin-sheng-pao [Taiwan New Life Daily]. Issues of Jan. 1, 1947, Jan. 9, 1947, Jan. 10, 1947, Jan. 25, 1947, Feb. 12, 1947, Feb. 19, 1947, Feb. 20, 1947, Feb. 24, 1947, Mar. 1, 1947, Mar. 3, 1947, Mar. 8, 1947, Mar. 9, 1947, Mar. 11, 1947, Mar. 16, 1947, Apr. 1, 1947, Apr. 6, 1947, Apr. 13, 1947, May 19, 1947, May 23, 1947, May 31, 1947, June 3, 1947, Oct. 25, 1947, May 23, 1950, June 18, 1950.
T'ai-wan hsin-sheng-pao-she ts'ung-shu pien-tsuan wei-yüan-hui, comp. *T'ai-wan nien-chien* [Taiwan Yearbook]. Taipei: T'ai-wan hsin-sheng-pao-she, 1947.
T'ai-wan min-chu tzu-chih t'ung-meng, ed. *Li-shih ti chien-cheng* [Eyewitnesses to History]. Beijing: T'ai-wan min-chu tzu-chih t'ung-meng, 1987.
T'ai-wan nien-chien [Taiwan Yearbook]. Taipei: T'ai-wan hsin-sheng-pao she, 1947.
T'ai-wan yen-chiu chi-k'an [Taiwan Study Quarterly]. Hsia-men: Hsia-men ta-hsüeh T'ai-wan yen-chiu-so, vol. 1, 1986.
T'ai-wan-sheng chieh-shou wei-yüan-hui Jih-ch'an ch'u-li wei-yüan-hui, ed. *T'ai-

wan-sheng chieh-shou wei-yüan-hui Jih-ch'an ch'u-li wei-yüan-hui chieh-shu tsung-pao-kao [A Complete Report of the Commission to Handle Japanese Property]. Taipei: T'ai-wan-sheng chieh-shou wei-yüan-hui jih-ch'an ch'u-li wei-yüan-hui, 1947.

T'ai-wan-sheng hsing-cheng chang-kuan kung-shu hsin-wen-shih [Taiwan Provincial Administrative Executive Office Agency for Information], comp. *T'ai-wan pao-tung shih-chien chi-shih* [A True Record of the February 28th Incident in Taiwan]. Taipei: T'ai-wan-sheng hsing-cheng chang-kuan kung-shu hsin-wen-shih, 1947.

T'ai-wan-sheng hsing-cheng chang-kuan kung-shu hsüan-ch'uan wei-yüan-hui [Taiwan Provincial Administrative Executive Office Propaganda Commission], comp. *T'ai-wan chih-nan* [Taiwan Guide]. Taipei: Hsüan-ch'uan wei-yüan-hui t'u-shu fa-hsing-so, 1946.

———. *T'ai-wan i-nien lai chih jen-shih hsing-cheng* [Personnel Administration After One Year in Taiwan]. Taipei: Hsüan-ch'uan wei-yüan-hui t'u-shu fa-hsing-so, 1946.

———. *Wai-kuo chi-che-t'uan yen-chung chih T'ai-wan* [Taiwan as Seen by a Team of Foreign Reporters]. Taipei: Hsüan-ch'uan wei-yüan-hui t'u-shu fa-hsing-so, 1946.

T'ai-wan-sheng hsing-cheng chang-kuan kung-shu kung-pao [Taiwan Provincial Administrative Executive Office News Gazette]. *Hsia-chi-pao* [The Summer Quarterly]. Issues of Apr. 8, 1947, Apr. 12, 1947, Apr. 15, 1947.

———. Issue no. 13 (Apr. 15, 1947).

T'ai-wan-sheng hsing-cheng chang-kuan kung-shu kung-pao, "Cheng-wu hui-i chi-yao: chang-kuan chih-tzu" [Government Affairs Conference Report: The Governor General's Instructions]. *T'ai-wan-sheng hsing-cheng chang-kuan kung-shu kung-pao* [TPA News Gazette], Apr. 12, 1947, p. 147.

T'ai-wan-sheng hsing-cheng chang-kuan kung-shu t'ung-chi-shih [Taiwan Provincial Administrative Executive Office Statistical Bureau], comp. *T'ai-wan-sheng t'ung-chi yao-lan* [A Statistical Summary of Taiwan Province]. Taipei: T'ai-wan-sheng hsing-cheng chang-kuan kung-shu t'ung-chi-shih, 1946. No. 1 (Oct. 1946); no. 2 (Dec. 1946), no. 3 (Mar. 1947).

———. *T'ai-wan-sheng wu-shih-i-nien lai t'ung-chi t'i-yao* [A Statistical Summary of Statistics for Taiwan Province for the Last 51 Years]. Taipei: T'ai-wan-sheng hsing-cheng chang-kuan kung-shu, 1946.

———. *T'ai-wan wu-chia t'ung-chi yüeh pao* [Taiwan Commodity Price Statistics Monthly]. Taipei: T'ai-wan-sheng hsing-cheng chang-kua kung-shu, 1947.

T'ai-wan-sheng liang-shih t'iao-chi wei-yüan-hui mi-shu-shih [Secretariat of the Taiwan Province Food Grain Regulatory Commission]. "T'ai-wan-sheng liang-shih tiao-chi wei-yüan-hui kung-tso pao-kao" [Work Report of the Food Grain Regulatory Committee of Taiwan Province]. *Cheng-ch'i pan-yüeh-k'an* [Righteousness Semimonthly], 1, no. 3 (May 1, 1946), pp. 18–19.

T'ai-wan-sheng pao-an ssu-ling-pu [Taiwan Provincial Security Headquarters], comp. *T'ai-wan erh-erh-pa p'an-luan chi-lüeh* [A Brief Account of Taiwan's February 28th Riot]. Typescript, 1956.

T'ai-wan-sheng wen-hsien wei-yüan-hui [Taiwan Provincial Historical Commission], comp. *T'ai-wan-sheng t'ung-shih* [A History of Taiwan Province]. Taipei:

T'ai-wan-sheng wen-hsien wei-yüan-hui, 1971. Vol. 3, sect. 2 (Cheng-shih-chih tsung-shuo p'ien).
Tan Kah-kee. *Nan-ch'iao hui-i-lu* [Autobiography by Tan Kah-kee]. N.p., 1946.
T'ang Hsien-lung. *T'ai-wan shih-pien nei-mu-chi* [An Inside Story of the Taiwan Incident]. Nanking: Chung-kuo hsin-wen-she ch'u-pan-pu, 1947.
Teng K'ung-chao. "Shih-lun T'ai-wan erh-erh-pa shih-chien chung ti min-chu yü ti-fang tzu-chih yao-ch'iu" [A Provisional Study on the Demands for Democracy and Self-Rule in Taiwan During the February 28th Incident], *T'ai-wan yen-chiu chi-k'an*, no. 2 (1987), pp. 1–11.
TNC. See *T'ai-wan nien-chien* [Taiwan Yearbook].
Ts'ai Ch'ien. *Jih-pen ti-kuo chu-i chih chih-min-ti: T'ai-wan* [A Colony Under Japanese Imperialism: Taiwan]. N.p., Hsin-hua shu-tien, 1942.
Ts'ai P'ei-huo et al. *T'ai-wan min-tsu yün-tung-shih* [A History of Taiwan's Nationalist Movement]. Taipei: Tzu-li wan-pao ts'ung-shu pien-chi wei-yüan-hui, 1971.
Tso. *See* Chu Wen-po.
TT. See Ch'in Hsiao-i, comp.
Tu Ts'ung-ming. *Hui-i-lu* [Memoirs]. Taipei: Dr. Tu Ts'ung-ming Scholarship Foundation, 1982.
T'ung-chi t'i-yao. See T'ai-wan-sheng hsing-cheng chang-kuan kung-shu t'ung-chi-shih, comp., *T'ai-wan-sheng wu-shih-i-nien lai t'ung-chi t'i-yao*.
Tzu-ch'iang-pao [Self-Strengthening Tribune]. Issues of Aug. 8, 1946, Sept. 11, 1946.
Tzu-yu shih-pao [Freedom Times]. Issues of Dec. 15, 1988, Dec. 16, 1988.
Wang K'ang. "Erh-erh-pa shih-pien ch'in-li-chi" [A Personal Historical Record of the February 28th Incident], in *Erh-erh-pa chen-hsiang* [The Real Facts About the February 28th Incident]. N.p., n.d. Pp. 304–39.
———. "Li-shih ti cheng-yen: Erh-erh-pa shih-pien ch'in-li-chi" [A Testimony on History: A Personal Historical Record of the February 28th Incident]. *Ch'ang-liu pan-yüeh-k'an*, no. 922 (July 1, 1988), pp. 11–14; no. 923 (July 16, 1988), pp. 8–11; and no. 924 (Aug. 1, 1988), pp. 9–12.
Wang Shih-hsün. "Erh-ch'i pu-tui chih hui-i" [A Personal Memoir of the Twenty-seventh Militia Corps], *T'ai-wan hsin wen-hua* [Taiwan's New Culture], no. 6 (Feb. 1987), p. 12.
Wang Shih-lang. *Wang Shih-lang ch'üan-chi* [The Complete Works of Wang Shih-lang]. Kaohsiung: Te-hsin-shih ch'u-pan-she, 1980.
Wang Yü-te. *T'ai-wan: k'u-men ti li-shih* [The Agony of Taiwan History]. Tokyo: Kyūko shobo, 1979.
WCT. *See under* T'ai-wan-sheng hsing-cheng chang-kuan kung-shu hsüan-ch'uan wei-yüan-hui.
Wei Ming, comp. *T'ai-wan ti erh-erh-pa shih-chien* [The February 28th Incident in Taiwan]. Hong Kong: Ch'i-shih nien-tai tsa-chih-she, 1975.
Wen-hui-pao [Wen-hui Daily]. Issue of Mar. 1, 1975.
Wu Cho-liu. *Wu-hua-kuo* [The fig]. Irvine, Calif.: T'ai-wan Publishing Co., 1984.
Wu Hsin-jung. *Wu Hsin-jung ch'üan-chi* [The Complete Works of Wu Hsin-jung]. Taipei: Yüan-ching shih-yeh kung-ssu, 1981.
Wu Kuo-an. "Lun T'ai-wan t'ung-pao ts'an-chia tsu-kuo k'ang-Jih chan-cheng ti

huo-tung chi ch'i li-shih i-i" [An Essay on the Activities of Our Taiwan Brethren Participating in the Mother Country's War of Resistance Against Japan, and Its Historical Significance], *Chin-tai-shih yen-chiu* [Research on Modern History], no. 3 (May 1986), pp. 216–31.

Wu Shih-ch'ang. "Lun T'ai-wan ti tung-luan" [On Taiwan's Turbulence], *Kuan-ch'a* [The Observer], 2, no. 4 (Mar. 22, 1947), pp. 8–9.

Wu Wen-hsing. "Jih-chü ch'u-ch'i T'ai-wan she-hui ling-tao chieh-ts'eng chih ssu-ying yü pien-tung" [The Response and Adjustments Made by the Leading Social Elite in Taiwan in the Early Period of Japanese Rule], *Kuo-li T'ai-wan shih-fan ta-hsüeh li-shih hsüeh-pao*, no. 15 (June 1987), pp. 285–349.

——. "Jih-chü shih-ch'i T'ai-wan tsung-tu-fu t'ui-kuang Jih-yü yün-tung ch'u-t'an" [A Preliminary Examination of the Campaign by the Governor General's Office to Promote the Learning of Japanese in Taiwan During the Period of Japanese Rule], *Tung-hai ta-hsüeh li-shih hsüeh-pao*, no. 7 (Dec. 1985), pp. 77–122.

Ya San [pseud. of Shen Yün-lung]. "Erh-erh-pa shih-pien ti t'ou-shih" [An Incisive Account of the February 28th Incident], *T'ai-wan yüeh-k'an* [Taiwan Monthly], no. 6 (Apr. 10, 1947), pp. 1–15.

Yang Chao-chia. *Yang Chao-chia hui-i-lu* [A Memoir by Yang Chao-chia]. Taipei: San-min shu-chü, 1968.

Yang Chin-hu. *Ch'i-shih hui-i* [A Memoir at Seventy]. N.p., n.d.

Yang Hsing-t'ing. *T'ai-wan ch'ing-nien pai-p'i-shu* [Taiwan Youth White Paper]. Unpublished manuscript dated Aug. 20, 1950, in the Hoover Institution's East Asian Collection, Stanford, Calif.

Yang I-chou. "Hui-i erh-erh-pa min-pien ko-ming san-shih-nien" [Remembering the February 28th Incident's People's Uprising Thirty Years Later], *Wang-ch'un-feng* [Mayflower], no. 90 (Feb. 20, 1977), pp. 14–17.

Yang Liang-kung and Ho Han-wen. Apr. 1947 report on the February Uprising, reprinted in *Shih-chieh jih-pao*, Mar. 11, 1988, pp. 6–7.

Yao Chia-wen. "T'ai-wan hai-hsia hua-fen shih-chieh hai-lu-ch'üan" [The Taiwan Straits as the Intersection Between Continental and Maritime Power in the World]. *T'ai-wan kung-lun-pao* [Taiwan Tribune], Jan. 18, 1988, p. 7.

Yeh Jung-chung. *Lin Hsien-t'ang hsien-sheng chi-nien-chi* [The Collected Works to Commemorate Mr. Lin Hsien-t'ang]. Taichung: Committee to Commemorate Mr. Lin Hsien-t'ang, 1960.

Yen Yen-ts'un. "Erh-erh-pa shih-pien ti ch'in-li yü fen-hsi" [A Personal History and Analysis of the February 28th Incident], *Ch'üan-chi wen-hsüeh* [Biographical Literature], 50, no. 6 (June 1987), pp. 40–44.

Yin P'ing. "T'ai-wan yao tu-li?," in *Shih-chieh chou-k'an*, no. 216 (May 8, 1988), pp. 6–12.

Ying [pseud.]. "Kao-hsiung ch'i-jih" [Kaohsiung's Seven Days], in T'ai-wan cheng-i ch'u-pan-she, ed., *T'ai-wan erh-erh-pa shih-chien ch'in-li-chi* [A Personal Memoir of the February 28th Incident]. N.p.: T'ai-wan cheng-i ch'u-pan-she, 1947. Pp. 188–94.

Bibliography   261

Japanese-language Materials

Haisengo no Nihon wa dō natte iru [Where Does Japan Stand After the Defeat?], Feb. 1947.
Inō Kanori. *Taiwan bunkashi* [A Cultural History of Taiwan] Tokyo: Tōkōshoin, 1965.
Kokumin taikei: Chū-Bei shōyaku to kahei kaikaku mondai [The Nationalist Party People's Congress: The China-U.S. Commercial Treaty and the Problem of Reforming the Currency System], Dec. 1946.
Kōnan Shinbunsha. *Taiwan jinshikan* [Outstanding People of Taiwan]. Taihoku: Kōnan Shinbunsha, 1943.
Kō Shō-dō. *Taiwan Sōtokufu* [The Governor-General's Office of Taiwan]. Tokyo: Kyōikusha, 1981.
Kokufu no kaiso to Taiwan-shō seifu no seiritsu [Establishing Governance in Taiwan Province and Reform of the National Government], June 1946.
Kuwata Etsu and Maehara Tōru, comp., *Dai Tōa sensō ni okeru chiiki betsu heiin oyobi shibotsu gaisu* [Summary Data of Deaths and Various Military Personnel by Region During the Great East Asia War]. Tokyo: Hara Shobo, 1982.
Minshushugi Kenkyūkai. *Taiwan ni okeru Nihon tōchi to sengo naigai jōsei* [Japanese Rule in Taiwan and the Domestic and International Conditions After the War]. Tokyo: Minshushugi Kenkyūkai, 1963.
Nagae Seigo. *Taiwan no gunpu* [Military Laborers of Taiwan]. Hsin-chu City: Nagae Seigo, 1941.
Nihon no baishō mondai [The Talking of Japanese Reparations], July 1946.
Rengōkoku Rōmubu sono seiritsu to keika [The General Assembly of the Allied Powers: Its Establishment and Evolution], Nov. 1946.
Rinji Rōmubu. "Jihenka ni okeru hontō no rōmu jijō" [Labor Conditions in Taiwan After the Taiwan Incident]. *Buhō*, no. 6 (Nov. 1, 1937).
Sanchu zenkai seiji keizai kaikaku hōan [Proposals for Political and Economic Reform by the Third Plenary of the Central Committee of the Kuomintang], May 1946.
Taiwan Ginkō Chōsabu, July 28, 1945, p. 2.
TKN 1942–43. Taiwan Keizai Nenpō Kankōkai, comp. *Taiwan keizai nenpō: Shōwa jūnananenhan* [Taiwan Economic Yearbook, 1942]. Tokyo: Kokusai Nihon Kyōkai, 1942–43.
TKN 1944. Idem, *Taiwan keizai nenpō: Shōwa jūkyū nenhan* [Taiwan Economic Yearbook, 1944] Taipei: Taiwan Shuppan Bunka Kabushiki Kaisha, 1945.
TNS. *Tai'wan Nichi Nichi Shin pō* [Taiwan Daily]. Issues of Jan. 1942, Feb. 1942, Jan. 1943, Jan. 1944, Feb. 1944, Feb. 1945, April 1945.
TS. *Taiwan Shinpō* [Taiwan Daily]. Issues of 1944–45.
Taiwan seinen [Taiwan Youth]. Issue no. 6 (Feb. 28, 1961).
Taiwan Sōtokufu [Governor-General's Office]. *Taiwan jijō* [Taiwan's State of Affairs]. Taipei: Taiwan Sōtokufu Kanbō Jōhōka, 1943.
———. *Taiwan Jūyō Sangyō Chōsei Iinkai kaigiroku* [Records of the Meetings of the Taiwan Important Industry Control Commission]. Taipei: Taiwan Governor-General's Office, 1938.
———. *Taiwan seinen tokuhon* [Taiwan Young People's Reader]. Taipei: Taiwan Kyōikukai, 1943.

———. Sōtokufu, *Taiwan tōchi gaiyō* [A Summary of Japanese Rule Over Taiwan]. Taipei: Sōtokufu, 1945.
Taiwan Sōtokufu Jōhōbu [Governor-General's Office, Information Department]. *Jikyokuka Taiwan no genzai to sono shōrai* [The Current Status of Taiwan's General Situation and Her Future]. Taipei: Sanwa Insatsujo, 1941.
Terasaki Ryūji, comp. *Hasegawa Kiyoshi den* [The Biography of Hasegawa Kiyoshi]. Tokyo: Hasegawa Kiyoshi den, 1972.
Tomisawa Shigeru. *Taiwan shūsen hishi* [A Private History of Taiwan Around the End of World War II]. Tokyo: Tōkyō Inshokan, 1984.
Tōnan Ajia no minzoku kaihō undō [National Liberation Movements of East Asia], Jan. 1947.
Umehara Ikuo, comp. *Taiwan seinen no sakebi* [Taiwan Youth Speak Out]. Taipei: Nikkōdō, 1942.

English-language Materials

Aristotle, *Poetics*, in T. S. Dorsch, ed. and trans., *Classical Literary Criticism*. Baltimore: Penguin Books, 1965.
Atwell, Pamela. *British Mandarins and Chinese Reformers: The British Administration of Weihaiwei (1893–1930) and the Territory's Return to Chinese Rule*. Hong Kong, Oxford, and New York: Oxford University Press, 1985.
Barclay, George W. *Colonial Development and Population in Taiwan*. Princeton, N.J.: Princeton University Press, 1954.
Bate, H. Maclean. *Report from Formosa*. London: Eyre & Spottiswoode, 1952.
Boorman, Howard L., et al., eds. *Biographical Dictionary of Republican China*. New York: Columbia University Press, 1967. Vol. 1 and vol. 3.
Cavendish, Patrick. "The 'New China' of the Kuomintang" in Jack Gray, ed., *Modern China's Search for a Political Form*. London: Oxford University Press, 1969.
Chai, Trong R. "Taiwan for the Taiwanese: The Taiwan Independence Movement, Its Character and Prospects," *Proceedings of the Symposium* (Nov. 6, 1975). East Lansing: Asian Studies Center, Michigan State University, 1975. Chai was a representative of World United Formosans for Independence.
Chang Kia-ngau. *The Inflationary Spiral: The Experience in China, 1939–1950*. Cambridge: Mass.: MIT Press, 1958.
Chang, Maria Hsia, and James Gregor. "The Taiwan Independence Movement: The Failure of Political Persuasion," *Political Communication and Persuasion*, 2, no. 4 (1985), pp. 363–91.
Chen, Edward I-Te. "Formosan Political Movements Under Japanese Rule, 1914–1937," *Journal of Asian Studies*, 31, no. 3 (May 1972), pp. 477–97.
Ch'en San-ching. "Prelude to the Recovery of Taiwan: Preparations and Takeover of Taiwan," *Proceedings of the Conference on Dr. Sun Yat-sen and Modern China*. Taipei: China Cultural Service. Vol. 4, pp. 293–320.
Chen Yung-fa. *Making Revolution: The Communist Movement in Eastern and Central China, 1937–1945*. Berkeley, Calif.: University of California Press, 1986.
Ch'i Hsi-sheng. *Nationalist China at War: Military Defeats and Political Collapse, 1937–1945*. Ann Arbor, Mich.: University of Michigan Press, 1982.

Ch'ien Tuan-sheng. *The Government and Politics of China, 1912–1949*. Stanford, Calif.: Stanford University Press, 1970.
The China White Paper: August 1949. Stanford, Calif.: Stanford University Press, 1967.
Chinese-American Joint Commission on Rural Reconstruction [JCCR]. *Taiwan Agricultural Statistics, 1901–1965*. Taipei: JCCR, 1966.
Chiu Hungda, *China and the Question of Taiwan: Documents and Analysis*. New York: Praeger Publishers, 1973.
Chou, Yang-sun, and Andrew J. Nathan. "Democratizing Transition in Taiwan," *Asian Survey*, 27, no. 3 (Mar. 1987), pp. 277–99.
Clough, Ralph N. "The Political System of Taiwan," in James C. Hsiung, ed. *Contemporary Republic of China: The Taiwan Experience, 1950–1980*. New York: Praeger Publishers, 1981.
Copper, John F., with George P. Chen. *Taiwan's Elections, Political Development and Democratization in the Republic of China*. Occasional Papers/Reprints Series in Contemporary Asian Studies. Baltimore, 1984.
Davidson, James W. *The Island of Formosa: Historical View from 1430–1900*. Taipei: World Book Company, 1960.
Eastman, Lloyd E. *Seeds of Destruction: Nationalist China in War and Revolution, 1937–1949*. Stanford, Calif.: Stanford University Press, 1984.
Fairbank, John King, ed. *The Cambridge History of China. Vol. 12: Republican China, 1912–1949, Part I*. New York: Cambridge University Press, 1983.
———. *The Great Chinese Revolution: 1800–1985*. New York: Harper & Row, 1986.
——— and Albert Feuerwerker, eds. *The Cambridge History of China. Vol. 13: Republican China, 1912–1949, Part II*. New York: Cambridge University Press, 1986.
Formosa: Internal Affairs, 1945–1949. See *United States State Department Central Files*.
Gouldner, Alvin W. *Wildcat Strike: A Study in Worker-Management Relationships*. New York: Harper & Row, 1965.
Graff, Henry F. *American Imperialism and the Philippine Insurrection*. Boston: Little, Brown and Company, 1969.
Gray, Jack, ed. *Modern China's Search for a Political Form*. London: Oxford University Press, 1969.
Gregor, James A., Maria Hsia Chang, and Andrew B. Zimmerman. *Ideology and Development: Sun Yat-sen and the Economic History of Taiwan*. Berkeley: Center for Chinese Studies, University of California, 1981.
Ho, Samuel P. S. *Economic Development of Taiwan, 1860–1970*. New Haven, Conn.: Yale University Press, 1978.
Hsieh, Chiao-min. *Taiwan-Ilha Formosa: A Geography in Perspective*. Washington, D.C.: Catholic University of America, 1964.
Hsü, Immanuel C. Y. *The Rise of Modern China*. New York: Oxford University Press, 1975.
Keiji Furuya. *Chiang Kai-shek: His Life and Time*. Jamaica, N.Y.: St. John's University Press, 1981.
Kerr, George H. *Formosa Betrayed*. Boston: Houghton Mifflin Company, 1965.
———. *Formosa: Licensed Revolution*. N.p., 1945.

———. "Formosa's Return to China," *Far Eastern Survey*, Oct. 15, 1947, p. 207.

Kuo, Tai-chün, and Ramon H. Myers. "The Great Transition: Political Change and Prospects for Democracy in the Republic of China on Taiwan," *Asian Affairs*, 25, no. 3 (Fall 1988), pp. 115–34.

Kuznetz, Simon. "Growth and Structural Shifts," in Walter Galenson, ed., *Economic Growth and Structural Change in Taiwan*. Ithaca, N.Y.: Cornell University Press, 1979.

Lamley, Harry J. "Assimilation Efforts in Colonial Taiwan: The Fate of the 1914 Movement," *Monumenta Serica*, 29 (1970–71), pp. 496–520.

———. "The Taiwan Literati and Early Japanese Rule, 1895–1915." Ph.D. diss., University of Washington, 1964.

Lee Yu-chi. *A Taiwanese Scholar Assails Powell's Riot Write-Up*. Taipei: The Taiwan News Service, 1947.

Legge, James. *The Chinese Classics: The Works of Mencius*. Taipei: World Book Co., n.d.

Li Thian-hok. "The China Impasse: A Formosan View," *Foreign Affairs*, 36, no. 3 (Apr. 1958), pp. 437–48.

Liu Fu-chi. *Essays on Monetary Development in Taiwan*. Taipei: China Committee for Publication Aid and Prize Awards, 1970.

Mao Tse-tung. *Five Essays on Philosophy*. Peking: Foreign Languages Press, 1977.

Mendel, Douglas. *The Politics of Formosan Nationalism*. Berkeley: University of California Press, 1970.

Metzger, Thomas A. "Developmental Criteria and Indigenously Conceptualized Options: A Normative Approach to China's Modernization in Recent Times," *Issues and Studies*, 23, no. 3 (Feb. 1987), pp. 19–81.

Myers, Ramon H. "The Contest Between Two Chinese States," *Asian Survey*, 23, no. 4 (Apr. 1983), p. 536–52.

———. "Political Theory and Recent Political Developments in the Republic of China," *Asian Survey*, 27, no. 9 (Sept. 1987), pp. 1003–22.

———. "Taiwan Under Ch'ing Imperial Rule, 1684–1895: The Traditional Order," *Journal of the Institute of Chinese Studies of the Chinese University of Hong Kong*, 4, no. 2 (1971).

———. "Taiwan Under Ch'ing Imperial Rule, 1684–1895: The Traditional Society," *Journal of the Institute of Chinese Studies of the Chinese University of Hong Kong*, 5, no. 2 (1972), pp. 413–53.

———. "Taiwan's Agrarian Economy Under Japanese Rule," *Journal of the Institute of Chinese Studies of the Chinese University of Hong Kong*, 7, no. 2 (1974), pp. 461–74.

———. "Taiwan as an Imperial Colony of Japan: 1895–1945," *Journal of the Institute of Chinese Studies of the Chinese University of Hong Kong*, 6, no. 2 (1973), pp. 425–53.

———, and Mark R. Peattie, eds. *The Japanese Colonial Empire, 1895–1945*. Princeton, N.J.: Princeton University Press, 1984.

P'eng Ming-min. *A Taste of Freedom: Memoirs of a Formosan Independence Leader*. New York: Holt, Rinehard and Winston, 1972.

Pepper, Suzanne. *Civil War in China: The Political Struggle, 1945–1949*. Berkeley: University of California Press, 1978.

Ravenholt, Albert. "Formosa Today," *Foreign Affairs*, 30, no. 4 (July 1952), pp. 612–24.
Rawski, Thomas G. *Economic Growth in Prewar China*. Berkeley: University of California Press, 1989.
Riggs, Fred W. *Formosa Under Chinese Nationalist Rule*. New York: Macmillan, 1952.
Sneider, Vern. *A Pail of Oysters*. New York: G. P. Putnam's Sons, 1953.
South China Morning Post. Vol. 3, no. 58 (Mar. 1, 1947); vol. 3, no. 60 (Mar. 3, 1947).
Tsurumi, E. Patricia. *Japanese Colonial Education in Taiwan, 1895–1945*. Cambridge, Mass.: Harvard University Press, 1977.
United Formosa for Independence (Philadelphia). "A Declaration of Formosans," in Douglas Mendel, ed., *The Politics of Formosan Nationalism*. Berkeley: University of California Press, 1970.
United States State Department Central Files. Formosa: Internal Affairs, 1945–1949. Washington, D.C.: University Publications of America, 1985. Reel 1 ("Political Affairs Reports for 1946 and January 1947").
Wakeman, Frederic, Jr. *The Great Enterprise*. Berkeley: University of California Press, 1985.
———, and Carolyn Grant. *Conflict and Control in Late Imperial China*. Berkeley: University of California Press, 1975.
Wickberg, Edgar. "The Taiwan Peasant Movement, 1923–1932: Chinese Rural Radicalism Under Japanese Development Programs," *Pacific Affairs*, 48, no. 4 (winter 1975–76), pp. 558–82.
Yang, C. K. "Some Preliminary Statistical Patterns of Mass Actions in Nineteenth-Century China," in Frederic Wakeman, Jr., and Carolyn Grant, eds., *Conflict and Control in Late Imperial China* (Berkeley: University of California Press, 1975), pp. 174–210.
Young, Arthur N. *China and the Helping Hand, 1937–1945*. Cambridge, Mass.: Harvard University Press, 1963.
Yü, Ying-shih, *Trade and Expansion in Han China*. Berkeley: University of California Press, 1967.

Index

In this index "f" after a number indicates a separate reference on the next page, and "ff" indicates separate references on the next two pages. A continuous discussion over two or more pages is indicated by a span of page numbers, e.g., "pp. 57–58." *Passim* is used for a cluster of references in close but not consecutive sequence.

Alliance for the Re-Liberation of Taiwan (T'ai-wan tsai-chieh-fang t'ung-meng), 189
Alliance of Youth for the Self-Government of Taiwan, 116f
Andō Rikichi, 36ff, 63
A-shan *see* Mainlanders
Assimilation Society, 22, 24
Association for Performing Public Work in Industry (Sangyō kōkōkai), 39
Association for Rendering Public Service for the Emperor (Kōmin hōkōkai), 30–31, 36
Association for Rice Delivery (Beikoku nōnyū kimiai), 40
Atwell, Pamela, 219, 261

Barkley, Thomas, 185
Beikoku nōnyū kimiai (Association for Rice Delivery), 40
Blake, Ralph J., 97, 218, 229, 232, 234
Boorman, Howard L., 228, 245, 261

Cairo Declaration, 56
Cavendish, Patrick, 229, 263
Central Investigation and Statistics Bureau (Chung-t'ung-chü), 144, 155
Chang Ch'ao, 181
Chang Chen, 144, 155
Chang Chih-chung, 137
Chang Ch'i-lang, 134
Chang Ch'ing-chuan, 111f
Chang I-chih, 155
Chang Kia-ngau, 227, 262
Chang, Maria Hsia, 218, 262

Chang Mu-t'ao, 111, 120–21
Chang Po-ya, 2
Chang Ts'an-hung, 189
Chang Wen-cheng, 131–33
Chang Wen-ch'i, 181, 242
Chang Yen-hsien, 180
Chang-lao chiao-hui, *see* Presbyterian Missionary Association
Chao Ch'eng, 124
Chao Lien-fang, 110
Chao Nai-ch'uan, 58, 61, 79
Chao Shao-k'ang, 184
Chen, Edward I-te, 220, 262
Ch'en Ch'eng, 166
Ch'en Ch'i, 116
Ch'en Chin-neng, 157
Ch'en Fang-hsien, 53
Ch'en Hai-ho, 111
Ch'en I, 57–63, 67–68, 70, 74–79, 84, 87, 89, 97–98, 143f, 150–52;
—and Uprising: reactions to, 9, 102; radio broadcasts during, 109f, 112, 119–20, 149–50, 201–5; and reply to Taipei Resolution Committee's demands, 116f; and communication with Chia-i mayor, 129; his view of Uprising's causes, 139; his role in suppressing Uprising, 148–49; and closing of Taiwan newspapers, 154; initiates new census, 154; and responsibility for Uprising casualties, 160f; leadership of, 171; role of during Uprising, 176–78; his fate, 180–82; speech at administrative conference, 206–11; message to personnel, 212–13
Ch'en Ken-huo, 111

Ch'en Kiang-shan, 164
Ch'en Kou-fu, 61
Ch'en P'i-nan, 111
Ch'en Sung-chien, 103
Ch'en Tung-sheng, 159
Ch'en Wen-hsi, 103, 148
Ch'en Yung-fa, 226–27
Cheng Ch'eng-kung (Koxinga), 13f
Cheng I-lin, 17
Cheng-chih chien-she hsieh-hui (Political Construction Association), 78, 111f
Ch'i Hsi-sheng, 226f, 262
Ch'i-p'ao (Chinese Robe), 128
Chia-i Uprising, 128–29
Chiang Ching-kuo, 190, 193
Chiang Kai-shek, 8, 142, 147–49, 152f, 177f
Chiang Kung-liang, 2
Chiang Meng-lin, 153
Chiang Mu-yün, 157, 252
Chiang Wei-ch'uan, 111f, 114, 116
Chiang Wei-shui, 24f, 111f, 167
Chien Sheng-yü, 111
Chien-t'u (traitors), 140
Ch'ien Tsung-ch'i, 61, 79
Ch'in Hsiao-i, 241, 252
China White Paper, 5, 218, 262
Chinese-American Joint Commission on Rural Reconstruction, 233, 262
Chinese Communist Taiwan Provincial Work Committee (Chung-kung T'ai-wan-sheng kung-tso wei-yüan-hui), 137
Chinese Robe (Ch'i-p'ao), 128
Ch'ing-hsiang kung-tso (The Work of Cleansing Society), 8
Ching-pei tsung-ssu-ling-pu (Garrison Command), 12, 57f
Chiu Hungdah, 228, 261
Ch'iu Nien-t'ai, 72, 158, 167, 179, 231, 252
Ch'iu Pin-ts'un, 167
Chō (department), 16
Chōhei seido (military recruitment system), 37
Chou I-o, 58, 61, 68, 78–79, 107, 110
Chou Pai-lien, 111
Chou Yen-shou, 108f, 111f
Christian Association for Taiwanese Self-Determination, 190
"Chu" ("pigs," or Mainlanders), 93
Chu Kao-cheng, 191, 193
Chu Wen-po, 107, 123, 239, 252
Ch'u-li wei-yüan-hui, *see* Resolution Committees
Chuang Chia-nung, 157, 240f, 244, 252

Chuang Ch'ui-sheng, 127
Chün-cheng-pu (Military-Political Department), 59
Chung I-jen, 138, 180, 240–46 *passim*, 253
Chung-i fu-wu-tui, *see* Righteous Service Corps
Chung-kung T'ai-wan-sheng kung-tso wei-yüan-hui (Chinese Communist Taiwan Provincial Work Committee), 137
Chung-t'ung-chü (Central Investigation and Statistics Bureau), 144, 155
Chung-wei jih-pao, 123, 154
Clough, Ralph, 184, 262
Commemorating the Uprising, 1f
Commodity Supply Bureau (Wu-tzu kung-ying-chü), 166. *See also* Trade Bureau
Communists (Kung-fei), 3, 55, 135–40. *See also* Taiwanese Communist Party

Dai seishin (Japan's "Great Spirit"), 36
Davidson, James W., 220, 262
Democratic Progressive Party, 1f, 184, 191, 193
Den Kinjirō, 24

Eastman, Lloyd E., 227, 262
Economic recovery of Taiwan, 80–93
Elections in Taiwan, 26, 67–68
Erh-ch'i pu-tui (Twenty-seventh Militia Corps), 127f, 138
Erh-mu p'ai-ch'u-so (T'ai-p'ing Street police station), 105

Fairbank, John King, 226f, 262
Fan Shou-k'ang, 94
Farmers Union (Taiwan nōmin kumiai), 25
Feng Yu-lan, 3
Feuerwerker, Albert, 227, 262
Formosa (Mei-li-tao), 190
Formosa: Internal Affairs, 1945–1949, 231f, 234ff, 262
Formosa Betrayed, 218, 263. *See also* Kerr, George H.
Formosan Association of Public Affairs (T'ai-wan-jen kung-kung shih-wu hsieh-hui), 190
Fu Hsüeh-t'ung, 103

Garrison Command (Ching-pei tsung-ssu-ling-pu), 12, 57f
Giyudan (People's Volunteer Corps), 37f
Glorious Nightclub (Ta-hua chiu-chia), 137
Graff, Henry F., 219, 263

Gray, Jack, 229, 263
Greater East Asia Co-Prosperity Sphere, 27f
Gregor, James, 218, 262

Han, Shih-ch'üan, 71, 94, 253
Hasegawa Kiyoshi, 27–29, 36, 221ff, 226, 261
Ho Han-wen, 159f, 192, 245, 258
Ho P'ing-ju, 161f, 245
Ho, Samuel P. S., 220, 263
Hokō (household system), 16, 37, 91. *See also* Pao-chia
Hōkō Sōnendan (Young People's Association for Public Service), 31
Hōkōhan (squads of KHK personnel), 30
Hōkoku seinentai (Youth Corps), 40
Ho-p'ing jih-pao (Peace Daily), 76f, 125, 154
Hsieh A-shui, 218, 253
Hsieh Chiao-min, 219, 263
Hsieh Hsüeh-hung, 100, 125ff, 136–38, 189, 240
Hsieh Kuan-sheng, 167
Hsieh Nan-kuang, 56
Hsieh O, vii, 108f, 111, 237
Hsieh Tung-ming, 167
Hsü Chen-ch'ing, 111
Hsü Ch'ing-ch'un, 167
Hsü Ch'ing-feng, 111
Hsü Ch'iu-chung, 157
Hsü Hsi-ch'ien, 133f
Hsü Hsiang-ch'ien, 3
Hsü Hsin-liang, 190
Hsü Hsüeh-yü, 58, 61, 79
Hsü, Immanuel C. Y., 226, 263
Hsü Te-heng, 3
Hsü Te-hui, 113f
Hsüeh Mu, 74, 231, 236, 253
Hu Ch'iu-yüan, 84
Hu Fu-hsiang, 58, 61, 79, 110
Hu Tien-p'eng, 16
Hu Yün-kung, 180
Hua-lien Resolution Committee, 131–34
Huan-lien Uprising, 131–34
Hua Yün-yu, 155
Huang Ch'ao-ch'in, 56f, 68, 108, 111, 143, 254
Huang Ch'ao-sheng, 111
Huang Chen-chung, 234, 254
Huang Ch'un-ch'ing, 16
Huang Chung-t'u, 130
Huang Hua, 191
Huang Huo-ting, 111

Huang K'o-li, 127–28, 159
Huang Ts'un-hou, 237f, 254
Huang Tz'u, 157
Huang Wen-hsiung, 190
Huang Wu-tung, 156, 254
Huang Yu-jen, 189
Huang Yüeh-ch'in, 184
Hung I-nan, 17
Hung Tzu-min, 125f

I-lan Uprising, 123
"Incident," 7, 217
Incident at the Square (Kuang-ch'ang shih-chien), 106, 109
Interpreting the Uprising, 3–6
Isshi dōjin (single vision of unified benevolence), 30
Itagaki Taisuko, 22, 24

Japanese colonial rule, in Taiwan and Korea compared, 46f. *See also* Taiwan under Japanese rule
Japanese education in Taiwan, 23–24, 33–35
Japanese repatriation from Taiwan, 63
Jen Hsien-ch'ün, 110
Jen Po, 238, 254
Jimmu Tennō, 34

Kami shibai kyōkai, 31
Kao ch'üan-kuo t'ung-pao-shu (March 6 resolutions of Taipei Resolution Committee), 118
Kaohsiung Uprising, 130–31
Keelung Uprising, 107, 121–22
Keiji Furuya, 228, 263
Ken (prefecture), 16
Kerr, George H., 197, 218, 230, 235, 245, 263
Kitashirakawa (Prince), 29
Ko Ching-en, 58, 61, 79, 107
K'o Yüan-fen, 108, 111, 115, 146–47, 150, 254, 276
Kōgakkō (unified primary school system), 34
Kokutai (Japanese essence), 28, 38
Kōmin (imperial subjects), 28, 37
Kokumin gakkō (public elementary schools), 34
Ko-lao-hui (local secret societies), 54
Kōmin hōkō undō (public service for the emperor), 29
Kōmin hōkōkai (Association for Rendering

Public Service for the Emperor), 30–31, 36
"Kou" ("dogs," or Japanese), 93
Koxinga (Cheng Ch'eng-kung), 13f
Kuang-ch'ang shih-chien, 106, 109
Kung-fei, *see* Communists
Kung-mai-chü (Public Sales Bureau), 166. See also Monopoly Bureau
Kuo I-min, 56
Kuo Kuo-chi, 69ff, 155
Kuomintang, 4–5, 26, 50, 170, 179, 192–93, 218. See also Nationalists
Kuznets, Simon, 231, 263

Labor Cooperative Association (Rōdō kyōkai), 39
League for Establishing a Taiwan Parliament, 24f
League for the Attainment of Local Autonomy, 25
Lee, Joshua, 189
Lee Teng-hui, 1
Lee, Thomas (Liao Wen-i), 189
Li Chiung-chih, 103
Li I-chung, 61, 144f
Li Jen-kuei, 111
Li Liang-jung, 152
Li Shih-chieh, 183, 255
Li Wan-chü, 62, 68, 105, 111, 113, 117
Li Yu-pang, 155
Li Yu-san, 136
Liang Ch'i-ch'ao, 21, 23
Liang K'o-ch'iang, 74
Liao Wei-i, 155
Liao Wen-i (Lee, Thomas), 189
Lien Chen-tung, 68
Lien Heng, 16
Lien-tso-fa (principles of collective responsibility), 154
Lin and *li* (neighborhood watchdog associations), 109f
Lin Chang-en, 111
Lin Ch'ao-ming, 111
Lin Ch'eng-lu, 24
Lin Chia, 164
Lin Chiang-mai, 103, 159
Lin Chung, 62, 77, 109, 111, 113, 255
Lin Hsien-t'ang, 22–23, 36, 127
Lin Jih-kao, 111, 122, 167
Lin, Kenneth S., 233
Lin Lien-tsung, 125
Lin Mao-sheng, 154
Lin Ming-yung, 133
Lin Mu-shun, 236, 238f, 255

Lin Shih-tang, 113
Lin Shui-t'ien, 111
Lin Tsung-hsien, 111, 113, 117, 122f
Lin Wu-ts'un, 114, 116
Lin Yao-t'ing, 16
Liu Ch'ing-shan, 125–26
Liu Fu-ch'i, 230f, 263
Liu Ming-ch'ao, 113
Liu Ts'un-hou, 125f
Liu Wen-tao, 154
Liu Yü-ch'ing, 142, 145, 151ff
Liu-mang (underworld elements), 92
Lo Ching-mo, 155
Lo Hsiu-hui, 16
Lo Shui-yüan, 111, 113
Lü Po-hsiung, 113

Ma Yu-yüeh, 131, 133
Mainlanders (A-shan), 6–7, 62, 169, 183
Man Hsi, 239, 255
Mao Jen-feng, 180
Mao Sen, 180, 246f
Mao Tse-tung, 6, 174, 182
Mei Ch'un, 244, 255
Mei-li-tao (Formosa), 190
Mendel, Douglas, 248f, 263
Methodology to examine Uprising, 6–11
Military-Political Department (Chün-cheng-pu), 59
Military Works Division (Ping-kung-shu), 59
Min-chung-tang (Popular Party), 25
Min-pao, 94, 154
Monopoly Bureau, 102–3, 104f, 166
Morikawa (department head in Japanese colonial administration), 221–22
Movement for Taiwanese Self-Government (T'ai-wan tzu-chih yün-tung), 187
Myers, Ramon H., 220f, 226, 263–64

Nabeyama Sadachika, 136
Nationalists: view of Taiwan of, 48–51 *passim*; control of Mainland by, 52–56; arrival on Taiwan of, 62–63; Taiwan administration by, 63–67; military forces of, on Taiwan, 67, 73–75; and disposition of Japanese assets, 71–73; corruption, 73f; economic management of, 80–89; police personnel of, 89–91; language and cultural difficulties of, 93–96; and response to Uprising, 121, 142–51; policies of, 170–71. See also Kuomintang
New People's Society, 24f

Index 271

Operation Ichigō, 54
Ou-yang Cheng-chai, 142

Pai Ch'ung-hsi, 4–5, 8, 150, 153, 164–65, 218f, 256
Pan-ch'iao Uprising, 107, 122f
P'an Ch'ü-yüan, 111
P'an Hua, 155
Pan-shan (Taiwanese returned from Mainland in 1945), 62, 183
Pao K'o-yung, 79, 107
Pao-chia, 16. *See also* Hokō
Pao-min (rebels during Uprising), 159
Peace Daily (Ho-p'ing jih-pao), 76f, 125, 154
Peattie, Mark, 221, 226, 264
P'eng Ch'ing-k'ao, 18, 21, 130
P'eng Meng-chi, 120, 130–31, 140f, 161, 164, 166
P'eng Ming-min, 4, 18–22, 155–56, 185–88, 218ff, 243, 248, 256
People's Volunteer Corps (Giyūdan), 37f
Pescadore (P'eng-hu) Islands, 134–35
Pepper, Suzanne, 230, 246, 264
Ping-kung-shu (Military Works Division), 59
Political Construction Association (Cheng-chih chien-she hsieh-hui), 78, 111f
Popular Party (Min-chung-tang), 25
Powell, John W., 156, 159, 244
Presbyterian Missionary Association (Chang-lao chiao-hui), 14f, 190
Provisional Committee for Maintaining Order in Taipei City (T'ai-pei-shih lin-shih chih-an wei-yüan-hui), 114
Provisional Education Investigation Commission, 33–34
Public Sales Bureau (Kung-mai-chü), 166; see also Monopoly Bureau

Rawski, Thomas G., 221, 264
Reforms, after Uprising, 166–67
Resolution Committees (Ch'u-li wei-yüan-hui), 99; *see also under names of specific cities*
Resource Commission (Tzu-yüan wei-yüan-hui), 84
Beikoku haigō kumiai, *see* Association for Rice Delivery
Riggs, Fred W., 246, 264
Righteous Service Corps (Chung-i fu-wu-tui), 114, 117
Rōdō kyōkai (Labor Cooperative Association), 39

Sangyō hōkōdan, 31
Sangyō kōkōkai (Association for Performing Public Work in Industry), 39
San-min chu-i ch'ing-nien-t'uan (Three Principles of the People Youth Corps), 155
Secret societies, local (Ko-lao-hui), 54
Self-Administration Forces, 124
Self-Strengthening Tribune (Tzu-ch'iang-pao), 76, 258
Shao Yin, 73
Shen Chung-chiu, 59, 180
Shen Yün-lung, 231, 234, 239, 256. *See also* Ya San
Shi, Paul K. T., 226, 264
Shih Hung-hsi, 77, 122
Shih-chieh T'ai-wan t'ung-hsiang lien-ho-hui (World Federation of Taiwanese Associations), 190
Shu-yüan, 14
Soong, T. V., 142
Southern Alliance Association, 129f
Ssu-shu (The Four Books), 16
Student Association, 111
Su Shao-wen, 124
Sun Yat-sen, 51f, 58, 60, 76, 84, 169f, 179
Suppression, of the Uprising, 155–57

Ta-hua chiu-chia (Glorious Nightclub), 137
Tai Chi-t'ao, 23
"Tai di" ("Kill the pigs!"), 106
Taichung Uprising, 124–28
"T'ai-jen chih T'ai" ("Home rule for Taiwan"), 184
Tainan Uprising, 129–30
Taipei City Council, 180f
Taipei Resolution Committee, 112, 114f, 118, 120f, 145–46, 175–76, 197–200
Taipei Uprising, 146
T'ai-pei-shih lin-shih chih-an wei-yüan-hui (Provisional Committee for Maintaining Order in Taipei City), 114
T'ai-p'ing Street, 103ff
T'ai-sheng pu-pi nei-ti (Taiwan Is Different from Mainland Provinces), 98
T'ai-tu lien-meng (Taiwan Independence Alliance), 189f
Taiwan Central Labor Cooperation Association (Taiwan chūo rōdō kyōkai), 39
Taiwan chūo rōdō kyōkai (Taiwan Central Labor Cooperation Association), 39
Taiwan Cultural Association, 24f, 137

Taiwan Heavy Industry Control Commission (Taiwan jūyō sangyō chōsei iinkai), 40
Taiwan Heroic Army (T'ai-wan i-yung-chün), 137
Taiwan ikka, 30
Taiwan Independence Alliance (T'ai-tu lien-meng), 189f
Taiwan Independence Movement, 4, 188–91
Taiwan Investigation Committee, 56f
Taiwan jūyō sangyō chōsei iinkai (Taiwan Heavy Industry Control Commission), 40
Taiwan Liberation Alliance (T'ai-wan chieh-fang t'ung-meng), 137
Taiwan nichi-nichi shimpō, 32, 261
Taiwan nōmin kumiai (Farmers Union), 25
Taiwan People's Association, in Mainland China, 96
Taiwan Provincial Administration, 57f, 66
Taiwan Provincial Administrative Executive Office (T'ai-wan-sheng hsing-cheng chang-kuan kung-shu), 57f
Taiwan Provincial Construction Committee (T'ai-wan-sheng chien-she-hui), 119
Taiwan Provincial Council, 108, 118
Taiwan Provincial Work Committee (T'ai-wan-sheng kung-tso wei-yüan-hui), 136
Taiwan Study Committee, 56
Taiwan under Japanese rule, 15–16, 23–29 *passim*, 32, 35–48 *passim*
Taiwan Work Team (T'ai-wan kung-tso-t'uan), 137
T'ai-wan chieh-fang t'ung-meng (Taiwan Liberation Alliance), 137
T'ai-wan chien-kuo lien-ho chen-hsien (United Front for Establishing Taiwan as a Nation), 190
T'ai-wan hsin-sheng-pao, 62, 71, 73, 105, 176, 257
T'ai-wan i-yung-chün (Taiwan Heroic Army), 137
T'ai-wan kung-tso-t'uan (Taiwan Work Team), 137
T'ai-wan tsai-chieh-fang t'ung-meng (Alliance for the Re-Liberation of Taiwan), 189
T'ai-wan tzu-chih yün-tung (Movement for Taiwanese Self-Government), 187
Taiwanese Communist Party, 25–26. See also Communists
Taiwanese Communist Youth League, 137
Taiwanese elite, 15–23, 44–45, 47–48, 172
Taiwanese Independence Alliance (T'ai-tu lien-meng), 189f
T'ai-wan-jen kung-kung shih-wu hsieh-hui (Formosan Association of Public Affairs), 190
T'ai-wan-sheng chien-she-hui (Taiwan Provincial Construction Committee), 119
T'ai-wan-sheng hsing-cheng chang-kuan kung-shu (Taiwan Provincial Administrative Executive Office), 57f
T'ai-wan-sheng kung-tso wei-yüan-hui (Taiwan Provincial Work Committee), 136
Tang-wai (non-KMT politicians), 192
T'ang En-po, 180f
T'ao-yüan Uprising, 123–24
Terasaki Ryūji, 221f, 225, 261
TIM, *see* Taiwan Independence Movement
Three Principles of the People Youth Corps (San-min chu-i ch'ing-nien-t'uan), 155
Tien Hung-mao, 226, 264
Ting Ming-nan, 180f
Ting Wen-chih, 154
Tomisawa Shigeru, 33, 261
Tosei Keizai, 28
Trade Bureau, 85f, 166. *See also* Commodity Supply Bureau
Treaty of Shimonoseki, 15f
Tsai-lai, 81
Ts'ai Hsiao-chien, 136f
Ts'ai Kuo-li, 17
Ts'ai P'ei-huo, 25
Ts'ai T'ung-jung, 189
Tseng Feng-ming, 130
Tu Ts'ung-ming, 94, 111, 258
Tu Wei-ming, 179, 246
T'u Kuang-ming, 130
T'ung-meng-hui, 16
Twenty-seventh Militia Corps (Erh-ch'i pu-tui), 127f, 138
Tzu-ch'iang-pao (Self-Strengthening Tribune), 76, 258
"Tzu-chih, tzu-yang, tzu-ch'uan" ("Self-organization, self-cultivation, self-promotion"), 14
Tzu-yüan wei-yüan-hui (Resource Commission), 84

Ulanfu, 3
United Front for Establishing Taiwan as a Nation (T'ai-wan chien-kuo lien-ho chen-hsien), 190
Uprising: events and suppression of, 8f;

moral aspects of, 10–11, 178–79; historical sources on, 11–12; chronology of, 100–104; causes of, 168–75; process of, 175–78; Chinese reactions to, 182
Uprising casualties, 140, 155–64, 178
Urban violence, in Chinese history, 9f

Wakeman, Frederic, Jr., 219, 264
Wang Chao-chia, 58, 61
Wang Chih-hsiung, 190
Wang Ching-wei, 173
Wang Ch'ung-hui, 143
Wang Jo-wang, 193
Wang K'ang, 106–7, 241, 244, 259, 276
Wang Kuei, 111
Wang Min-ning, 62
Wang P'ing, 155
Wang P'ing-shui, 131
Wang Shih-lang, 16, 220, 259
Wang Shih-ting, 157
Wang T'ien-teng, 100, 109, 113, 117, 119, 154, 163
Wang Yü-te, 189, 237, 239, 244, 259
Wang Yü-yün, 190
Warlords, Chinese, 52
Wedemeyer, Albert Coady, 5, 8, 171, 175
Wei Tao-ming, 101, 151, 165ff, 245
Weihaiwei, 10
Weiner, Myron, 193
Weng, Wen-hao, 89
Wickburg, Edward, 221, 264
Wilbur, C. Martin, 226
The Work of Cleansing Society (Ch'ing-hsiang kung-tso), 8
World Federation of Taiwanese Associations (Shih-chieh T'ai-wan t'ung-hsiang lien-ho-hui), 190

Wu Chen-wu, 125
Wu Chin-lien, 105
Wu Cho-liu, 67, 96, 230, 236, 259
Wu Hsin-jung, 32
Wu Kuo-an, 221, 259
Wu Te-kung, 17
Wu Ting-ch'ang, 167
Wu Tsong-min, 233
Wu Yu-k'o, 111
Wu Yüan, 242, 259
Wu-tzu kung-ying-chü (Commodity Supply Bureau), 166. *See also* Trade Bureau

Ya San, 239; *see also* Shen Yün-lung, 259
Yang, C. K., 9, 219, 264
Yang K'o-huang, 137
Yang K'o-p'ei, 137
Yang Liang-kung, 8, 45, 120, 139, 146, 164, 192, 219, 260
Yang Yüan-ting, 122
Yao Chia-wen, 188, 191, 249, 260
Yeh Chien-ying, 3
Yeh Ming-hsün, 77, 228, 232
Yen Chia-kan, 58, 61, 107
Yen Chia-li, 181, 246
Yen Ch'un-hui, 167
Yin Hai-kuang, 12
Yin-hsieh-wen-hua ("sinister culture"), 191
Young, Arthur N., 227, 264
Young People's Association for Public Service (Hōkō Sōnendan), 31
Youth Association, 113
Youth Corps (Hōkoku seinentai), 40
Yu Mi-chien, 105
Yü Ying-shih, 219, 264

Library of Congress Cataloging-in-Publication Data
Lai, Tse-han.
  A tragic beginning : the Taiwan uprising of February 28, 1947 /
Lai Tse-han, Ramon H. Myers, Wei Wou.
    p. cm.
  Includes bibliographical references and index.
  ISBN 0-8047-1829-6 (cloth : alk. paper)
  1. Taiwan—History—February Twenty Eighth Incident, 1947.
I. Myers, Ramon Hawley, 1929–   . II. Wei, Wou. III. Title.
DS799.823.L35   1991
951.24'905—dc20   90-39218
                                                            CIP

∞ This book is printed on acid-free paper.